The Balkanization of the West

From a purely clinical viewpoint, the violence which has occurred in the former Yugoslavia does not deserve special attention compared with, for example, the genocide in Cambodia and Iraq, and World War II. Yet from the perspectives of postmodernism and postcommunism that are central to this discussion, the butchery in former Yugoslavia is a special case because this violence is occurring in the heart of Europe which had promised never to tolerate such a bloodbath again. "Rational" solutions seem incapable of getting to grips with the problem. The author argues that the media has reduced the world to a collective voyeur that passively watches and monitors horrible crimes against humanity. The Balkan War has produced the Balkanization of the West with the leading Western powers seemingly paralysed by the spectacle of internecine warfare. Meštrović claims that the Balkan war has derailed the movement for unification in Europe. The Islamic world has seen that the West is quite willing to bomb Muslim targets, from Iraq to Somalia, but absolutely unwilling to wage a "just war" to save the Bosnian Muslims. The author concludes that the Balkan War is a key catalyst in the unravelling of the West.

Stjepan Meštrović is Professor of Sociology at Texas A&M University.

The Balkanization of the West

The confluence of postmodernism and postcommunism

Stjepan G. Meštrović

London and New York

First published 1994
by Routledge
11 New Fetter Lane, London EC4P 4EE

Simultaneously published in the USA and Canada
by Routledge
29 West 35th Street, New York, NY 10001

© 1994 Stjepan G. Meštrović

Typeset in Baskerville by
NWL Editorial Services, Langport, Somerset

Printed and bound in Great Britain by
Biddles Ltd, Guildford and King's Lynn

British Library Cataloguing in Publication Data
A catalogue record for this book is available from the British Library

Library of Congress Cataloging in Publication Data
has been applied for

ISBN 0–415–08754–6 (hbk)
ISBN 0–415–08755–4 (pbk)

Contents

To the memory of my fathers

Preface and acknowledgements

From a purely clinical point of view, the crimes against humanity that have occurred in the former Yugoslavia do not deserve any special attention compared with, for example, the genocide in Cambodia and Iraq, World War II Europe, or other sites in the world. Yet from the perspective of postmodernism and postcommunism that are central to the present discussion, the moral crimes in former Yugoslavia are a special case, for the following reasons: these crimes are occurring in the heart of post-World-War-II Europe which had promised to never tolerate such crimes again. The West had placed its credibility on the line by attempting to solve the current Balkan War through pure negotiation and other rational means derived from Enlightenment narratives. Whereas many can argue that they do not have sufficient information concerning genocide in Cambodia or Hitler's Europe or any other historical or current site of genocide, the miracle of the electronic age has made sure that the entire world can follow the genocide in the former Yugoslavia. Thus, the credibility of the same Enlightenment narratives that is at stake in the postmodern discourse is also at stake in the West's actions *vis-à-vis* the current Balkan War. This claim constitutes the crux of the present study.

Without seeking to repeat any of the arguments in this book, I believe that a few prefatory remarks concerning the motives, background, and context for writing it would be helpful to most readers. Its central ideas occurred to me way back in 1989, as the so-called Velvet Revolution or the fall of communism had just begun. Not for an instant did I believe the widespread views promulgated by American opinion-makers that communism would be transformed easily and swiftly into American-style democracy and free-market institutions. Instead, I told my friends, colleagues, and audiences that a brutal war would emerge in the former Yugoslavia; that it would be a prelude to a much larger and bloodier unraveling of the former Soviet Union; and that Balkanization would eventually engulf the Western world as well. Ridicule emerged as the most dominant reaction from my listeners. Why was I such a pessimist? What was wrong with me?

There was nothing magical about my ability to prophesy. I had simply clung stubbornly to the most fundamental premise of classical sociology, that society consists of habits and traditional ways of thinking and doing things. The lands that had been ruled by communism did not have a tradition of democracy but did have a tradition of savagery. Postcommunist societies looked to so-called Western Europe in general and the United States of America in particular for guidance in establishing democracy on the ruins of communism. Thus, postcommunist nations lived their democratic fantasies vicariously, through the West. Alas, the cynical West had long ceased seeing itself as a moral power in the world, and Western intellectuals have been writing about narcissism and the end of democracy in their nations for many years now. So the outcome of the fall of communism was easy to predict, or so it seemed to me: most postcommunist nations would not succeed in making the transition to democracy and, for the most part, the West would just monitor their disintegration into chaos. But the American opinion-makers, as well as my colleagues, clung just as stubbornly to the Enlightenment narratives which predicted the end of history, the end of culture, and the ability to transcend habits and traditions. Only they would not admit that these Enlightenment narratives are themselves habits and traditions characteristic of American, British, and French cultures. This is because the Enlightenment, almost by definition, rebelled at the notion that culture and history can constrain the individual. Thus, disciples of the Enlightenment are unconscious traditionalists, conservative despite themselves, and despite their loud commitment to liberalism.

In any event, the tragic war currently being waged in the Balkans vindicates my first prediction, and the ever-increasing bloodshed in the former Soviet Union is beginning to vindicate my second. But the Balkanization of the West? Impossible. Why, the very term, Balkanization, was invented to denote *those people* in the Balkans who seem to like to slaughter each other, as opposed to the civilized Americans, French, and British. I fully expect that most readers who pick up this book will experience some variation of this reaction to my thesis. Yet I insist, knowing full well that fifty to a hundred years from now nobody will remember my argument if I am proven wrong by future events. But if I am right, then I am writing for readers at some future time, not my contemporaries.

Perhaps it is not necessary to wait that long. Without repeating the arguments I make later in the book, let me offer two short reasons why the reader might wish to take my thesis seriously. The first is that my argument falls into that broad discourse called postmodernism, which concerns itself with the end of the Enlightenment project, and which can no longer be ignored. Indeed, the disciples of the Enlightenment who make up the corps of American opinion-makers have projected the most fantastic apocalyptic fears onto this Balkan War (again, despite themselves): it is supposed to signal the end of Europe, the UN, NATO, the New World Order, civilization, and morality. It is also alleged to symbolize the return of Nazism, the Crusades, and the extermination of Islam. One could argue that none of these claims can be defended logically. After all, the current war in the Balkans pales in comparison, quantitatively speaking, with the ongoing genocide in Cambodia and Somalia, or with other historical instances of genocide. But logic is quite beside the point, and besides, recourse to statistics in discussions of genocide is a nasty business. It really should not matter whether millions or thousands of people are wiped out because of ethnic hatred. When one examines what has been said and written in the postmodern information media, one is confronted with the fact that this relatively limited war in a small corner of Europe has taken on enormous symbolic significance. I shall argue that all this attention and paralysis *vis-à-vis* the Balkans suggests a terror in the Western mind that it is about to succumb to Balkanization.

This leads to my second reason. Consider the definition of Balkanization as the breaking up of a unit into increasingly smaller units that are hostile to each other. There is no good reason to understand Balkanization literally, as something that must apply only to the Balkans. Indeed, the last few years offer a plethora of events that suggest disintegration of alliances and globalizing tendencies that used to be taken for granted. For example, France and Britain blamed Germany in large measure for the current Balkan War, and the strains among these countries caused serious rifts in the plans for establishing a sort of United States of Europe. Various members of NATO, such as Greece and Turkey, renewed their old antagonisms, again largely owing to differing sympathies for parties involved in the Balkan conflict. Even in the United States, California is on the verge of breaking up into three separate states; Hawaii is seeking secession; there is serious talk in Texas of the Southern, Hispanic half seceding from the Northern, Protestant half, and so on. Quite apart from regional hostilities, which are growing louder every day throughout Europe, the USA, and the rest of the world, consider other forms of divisiveness: women, gays, and other minority groups have practically taken on the metaphorical status of ethnic groups within the USA, and are engaged in very hostile relationships with their enemies, including men, straights, and other ethnic groups. President Clinton frequently bemoans the divisiveness within American society, and linked conceptually the Los Angeles riots with the ethnic hatred in the Balkans. Xenophobia and contempt for foreigners is undisguised in Western Europe. Again, I do not wish to engage in a long-winded argument here. My point is simply that it is really not all that funny to consider that the West is slowly succumbing to Balkanization when one takes into account the hate crimes, violence, and savagery in various Western cultures. For example, is the Irish Republican Army practice of shooting people in the kneecaps really that different from the savagery exhibited by Serbs against Muslims?

Another issue that must be confronted honestly is the background of the author. I have grown somewhat used to the ethnic prejudice directed against me, at least initially, by my University students. For example, I evoke a lot of nervous laughter on the first day of classes when I begin with the line, "Don't worry, I really do speak English, despite the strange spelling of my name." I am still somewhat surprised and saddened by the fact that many of my colleagues are just as ethnocentric and prejudiced as my students. Sociologists really ought to know better. For example, a reviewer of one of my other books dismissed it as an essentially Catholic and Croat argument. I realize that even bringing this issue up is going to be perceived as disconcerting by many readers. But the issue is unavoidable: here is an author born in the Balkans (raised in the USA) who has written a book about the Balkanization of the West. Why shouldn't he be dismissed as a crank?

There exist many reasons. First, my argument is amply documented and, after all, it is an *argument*, and as such, something to be judged on the basis of its merits, not the author's background. Second, an author's place of birth should not preclude his or her being objective any more than being a father and a husband, for example, should prevent one from teaching a sociology course on marriage and the family. Third, the entire issue of objectivity *vis-à-vis* postmodernism and the Enlightenment is infinitely more complex than one's ethnicity, and it is an issue that I treat at length in this book. Fourth, the unthinking expectation that someone from the Balkans will be biased concerning the Balkans betrays a widespread form of ethnocentrism found in nations in which the Enlightenment project took root. This form of ethnocentrism supposes that one is objective if one writes from nobody's point of view. Yet this belief – that one can write from nobody's point of view – is a typically Enlightenment-based point of view, derived from René Descartes' rejection of culture (Gellner 1992a). As such, it is hypocritical, because it holds up a standard of neutrality that is impossible to meet in reality, yet favors the arrogant imposition of American, British, and French points of view in the guise of being nobody's points of view. Consider, for example, the plethora of books by Western authors about postcommunist developments versus the handful of books by native authors.

Fifth, my purpose is less to win an argument – even though one is trained to win arguments in Western academe – and more to open lines of communication that would otherwise remain closed. For example, to sensitize my classes to alternatives to ethnocentrism, I often bring up the fact that when my American wife asks me to take her and our daughter to Disneyworld or some other fun theme park, I comply, but never enjoy the experience as fully as she does. I do not have fun in Disneyworld. Invariably, my classes gasp – collectively and literally. One can scarcely think of a more un-American statement than the admission that one does not enjoy Disneyworld. Even criticizing Presidents Bush and Clinton is okay, by comparison. But to fail to have fun at Disneyworld – that really gets a discussion going. I explain to my students that my purpose is not to criticize Disney or them, but to point out that I was not raised in a fun-culture, and they were. From that insight, can we build dialogue? Usually, we can.

Sixth, and closely related, one can take a completely different attitude toward this author. Was there never a time in which people would approach a stranger with the aim of learning something from them precisely because they think differently to the natives? Why can't a foreigner be exotic, instead of threatening? I am thinking of Georg Simmel's and David Riesman's mutual claim that strangers – as those who are simultaneously in and out of the mainstream group – often make the best sociologists, judges, and other professionals, precisely because they are different at the same time that they are like everybody else. Little wonder, then, that most of the founding fathers of sociology were Jewish, because Jews have consistently experienced this role as strangers, participating in the group, yet always outside it. Let us assume, for the sake of argument, that my place of birth gives me a particular "bias." At the same time, my thoroughly American education gives me a perspective on that bias that a native American will never possess. Combining the two perspectives may lead to new insights. That is my hope, in any event, and that constitutes a much more charitable and broad-minded approach than ethnocentric prejudice, which is all too common.

Allow me to give one more illustration of what I mean. In the 1920s, the city fathers of Chicago asked my grandfather, who was a famous sculptor by then, to sculpt a monument of an American President. He told them that America had enough monuments to its Presidents, and suggested that they commission a memorial to the true American hero, the American Indian – today, called the Native American in the lexicon of political correctness. Imagine, a Croat telling Americans that they needed a grand monument to the people they had nearly exterminated! The city fathers agreed, and Ivan Meštrović's monument to the Native American still stands on the shores of Lake Michigan in Chicago. Furthermore, he portrayed the Native American as a noble, muscular warrior seated on a full-bodied Roman horse, not the mustangs that they really rode. My grandfather was postmodern before his time. The important point is that it would be narrow-minded and foolish to dismiss this statue as typically Croat, for it is quite atypical, and cannot be reduced to any cultural point of view. It constitutes the insight of a stranger who reminded the Americans of something that they have quite literally forgotten.

Similarly, this book and my other books are not typically this or that. And I regard myself very much as a citizen of the world. If my religious preference must be known, it is for the Celtic worship of tree spirits. It is regrettable that such issues must be brought up, but it will be of historical interest to my readers in the distant future that I have little choice than to confront ethnic prejudice directed at me daily as a university professor and author. Despite all the *talk* of tolerance and multiculturalism nowadays, in reality one confronts bigotry, hatred, and prejudice on a daily basis, much of it subtle. I have found that eventually, I am able to reach a level of humane dialogue with my students. But my colleagues in sociology strike me as an especially mean-spirited lot.

To avoid misunderstanding on this point as well, let me note that I do not ascribe meanness as a personal trait to academicians. Personal motives are irrelevant to the point I am making. Rather, the training that university professors receive puts a premium on holding one's emotions in check – especially tender-hearted emotions – for the sake of neutrality, impartiality, and objectivity. But an unintended outcome of this training is an institutionalized proclivity toward sadism. For almost by definition, sadists are indifferent and "neutral" toward human suffering. I shall not elaborate further here on this point, but wish to emphasize that even when I discuss this topic later in the book, I follow standard academic procedure by documenting many thinkers who were concerned with sympathetic understanding versus cold objectivity, from Max Weber and Emile Durkheim to Pitirim Sorokin. Thus, even when I criticize academic neutrality, I employ neutral methods.

In any event, throughout this book I problematize notions and concepts that are otherwise taken for granted, including but not limited to, objectivity, Western, the Enlightenment, fundamentalism, rape, and truth. The aim is not to win an argument or arrive at dogma, but to ignite the reader's imagination and to engage in constructive dialogue.

Out of all these concepts that are problematized, perhaps rape is the most important for the purposes of the discussion that follows. I will be discussing rape, not from the feminist point of view, i.e. as a reflection of male dominance, but from an ethnic one, the perception by Bosnian Muslims that they are being symbolically raped. As illustration of what I intend, allow me to quote from a speech given by the Bosnian Ambassador to the United Nations, Mr Muhamed Sacirbey, to the United Nations Security Council on 24 August 1993:

> The last time that I spoke before this Council, the Republic of Bosnia and Herzegovina was told, in a perversion of the UN Charter and the principles of international justice, that its right to obtain defensive weapons and fully exercise self defense would pose a threat to the UN forces in my country and would prolong the war. Now, in the climax of this continuing perversion, it is subtly suggested that the re-emphasis of principles of the UN Charter, international law, the CSCE, Security Council resolutions, the Decisions of the International Court of Justice and the London Conference on the former Yugoslavia would somehow undermine the chances of a negotiated settlement. *The legal absurdity and moral degradation of this argument can only be compared to a policeman being instructed not to interpret a gang rape because, after resisting, the victim is finally ready to coolly submit to the inevitable. Under this theory, the most heinous of crimes, a gang rape, becomes an act of seduction. Excellencies, Bosnia and Herzegovina is being gang raped.* Once forced into a submissive position by acts of violence and aggression, one does not become any less of a victim of a criminal act just because the victim is exhausted by the struggle. The victim calls out for help. The strong and gallant hear the cries and rush to the scene of the crime. They plead with the criminals to stop. The criminals respond even more loudly with a fierce and perverse determination. Afraid to confront the criminals, the strong avert their eyes. The gallant explain their inaction by the age-old excuse that the "victim was really asking for it." Having failed to confront the rapists, they now hope that the criminals are fatigued from and satisfied with the criminal orgy and prepared to return to the life of a law-abiding member of the community. Excellencies, all have heard the cries of the victim in Bosnia and Herzegovina. . . . I do not lightly apply the analogy of a gang rape to the plight of the Republic of Bosnia and Herzegovina. As we know, systematic rape has been one of the weapons of this aggression against the Bosnian women in particular.
>
> (emphasis added)

I would like to thank Chris Rojek and Barry Smart for taking me seriously and not ridiculing me when I proposed this project to them, as well as for their constructive criticisms. I also benefited from the insights offered by the following colleagues: C.G. Schoenfeld, Slaven Letica, Miroslav Goreta, Philip Cohen, Barry Glassner, David Riesman, Susan Greenwood, Akbar Ahmed, Michael Weinstein, and last, but certainly not least, my wife, Amber. Of course, I am solely responsible for all the views put forth in this book, and they deserve none of the criticisms. Special thanks to Amber's grandmother, Doris K. Lee, for meticulously keeping track of and clipping newspaper articles for me.

I am grateful to the Council for the International Exchange of Scholars for a Fulbright grant that enabled me to live, teach, and conduct research in Croatia in 1992. I am also grateful to Texas A&M University for funding three other, shorter trips to the former Yugoslavia, and to the Heads of my Department, Ben Crouch and Dudley Poston, for their enthusiastic support of my research. The reader will notice that the endnotes, as well as the text itself, are crammed full of verbatim quotations from newspapers and magazines concerning postcommunism. The reason that I use verbatim quotes instead of summarizing the thoughts of others is that I wish to maintain a historical record for future generations. I am certain that the revolution initiated by the fall of communism since 1989 will go down in history as one of the most important events in the past few centuries. It will be important for future researchers and interested laypeople to know exactly what was being said and written during this revolution, which has not yet reached its zenith. In the interest of the historical record, I wish to conclude this preface by listing the publications that rejected essays authored by me that I eventually incorporated into this book. I realize that this is an unorthodox move, but my motives are as follows. Opinion-makers are already making the false claim that nobody had predicted the fall of communism and its consequences. I suspect that there were many others who, like me, had made such predictions, but were not given an opportunity to put their views in print. If that is true, it is an important piece of the historical record. Furthermore, if the predictions that I make in this book turn out to be somewhat accurate, I wish to offer a counter to the claims that will undoubtedly be made in the future that nobody suspected the pessimistic scenarios that I offer.

I sincerely hope that I am wrong, because the scenario I offer is frightening even to me. In any event, here are the publications that rejected the ideas which form the basis of this book: *Foreign Affairs*, *The World and I*, *New York Times*, *New York Review of Books*, *Wall Street Journal*, *Freedom Review*, *Orbis*, *Policy Review*, *The National Interest*, *Sociological Inquiry*, *The New Yorker*, *New Republic*, *Commentary*, and *Harper's*. The only exception is the publication of my "West as Post-modern Voyeur" by *Impact International*, 23 (July/August 1993): 27–8. Finally, I would like to quote the response from the President-elect of the American Sociological Association to my offer to establish a session on the current Balkan War and its significance:

Thank you for your January 23 letter suggesting a session on "Sociological Perspectives on the Balkan War of 1991–1993" for the American Sociological Association meetings in Los Angeles, August 5–9, 1994. The Program

Chapter 1

From the postmodern culture of fun to the grim realities of postcommunism

The collapse of communism at the present *fin de siècle* coincided with widespread interest among intellectuals in a phenomenon known as postmodernism, itself a confluence of apocalyptic themes found in the previous *fin de siècle* (Meštrović 1991) and the fun-culture uncovered by David Riesman in his *Lonely Crowd* (1950). The confluence of these two phenomena, postcommunism with postmodernism (as a fun version of the apocalypse), produced the giddy, optimistic belief that democracy and tolerance would emerge from the ruins of communism, a widespread belief that only a fun-culture could produce. This nexus of sometimes contradictory cultural forces, and their consequences, will be the theme of the rest of this book, yet it requires some immediate clarification.

First, the "collapse of communism" was not complete, because communism continues to rule China, Cuba, North Korea and other nations in the world. Communism's apparent demise in Eastern Europe and the former Soviet Union does not rule out the possibility that the cultural roots of communism have remained in the countries that were once ruled by this ideology, nor the possibility that these same cultural roots will sprout new forms of authoritarianism.[1] In the words of Aleksander Solzhenitsyn, "Time has finally run out for communism, but its concrete edifice has not yet crumbled. And we must take care not to be crushed beneath its rubble instead of gaining liberty" (1991: 3). Second, it is nearly impossible to settle on a consistent definition of "postmodernism" (Rosenau 1992),[2] even though this concept seems to imply the collapse of modernism. As with the alleged collapse of communism, this characterization does not preclude the possibility that the cultural roots of what is called modernity will sprout new forms of modernism – despite the rhetoric of protest found in postmodern discourse. Yet, with the notable exception of Akbar Ahmed (1992), most intellectuals involved in this discourse have overlooked Islam as a distinct form of postmodernism or anti-modernism. Third, the French term, *fin de siècle*, which binds much of the rhetoric of protest across the two end-points of the twentieth century, implies so much more than the straightforward translation: end of the century. It connotes a spirit or world-view characterized by anxiety, uneasiness, pessimism and disgust at some of the unwelcome consequences of modernity. Thus, the dramatic, contemporary confluence of the purported endings of communism, modernity, the twentieth century – even the millennium – demand a new and creative analysis of social phenomena that often have been taken for granted.

A discussion of the sort being proposed here would be crippled from the outset if one were to limit it to the analytic issue of whether postmodernism – whatever it is – constitutes a rebellion or extension of modernity. The way this problem is posed in the existing literature betrays the very Enlightenment narratives that are in question,[3] for it assumes a "before" and "after" to modernity, as well as a linear progression to history. We shall gain much more room for discussion, and may be able to learn something new, by allowing the possibility that tradition, modernity, and postmodernity (or various forms of postmodernity) are able to co-exist. True, such an assertion seems illogical from the many perspectives found in modernist theories that assume progress from "primitive" to "civilized" societies. Yet the notion of linear progress is one of the assumptions that is called into question by the postmodern rebellion against narratives spun from the Enlightenment. Besides, it often seems that in the present *fin de siècle*, one finds that fundamentalism,[4] nationalism, and many other sorts of traditional cultural phenomena *do* thrive alongside modernity.

Let us return to the coincidence that was noted in the first sentence of this chapter: namely, that communism seems to have collapsed at nearly the same time that postmodernism asserted itself in intellectual discourse. In rough tandem, the high priest of postmodernism, Jean Baudrillard (1986), declared the *end of modernity and of culture*, Francis Fukuyama (1992) declared the *end of history*, and the high priest of foreign affairs, Zbigniew Brzezinski (1989), pronounced the death and *end of communism*. All these dramatic endings seem to have coincided with the end of the millennium, at a time when the prestige of sociology relative to the other social sciences – not to mention the so-called "hard sciences" – seems to be at an all-time low (Kantrowitz 1992). Thus, one might add the *end of sociology* to the long list of dramatic endings that seem to be invoked in contemporary intellectual discourse (see also Bauman 1992).

To be sure, the meaning of all these alleged endings is far from clear, and such claims provoke controversy in any case. In contradistinction to Baudrillard, Anthony Giddens (1990, 1992) and other modernists deny the existence of any break with modernity, and prefer to speak of "high modernity." To contradict Fukuyama's claim that humanity had finally reached the end of history – by which he means that with the end of the Cold War, liberal democracy had triumphed over racism as well as historical wars for ideology, nationalism, and imperialism – one has only to consider the brutal war that has continued in former Yugoslavia since 1991, among many other nationalistic wars currently raging in the world, from formerly Soviet Georgia to Somalia.[5] Indeed, the race riots that spread from Los Angeles to many other cities in the USA in April 1992 led many commentators to remark, with considerable amazement, that America suddenly seemed like the Balkans – that they could not believe that the United States of America could be racked by ethnic conflict this late in its historical development. The Western media frequently referred to the Balkan crisis as contagious, as if ethnic hatred were some sort of virus.[6] I shall have more to say in Chapter 2 and elsewhere on this postmodern use of metaphors such that the modern West became Balkanized while the reality of the current Balkan War became a mere metaphor. At this point in the discussion, it is worth stressing that this ominous conceptual linkage between Los Angeles and the former Yugoslavia was strengthened by President Clinton on 17 April 1993, on the occasion of the reading of the verdict in the second trial of the policemen who abused Rodney King. Mr. Clinton said that the second verdict, in which two officers were found guilty of violating Rodney King's rights, proved that America would not succumb to the ethnic hatred that consumed the former Yugoslavia.[7] But why should he have made such a statement were it not for the fear, largely unconscious, that the USA *could* fall victim to the "virus" of ethnic hatred? In any event, countering Fukuyama, Alan Ryan (1992: 7) writes that "the most obvious complaint against the view that the whole world is committed to liberal democracy is that most of it is not."[8]

Consider Mikhail Gorbachev's ominous warning, made on the occasion of his resignation as President of the Soviet Union on Christmas Eve, 1991, that the former Soviet Union would follow in the bloody wake of the Balkans. Indeed, the turmoil in the Balkans seems to have foreshadowed ominously the potential for widespread racism and ethnic conflict throughout the world, from China and Africa to Western Europe and the United States. In addition, the news media reported noticeable increases in hate crimes committed by skinheads in Britain, neo-Nazis in Germany, "gaybashers" in the United States military, and anti-Semites in France, among many others. By 1993, the cheerful confidence concerning a New World Order based on rationality and tolerance, which was popularized by postmodern writers as well as by President George Bush in 1991, turned into a cynical pessimism in relation to a New World Disorder (*Wall Street Journal*, 1 June 1992: A13).

Neither Mr. Gorbachev nor popular opinion-makers have explained *why* the Balkans emerged as the paradigm for dissolution and hatred in a world that was assumed to be moving in the contrary direction of postmodern tolerance, the modernist unification of markets, and the growth of democracy. The remainder of this book is devoted to explicating this unexpected turn of events, so that only a thumbnail sketch of the argument will be offered in this chapter.

Let us begin with the widespread understanding of postmodernism as rebellion against the grand narratives of the Enlightenment (Gellner 1992b, Lyotard 1984, Rosenau 1992). Again, this is a deceptively simple definition that begs many questions which will be taken up later, including the following: are these "narratives" mere fictions or are they truths rooted in reality? In other words, are these "narratives" actually "traditions," such that the Enlightenment constitutes a tradition even though the hallmark of the Enlightenment was rebellion at all traditions, customs, and other components of culture? Does the period referred to as the Enlightenment signify a particular time and place in European history, as argued by Ernest Gellner (1992a), or does it imply a universal stage of development through which all of humanity passes on the road from traditionalism to modernity? Is the postmodern focus on circulating fictions really new, or merely the latest version of Sophistry that even Plato had to contend with? Let us set aside these important issues for now, and focus on how rebellion at Enlightenment narratives might lead to the unwelcome turn of events described above, as opposed to tolerance and democracy.

One of the most notable, and ironic, examples of promoting tolerance through intolerant methods is the following: "Speaking on the opening day of the first World Conference on Human Rights in 25 years, Secretary of State Warren Christopher said the universality of human rights set a single standard of acceptable behavior around the world, a standard Washington would apply to all countries" (*New York Times*, 15 June 1993: A1). He added that "we cannot let cultural relativism become the last refuge of repression" (ibid.). But representatives of other nations at this conference accused the West of applying double standards with regard to human rights and, in general, of using the notion of universality as "a mask for Western domination" (ibid.). Ironically, the US was intolerant in pushing its version of tolerance, such that the US "seems to be developing a flexible carrot-and-stick approach, using incentives to modify the behavior of countries it considers capable of improvement, like Turkey and China, while punishing those it considers renegades, like Iran" (ibid.). One should note that sociologists routinely accept the notion that no standards are universal and that all social phenomena are culturally relative. Hence, the official actions of the US government, while promoting the Enlightenment project, go against the grain of a century's worth of sociological theorizing and research.

The ethnocentrism in America's approach lies in the fact that the US focuses almost exclusively on civil and political rights such as free speech, press, and elections, while it does not recognize the tendency in most of the rest of the world to view human rights as a matter of employment, education, housing, and food (Stephens 1993). Moreover, "although most nations have banned the death penalty, [the US] refuses to acknowledge international law on this issue" and the US ignores the international requirement that refugees be given an opportunity to apply for political asylum, particularly with regard to Haitian refugees (ibid.).

Communism emerged as an important narrative spun from the Enlightenment, with its utopian assumptions, emphasis on central planning and bureaucracy, and disdain for the traditionalism suggested by nationalism and religion, among other characteristics (Bauman 1992). Barry Smart (1992) is right to conclude that neither socialism nor communism was a fundamental alternative to capitalism, and that all three politico-economic systems were refractions of modernity. It seems to follow logically that rebellion against communism as a modernist system would unleash the anti-modernist forces that communism tried to contain, among them Islamic cultural identity, nationalism, fundamentalism, separatism, anti-Semitism and other phenomena up to and including the white heat of hatred demonstrated in the Balkans since 1991. Moreover, if it is true that communism, socialism, and capitalism are all modernist doctrines, and if all three doctrines are collapsing as part of a postmodern rebellion against modernity, then Islamic cultural movements, nationalism, fundamentalism, and other anti-rational phenomena ought to affect the USA and Western Europe, not just the Balkans and the former Soviet Union. How is it that this obvious connection was missed so completely by analysts who took up Fukuyama's concept of the end of history as their banner? In other words, why did so-called Western nations gloat at the collapse of communism without realizing that the infrastructure of capitalism might be collapsing alongside communism?

One reply is that the so-called capitalist and socialist nations of the industrialized West perceived communist nations as the Evil Empire (to borrow a phrase from former President Ronald Reagan). The Cold War pitted Western capitalism against a supposedly Oriental communism (we shall deconstruct this false polarity of West and East later). Western intellectuals and politicians interpreted the demise of communism as victory for capitalism. This attitude might be termed cosmopolitan provincialism, because it assumes that Western capitalism and democracy are universal occurrences superior to all others. Such an ethnocentric assumption ignores the obvious: communism, socialism, and capitalism are modernist doctrines that are opposed by many anti-modernist happenings, from nationalism to fundamentalism and a good portion of the Islamic world. Thus, as predicted by Emile Durkheim in his 1928 treatise, *Socialism and Saint-Simon*, socialism, communism and capitalism are all destined to fall because they are erected on the incorrect, modernist premise that rationalism and egoism can eradicate and replace the traditions and habits that comprise culture.

FROM THE COLD WAR TO THE ISLAMIC THREAT?

The conclusion that capitalism is next in line for demolition strikes terror in the hearts of so-called Westerners, even if it flows logically from the premise that all narratives spun from the Enlightenment are in serious jeopardy in the postmodern era. Yet evidence abounds to support this hypothesis, even if it is disturbing and therefore rarely admitted openly (Kennedy 1992, Lukacs 1992, Paepke 1992). For example, following the end of the Cold War, capitalist, socialist, and formerly communist nations have focused on Islamic fundamentalism as a threat, sometimes even as a common enemy. Akbar Ahmed (1992) as well as Gellner (1992b) have depicted Islamic culture as the opposite of modernity.[9] In a sense, contemporary Islam constitutes a genuinely postmodern phenomenon in that it rebels at Western, modern cultures. Consider the following passage from a report to the United States House of Representatives by the Task Force on Terrorism and Unconventional Warfare:

In Western Europe, Muslim communities will constitute 25 per cent of the population by the year 2000. (At present, Muslims constitute 7–9 per cent of the population in the US, and 8–10 per cent in France.) Moreover, the Muslim emigre community, and especially the younger, European born, generation is rapidly becoming militant Islamist in outlook. The fundamental source of the problem lies in the irreconcilable difference between Muslim society and the West European environment. The Islamists in Europe have fundamental and uncompromising differences with the society in which they live. The Islamists consider democracy as "the worst scourge the West inflicted on Muslim society in order to destroy it from the inside and annihilate its ancestral values," and are therefore determined to strike it at its core. The Muslim communities demand to be allowed to retain all aspects of Islam, including laws unacceptable in the West.

(3 September 1992: 1)

It is instructive that since the end of the Cold War, Western nations have waged war against Iraq, a Muslim nation – albeit, not a fundamentalist one – but hesitated for three years to wage war to rescue the Muslims in Bosnia-Herzegovina from Serbian aggression. To put the matter another way, "the world goes to war so Kuwait won't disappear, but Bosnia-Herzegovina disappears and the world does nothing" (*New York Times* 17 July 1992: A8). President Bush bombed Iraq during the last days of his tenure in office, in January 1993, ostensibly to enforce a no-fly zone and other United Nations resolutions imposed on Iraq. But no Western power bombed Serbia in order to enforce a similar no-fly zone over Bosnia-Herzegovina and other United Nations resolutions that were imposed – but never effectively enforced – against Serbia.[10] President Clinton bombed Iraq in June 1993 as an act of "self-defense"[11] justified by Article 51 of the United Nations Charter, but would not invoke this same article to allow the Bosnian Muslims to defend themselves. Alexander Cockburn labeled President Clinton's action as American-style state-sponsored terrorism:

> Thus far, bloodletting appears to be the dynamic core of his [President Clinton's] politics of meaning whether in Waco, Mogadishu or Baghdad. The president has also grasped the important principle that it's better to pick on targets emphatically not your own size and to shoot from a safe distance.... Among the usual attributes of a civilized country is its determination to abide by the law. The missile attack [on Baghdad] was entirely lawless, as exemplified by the ludicrous invocation of the self-defense provisions in Article 51 of the UN Charter.
>
> (*Wall Street Journal*, 1 July 1993: A15)

According to the *New York Times*, "The Egyptian Foreign Minister, Amr Moussa, said he hoped US policy would be as firm toward the crimes the Serbs of Bosnia and Herzegovina are committing in violation of legitimacy and all international charters" (28 June 1993: A5). Albert Wohlstetter argued that the United States was employing a double standard:

> The [weapons] embargo was imposed at the request of the Serbs before Slovenia, Bosnia, Croatia, Macedonia, *et al.* became independent states and members of the UN with the right under Article 51 to receive arms for

individual or collective self-defense. That is the article that President Clinton cited when he justified unilateral action in air strikes against Baghdad.

(*Wall Street Journal*, 2 July 1993: A12)

In fact, the only UN resolution that was truly and strictly enforced relative to former Yugoslavia was the one that prevented the Muslims and Croats from defending themselves against Serbian aggression.[12] According to the editors of the *Wall Street Journal*,

> The talk from the West about an air strike against Saddam comes in the wake of Europe's feckless handling of the Serbs' increasingly horrifying predations. What is mainly being lost here is the West's credibility. The people who would destroy any New World Order seem to have noticed.
>
> (22 July 1992: A12)

Islamic nations concluded that the West operates on a double standard: Muslims are punished for violating United Nations resolutions while Christian nations, such as Serbia, flout similar resolutions with impunity. According to George Kenney, former State Department official for Yugoslavia,

> The West has tended to seriously underestimate another issue at stake, namely that citizens of Islamic countries are enraged by the Western failure to stop Serbian aggression directed primarily at Muslims. Many in the Islamic world are quick to point out the double standard when the West bombs Saddam Hussein but ignores Bosnia's plight. On a pragmatic level that may mean an end to the cooperation of Mideast states regarding Iraq. In turn, that could jeopardize our energy security.
>
> (*Wall Street Journal*, 18 February 1993: A18)

Leaders of Islamic nations that are keen on some degree of modernization and cooperation with the West, such as Turkey and Egypt, found themselves under pressure from so-called Islamic fundamentalism, thought to emanate mostly from Iran, as a result of these and other inconsistencies.

Consider the contents of a full-page advertisement in the *New York Times* (30 May 1993: E12) paid for by the Royal Embassy of Saudi Arabia, in which the Saudi Ambassador to the United States, Bandar bin Sultan, charges that "The United States prides itself on being open-minded and believing in pluralism. Yet the media and many in your [USA] political elite abound in stereotypes and the most elementary misunderstandings about Islam." He illustrates this claim by pointing out that

> Whenever suspects in the deplorable World Trade Center bombing are mentioned in the media, they are always described as Muslims, Muslims, Muslims. Yet when news coverage and public discussion turned to Waco, Texas,[13] the central figures there were rarely referred to as Christians, even though that was their overriding commitment. The contrast speaks for itself.
>
> (ibid.)

The Ambassador draws special attention to the Islamic world's great concern for its brethren in Bosnia, who are under threat of extinction. Curiously, instead of calling for Islamic leadership in resolving the threat to Bosnian Muslims, he calls for American leadership. We shall have more to say on the fiction-reality of America as the leader of the postcommunist world. For the present, let us observe that in general, many Muslim leaders have added up perceived defeats and tragedies in Kashmir, Palestine, Afghanistan, Somalia, and Bosnia-Herzegovina to conclude that the West – socialist, communist, as well as capitalist – seeks to exterminate Islam.[14]

Thus, by 1993, it became increasingly clear that the predominantly *economic* Cold War between capitalist and communist nations was being replaced a predominantly *religious* war between the Christian West versus Islam. (Yet one should note that Ahmed 1993 also faults the Islamic nations for their own lack of heart regarding the plight of Muslims in Bosnia-Herzegovina.) Even so, the old-fashioned concept, religion, does not capture the postmodern melting of politics and religion into a new alloy that resembles Robert N. Bellah's (1967) concept of civil religion. This is because all of the world's major religions teach love of neighbor as one's self, whereas this new postmodern religious alloy seems to be advocating suspicion, paranoia, and sometimes even hate of neighbor. We shall have more to say on this later in the book.

How should one conceptualize this dramatic shift in antagonism from the United States versus the former Soviet Union, and their various allies, to the modern and postmodern West versus Islam and various other traditional, fundamentalist, and nationalist entities? Karl Marx's economic reductionism might have been relevant, or at least interesting, during the Cold War. But the new and dangerous mixing of politics with religion calls for a sociological theory that takes religion *and its cultural derivatives* seriously. Yet most social theories derived from the Enlightenment held that religion would disappear from the face of the Earth with the advent of modernity. Only one major sociological theorist – albeit a neglected one, relative to Marx – had argued that in principle, everything is religious. That sociologist was Emile Durkheim. The spirit of Durkheim's overlooked sociology will inform the bulk of the present discussion for the straightforward reason that his emphasis on culture, collective consciousness, and the importance of religion seems better suited for capturing the gist of contemporary developments than the modernist bias in sociological theory.

GOOD VERSUS BAD NATIONALISM

In addition to civil religion, the other powerful anti-modernist force that has been unleashed in our postmodern era is nationalism. At the present juncture in history, it is difficult to argue which is the more powerful social force, religion or nationalism. Nevertheless, I agree with Liah Greenfeld (1992) that nationalism is here to stay so that one must choose between good and bad forms of nationalism. Greenfeld is also right to argue that even France, Britain, and the USA, whose political structures were ostensibly built on the Enlightenment premise that democracy would overcome nationalism, turn out to be highly nationalistic states. Moreover, Western nations are threatened with nationalist and secessionist movements within existing borders, even if these threats are not yet as grave as the forces that tore apart the former Yugoslavia and Soviet Union.

John Lukacs (1992) argues that Soviet communism was just a veneer for Russian nationalism. A similar argument has been made for Yugoslav communism as a cover for Serbian nationalism, even internal imperialism (Meštrović, Goreta, and Letica 1993a). It could be the case that "because we didn't understand that communism wasn't a threat to us, we built the military–industrial–national security state that Eisenhower warned us about, and thereby prolonged the Cold War far longer than necessary" (Ledeen 1993: A12). Moreover, the possibility exists that even if the communist veneer has collapsed, Russian, Serbian, and presumably other nationalist roots for communism have not expired. Thus, the quest for Greater Serbia reared its ugly head in 1991, and foreshadowed the drive for Greater Russia which began to be apparent in 1993 (with Russia's open declaration of support for Serbia).[15] The Cold War ideologues may have got it all wrong: it may never have been the capitalist West in struggle with the communist Evil Empire, but "good" nationalisms versus "bad" nationalisms, within communist empires as well as on the other side of the Iron Curtain.

Of course, the task of distinguishing "good" from "bad" nationalisms seems daunting in a postmodern era that eschews all such distinctions as oppressive. Because this distinction constitutes an important dimension of the remainder of this book, I shall offer only a brief sketch of the proposed reply to the post-modernists. The distinction between good and evil need not hide an imperialist or otherwise intolerant tendency. The cultural relativists need not get defensive about whose societal category of good and evil should be used. Rather, and in line with Durkheim's ([1925] 1961) sociological theorizing, good nationalisms are those that promote compassion and peaceful co-existence with other nations as opposed to nationalisms that are erected on egoistic principles and megalomania relative to other nations. And compassion always co-exists with its opposites, including egoism and anomie, such that Durkheim's insistence on the concept of the dualism of human nature precludes any adherence to utopian thinking (see Meštrović 1993). In other words, good nationalism will always be locked in struggle with bad nationalism, the kind that leads to megalomania and oppression. The important point is that nationalism is inescapable, because without it no society could possibly be anything more than an aggregate of individuals who are perpetually hostile to each other. And if nationalism is inevitable, then it is ludicrous to pretend that it does not exist simply because one would be forced to choose between good and evil.

To be sure, a key narrative in the Enlightenment project that is in trouble in the current, postmodern era is that the lonely, isolated individual is born with "natural rights" and *a priori* moral principles so that he or she really does not need the nation or culture for guidance. (But defenders of this position do not seem overly bothered by the fact that this narcissistic individual is often aggressive, and needs the state to police his or her actions.) This myth has been around at least since Immanuel Kant, John Stuart Mill, and Jean Jacques Rousseau. Democracy was supposed to have emerged equally naturally and harmoniously from the recognition of these natural rights. Yet, former French President Valéry Giscard d'Estaing seems to have a point when he says that "we are facing a crisis of representative democracy" around the world in the present *fin de siècle*, when one considers the widespread dissatisfaction among the voters in the world's democracies (*Wall Street Journal*, 2 July 1993: A1).

The United Nations is the latest social institution that was built on the modernist premise that bureaucracy and rationality can control nationalist passions which are presumed to lead to war, and promote the natural rights of the world's individuals. But as of 1993, United Nations efforts to promote peace based on these principles derived from the Enlightenment were judged to be an abysmal failure in the Middle East, Kashmir, Cyprus, the Golan Heights, Lebanon, Iraq, Angola, San Salvador, the Western Sahara, Cambodia, Somalia, Mozambique, and of course, the former Yugoslavia (*New York Times*, 7 February 1993: A12). These failures should not be surprising if one recalls Sigmund Freud's ([1932] 1963) prediction that the League of Nations – the predecessor of the United Nations – and its successors would fail for the simple reason that the id is stronger than these organizational efforts to establish a substitute for the super-ego. If Freud and his pessimistic contemporaries from the previous *fin de siècle* are correct, it follows that successful international relations in the future must be practiced on a non-modernist assumption: that the id and its derivatives, including nationalism, cannot be eliminated, but must somehow be harmonized and incorporated into cultural and societal institutions. The world's vastly different cultures must somehow cooperate, advance common interests, and merge into a just division of labor that spans the entire globe. We are far from realizing how such harmony should occur. It is important, at this point, to consider that present-day, modernist arrangements might be doomed to fail, and that creative, new solutions should be sought.

THE NEW INTOLERANCE OF ORGANIZED TOLERANCE

The postmodern program of promoting *organized* tolerance is fundamentally flawed, and doomed to failure. This is because any and all organized systems of tolerance will automatically be intolerant of some groups and of all traditional cultures. For example, the campaign for tolerance toward homosexuals in the United States is intolerant of fundamentalist Christian, Hispanic, and other cultural groups who do not tolerate homosexuality. Charles Moskos writes that "Enlightened gay advocates shouldn't argue for compulsory intimacy among persons of openly different sexual orientation," and notes that the US is being torn apart by a strong religious right versus an active gay movement on the political left (*Wall Street Journal*, 23 June 1993: A1). Similarly, the organized campaign to ensure that women would be tolerated as ambitious in the American workplace led to the passage of restrictive laws in some universities that prohibited any and all dating between professors and students. Some university women objected that such laws restricted their freedom to enter into romantic and/or sexual relationships of their choosing.[16] The seemingly compassionate drive on many college campuses to control speech and writing so that it shall not offend anyone may actually be interpreted as a disguised form of authoritarianism, if not a revival of the Inquisition (Rauch 1993).[17] The postmodern focus on tolerance may have resulted in the paradox that extreme forms of intolerance are tolerated because even the intolerant have a point of view that must be heard. We shall have more to say later on the paradoxical intolerance of postmodern tolerance.

For now, let us note that tolerance denotes an air of contemptuous superiority on the part of those who do the tolerating. To tolerate is to put up with something or someone, not to sympathize or understand. Enlightened tolerant persons will fall unwittingly into the trap of narcissism because by being tolerant they feel that they are better than traditional persons. Yet narcissism opens the door to all sorts of ethnocentrism and bigotry which, in the end, will result in the repetition of the alleged evils of traditional bigots.

Marxism is another narrative spun from the Enlightenment that has been affected by both postmodernism and the collapse of communism – and Marxism also tried to instil compulsory tolerance at the same time that it would not tolerate tradition (Bauman 1992). Thus, postmodernism is frequently associated with the concept of post-Marxism. Yet the concept of post-Marxism is as murky as the concept of postmodernism, and for similar reasons: is post-Marxism a rebellion against or an extension of Marxism? Up to the present, Marxists have thrived in academia although there have been challenges to them (Hollander 1992). Despite the apparent collapse of communism, Marxists deny that their project is dead, even if it seems discredited at the present time. Nevertheless, the many Marxist spin-offs that focus on class equality regarding race and gender are challenged by conservative, even fundamentalist, movements as well as organized outbreaks of hate crimes against women and minorities. Besides, even old-fashioned communism – rejected by enlightened Marxists – is alive and well in China and other regions of Asia. There exists the real threat that communism may transform itself into a new system of authoritarianism in the former Soviet Union and the Balkans (Meštrović, Goreta, and Letica 1993b; Tomašić 1948a).

Narcissism is a neglected dimension of capitalist as well as communist efforts to promote organized tolerance. Christopher Lasch's unmasking of the West's "culture of narcissism" (1979) needs to be compared with Jovan Rasković's (1990) unmasking of communist and Marxist narcissisms: advocates of both systems (capitalism and communism) boasted that they were superior to the other, and had produced the best socio-political system in the world. (Herein lies the secret of the fact that Francis Fukuyama could write a Marxist defense of US capitalism!) But one should keep in mind Sigmund Freud's admonition that excessive narcissism is a pathological phenomenon that invariably leads to aggression, *not* tolerance. Thus, the postmodern and postcommunist programs aimed at promoting tolerance

– by force, if necessary – have resulted in appreciably less tolerance in a world that seems to be tormented by ethnic hatred. The key point is that genuine tolerance flows from compassion, which is the opposite of narcissism. Both communism and capitalism, as modernist systems, are erected on premises that lead to narcissism, and narcissism *cannot* yield tolerance.

Sociology presents a special case of the near extinction of this Enlightenment narrative that begins and ends with the individual. It is a strange paradox that sociology, as the science of societies, has mirrored the West's intolerance of conceptualizing cultures as phenomena that transcend or constrain the individual. Hence, the most sociological of the sociologists, Emile Durkheim, was completely eclipsed by the most psychological sociologist, Karl Marx, who regards the notion of culture as reification, and who sought to restore the individual to his or her self (see Fromm 1962). Barely a hundred years old, sociology may well expire by the end of this century along with communism and capitalism.

The reasons for sociology's pathetic decline are not difficult to fathom. Since its inception, sociology had wed itself to the Enlightenment legacy of Auguste Comte, and its biggest export was Marxism, another Enlightenment-based theory. Parsonian functionalism is yet another, once-popular modernist doctrine that was promulgated by twentieth-century sociologists. Sociology tried to gain popularity and acceptance in academia by adopting the statistical methodology of the natural sciences. The philosopher-turned-sociologist, Georg Simmel, spotted this tendency in the social sciences as early as 1905:

> This primacy of technique has infected even the purely intellectual branches of knowledge: in the historical sciences, as in that of experimental psychology, investigations, essentially worthless and, as regards the ultimate end of all research, most unimportant, frequently enjoy a quite disproportionate degree of recognition, provided only that they be carried out by means of perfect methodical, technical processes.
>
> (1905: 25)

Now that positivism, Marxism, and science are under increasing attack from populism, fundamentalism, and other anti-Enlightenment forces, sociology finds itself sinking along with the Enlightenment narratives it promoted. Sociologists rationalize their low status in academia by claiming that they tolerate all points of view. But that is not true, because quantitative studies are still considered to be more prestigious than qualitative, cultural studies. Sociology's professional narcissism – the belief among its aging elite that positivism is a method of inquiry superior to all others – has led to consequences on a par with the cultural narcissism of communism and capitalism, namely, aggression and paranoia toward scholars who refuse to adopt mainstream thinking and methodology that drives away followers. And far from looking for new bearings by seeking out its own cultural roots, sociology pretends that it can still save itself by clinging to the same Comtean narratives that have brought it to its present lack of distinction.

With regard to the fate of sociology, I shall extend the argument here that I began elsewhere (Meštrović 1988, 1991, 1992): Auguste Comte may have given sociology its name and tried to pass it off as an Enlightenment doctrine. And Karl Marx promulgated this same Enlightenment dream, albeit with a German, specifically Hegelian, twist. But the world's first bona fide professor of sociology was Emile Durkheim, and he christened sociology with the anti-Enlightenment *fin de siècle* spirit of the times in which he lived, and in particular, Arthur Schopenhauer's philosophy. Durkheim's sociological colleague, Georg Simmel ([1907] 1986), makes it clear that at the previous turn of the century, Arthur Schopenhauer's anti-Enlightenment philosophy paved the way for Nietzsche,[18] and both philosophies had supplanted the dominance of Hegel, Kant, and Comte. Thus, in seeking out the roots of sociology, one encounters a polemic between Comtean, pro-Enlightenment visions of social order versus Durkheimian, anti-Enlightenment sociology that is very similar to contemporary debates concerning postmodernism.

CONTRADICTIONS AND INCONSISTENCIES IN THE POSTMODERN DISCOURSE

How can one make sense of the alleged fall of communism in such intellectually confusing times? Did liberal democracy finally "win" over history, as claimed by Fukuyama, or is humanity unknowingly poised for another round of Nietzsche's recurrence of the same? One can make the case that the world is moving in several directions simultaneously, and that some of these are opposed to the rational myths of progress that would lead to a utopia of peace and democracy, yet intellectual concepts in general and sociological concepts in particular are lagging behind these tendencies by clinging to outmoded narratives spun from the Enlightenment.

For example, if communism is dead, as Brzezinski (1989) and others claim, what will replace it? The unthinking answer thus far has been, capitalism and democracy – in fact, the American versions of these phenomena, as if no other sorts exist. A more cautious and thoughtful analysis suggests that capitalism and democracy are generally considered to be cultural products of the Enlightenment, but then, Marxism as well as communism is also a variation of the Enlightenment project. All of these are ideologies that worship Science with a capital "S" and Rationality with a capital "R" (Bauman 1992). Yet the postmodernists claim that the Enlightenment project itself is bankrupt, and has been responsible for widespread, organized terror and oppression, from the French Revolution through to the communism experiment in the Soviet Union (Gellner 1992b). If the postmodernists are correct, they deliberately do not point to an alternative to the Enlightenment project. Instead, they urge one to be comfortable in the absence of certainty (Rosenau 1992). Tolerance is supposed to emerge spontaneously from this postmodern overthrow of Enlightenment narratives (Bauman 1991).

Such optimistic conclusions are little more than wishful thinking, and constitute a disguised version of utopianism – perhaps even Marxism – against which postmodernism was supposed to have rebelled. If the Enlightenment project opposed tradition and culture, as claimed by Gellner (1992a) and others, then one would expect that a postmodern revolt against the Enlightenment would seek to revive tradition and culture. Instead, many proponents of postmodernism continue to write in the pro-Enlightenment habit of eschewing tradition and culture. Far from being obvious that anti-cultural modernism can sustain tolerance, it seems that the opposite might be true: the sustained modernist contempt for tradition and culture is itself highly intolerant, and signals the contours of the postmodern future in which intolerance will be disguised as tolerance.

For example, Jean Baudrillard, frequently cited as *the* spokesperson for postmodernism (Gane 1991), likens the postmodern future in general and of America in particular to a cultural desert, a society that exists without cultural mores (1986: 99). Far from promoting tolerance, this lack of culture can promote cruel indifference and new forms of intolerance:

> But this easy life knows no pity. Its logic is a pitiless one. If utopia has already been achieved, then unhappiness does not exist, the poor are no longer credible. . . . The have-nots will be condemned to oblivion, to abandonment, to disappearance pure and simple. This is "must exit" logic: poor people must exit. The ultimatum issued in the name of wealth and efficiency wipes them off the map. And rightly so, since they show such bad taste as to deviate from the general consensus. . . . No need to feel guilty. . . . Long live the Fourth World, the world to which you can say, "Right, utopia has arrived. If you aren't part of it, get lost!"
>
> (Baudrillard 1986: 111)

According to Arthur Kroker, Baudrillard's America as the metaphor for the postmodern world of the future exists as a "quantum society: no history, only a virtual culture; no time, only a perfectly spatialized politics; no justice, only a contractual theory of political rights; and finally, not even a mass society, but a society of masses, typified by the random and violent struggle of predators and parasites" (1992: 71).

Fukuyama's "end of history" concept is often apprehended similarly in the context of postmodernism, because both concepts imply the end of tradition and culture – and tradition and culture are regarded by modernists as well as postmodernists in pejorative terms, as primitive phenomena to be outgrown by an aging, supposedly more sophisticated humanity. If Fukuyama is correct that liberal democracy has replaced history, that seems to imply that democracy is no longer rooted in the cultural "habits of the heart" of Americans or other peoples, as claimed by Alexis de Tocqueville ([1845] 1945) and other founding fathers of sociology from the previous *fin de siècle*. Fukuyama and the postmodernists beg the question of how a postmodern culture is reproduced or transmitted across generations if it exists without the help of habits and traditions. According to Fukuyama, "contemporary liberal democracies did not emerge out of the shadowy mists of tradition" (1992: 153). If that is true, then what props up liberal democracy? How does one learn to be democratic if democracy is not a tradition?

Contrary to all the work by anthropologists and other students of culture, Fukuyama would have us believe that democracy exists as a rootless, universal abstraction, self-begotten and self-sustaining entity, severed completely from culture and history. This is simply an impossible state of affairs.

Fukuyama draws on two well-known defenders of the Enlightenment, Hegel and Marx, to construct the intellectual scaffolding for his problematic argument. It is ironic that the Bolsheviks drew on these same two philosophers of progress and enlightened social engineering for their failed experiment in utopia, as well as for their jaundiced view of all traditions. Apparently unaware of the full extent of this irony, Fukuyama admits that in his defense of liberal democracy and capitalism, he offers "a kind of Marxist interpretation of history that leads to a completely non-Marxist conclusion" (1992: 131). But one wonders how Marxism can lead to non-Marxist goals, and besides – hasn't the world suffered through enough efforts to refract some pure, distilled version of Hegel and Marx that will finally work?

Yet, with apparent sincerity, Fukuyama – who was once employed by the US State Department – attempts to derive the ideals of liberal democracy from Marx and Hegel's often harshly oppressive philosophies. As much as some intellectuals seek to defend the "young" Marx who was supposedly a humanist, there is no doubt that in *The Communist Manifesto* – and elsewhere – Marx writes of the need to fight against democracy, and already approved of forced labor, abolition of all right of inheritance, centralization of all credit in the hands of the state, the dissolution of the family, as well as the forced "abolition of all the distinction between town and country," among many other goals that are frankly totalitarian (1983: 227).

Similarly, one must keep in mind that even if Hegel did write of freedom in *Philosophy of History* ([1899] 1965), his version of freedom had a peculiarly Prussian flavor to it: "Morality and Justice in the State are also divine and commanded by God, and [in] point of substance there is nothing higher or more sacred" (p. 422). Moreover, Hegel predicted that the Protestant countries in general and the Protestant regions of Germany in particular would achieve this desired state that he called the end of history, while other regions of the world would not. Hegel dismissed the Americas, Africa, Asia and most of Europe as being unsuitable for sustaining what he called freedom. According to Hegel, "the German world appears at this point of development – the fourth [and final] phase of World-History" (ibid. 108). With all due respect to Hegel's philosophical skills, it cannot be denied that his philosophy inspired Nazism as well as communism, two of the most monstrous and inhumane doctrines of the twentieth century. Herein lies still another irony that Fukuyama seems not to acknowledge: Hegel's "end of history" presupposes the very ethnocentrism and nationalism that Fukuyama claims will disappear with the end of history! There can be little doubt that Hegel was proposing a distinctively *German* and ethnocentric "end of history." In following the popular efforts of his mentor, Allan Bloom (1987), to revive those portions of German philosophy that Nietzsche had vanquished, Fukuyama proposes an Americanized version of this threatening idea.

Despite these rather obvious, glaring, and somewhat bizarre contradictions, the dustjacket of Fukuyama's book boasts praise from Charles Krauthammer, George F. Will, Tom Wolfe, Irving Kristol, Allan Bloom, and Eduard Shevardnadze. In a discussion of this sort, it should be noted that Mr. Shevardnadze replaced by military force the democratically elected leader of formerly Soviet Georgia in 1991, and is regarded by many Georgians as a dictator. In any event, Fukuyama achieved practically instant fame for his not so subtle revival of Marxism at a time when Marxism was presumed to be dead. How was this possible? An answer seems to be that Fukuyama defends the Enlightenment project's faith in the victory of grand, modernist, social engineering over tradition and culture that was assumed by the Bolsheviks and continues to be assumed by many intellectuals who consider themselves to be postmodern defenders of liberal democracy. Yet the "grand failure" of Marxist-based communism (from Brzezinski 1989) should make one wonder whether genuine liberalism can be derived exclusively from an Enlightenment-based philosophy that is hostile to the idea of culture.

Moreover, genuine liberalism presupposes an *emotionally* charged, even *irrational*, high regard for the individual and for human rights that is not really commensurate with the value placed upon intellectual detachment that is usually associated with the Enlightenment. Intellectual detachment deteriorates easily into old-fashioned sadism or other forms of cruel indifference to the plight of minorities and others who suffer oppression. Liberalism cannot be derived from itself, but must be rooted in culture. In this regard, too, Durkheim offers the unusual alternative to the stale debates between liberals and conservatives by positing a "communitarian liberalism" (Cladis 1992). For Durkheim, liberalism is not opposed to tradition, but is itself a tradition (Meštrović 1991, 1992).

Durkheim's thoughtful and philosophical analysis does not inform contemporary, faddish efforts at multiculturalism. Postmodern, politically correct multiculturalism is actually hostile and intolerant to old-fashioned culture even as it preaches tolerance. According to Kay S. Hymowitz (1993), "multiculturalists who hope to advance the cause of oppressed minorities face a simple, if unwelcome truth: culture is an essentially conservative force. It binds people to a past laden with powerful traditions and beliefs and often obligates them to strict, customary discipline". Thus, the attempt to transform the traditional celebration of Irish culture in New York City's St. Patrick's Day parade into a multicultural event that would tolerate gays and lesbians is every bit as intolerant as the melting-pot, assimilation model that the multiculturalists criticize. There is no escape from the fact that every organized system of avowed tolerance is also going to be intolerant.

The problem comes down to the following: if the Enlightenment is not an adequate or even true bedrock upon which the ideals of liberal democracy can or should be built, what is? It may well be the case that Tocqueville and Durkheim – in opposition to Hegel and Marx – were right to claim that democracy in general and American freedoms in particular are nurtured by cultural "habits of the heart" that are found in religion, family, the community, and other cultural institutions based upon compassion. It is no longer common knowledge that except for Karl

Marx, the original founding fathers of sociology frequently referred to various derivatives of "habits of the heart" – *not* habits of the mind glorified by the Enlightenment – as the structural basis of society itself as well as its major institutions, including democracy. These derivatives include mores, folkways, culture, collective representations, and even Durkheim's notion of a collective consciousness. In other words, and in direct opposition to Hegel and Fukuyama, Tocqueville and Durkheim would have one believe that democracy *does* emerge out of tradition, even that democracy itself *is* a tradition that needs to be self-consciously nurtured in a postmodernist era that seeks to abolish all cultural traditions.

Of course, the characterization of liberalism and democracy as rooted in culture and traditions raises the question whether all "habits of the heart" are benign. Tocqueville, Durkheim and other sociologists who valued tradition were clearly aware that some cultural phenomena are destructive. For this reason, Tocqueville distinguished between "good" versus "bad" habits of the heart in the USA, and Durkheim ([1897] 1951) distinguished between healthy, normal social facts and anomic, pathological ones. Both thinkers have been criticized vigorously for making these distinctions. Here one arrives at another aspect of the postmodern scene, the acceptance of cultural and ethical relativism that regards all distinctions and differences as automatically oppressive (Gellner 1992b). At this point in the discussion, we shall only note a serious problem that must be taken up later.

To summarize this segment of the discussion: much of the postmodernist discourse is contradictory and inconsistent because it unwittingly promotes the same Enlightenment agenda that it pretends to rebel against. I have pointed to important sociologists from the previous *fin de siècle* who make a more convincing argument that liberalism and tolerance must be rooted in culture. Yet culture and tradition have been given such a negative reputation by modernists that this claim is not immediately convincing, and it raises the fear that what might seem to be a "good" or benign cultural value to a particular individual will be "evil" and oppressive to another. This problem constitutes one reason among many why postmodernists dismiss all distinctions, dualisms, and categories as inherently oppressive (Lyotard 1984).

But what are the alternatives to the cultural approach to social life? Consider Zygmunt Bauman's (1992) elaboration on the theme that the collapse of communism is a symptom of postmodernity defined as rebellion against Enlightenment narratives. He depicts the communist dream of the perfect society as a manifestation of the *modernist* experiment in social engineering. If that is true, then the people who celebrate the collapse of communism "celebrate more than that without always knowing it. They celebrate the end of modernity actually, because what collapsed was the most decisive attempt to make modernity work; and it failed" (1992: 222). For the sake of argument, let us assume that Bauman is correct. In that case, efforts to export democracy and free-market institutions to postcommunist nations would be reduced to unwitting efforts to replace a dead with a dying system of modernity. In order to avoid this unwelcome conclusion, Bauman calls for the softened Marxist goal of "modernity emancipated from false consciousness" (p. 188) that is supposed to lead to freedom. Yet this Marxist goal commits the same modernist mistake that we had exposed above: it posits a mythical freedom from culture in the form of "true consciousness" without explaining the origins or reproduction of such enlightened consciousness. But more importantly, and far from celebrating the collapse of modernity, most persons would regard such a collapse of modernity as inherently frightening. How does one avoid anomie, chaos, and the war of all against all once modernist forces are removed? Bauman has not transcended the utopianism inherent in Marxist thinking – despite his criticisms of Marxism – that leads to the unsubstantiated conclusion that the human who is completely emancipated from culture will be only kind and tolerant. The Freudian and Durkheimian counterarguments must be considered as well: a human untouched and unfettered by culture is at the mercy of his or her savage id and anomic tendencies.

Instead of being seduced by Marxism and modernism yet again, let us search for a non-Marxist, non-modernist alternative to the lacunae that are exposed by postmodern controversies.

THE CULTURAL DECLINE OF CULTURAL EXPLANATIONS

Missing in Fukuyama's, Baudrillard's, Bauman's, and other postmodern, highly abstract, and jargon-filled accounts of dramatic endings is the traditional notion of culture. To be sure, intellectuals write of postmodern culture, but unlike the traditionalists, they mean that culture consists of rootless, circulating fictions and signs that do not refer to anything permanent (Baudrillard 1981, 1988a, 1990). One thinks of the oxymorons, "television heritage" or "electronic town meeting" as illustrations of this contemporary bastardization of the concept of culture. Here again, despite the rhetoric of protest, the postmodernists merely extend the modernist disdain for the rootedness of culture. In a sense, postmodernism signifies the triumph of sophistry, such that appearance counts far more than old-fashioned reality. Postmodern culture conceived as a mess of circulating fictions is a feeble copy of what Tocqueville termed habits of the heart. For the sake of clarity in this discussion, we shall refer to postmodern fictions in opposition to the notion of culture as used by Tocqueville, Durkheim, and other sociologists from the previous *fin de siècle*.

Arthur Kroker captures some of the irony involved in the postmodern discussion of culture with this characterization of Baudrillard: "This is to suggest that Baudrillard is really the Oswald Spengler of the cyborg age. Not so much the author of the *Decline of the West* (that would privilege the finality of the referent), but the digital historian of the Ecstasy of the Decline" (1992: 57).

Phenomena that were depicted as habits of the heart or collective representations or some other cultural product a century ago tend to be depicted by contemporary, postmodern intellectuals as if they were reified, self-begotten, *a priori* categories, floating through history like clouds. For example, it does not seem to have occurred to Brzezinski (1989) that an authoritarian culture might have preceded communism, and that this same culture might fester secretly beneath the surface victory of democracy in Eastern Europe and the former Soviet Union. It is ironic that, following Max Weber ([1904] 1958), thousands of studies have examined the cultural roots of capitalism, yet the notion that communism might have sprung from cultural roots is practically unexplored, with the notable exception of neglected works by Dinko Tomašić (1948a, 1953). In other words, communism might well draw on certain, specific cultural values, much as Tocqueville associated slavery in America with the authoritarianism and aristocracy of the Old South. Similarly, democracy might draw on equally specific cultural values, even geographical settings, as was the case with Puritan America – and not all of these cultural values are necessarily benign.

Foreign policy experts seem to have overlooked the possibility of a counterrevolution that would bring back communism to the nations in which it fell all too easily in the late 1980s – even though it may not be called communism the second time around, even if most of the same ex-communists have been elected to office and rule the very nations they used to rule, under the new banner of democracy. The important point is that old habits die hard. This rule applies to the authoritarian habits that comprised communism, which was a cultural system, not just an abstract ideology.

Similarly, Bauman (1992) does not consider that even if communism is a modernist doctrine, it failed to modernize or change dramatically the medieval mind-set of the people it ruled. Almost as soon as communism fell in Eastern Europe in the 1980s, the postcommunist nations stepped *back into history*, and did not make appreciable strides in becoming like the modern West. From the cultural framework adopted here, this is not surprising. For the most part, the nations that were ruled by communism had never developed the traditions of human rights and the rule of law that are taken for granted in the West. In fact, because they lacked anything like an Enlightenment tradition, Russia, Croatia, Slovenia, Poland and other nations that emerged from the tyranny of communism looked to Western Europe and the United States for guidance in establishing democracy and free markets. But since 1989 the United States has been preoccupied with its domestic problems, and has not exercised its traditional role, first cited by Tocqueville ([1845] 1945: 32), as the beacon of democracy in the world. And for the most part, Western Europe shunned the nations that had recently emerged from communism.

Many contemporary Americans are cynical about this traditional role that America still plays in the world – albeit, a fictional role, because America is seen by the oppressed as much more democratic and committed to human rights than it really is. This contrast became painfully obvious in May 1993 when President Clinton abdicated America's leadership to Russia and the Europeans with regard to putting an end to Serbian aggression in the Balkans. America's abnegation following the end of the Cold War

left a vacuum that the European Community simply could not fill. . . . That means that pirates or rogues such as Slobodan Milošević will be able to pursue their goals challenged mainly by conciliatory delegations of European Community foreign ministers, half-hearted economic embargoes and hollow condemnations. The blood from the Balkans is seeping under Europe's door. If Europeans won't stanch the flow, then America has to lead them in a joint rescue.

(New York Times, 23 July 1992: A10)

Similarly, according to William Safire, "Wherever in the world brutality is inflicted on millions of people, America's place is in the vanguard of marshalling civilization's response" (*New York Times*, 21 May 1992: A15).[19]

For example, despite the rhetoric of supporting democratic reform, the United States mistakenly backed the communist governments of Gorbachev and a Serbian-dominated Yugoslavia as long as it could. Richard Nixon (1992a) has observed that even when Yeltsin and the leaders of Croatia and Slovenia openly sought inclusion in the democratic orbit of values they perceived as Western, the United States as well as Europe excluded them from their markets and other organizational structures.[20] The futures of postcommunist Russia and Eastern Europe were conspicuously absent in the Presidential Campaign of 1992. As late as the Spring of 1993, the United States would not promise much more than $3 billion to rescue Russia's ailing economy and guarantee peace for future generations even though the Western allies had spent over $50 billion in the mostly fruitless war against Saddam Hussein. Similarly, the cost for maintaining the North Atlantic Treaty Organization (NATO) comes to over $100 billion per year.

In the absence of a democratic system of cultural values to replace the values that fed Bolshevism, there emerged within postcommunist nations nationalism, ethnocentrism, fundamentalism, Balkanization, and other phenomena that Fukuyama and other analysts had declared dead – and these sinister forces returned with a vengeance. Caught almost completely off guard, the West responded with denial and paralysis.

For example, with regard to the third Balkan War that began in 1991, and continues to rage in former Yugoslavia as I am writing, the former US Ambassador, David Anderson wrote, "The US hopes that the whole dirty business will go away."[21] Pretending that both history and communism really did come to some magical, postmodern end, United States as well as European policy-makers refused to acknowledge evidence to the contrary, and also refused initially to fault and isolate the hardline Serbian government's documented aggression against its neighbors. The United States waited until 7 April 1992 to finally go along with its European friends and allies in recognizing the efforts by Slovenia, Croatia, and Bosnia-Herzegovina to break away from a Serbian-dominated, communist Yugoslavia. (The USA, Britain, and France also consistently second-guessed and expressed regret at the decisions to recognize these nations.)

The United States placed the blame for the war equally on the Croats, Serbs, and Bosnians, even though respected newspapers such as the *New York Times* made it clear that the Serbian government and the Serbian-dominated federal army were and continue to be the aggressors in the current Balkan War. For example, on 23 April 1992, "The State Department condemned Serbian forces again today for the violence in Bosnia-Herzegovina, but extended its criticisms to the republic's Croats and Muslims as well. 'No party is blameless for the current situation,' the department spokeswoman, Margaret D. Tutwiler, said" (*New York Times*, 23 April 1992: A4).

The European Community was only slightly less tardy than the US, waiting six months to grant diplomatic recognition to pro-Western Slovenia, Croatia, and Bosnia-Herzegovina. On 28 June 1991, war broke out in the Balkans, but the USA refused for months to give up on the idea of Yugoslavia, even after Yugoslavia was reduced to only Serbia and Montenegro. And in delaying recognition of Slovenia, Bosnia-Herzegovina, and Croatia, as well as imposing sanctions on them – acts that, in effect, punished them for seeking democracy and self-determination – the so-called West gave tacit support to a hardline, communist regime emanating from Belgrade. Similarly, former President Richard Nixon (1992b) noted that the West had not made appreciable efforts to ensure that Boris Yeltsin would succeed in his bold experiment in democracy. Why should it, when the prevailing mood in the early 1990s was euphoria in response to the fiction that the danger of totalitarianism had passed completely?

In summary, following the collapse of communism, leading intellectuals in Western nations seem to have clung uncritically and unwittingly to major tenets of Comtean positivism, Marxism, Hegelianism, and other derivatives of modernism. And all this, despite the vocal rhetoric of rebellion at Enlightenment narratives represented by postmodern doctrines! Like the positivists, post-Cold-War postmodernists assumed incorrectly that religion in general and religious fundamentalism in particular were no longer social forces to be taken seriously. Like the Marxists, Western analysts failed to take nationalism seriously, even though nationalism is emerging as one of the strongest social forces in the post-Cold-War, postmodernist era. Hegel, the Bolsheviks, and Fukuyama proclaimed the end of history, even though history was repeating itself, with a vengeance, all over the world. More surprisingly, the same intellectuals who had opposed communism and demonized Marxism now praised Fukuyama and accepted his version of Marxism![22] Given the dominance of various derivatives of soft Marxism found in academia (Hollander 1992), from Fukuyama to the postmodernists, how could anyone have expected the resurgence of nationalism, racism, genocide and other evils in the post-Cold-War world? Like the Bolsheviks of old, many intellectuals on this side of the former Iron Curtain discounted the power of nationalism, fundamentalism, and other aspects of what Hegel and Fukuyama dismiss as mere history. As a result, while the West was congratulating itself on its victory in the Cold War, these neglected forces began to lead to unwelcome ends: Balkanization, conflict, isolation, separation, chaos, racism, and genocide – even the emergence of new totalitarian states.

Modern sociology seems ill-equipped to offer guidance, because it is as uncritically anti-cultural as the rest of contemporary Western intelligentsia.

Contemporary sociology pays lip-service to its classical founding fathers – among them, Tocqueville, Veblen, Weber, Durkheim, and Simmel – but it does not take seriously their cultural approach to social phenomena. For example, the Enlightenment-based legacy of Karl Marx overpowered the tradition-based legacies of Tocqueville and Durkheim among the sociologists. Instead of studying what Tocqueville called the "habits of the heart" of various peoples that were ruled by communism, twentieth-century sociology has tried to emulate the allegedly pristine and "value-free" science exemplified by physics and other natural sciences. Both Marxism and Parsonian functionalism seized upon this modernist mood, and dominated sociology in the present century. Society was supposed to be explained through simple and elegant mathematical formulas. Alas, as postmodern social life proved to be too complex for the oversimplified rationalism that took over the Universities, sociology lost stature, and is deemed by the general population practically irrelevant to the catastrophes and socio-political drama unfolding in the present *fin de siècle*. Because sociology in formerly communist nations was little more than disguised Marxist ideology, it never gave rise to anything like the Chicago School tradition of qualitative studies and ethnographies. As a result, and despite a hundred years of sociology, the post-Cold-War world finds itself in the incredible position of knowing practically nothing of the life experiences of the peoples that were ruled by communism. For example, there exists no Russian or Yugoslav equivalent of David Riesman's *Lonely Crowd* (1950), Seymour Martin Lipset's *Continental Divide* (1989), or other studies of American social character.

COPING WITH THE RETURN OF HISTORY

But in fact, and contrary to Fukuyama and the other modernists, history is repeating and reasserting itself in the present *fin de siècle* with a vengeance. Nations that were assumed to have disappeared over a century ago lay apparently submerged beneath communist modernism, and they awoke with more vigor than ever. Almost as soon as communism fell, nationalism replaced it as one of the strongest and most important social forces in the world today. Communism did *not* brainwash the masses – as many intellectuals had feared since the 1950s (Riesman 1954) – and seems hardly to have made a dent in the traditional cultures of the peoples it apparently ruled. Religion, fundamentalism, ethnocentrism, even racism, have also become noisier in recent years – even in Western nations, which regarded these things as beneath them for a long time. For example, following the notorious Los Angeles riots of 1992, Americans no longer discuss assimilation or anything like the old-fashioned "melting-pot" goal for America's ethnic groups. Instead, contemporary politicians ask the question posed by Rodney King,[23] "Can we all just get along?" Getting along is the bare minimum necessary for social functioning. There can be little doubt that the present *fin de siècle* will prove to be every bit as tumultuous as the previous one.

If the modernists and postmodernists are not able to capture the direction of world events today, to whom should one turn for intellectual meaning? A good strategy to follow is simply to consider the intellectuals and theories that these modernists and postmodernists had eclipsed – to seek out the lacunae that have been left in social consciousness as a result of a misguided quest for oversimplified rationalism. For example, almost everyone seems to have forgotten Hegel's rival and severe critic, Arthur Schopenhauer. By most historical accounts, it was Schopenhauer, *not* Hegel, Nietzsche, or Kant, who ruled the intellectual Western world of the 1880s and 1890s. Similarly, Emile Durkheim, *not* Karl Marx or Max Weber, ruled the sociological world of the previous *fin de siècle* (Meštrović 1988). Baudrillard has set himself and his anti-cultural postmodernism in direct and self-conscious opposition to Alexis de Tocqueville and Thorstein Veblen, who argued for the primacy and rootedness of cultural habits. With the notable exception of Charles Schoenfeld,[24] few intellectuals have applied Sigmund Freud's and other psychoanalytic writings to understanding nationalism, sovereignty, crime, and other political phenomena. Yet it should be obvious that the unconscious, aggressive, and non-rational aspects of human life that Freud studied should and do apply to nations and their political leaders. Finally, Talcott Parsons displaced the importance of Pitirim Sorokin, the Russian-born sociologist who hired him and established the sociology department at Harvard University in the 1930s.

By analogy, we might say that much as the communists and other modernists were wrong to believe that nations would disappear and merge into some giant, abstract, global society, the postmodernists and modern sociologists are wrong to claim that all of the classical founders of sociology except for Karl Marx are now irrelevant. Much as Bosnia-Herzegovina, Croatia and Slovenia escaped the clutches of a Serb-dominated and communist Yugoslavia – to some degree, even if they paid a high price for freedom – the repressed legacies of Schopenhauer, Durkheim, Veblen, Freud, Tocqueville, and Sorokin need to break through the repression imposed by Parsonian, Marxist and other hyper-abstractionist sociologies.

For example, Bryan Magee claims that "by the turn of the [previous] century, Schopenhauer was an all-pervading cultural influence" whose impact could be traced from Sigmund Freud and Emile Durkheim to Leo Tolstoy, Thomas Mann, Max Horkheimer, and Albert Einstein (1983: 264). This is because Schopenhauer, in direct opposition to Hegel and Kant, taught that the heart (signifying the unconscious, emotions, and all that opposes rationality) is stronger and more important than the mind glorified by the Enlightenment. In fact, Schopenhauer often referred to "that miserable Hegelism, that school of dullness, that center of stupidity and ignorance, that mind-destroying, spurious wisdom" in strongly critical terms ([1818] 1965b: 616). Unlike Hegel, Schopenhauer taught that the state could never be trusted to make people moral, only to punish lawbreakers. Contrary to Hegel, Schopenhauer insisted that the individual person is far more important than the state. Schopenhauer took seriously the ethical message preached by all the world's major religions, that the essence of morality is compassion, not egoism. He concluded that utopia could never be reached, and that history would never come to an end. Instead, human evil and irrationality would have to be managed within tolerable limits, because they could never be eliminated completely. Obviously, Schopenhauer's philosophy seems much more sobering and realistic than the utopian visions of Hegel, Marx, and other modernists.

If one examines contemporary sociological treatises, one will find that they draw primarily upon Kant, Hegel, Marx, and Nietzsche – as if Schopenhauer and his disciples never existed, and had never exerted the profound influence that historians attribute to them. Similarly, Jean Baudrillard makes it clear that his book, *America*, is meant to supplant Alexis de Tocqueville's *Democracy in America*. Tocqueville argued that democracy is rooted in traditions, whereas Baudrillard argues that social life is made up of circulating, rootless fictions, and that democracy is one such fiction among many. Yet Tocqueville's assessments seem so much more hopeful, and relevant to contemporary problems, than Baudrillard's cruel dismissal of culture. In his 1845 classic, *Democracy in America*, Tocqueville warned against the excesses of democracy unchecked by moral principles: democracy can degenerate into despotism when elected officials seek office for private gain at public expense. One might claim that, in recent years, the United States seems to have reached this distressing state of affairs. And this is possible in democracy because unrestrained self-interest "tends to isolate men from each other so that each thinks only of himself" ([1845] 1945: 444). Durkheim agrees with Tocqueville that society cannot exist solely on the basis of egoism. The very notion of society presupposes empathy, the identification of all of society's members with each other. Contrary to Tocqueville and Durkheim, the postmodern "Me-generation" of the 1980s and 1990s is attempting to erect a liberal, democratic world order on the basis of egoism and narcissism, not empathy and compassion. This misguided effort is doomed to fail.

Tocqueville also made the disheartening prediction that race relations in America would not be resolved until blacks and whites intermingle completely:

> These two races are fastened to each other without intermingling; and they are alike unable to separate entirely or to combine. The most formidable of all the ills that threaten the future of the Union arises from the presence of a black population upon its territory; and in contemplating the cause of the present embarrassments, or the future dangers of the United States, the observer is invariably led to this as a primary fact.
>
> ([1845] 1945: 370)

Consider the powerful resonance for today's social problems in Tocqueville's observation that "the legal barrier which separated the two races is falling away, but not that which exists in the manners of the country; slavery recedes, but the prejudice to which it has given birth is immovable" (p. 373). He predicted that, "if oppressed, [blacks] may bring an action at law, but they will find none but whites among their judges" (ibid.). In these and other ways, Tocqueville continues to speak directly to us today, but who reads Tocqueville seriously anymore?[25]

Similarly, Pitirim Sorokin was almost completely eclipsed by his American student, the economist-turned-sociologist, Talcott Parsons. It is not beside the point to consider the pre-communist "Russianness" of Sorokin's theory versus the glib, and in many ways typically American, optimism found in the modernist writings of Parsons. In his *Russia and the United States*, first published in 1944, Sorokin predicted the end of the Cold War and a close friendship between the United States and Russia. In his autobiography, Sorokin (1963) recalled his life during the tumultuous Bolshevik revolution, and depicted accurately the thug mentality of the Bolsheviks at a time when many American intellectuals were seduced by Lenin and Stalin. In *Social and Cultural Dynamics*, Sorokin (1957) predicted that the twentieth century would be the most violent century in recorded human history. In *The Reconstruction of Humanity* (1948) and other books, he urged sociologists to conduct more research into empathy, compassion, and love, the topics that are most neglected by social scientists yet vital to all the humanistic and political programs of liberal democracies. More than any other twentieth-century sociologist, Sorokin understood the power of the human heart to effect monstrous evil as well as the fundamental goodness that is necessary to sustain social life in all its manifestations, from the family to the state.

IMPLICATIONS

The present *fin de siècle* is repeating many of the dramatic, apocalyptic themes of the previous one. Sexual, racial, and political anarchy threaten the social order across the globe. In the words of Emile Durkheim, "The old gods are growing old or are already dead, and others are not yet born" ([1912] 1965: 475). The intellectual responses to the many dramatic turns of events in our *fin de siècle* have been inadequate. No new prophets have arisen, and capitalism has failed thus far to inspire the faith, even fanaticism, that old-fashioned Marxism once inspired. Instead, the postmodernists have proved that they are experts at deconstructing the Enlightenment narratives that justify Western culture, but they rarely re-construct. Hardline Marxism has given way to soft Marxism, even in America, which continues to imply that the state and Rationality will solve all social ills, despite the mounting cynicism regarding both phenomena. Following Brzezinski and Fukuyama, foreign policy experts have not prepared contingency plans for the possible return of authoritarian and, worse, totalitarian regimes in postcommunist lands. In accepting the false premise that history had come to an end, the United States, in particular, relinquished its traditional role, cited by Tocqueville, as the beacon of democracy in a world that looked up to it as the premier example of freedom. And sociology itself lost its traditional leadership and therapeutic roles that stem from the *cultural* analyses of Tocqueville, Durkheim, Simmel, Freud, Veblen, Sorokin, and Weber.

The legacy of these forgotten founders of sociology should be re-examined in these troubled times. I do not mean to imply that their works offer any sort of blueprint for the "right" type of social engineering. On the contrary, they would all agree that genuine and constructive human change occurs though a fundamental *change of heart*, not the mere changing of one's collective mind as found in the abstract imposition of legislation, government regulations, police or military force. If people act primarily from duty or fear of punishment, then the underlying basis of their behavior is egoism, which is insufficient for long-term moral progress. Genuinely moral and democratic values must act like magnets that attract people, that make them *want* to preserve the moral and social order – spontaneously, and never out of fear. The real lesson of the fall of communism – missed thus far in the many analyses – is that it tried to legislate, coerce, and force human sympathy and goodness. The heart cannot be compelled. In the absence of genuine goodwill, the darker forces of the heart, ranging from a desire for revenge to old-fashioned hatred, festered beneath the surface of the promised land that communism was supposed to be. When the forces that sustained communism finally crumbled, these darker forces were unleashed, and continue to rule unchecked in postcommunist lands. Although Western, democratic governments can never be compared to the communist regimes that fell in recent years – capitalism has not resulted in Gulags, after all – one should heed Tocqueville's and Durkheim's warnings that, left unattended, even democracies can degenerate into despotisms. The present *fin de siècle* is witnessing the dramatic return of history, all the things that modernists thought they had overcome.

Confronting the return of history portends risks in the modernist project, but realistic opportunities as well. It represents a kind of "return of the repressed," using Freud's terminology. The communists as well as other modernists have been suppressing nationalist aspirations for well over a century now, on both sides of the former Iron Curtain. Now that the two grand ideologies, capitalism and communism, have weakened, their repressive functions have been weakened as well, so that ethnicity, religion, and various other traditional forces are emerging again all over the world. If the response to this challenge is along modernist lines, to impose more social control on these anti-modernist forces, the result cannot be anything other than a new wave of Fascism and totalitarianism in the world.

The present discussion will seek an alternative to this unwelcome response. Instead of perpetuating the modernist aim of trying to tame and control various derivatives of the heart – the passions that are crystallized in religion, nationalism, and other traditional phenomena – at the cost of perpetuating terror, it may be high time to abandon the modernist project in this form. The alternative is to embrace the best part of many traditional phenomena that are typically considered to be anti-modern, such as Islamic culture (Ahmed 1992). But such a project necessitates making a distinction between "good" versus "bad" habits of the heart.

In other words, the crucial task for the present *fin de siècle* is for the world to identify and empathize with humanity all around the globe, not to continue to promote narcissistic self-interest as the basis for a liberal world order that must be enforced at the point of a gun. Note that this goal is fundamentally different from

Marxist, other modernist, and postmodernist goals of eliminating all ethnic and other differences through forced assimilation. And again, it is worth repeating that Emile Durkheim and other classical founders of sociology called for study into empathy and compassion – essential ingredients of moral individualism – over a century ago.

Tocqueville reflects the traditionally Western doctrine of *homo duplex* in distinguishing between the Good America of Democracy versus the Bad America that almost exterminated the Indians and promoted slavery. His characterization is much more credible than either the Marxist dismissal of all capitalist nations or the short-sighted denial of history. But every nation has its own *homo duplex* reflected in its national civil religion, its own strengths and weaknesses. Those who promote the end of history denigrate all forms of nationalism, and thereby rob nations of the benign, moral aspects of their traditions as well. They do not offer a viable alternative to the traditions offered by history. It seems more realistic to call for all nations affected by the end of the Cold War to continue with a constructive renewal of history, to draw upon the strengths in their traditions, and to confront their weaknesses honestly and courageously. For the United States, this means reaffirming its revolutionary tradition of standing up for freedom in the world as well as within its borders, and promoting it actively.

Chapter 2

Still hunting Nazis, and losing reality

The insights in Jean Baudrillard's essay, "Hunting Nazis and Losing Reality" (1989) ought to be extended to the present discussion, and particularly to the postcommunist developments in the Balkans. The former Yugoslavia became the postmodern screen for projecting all sorts of fictitious evils from history, from the extermination of Native Americans to Vietnam, but especially Nazism. Croatia's bid for independence was branded by many as a manifestation of its allegedly genocidal national character manifested during World War II (Kaplan 1991b, 1993). Serbia's aggression against its neighbors was also frequently likened to Nazism. Four of the five nations that came up with the failed Washington Peace Plan on 23 May 1993, which was designed to end the fighting in former Yugoslavia, were the anti-Nazi allies from World War II: Britain, France, Russia, the USA, and Spain. From a more cynical perspective, most of these nations also capitulated to Hitler in the years prior to World War II, and arguably capitulated to Slobodan Milošević of Serbia in the 1990s. History was repeating itself with a vengeance. Despite these and other revivals of ghosts from the past, and despite the often heard refrain, "Never Again," genocide in the Balkans continued unabated – with the full and conscious knowledge of the postmodern world's television-viewing public. The hunt for Nazis in the Balkans was fictitious in the sense that it never connected with the moral outrage necessary to put a stop to the real genocide that was occurring in former Yugoslavia.

To phrase the matter in a different way, postmodern politicians and diplomats in the 1990s expressed great worry about Nazism, but seemed indifferent to Europe, even to . . . communism. The fighting in former Yugoslavia caused deep divisions within the European Community, and these divisions were a strong echo of a divided Europe from earlier in this century. Specifically, Germany, Italy, Austria, and Japan – all formerly pro-Axis powers – were left out of the 23 May 1993 "peace plan" – labeled as capitulation to Serbia by its critics – put forth by the "Allies." Franco-German tensions, in particular, affected European policy on the current Balkan War.[1] There was nothing subtle in this effort to place some of the blame for the cruel war in former Yugoslavia onto Germany. In the words of US Secretary of State Warren Christopher:

There were serious mistakes made in the whole process of recognition, quick recognition, and the Germans bear a particular responsibility in persuading their colleagues and the European community. We were not in office at that time, but many serious students of the matter think the beginning of the problems we face here today stem from the recognition of Croatia and thereafter of Bosnia.

(*USA Today*, 17 June 1993: 11A)

An important counter to Mr. Christopher is offered by Albert Wohlstetter:

In response to Serbian conquest and ethnic cleansing in the former Yugoslavia, the EC and the UN, led by France, Britain and the US, have for 21 months kept arms from the victims, not the perpetrators, of ethnic cleansing in Bosnia. . . . Mr. Christopher would be closer to the truth if he said that it was US and EC assurance to Belgrade that we [the US] would not recognize the secession of any republic (and so would not allow the republics to arm themselves) that encouraged three successive invasions by Milošević's Yugoslav People's Army. . . . The myth that is now spreading about German war guilt in Bosnia exculpates Britain, France and the US and distorts the past in a way that is likely to continue to divide the alliance.

(*Wall Street Journal*, 1 July 1993: A14)

Even after it had been demolished, communism was never reviled in Europe to the same extent as Nazism. But Nazism is itself a historical ghost! Baudrillard only touches on some of these ironies when he writes that

We shall never know if Nazism, the concentration camps or Hiroshima were intelligible or not. We are no longer in the same mental universe. . . . Even if the facts were there staring us in the face, we would not be convinced. Thus, the more we have pored over Nazism and the gas chambers in an effort to analyze those things, the less intelligible they have become and we have in the end arrived quite logically at the improbable question: "When it comes down to it, did all these things really exist?" The question may be stupid, or morally indefensible, but what is interesting is what makes it logically possible to ask it. . . . It exactly expresses the situation of an entire culture – the dead-end that our *fin de siècle* has got itself into, fascinated as it is to the point of distraction by the horror of its own origins.

(1988b: 17)

Baudrillard concludes that nostalgia for Fascism is not dangerous, but

what is dangerous and lamentable is this pathological revival of the past, which everyone – both those who deny and those who assert the reality of the gas chambers, both Heidegger's critics and his supporters – is currently participating (indeed virtually conniving) in, this collective hallucination which transfers the power of imagination that is lacking from our own period, and all the burden of violence and reality, which has today become merely illusory, back to that earlier period in a sort of compulsion to re-live its history, a compulsion accompanied by a profound sense of guilt at not having been there.

(ibid.)

I agree with Baudrillard that contemporary violence in the Balkans, for example, seems to be regarded *as if* it were a fiction compared with the seemingly "real" yet equally illusory compulsions to relive past horrors. In sum, real genocide occurred in the Balkans even as Western intellectuals reviled Nazism. Where I part company with Baudrillard is on his almost pedantic but certainly purely academic tendency to stay trapped in the epistemological consequences of his postmodern framework. Baudrillard seems to be satisfied to conclude that neither Nazism nor contemporary evils can be understood at all, that all violence is fiction. In contradistinction to Baudrillard, I would point to the need to understand why Nazism stands out as the supreme evil in this, our postmodern, postcommunist era, and to claim that real people, not fictions, suffer from violence.

At this point in the discussion, I shall venture only a short summary of my reply to the question: Why is the world still hunting Nazis in the 1990s? One part of the answer has to do with the deep-seated antagonism of Britain and France toward Germany. If Britain and France experienced revolutions that gave us individualism and the rights of man, Germany had consistently been the counterrevolutionary force in Europe.[2] Drawing on Seymour Martin Lipset's (1989) study of American versus Canadian social characters as revolutionary and counterrevolutionary, respectively, one might speculate that Britain and France represent the Enlightenment narratives that Germany had consistently opposed. In this, our postmodern era, the collective values represented by Britain and France are in serious trouble, because it is no longer clear that individualism and rationalism are sufficient to sustain the good society. Hence, Britain and France – unconsciously, collectively – throw up Nazism as the deepest stain they can find against Germany, and they unite against Germany *vis-à-vis* the tragic conflict in the Balkans. For example, Germany led the way for the diplomatic recognition of Croatia, Slovenia, and Bosnia-Herzegovina, but Britain and France opposed Germany in this move and just as consistently backed Germany's arch-enemy, Serbia. The stain of Nazism and German war guilt in general was thrown on Croatia, which was once part of the Austro-Hungarian Empire, partly because of Germany's strong support for Croatia. Interestingly, French and Serbian Nazi collaboration during World War II is *not* invoked in discussions of this sort. The peace negotiators sent to the Balkans were consistently non-German, and the negotiating style was decidedly British: let us negotiate peace at any cost.

Croatia became Western Europe's whipping boy when they wanted to punish and contain Germany. And France and Britain were willing to overcome their traditional differences when it came to any action that opposed Germany. In an essay entitled "Germany Is Not to Blame for Bosnia," David Unger explains:

It is now conventional wisdom that Germany, by extending diplomatic recognition to Croatia and Slovenia in late December 1991, forced the breakup of the old Yugoslav federation, making the subsequent tragedy in Bosnia inevitable. That's a strained reading of the chronological record. Worse, it conceals the real dynamics of the crisis, inviting future policy mistakes. . . . But London, Paris, and Washington didn't see Germany's motives as benign. Instead, *they saw a repetition of the Nazis' sponsorship of a Croatian puppet state*. Washington, London and Paris had long seen a unified Yugoslavia as a geopolitical bulwark against first German, then Soviet expansionism. . . . The continued insistence by London and Paris that Bonn is to blame reflects the resurgence of historic European rivalries. When it comes to the Balkans, the European Community remains so driven by its own national and historical rivalries that it cannot offer coherent leadership or even followership.

(*New York Times*, 7 June 1993: A14; emphasis added)

Alan Riding (1993) exposed French hypocrisy regarding its own Nazi collaboration *vis-à-vis* the Paris murder of René Bousquet, the Vichy police chief, in June 1993:

The French establishment – a succession of governments as well as the judiciary – has always acted on the belief that the painful memories of the German occupation were best buried and forgotten. That at least helps to explain why the trials of Messrs. Bousquet, Papon and Touvier [suspected Nazi collaborators] were endlessly delayed and why, to date, no Frenchman has had to answer in court for wartime crimes against Jews. . . . A France that emerged from World War II as a "victorious" ally and went on to become a major European power seems reluctant to look back. . . . Urged to apologize in the name of France for the deportation of Jews, he [President Mitterrand] said the French Republic was not responsible for the acts of an illegitimate state. [Yet] the country's powerful bureaucracy remained intact throughout the [Nazi] Occupation working before, during and after the war for whoever was in charge. French railroads even asked for payment for supplying trains to carry Jews to Germany after France had been liberated.

(1993: E4)

In these and many other ways, it seems that postcommunism and Balkanization unconsciously perceived threats to the cultural legacies of two nations most responsible for the Enlightenment, Britain and France. Only in this way is it possible to explain what otherwise seems absurd: the widespread preoccupation with Nazism during a period of postcommunist genocide in the Balkans. I shall have much more to say on this later, but would now like to proceed at a more deliberate pace in making this complex argument. The important point is this: the war that began in former Yugoslavia in 1991 and still rages as I write came to be perceived eventually as the model for most postcommunist development. As I shall demonstrate shortly, this Balkan War was depicted in the media as having divided the West in a way that the formerly communist Soviet Union never did, and to have put an end to the dream of a united Europe, a New World Order, and American leadership in world affairs. To be sure, these are not logical assumptions at all, because the war in former Yugoslavia is one of over thirty wars that are currently raging in the world, including wars in the former Soviet Union. And this assumption represents a sudden and complete about-face from the postmodern optimism in 1991 that the tearing down of the Berlin Wall would usher in the democratic "end of history" (Fukuyama 1992). Nevertheless, the postmodernists are right to question the once sacrosanct distinction between fact and fiction. Let us analyze the widespread perception that the brutal events that characterize the war in postcommunist former Yugoslavia hold special symbolic meaning for this, our postmodern *fin de siècle*.

NEVER AGAIN, EXCEPT FOR BOSNIA

Let us begin with Zbigniew Brzezinski's (1993) essay, "Never Again – Except for Bosnia." The publication of Mr. Brzezinski's essay coincided with the opening of the Holocaust Memorial Museum in Washington DC on 22 April 1993. On this emotionally charged day, Mr. Brzezinski asserted:

> "Never again." These emphatic words echo and re-echo this week. . . . Yet what are we hearing? Is this truly a proclamation of a moral imperative? Or merely a pompous affirmation of hypocrisy? . . . The indifference to the slaughter in the [Polish] ghetto is mirrored in the passivity of the citizens who watch the agony of Srebrenica [Bosnia-Herzegovina] on TV and in the hypocrisy of evasive statesmen as they draft their "never again" speeches. . . . The feud [in former Yugoslavia], Defense Department spokesmen tell us, does not involve our national security interests. Neither did the slaughter of the Jews, some would have argued.
>
> (1993b: A21)

At the ceremony that marked the opening of the Holocaust Memorial Museum, Elie Wiesel, the Nobel Peace Prize winner, turned to President Clinton, and said: "Mr. President, I cannot not tell you something. I have been in the former Yugoslavia last fall. I cannot sleep since what I have seen. As a Jew I am saying that. We must do something to stop the bloodshed in that country" (*New York Times*, 25 April 1993: E1). It is interesting that Mr. Wiesel's plea was the pure, non-modernist voice of compassion in the sense that he was appealing to Mr. Clinton's emotions to get him to do something, anything, to stop the killing. In fact, following this plea from the heart, Mr. Clinton began to threaten that he would bomb the Serbian aggressor and arm the Bosnian victims – but changed his mind a month later.[3] Part of the reason for the change of heart was that his staff began to demand modernist criteria for a quick and easy victory, including well-defined objectives, a timetable, and a plan for exit from the conflict.[4] All of these modernist demands dampened the moral outrage so that eventually the West returned to its policy of capitulating to a Serbian victory, a policy that drew the sarcastic remark from Senator Daniel Patrick Moynihan, that at some future date the West would be building another museum, this time to honor Serbia's victims (*New York Times*, 28 April 1993: A4).

On the same day that Mr. Wiesel addressed President Clinton, President Franjo Tudjman of Croatia was assailed for attending this same opening ceremony (*New York Times*, 22 April 1993: A1). The criticism stems from the historical fact that during World War II, the Ustase regime in Croatia was affiliated with the Nazis – even though the critics failed to assail Serbia for its own Nazi collaboration during World War II (Vuković 1991). Moreover, every one of the other guests at this ceremony represented a Central or Eastern European nation that had succumbed to Nazism during World War II, yet neither they nor their nations were criticized. Why would postmodern intellectuals single out Croatia as the scapegoat for all of Europe's guilt about Nazism? We shall return to this question later. For now, let us note that the historical Nazi collaboration of Croatia as well as Serbia constitutes more than an interesting footnote to these incredible contemporary events. Instead, it shows just how unresolved the distinction between fact and fiction remains, despite the many years of historical research following World War II. It highlights the irony of how easily and quickly historical fact-fictions are invoked in an era that has declared the end of history, and it accentuates the postmodern aim to blur, not distinguish, fact from fiction. And regarding the matter at hand, linking Croatia with past Nazi horrors at the same time that Serbia was linked with contemporary horrors (yet exonerated from its own past Nazi horrors) meant that the distinction between contemporary victims (Croats) and aggressors (Serbs) was itself weakened, and thereby, the world community's resolve to act was diminished. Reality was again lost.[5]

Hence, the *New York Times* was right to run a headline that read, "Does the World Still Recognize a Holocaust?" (25 April 1993: E1). In addition to the Holocaust, there have been many instances of genocide in the twentieth century, including the massacre of more than a million Armenians at the hands of the Turks between 1915 and 1918, the extermination of millions of peasants by Stalin, and the killings of Cambodians by the Khmer Rouge in the 1970s. (The most neglected of all instances of genocide is that of the Native Americans, of course.) Why should the current genocide in former Yugoslavia be linked more directly than these others instances of genocide to the Holocaust? There is no rational reply. What is of interest is that this mental linkage is offensive to many survivors of the Holocaust, yet continues to be made by the news media and by politicians. If the real Holocaust is used as the yardstick for assessing human evil, no post-World-War-II event could measure up. Nevertheless, during a news conference, President Clinton was asked, "Do you see any parallel between the ethnic cleansing in Bosnia and the Holocaust?" The President replied:

I think the Holocaust is on a whole different level. I think it is without precedent or peer in human history. On the other hand, ethnic cleansing is the kind of inhumanity that the Holocaust took to the nth degree. The idea of moving people around and abusing them and often killing them, solely because of their ethnicity, is an abhorrent thing . . . and I think you have to stand up against it. I think it's wrong.

(New York Times, 24 April 1993: A5)

THE BERLIN WALL IN TEXAS

The postmodern flavor, the hysterical character of our times, is captured by other events that took place in the week of 20 April 1993. One could argue that the very idea of a museum to capture the horrors of the Holocaust is part and parcel of the museum culture that the postmodernists have described.[6] Does such a museum teach humanity a lesson, or merely desensitize the masses further by making even the Holocaust seem artificial? President Bush came to Texas A&M University, where I teach and am writing this book, on 21 April 1993. He spoke next to a huge piece of the Berlin Wall that had been shipped to Texas. This souvenir was meant to commemorate his role in "winning" the Cold War, and to sanctify the grounds of the Bush Presidential Library that would be built at Texas A&M University. Yet the audience was small, because Mr. Bush's "New World Order" had already become the butt of cynical jokes among opinion-makers. And despite the fact that America is undoubtedly a modern culture, there was something strange – one is tempted to say, primitive – in the fact that a piece of the Berlin Wall was being treated as almost a sacred relic of the Cold War. Indeed, this relic is situated next to a "sacred" burial ground at the University wherein its mascots are buried, and close to "sacred" grass that commemorates Aggies who died in wars ("sacred" in the Durkheimian sense that one is not allowed to walk on the grass, and one is supposed to show "respect"). One simply cannot avoid invoking Durkheim's ([1912] 1965) theories on totemism and sacredness to explain these seemingly strange, postmodern behaviors in ostensibly modern times.

The University was celebrating or responding to a number of other events simultaneously: Earth Day, Muster (a ceremony in which the names of all Aggies who had died in the previous year are called out), and even a Ku Klux Klan recruitment rally scheduled for 24 April 1993. In other words, the end of the Cold War had been absorbed into a plethora of competing spectacles. President Bush had presided over the apparent end of the Cold War and the demise of communism, but had he grasped the significance of these events? After all, he had referred to the war in postcommunist, former Yugoslavia as a "hiccup."[7] But fate decreed that the seemingly trivial "hiccup" in the postcommunist Balkans would take on enormous symbolic significance in a postmodern world. Thus, according to the editors of the Wall Street Journal, "Today's world is already full of Bosnias. Ethnic cleansing has also been taking place in Tajikistan, Armenia, Cambodia, Sri Lanka, Angola, Peru, Haiti, Rwanda, South Africa, and India" (11 May 1993: A14).

Mr. Bush's ceremony at the piece of the Berlin Wall in Texas did not receive widespread media attention compared with Mr. Clinton's attendance at the ceremony at the Holocaust Museum. One might be tempted to explain that this is because Mr. Bush was no longer President of the USA. But this explanation is inadequate because even when the Berlin Wall was torn down in 1991, Mr. Bush hardly had a thing to say about this dramatic symbolization of the fall of communism. Both communism and Marxism had too many supporters among the intellectual elite in the West for the masses to be swayed to celebrate their apparent downfall. Threatened by the collapse of an ideology they had supported for many years, many Western intellectuals began to revive an antipathy for Nazism that had buttressed Marxism since World War II. This, despite the fact that Nazism was now only a historical relic and that communist oppression was still struggling for survival in Serbia as well as among Boris Yeltsin's opponents in Russia.

In sum, Mr. Bush's self-proclaimed victory over communism and the Evil Empire that it had produced was never celebrated with gusto. Both the fall of communism and Mr. Bush's celebrations of that fall went out with a whimper, not a bang. Indeed, Mr. Bush had tried to preserve Mr. Gorbachev's communist Soviet Union as well as a communist Yugoslavia for as long as he could. When fighting broke out in both the former Soviet Union and the former Yugoslavia, neither the information media nor the politicians indicted the communists and so-called "former communists" in these countries for instigating conflict. On the contrary, former communists were elected democratically to a plethora of posts, and the West expected them – almost overnight – to achieve democratic and free-market institutions. Far from hunting communists, which would have been a realistic enterprise, the West turned to hunting Nazis and promoting a kitsch version of free-market and democratic institutions. This is the ultimate irony of Mr. Bush's "victory" over communism.

THE FORMER YUGOSLAVIA AS THE PARADIGM FOR – WHAT?

Mr. Bush's successor, President Bill Clinton, stated that "We have an interest in standing up against the principle of ethnic cleansing. If you look at the turmoil all through the Balkans, if you look at the other places where this could play itself out in other places of the world, this is not just about Bosnia" (*New York Times*, 17 April 1993: A5). The paradoxical notion that a moral stand is in the world's pragmatic self-interest reappeared in an editorial written by Anthony Lewis: "There are many horrors in the world today – but none worse than the unapologetic aggression and murder in Bosnia, and none so central to the established American interest in a peaceful Europe" (ibid., 19 April 1993: A11). President Clinton acknowledged that "the United States should lead"[8] because the Europeans had failed to respond adequately to the crisis in former Yugoslavia. Former Prime Minister Margaret Thatcher went so far as to describe the political leaders of the European Community as behaving "a little like accomplices to massacre"[9] because, she said, they had done nothing to stop the killing in former Yugoslavia. Leslie H. Gelb accused Europe and the USA of "waiting for the Serbs to win," and predicted that the resultant "cynicism will eat away at the Clinton Presidency and at US foreign policy. Bosnian Muslims will pay with their lives, and Americans with their faith."[10] Elsewhere, Mr. Gelb made the analogy that because of his failure to act quickly enough on the Bosnian issue, President Clinton was quickly becoming another Jimmy Carter.[11] William Safire made the truly sweeping generalization that the 1990s war in Bosnia shows that "Europe is entering the third millennium the same way it entered the second – with the Christians kicking the Muslims out."[12]

From the Muslim perspective as well, Bosnia has taken on enormous symbolic significance. According to Suroosh Irfani, "Locked in a two-front battle, of physical and political survival against Serbian aggression on the one hand, and inner struggle for coherence amidst chaos on the other, *Bosnian Muslims embody an epic of resistance unparalleled in Muslim history*" (emphasis added).[13]

According to former United States Ambassador to Yugoslavia, Warren Zimmermann, "Yugoslavia is a paradigm for other countries in Central Europe and the Soviet Union of a collectivist ideology of Communism replaced by another collectivist ideology, nationalism" (*New York Times*, 14 June 1992: E9). Even the destruction exhibited in this Balkan War seems to be symbolic: "Sarajevo was not just the destruction of a city or the destruction of the Bosnian state. It was the brutal destruction of the idea of Europe, the idea of tolerance and democracy" (*New York Times*, 13 June 1992: A3). Mr. Anthony Lewis concurs:

> The dream of a united Europe, powerful contributor in a better world, is dead. It died when the European Community refused to act against Serbian aggression – when it would not lift a finger to stop mass racial murder on its own continent. The Community survives, but it is a soulless creature. Its bureaucrats set standards for the butterfat content of ice cream.
>
> (*New York Times*, 29 March 1993: A11)

Elsewhere, Mr. Lewis claims that "the Serbian onslaught is, in fact, the model of the next great challenge to international peace and order" (*New York Times*, 3 August 1992: A15). In still another editorial entitled "Bush's 'New World Order' Evokes Only Cynicism," Mr. Lewis refers to Yugoslavia as Bush's greatest failure:

> The greatest failure, the one that will forever stain George Bush's reputation, has been in the former Yugoslavia. Bold American leadership, exercised in a timely way, could have prevented much of the political and human disaster. Mr. Bush wrung his hands [yet] it happened on George Bush's watch. How is it possible to square the feeble, feckless Bush of these events with the gung-ho President who rallied the world against Saddam Hussein? Does the difference come down to oil?
>
> (*New York Times*, 28 September 1992: A14)

Bosnia was also cited as the factor that reduced the North Atlantic Treaty Organization to "little more than an expensive fiction."[14] This is because President Clinton allocated about $100 billion to NATO for fiscal year 1994, yet the alliance that it represents seems unable to find a post-Cold-War role, and was certainly unable to put a halt to the carnage in the former Yugoslavia. A headline in the *New York Times* read, "Can the UN Survive Continued Failure in Bosnia?" (15 June

1993: A12).[15] Similarly, an editorial in the *Wall Street Journal* entitled "The New World Order Dies in Bosnia" concluded that "it is sheer deception to fly warplanes in Iraq in the name of a New World Order when Mr. Bush is indifferent to the carnage in Bosnia" (17 September 1992: A15). Leslie Gelb cited Western policy on Bosnia as a step toward the "end of civilization":

> The day will soon come when two groups of leaders are charged with crimes against humanity in Bosnia: the Serbs who are killing Muslims and driving them from their homes, and the Western leaders who are doing little to stop this unspeakable brutality. The Serbian policy of "ethnic cleansing" is worse than a crime; it is evil. The West's failure to confront this evil is worse than a blunder; it is an abdication of our humanity ... for if we allow evil to triumph in ex-Yugoslavia, we will breed a cynicism so pervasive and profound as to corrode the very basis of Western liberty and smash every hope of fashioning a better world. ... To countenance genocide, and that is what the Serbs are doing, is to say that evil does not matter, that nothing matters, and that therefore almost anything is acceptable. ... Our present leaders say we cannot commit greater force there for "merely humanitarian" reasons. Listen again, "merely humanitarian" reasons. When we come to think of humanitarian concerns as "mere," we are arriving at the end of civilization.
>
> *(New York Times*, 13 December 1992: E17)

In an essay entitled "Paying for the Fall of Communism," Roger Cohen summarizes the dramatic change in the world's 1993 political mood since 1989:

> The resurgence of nationalism and the changed economic conditions of a reunited Germany would demolish assumptions that had taken on the weight of truths that Western Europe was inexorably heading toward unity, that businesses could bank on a single market and currency, and that war had been banished from the Continent. The destruction of those convictions – rather than the actual financial cost to the West of building market economies in the East – now appears to be the heaviest price paid by Europe for its recent convulsion. For in the place of confidence, there is now malaise; in the place of the growth of the 1980s, lingering recession with rising unemployment; in the place of peace, the war in what was once Yugoslavia; in the place of a clear sense of direction, uncertainty.
>
> *(New York Times*, 27 September 1992: F1)

Yet the linkage between former Yugoslavia and the course of postmodernism and postcommunism that deserves the most attention is that Serbia's aggression against its former internal colonies within Yugoslavia foreshadowed Russia's growing aggression against the nationalities it used to dominate completely under the guise of communist ideology. Angelo Codevilla writes in the *Wall Street Journal*:

> When the US organized the expedition to Somalia [in December 1992], it

abetted Europe's flight from responsibility for its own backyard. Hence Russia's communist apparatchiks, who are now recouping their powers in Moscow and have already started border wars in Georgia and Moldova, have reason to believe that the West would stand by if they tried to reassert control over Ukraine and the Baltics, and that afterward Europe would pay them protection money. . . . The Clinton administration is likely to follow its predecessor in involving the UN rather than the American people in formulating its foreign policy and in hiding its judgments behind the supposed majesty of the UN. . . . But the UN has no legitimacy with ordinary people anywhere. . . . A little sense of our own self-interest and a little more attention to the fundamentals of international affairs would have been enough to conclude that the suffering in former Yugoslavia is just as humanly compelling as that in Somalia, that the Balkans' problems are more tractable by US military power, and their alleviation is likelier to save us bigger problems down the road.

(7 January 1993: A15)

A telling sign that this analysis is on the right track is that Serbia increased its attacks on Bosnian Muslims during Boris Yeltsin's power struggle with the Russian Parliament in March 1993: "The Serbs have been counting for months on Boris Yeltsin's defeat and ensuing support from Russia . . . [which is] a traditional ally of the Serbs" (*New York Times*, 26 March 1993: A1).

However, such conceptual linkages between the tragedy in postcommunist former Yugoslavia and the rest of the postcommunist project seem to have escaped the Clinton Administration. For example, in his first formal news conference in his new role as President of the United States, held in March 1993, Bill Clinton addressed the power struggle in Russia between Boris Yeltsin and the hardline Parliament, but said nothing concerning Serbian aggression in Bosnia-Herzegovina. William Safire adds, "The press fell short, too: not one question on dying Bosnia" (*New York Times*, 25 March 1993: A15). In fact Leslie Gelb has a point when he writes in the *New York Times* that in 1992, "almost everyone was proclaiming democracy's triumph and heralding Western European unity and a major free-trade agreement. At year's end, prospects for all three have plummeted. In early 1992, hardly anyone gave a thought to Bosnia or Somalia. Within months, they were called sites of genocide and ignited dramatic debates about using force for humanitarian ends" (4 Janury 1993: A12).

Consider the following phrases used in articles or television programs to describe the current Balkan War or the Balkans: "A World Gone Raving Mad';[16] "Yugoslavia: Land of the Demons';[17] this Balkan War as the "problem from hell';[18] or as a "morally ambiguous tribal war."[19] Of the peoples of former Yugoslavia, a French Foreign Ministry official blurted out: "They need to fight. They want to fight. They have hated each other for centuries."[20] But in fact, this Balkan War is *not* the result of Balkan tribalism. The West has tried to wash its hands of it, but the West is implicated in this most recent Balkan tragedy. This is because Russia,[21] Britain, and France took steps to ensure that Serbia should succeed in its aggression against its neighbors, and prevented the United Nations as well as the United States from taking tough steps to stop Serbia.[22] For example, the arms embargo that the West imposed on all of former Yugoslavia hurt Serbia's victims, and ensured that the "war" would be transformed into slaughter because of Serbia's military superiority. In plain terms, the West made sure that it was not a fair fight, and the West refused consistently and steadfastly to allow Bosnia and Croatia to arm themselves so that they could stand up to Serbian aggression. The West must confront the fact that it became an implicit ally of Serbia in this latest Balkan War. In the words of Leslie Gelb:

> Diplomacy without force is farce, but that is the present Western–UN course. It is cynical farce, for all the realists and neo-isolationists who espouse it know they are winking at Serbian genocide and merely delaying their inevitable confrontation with Serbia, at unforgivable cost in Muslim lives [and] genocide in Bosnia. . . . The US cannot simply abandon the prospect of using force because nasty Russian nationalists insist on supporting their Serbian brethren no matter what horrible crimes they commit. . . . I know that what I argue has almost no chance of winning over world leaders. They all rightly fear a Bosnian quagmire. They all correctly want to focus on their home-front horrors. But they have not found a decent answer to genocide in Bosnia, and they must.
>
> *(New York Times, 28 February 1993: E15)*

In subsequent chapters I shall develop further the disturbing fact that traditional alliances emerged in the postcommunist world despite the postmodern rhetoric that history had been overcome. At this stage, I should like to mention a prominent aspect of this historical revivalism. If it is true that Serbia was demonized in the British, French, and American media, it is equally true that Serbia's aggression was explained quite simply on the socio-psychological basis of fear of the Croatians: "Western diplomats based here [in Belgrade] agree that the Serbs have every reason to recall their barbarous treatment at the hands of the Croatian Ustashe."[23] This is another aspect of postmodern Nazi-hunting that needs to be analyzed.

CROATIA AS THE SCAPEGOAT FOR EUROPE'S NAZI PAST

To the extent that one hopes to engage in a serious and even-handed discussion of Nazism in Europe, one must account for the fact that most of Europe had succumbed to or collaborated with the Nazis prior to or during World War II. However, what stands out in the postmodern discussion – if it can be called that – of Nazism is that it focuses almost entirely on Croatia. There is no notable mention, much less analysis, in the contemporary information media of Nazi collaboration by France, Serbia, Austria, Italy, Greece, Bulgaria, or any of the other actors in the current, postcommunist drama in the Balkans. Indeed, there is hardly any explicit contemporary discussion of Germany's involvement in Nazism even though Germany's past is implicated in many contemporary political decisions. Instead, Western intellectuals responded enthusiastically to Serbia's charge that Croatia was a genocidal nation, supposedly evidenced by its Nazi collaboration during World War II (Rasković 1990). Misha Glenny (1990, 1992) and Robert Kaplan (1991b, 1993), in particular, pursued this stigmatic approach as an explanation for Serbia's war of aggression against Croatia. In the news media, one frequently came across the explanation that Serbia attacked Croatia in 1991 out of fear. This collective fear is supposed to stem from Croat Ustase atrocities against the Serbs during World War II as well as Turkish atrocities committed in 1389.[24] Writing in the *Wall Street Journal* Mark Heprin considers this rationalization of Serbian atrocities as outrageous:

> What do the Serbs want? The Serbs say they want to protect themselves, a response that seems grotesquely inadequate as an explanation for their relentless prosecution of a war largely against innocent civilians. . . . When Yugoslavia broke up, the Serbs' memories of the Second World War made them rush to the premature rescue of Serbs left outside the fold.
>
> (6 May 1993: A14)

One of the most ironic aspects of this explanation is that it was used by Hitler to justify his own war for conquest: the logic that all Germans should live in a purely German nation was echoed by the logic that all Serbs should live in a purely Serbian nation. According to Albert Wohlstetter,

> Our failure so far in the former Yugoslavia is the failure to deal with the consequences of the breakup of a communist dictatorship in which a tyrant [Serbia's Mr. Milošević] is using the mask of protecting an ethnic minority in a recognized sovereign state [Bosnia-Herzegovina] to capture lost territory, people and strategic facilities – to capture some of which he never had.
>
> (*Wall Street Journal*, 1 July 1993: A14)

Another irony is that whereas Croatia's symbols of nationhood were branded by Serbian propaganda as reminiscent of Nazism (Knežević 1992), many Serbs openly, self-consciously and defiantly wear and display Chetnik symbolism. Yet this never draws the wrath of the Western media, and is never connected with Nazism, even though the Chetniks were Serbia's pro-Nazi faction during World War II (Ramet 1992: 254). Finally, the attempt to justify contemporary Serbian aggression on the basis of historical fears seems rather incredible if one considers that France, the Netherlands, Poland, and other contemporary neighbors of Germany could use the same explanation to justify grabbing German territory in the 1990s because of Nazi atrocities in the 1940s. Perhaps the most incredible aspect of this attempt at justification is that it was tacitly accepted by the Western media and intellectuals – it was certainly not challenged effectively.

To be sure, there exist intelligent rebuttals to these Serbian attempts to portray their victims as Nazi clones who, by implication, deserve what they got (Finkielkraut 1992; Knežević 1992). Much more interesting is the case that one could make for the claim that Serbian ideology concerning the establishment of a Greater Serbia extends directly from the World War II Chetnik movement to the present (Cohen 1992, Knežević 1992, Vuković 1991).[25] An important part of this direct link is the powerful effect of Serbian propaganda that is rivaled only by German Nazi propaganda from World War II. For example, consider these passages from an advertisement printed in the *New York Times* (29 April 1993: A10) under the heading, "Mr. President, Do Not Bomb the Victims of Nazi/Croatian Genocide":

> Over 700,000 Serbs and 60,000 Jews were murdered (according to Simon Wiesenthal) by Nazi Croatians and Bosnian Muslims in W W II. Many died in Croatia's Jasenovac death camp. Muslim SS units joined in slaughtering Serbs, Jews and Gypsies in Bosnia (then part of the Nazi puppet state of Croatia). This genocide is why Serbs are no longer Bosnia's largest group. The Serbs have suffered enough. The brutalized people of the Balkans do not need more arms or additional violence from the sky. US generals say that will only increase killings, stop peace talks and may draw US ground troops into a Balkan quagmire. Jews and Serbs, whose ashes mingled in the crematoria of Jasenovac, were outraged when Croatia's Franjo Tudjman was recently invited to the Holocaust Museum and White House. Tudjman, who is quoted as saying that he is glad his wife is "neither a Serb nor a Jew," wrote in this 1989 book: "The establishment of Hitler's *new European order* can be justified by the need to be rid of the Jews (undesirable more or less in all European countries)." Using the term "judeo-nazism" he also claims that 900,000 Jews, not six million, died in the Holocaust. TODAY, with no sanctions, Tudjman is creating an ethnically cleansed "Greater Croatia," including 30 per cent of Bosnia, where Croat troops use "Sieg Heil" salutes and wear symbols from their Nazi W W II era (*Financial Times*, April 15). Mr. President, we condemn violence and atrocities, committed by all sides. Please look beyond the propaganda and scrutinize the arguments of those who say that war is peace. Call upon the three Bosnian factions to find a solution together. Summon their leaders to a peace conference in Washington.

In the pages of the *New York Times*, Diana Jean Schemo criticized the Croatian President, Franjo Tudjman, along similar lines.[26] However, when one contrasts the anti-Semitic statements that are attributed to Mr. Tudjman with what he actually wrote in his *Wilderness of Historical Reality: A Treatise on the History and Philosophy of Evil Brutality* (1990), it immediately becomes apparent that the quotes were taken out of context. Mr. Tudjman was attributing the anti-Semitic statements and figures to other persons, whom he criticizes, and not making them himself. Anto Knežević (1992) demonstrates this in painstaking detail by analyzing each and every passage that is misquoted from Tudjman's book and contrasting it with what he calls the "kitchen translation" that was sent by the Belgrade regime to the world's media centers. I should add that my own reading of Tudjman's *Wilderness of Historical Reality* leads me to conclude that it is an unmistakably scholarly book, and that it is not anti-Semitic. My opinion is shared with members of the Jewish community whom I interviewed in Zagreb, Croatia, in

May 1993. In fact, a prominent member of the Croatian Jewish community, Mr. Slavko Goldstein, stated on Croatian television that he had known Mr. Tudjman for over twenty years, and feels strongly that Mr. Tudjman is *not* an anti-Semite.[27]

The most telling irony regarding the effort to sort out fact from fiction *vis-à-vis* the use of Nazi imagery is that the World Jewish Congress published its own open letter to President Clinton on 22 April 1993, urging him to intervene militarily against Serbia and to lift the arms embargo against the Bosnians. The irony lies in the fact that the Serbian use of the Holocaust to cast a stain on Croatia – and, to a lesser extent, on Bosnian Muslims as well – was more effective than the open letter from the World Jewish Congress in that Mr. Clinton did not intervene militarily. In any event, passages from the World Jewish Congress letter are worth pondering:

> We write this Open Letter to you as friends. Your presidency has given new hope and vitality to our nation and to the world. You have challenged us to live up to our ideals, not to succumb to our fears. Regrettably, the courage and decency that have characterized your approach to the nation's challenges at home have so far found no resonance in our response to massive Serbian aggression and brutality in the Balkans. We know you are distressed by Serbian aggression, and you have urged a tightening of sanctions and the enforcement of a no-fly zone. But as the genocidal shelling of Srebrenica and Sarajevo resumes, it is clear these measures will not stop the massacre. Slobodan Milošević, president of Serbia, mockingly thanked you for not intervening in the slaughter. He and his Serbian allies in Bosnia believe they have been given a green light from America (European leaders gave them the green light long ago), and have resumed their onslaught on Srebrenica and Sarajevo with unrestrained brutality and fury.
>
> Observing the atrocities committed by the Serbs, Larry Hollingsworth, the senior UN refugee official in Sarajevo, said of the Serbs: "I hope that their sleep is punctuated by the screams of the children and the cries of their mothers." But what about us, Mr. President? Is our sleep disturbed by the screams of the children and the cries of their mothers?
>
> The question of why the world did nothing to prevent the Holocaust has haunted the civilized world. Tragically, we now know the answer to that question. It is for the same reason that the world is doing nothing, and that we in America are doing nothing, to stop the ethnic cleansing, the systematic rape of women and little girls, the slaughter of innocents, outrages that are now assuming genocidal proportions.
>
> It was cowardice, callousness, and a massive failure of the moral imagination in the Western world that made the Holocaust possible. Have we really learned nothing from that experience? Is the world's most powerful nation, its only superpower, helpless in the face of brutal Serbian aggression?
>
> (*New York Times*, 22 April 1993: A15)

SERBO-NAZISM, THEN AND NOW?

Not only Slobodan Milošević, but Radovan Karadžić as well, mockingly thanked Mr. Clinton for not intervening militarily against them. Given that Messrs. Milošević and Karadzić[28] are suspected war criminals, at the time of writing, one can hardly resist drawing a parallel with Hitler's own mockery of Neville Chamberlain and other European leaders when they capitulated to his aggression in the name of peace. To be sure, some Western opinion-makers and newspapers made the connection between Serbia and Nazism. I refer to well-documented and well-publicized conclusions such as this one, published in the *Wall Street Journal*: "United Nations investigators blame Serbs for the worst atrocities, from the creation of Nazi-like detention camps to forced deportation and systematic rape of Muslims" (23 February 1993: A1). Similarly, according to Anthony Lewis, writing in the *New York Times*:

> The Serbs are the aggressors. None of the ethnic groups in the conflict is above reproach. But it is the Serbs who have grabbed pieces of territory in Croatia and Bosnia. It is the Serbs who are shelling Sarajevo and Gorazde and other small towns in eastern Bosnia – and throttling relief supplies to them. . . . When they [the Serbs] began shelling the ancient Croatian city of Dubrovnik 16 months ago, the leaders of Western Europe could so easily have said: Stop or we shall intervene. But they lacked the courage, and the Serbs got the message. They went on to destroy Vukovar on the other side of Croatia, and then to savage Bosnia.
>
> (26 February 1993: A15)

Consider other, similar connections between World War II Nazism and contemporary Serbian aggression: Bosnia-Herzegovina's foreign minister, Haris Silajdzić, was quoted as saying that "the world was standing on the sidelines as it had done in the face of Nazi atrocities in the 1930s" (*New York Times*, 20 May 1992: A7). At an address given at Texas A&M University on 26 March 1993, former British Prime Minister Margaret Thatcher said that in the current Balkan War, "the Serbs use the same methods as the Nazis, which I never expected in my lifetime to see in Europe again" (*Bryan/College Station Eagle*, 27 March 1993: A1). Anthony Lewis wrote that the tragedy in Bosnia-Herzegovina is "the worst human disaster in Europe since the crimes of the Nazis" (*New York Times*, 26 March 1993: A13). Elsewhere, Mr. Lewis wrote:

> President Bush's spokesman said Governor Clinton was "unaware of the political complications in Yugoslavia." That Fitzwater phrase reminded me of Prime Minister Neville Chamberlain explaining in 1938 why Britons should not care about Nazi designs on Czechoslovakia: it was, Chamberlain said, "a quarrel in a faraway country between people of whom we know nothing." . . . President Bush has been a veritable Neville Chamberlain in refusing to face the challenge in Yugoslavia.
>
> (ibid. 3 August 1992: A15)

According to Roger Thurow and Tony Horwitz, writing in the *Wall Street Journal*,

> While rationalizing their deeds with reference to earlier genocide, Serbian nationalists themselves evoke eerie echoes of the Nazi era: with detention camps, ethnically cleansed towns, Hitler-like talks of a greater Serbia and the branding of war critics as "low-quality" Serbs.
>
> (18 September 1992: A1)

In an essay entitled, "Desecrating the Holocaust: Serbia's Exploitation of the Holocaust as Propaganda," Philip J. Cohen explains an important irony in the current, postmodernist hunt for Nazis in the Balkans:

> Even as Serbia courts Jewish public opinion, their propagandists conceal a tradition of well-ingrained anti-Semitism, which persists to the present. Moreover, Serbs portray themselves as victims in the Second World War, which indeed they were, but conceal the genocidal massacres that various Serbian formations perpetrated against several peoples, including the Jews. As such, Serbs have usurped for their own propaganda purposes the Holocaust that occurred in neighboring Croatia and Bosnia-Herzegovina, but do not give an honest accounting of the Holocaust as it occurred in Serbia.
>
> (1993: 3)

With painstaking documentation, Cohen traces an anti-Semitic "tradition" in Serbia from 1815 to the present, including Serbia's own Nazi puppet state during World War II, headed by Milan Nedić. The common thread that runs through this anti-Semitic tradition – anti-Semitic in the broadest sense, as anti-Jewish and anti-Muslim – is the quest for a Greater Serbia, which regards all non-Serbs, Jewish or non-Jewish, as a threat. It is in this sense that contemporary Serbian genocide may be compared with Nazism in a meaningful, not fictitious way: both doctrines draw on a long and well-established tradition of writings and cultural thought that laid the groundwork for subsequent genocide. Let us note the most important of these documents.

In an essay written in 1844, the Serbian politician, Ilija Garasanin, claimed that "A plan may be constructed which does not limit Serbia to her present borders, but endeavors to absorb all the Serbian people around her" (in Beljo 1992: 10).[29] In "Serbs All and Everywhere," published in 1849, the linguist Vuk Karadzić argued that even non-Serbian peoples in the Balkans unknowingly speak the Serbian language and are therefore Serbian (ibid.: 17–22). Similarly, the Serbian politician, Nikola Stojanović asserted in 1902 that "Croatians, therefore, are not and cannot be a separate nationality, but they are on the way to becoming part of the Serbian nationality" (ibid.: 27). Perhaps one of the most Nazi-like statements is the 1937 memorandum by Vaso Cubrilović entitled "Expulsion of the Albanians," and presented to the Royal Yugoslav government:

> Without a doubt, the main cause for the lack of success of our [Serbian] colonization in those regions [Kosovo] was that the best land remained in the hands of the Albanians. The only possible way for our mass colonization of

those regions was to take the land from the Albanians. . . . The mass removal of the Albanians from their triangle is the only effective course for us. To bring about the relocation of a whole population, the first prerequisite is the creation of a suitable psychosis. It can be created in many ways.

As is well-known, the Muslim masses, in general, are very readily influenced, especially by religion, and they are superstitious and fanatical. Therefore, first we must win over their clergy and men of influence, through money or threats, to support the relocation of the Albanians. Agitators to advocate this removal must be found, as quickly as possible, especially from Turkey, if it will provide them for us.

Another means would be coercion by the state apparatus. The law must be enforced to the letter so as to make staying intolerable for the Albanians: fines and imprisonments, the ruthless application of all police dispositions, such as the prohibition of smuggling, cutting forests, damaging agriculture, leaving dogs unchained, compulsory labor and any other measure that an experienced police force can contrive. From the economic aspect: the refusal to recognize old land deeds, the work with the land registrar should immediately include the ruthless collection of taxes and the payment of all private and public debts, the requisitioning of all state and communal pastures, and the cancellation of concessions. The withdrawal of permits to exercise a profession, dismissal from state, private and communal offices etc. will hasten the process of their removal. Health measures: the brutal application of all the dispositions even in homes, pulling down encircling walls and high hedges around houses, rigorous application of veterinary measures which would result in impeding the sale of livestock on the market etc. can also be applied in an effective and practical way. When it comes to religion, the Albanians are very touchy, and thus they must be harassed on this score, too. This can be achieved through ill-treatment of their clergy, the destruction of their cemeteries, the prohibition of polygamy, and especially the inflexible application of the law compelling girls to attend elementary schools, wherever they are.

(ibid.: 44–6)

Finally, one needs to consider the notorious 1986 Memorandum of the Serbian Academy of Arts and Sciences, authored primarily by the Serbian writer, Dobrica Cosić, who was later elected President of Yugoslavia until he was ousted from his post by Slobodan Milošević in June 1993. The major theme of this memorandum is that Serbian peoples outside Serbia proper are cruelly oppressed, especially by Muslims and Croats, and that "the complete national and cultural integrity of the Serbian people is their historic and democratic right, no matter in which republic or province they might find themselves living" (ibid.: 75). One can scarcely avoid making the comparison with Hitler's own rationalizations for "liberating" the German peoples of Austria, Czechoslovakia, and Poland.

The Mosaic of Betrayal, by Tomislav Vuković (1991), offers the best-documented account of how the ideology for a Greater Serbia meshed with

Nazi ideology during the World War II occupation of Serbia. The authors[30] document how Serbian priests of the Serbian Orthodox Church collaborated with Nazis as well as Serbian politicians during this period, and then later covered up their betrayal by presenting Serbia as an ally of France, Britain, the USA, and Russia. Little would be gained from dismissing this work as an instance of intellectual Serbia-bashing, even if it is documented and convincing, to offset Croatia-bashing and anti-German sentiments that persist into the 1990s. Far more is at stake, to the extent that one hopes to engage in a serious discussion of the role of Nazi-hunting in postcommunism, including the following issues and questions: if the Americans can be excused for their ill-conceived, tacit support of Serbian aggression in the 1990s due to their well-known ignorance of European history, France and Britain cannot be excused in this way. Surely every European knows that *all* of former Yugoslavia, along with most of Europe, was under Axis occupation during World War II. An enlightened population in the 1990s should not need a book such as *The Mosaic of Betrayal* to tell it what it already knows. Yet it does need such books, because contemporary French and British governments as well as media engaged in a veritable orgy of Croatia-bashing – almost all the guilt for Europe's Nazi past was thrown at Croatia's feet (see Finkielkraut 1992) – while Serbia was shielded repeatedly from US military intervention by France and Britain. But Britain and France are the traditional sources of the Enlightenment, which brings us squarely back into the mainstream of the present discussion. The Enlightenment tradition is implicated in France's own Nazi collaboration during World War II as well as its collaboration with Serbia in the 1990s and Britain's own still largely secret role in Serbia's Nazi collaboration (see Balfour and Mackay 1980) as well its contemporary efforts to keep Serbia strong in order to contain Germany and Germany's friends, such as Croatia. For example, in an article entitled "Thatcher Sought Alliance With France Against Germany," Michael Jones writes in the *Sunday Times* of 17 October 1993 that the then British Prime Minister Margaret Thatcher and French President François Mitterand worked together to thwart German influence in East and Central Europe (see also "Thatcher Tells of '89 Plan with Paris to Rein in Bonn" by John Darnton, *New York Times*, 18 October 1993: A10). In sum, one must confront the question: why does the Enlightenment tradition display such a remarkable tendency to appease and collaborate with dictatorial regimes that promulgate terror, from Hitler to Slobodan Milošević? That is a profoundly postmodern question, in that many postmodernists accuse the Enlightenment narratives of promoting terror, not the human rights they espouse.

Nevertheless, all the documentation in the world cannot act as a substitute for judgment in the postmodern era, which eschews the distinction between fact and fiction. To close this part of the discussion, pertaining to affinities between Serbian and Nazi barbarisms, consider the following poem by Branislav Petrović from *New Serbian Satire* (1987). Is it just satire, or a manifestation of the collective pathology that would lead to the ethnic cleansing in the Balkans in the 1990s? The poem is entitled "Contribution to European History":[31]

We oriented ourselves to the stars.
Trumpets and prison keys led us.
We strained to hear counsel from those below the earth.
We did not stop.

First, we discovered the skin of a woman.
Well cared for, woven of young snakes.
Then we found angel's wings
Lost by a soldier.

We came upon a deserted village,
Recognizing things from childhood.
Only an old man
Who had failed to escape
Was there to meet us.

We wanted drinking water
But the wells were polluted,
Filled to the top with dead people,
And their faithful animals.

We came upon a demolished church.
Here we peed.
We went on to the first school
Which we set ablaze to warm ourselves.

The school janitor woke us
With an indescribable scream.
We trampled him with our boots
And threw him in the ashes.

A teacher appeared with students.
Their astonishment betrayed them.
We did the same to the teacher
As to the janitor
And raped the students.

We saw a green meadow.
Here we stopped to rest.
We slaughtered a little among ourselves.
Chatting, sorting out memory.

Then we went on.
Toward the star which led us.
Our task was to be remembered for evil
By the people we visited.

We came upon a man without arm and legs
At a crossroads.
We ordered him to salute according to regulations.
When he could not, we shot him.

We passed through large cities,
Playing dumb.
We left cans with epidemics
And went on.

We came upon a widow
With three children in her arms.
We returned the children to the mother's insides
And threw the mother to our dogs.

So we went on,
Ahead of the weeping
We left in our wake.
Thus we arrived at a spring
Where we washed ourselves.

The owner of the spring appeared
And called us filthy dogs.
We saw he was our man
And took him with us.

To test him,
We found a child holding a lamb.
The man slaughtered them both with his teeth
And won our full confidence.

We had a sensitive youth
Who wept incessantly.
Gradually we steeled him,
Making a man out of him.

He completed each task
Better than the rest of us
But when he tore out a priest's tongue,
It was he and not the priest who shrieked.

We gave him an easier task,
To shoot students in the schoolyards.
Not even this filled him with joy.
We stripped him of his rank and spat upon him.

We came upon an isolated cemetery
And threw tear-gas bombs in the graves.
The dead leapt from their graves
And we killed them again.

Behind us, the senseless wails of the unworthy.
Before us, lofty goals
Elevated above the Beast who leads us
On the paths of the Lord.

We came upon a pregnant woman
Who impudently resembles the Virgin Mary.
We tear out the baby to raise it and teach it,
And she, unworthy, to the rats.

We come upon a human eye
Freed from its socket.
We bathe in its glance
And go on.

We come upon a human hand
Freed from an unworthy person.
The hand stroked us like a sister
And waved to us as we departed.

We come upon a human brain
Removed from a skull.
We recognize pure thought
And remember it.

We come upon a heart.
We did not know whose it was.
It thrashed around our feet
And wanted to enter our breast.

We throw a bomb at that heart.
We carve it up with knives
But it does not stop
Jumping after us.

We catch it and tie it.
Pour sulfur on it and ignite it
But it was ever stronger.
A stubborn sort of heart.

We offer it the breast of a rat
And then the breast of a dog
But it didn't want them.
It wanted to enter our breast.

We gave it to the breast of the youth
Whom we had stripped of his rank and spat upon.
With such a heart
He could be with us.

We came upon a nursing breast
Our predecessors had sliced off.
We kneeled, drank the proffered milk
And continued, fortified.

We still travelled a long distance
Behind us wails and rats,
Before us pure thought
And messages to the nations.

Unexpectedly, we wander on a mountain.
On the mountain, we come upon clear water.
We look at our faces in the clear water
And suddenly burst into sobs.

SEARCHING FOR THE PERFECT VICTIM

The sociological analyst is confronted with the following facts: the supposed end of communism did not result in a hunt for communists and the evils they had committed in the name of some modernist utopia. Instead, Western intellectuals turned to what Baudrillard called the hunt for Nazis. Serbs, Marxists, opinion-makers, the Jewish community and others made use of Nazism as a metaphor for apprehending the current Balkan War as the focal point for postcommunist development. Moreover, the conceptual linkage Croatia–Nazism was much more effective in drawing a negative reaction from the world community than was the conceptual linkage Serbia–Nazism. The proof lies in the fact that despite the parallels between the quest for a Greater Serbia and a Greater Germany, as well as the brutal methods used by both to achieve their aims, the world allowed Serbia to make its conquest while it tended to ignore Croatia's plight. Implicitly, the world agreed with Serbia that her expressed fears of Croats, as well as Muslims, were justified. For example, American news media coverage of Serbian aggression during 1992 and 1993 simply and notably omitted the almost daily Serbian bombing of Croatian cities such as Zadar, Gospic, and Sibenik, while it concentrated on Serbian bombing of Bosnian cities. President Clinton spoke of lifting the arms embargo on the Bosnian Muslims, but not on the Croats, even though Croats and Bosnians were both victims of Serbian aggression. The Croatian military fought against the Serbs in Bosnia-Herzegovina under a written agreement with the government of Bosnia-Herzegovina. Nevertheless, invited and formal Croat military presence in Bosnia was described in the Western news media as being on a par with Serbian paramilitary units. Herein lies another irony: the Bosnian Muslims tended to be depicted as almost perfect victims, even as metaphorical sacrificial lambs, whose role in Nazism was never brought up.[32] Even so, the West would not save the Bosnian Muslims from certain defeat at the hands of the Serbs.

If it is true that postmodern intellectuals, reporters, and analysts cast the postcommunist drama in the historical terms of Nazism, and thereby obfuscated postcommunist reality, the following were consequences of this collective escape into fiction: Croatia was perceived to be an imperfect victim when Serbia attacked her cities in 1991 due to the *perception* of Croatia as a Nazi, genocidal nation, and the complete absence of any discussion of Serbia's role in Nazism. (In fact, Serbia presented herself to the West as one of the allies of Russia, Britain, France, and the USA.) Hence, the bombing of the Croatian city of Vukovar by the Serbs never received the media coverage that the bombing of the Bosnian city of Sarajevo by the Serbs received. In fact, when CNN (Cable News Network) began bombarding the West with images of Serbian-run "concentration camps" in Bosnia-Herzegovina, everything became "crystal clear" in the West. Metaphorically speaking, the Serbs became the Nazis, and the Muslims became the Jews of World War II (with Croatia relegated to the background as an ambiguous case, still tainted by Nazism, despite her obvious generosity in accepting all those hundreds of thousands of Muslim refugees). And the world behaved toward the new, fictitious Jews – the Bosnian Muslims – much as it behaved toward the real Jews during World War II. Both Semitic peoples were abandoned to barbaric forces according to a script in which Western diplomats and intellectuals spoke of peace, negotiation, rationality, and other high-sounding Enlightenment narratives. Using Freud's terminology, one could accuse the postmodern West of engaging in a widespread, collective, *compulsion to repeat*. The West (England and France in particular) handed Bosnia over to Serbia according to much the same script of appeasement and capitulation that was used to hand the Jewish people over to Hitler.

For example, Britain, France, and Russia engaged in a "successful effort to defeat" a measure presented to the UN Security Council by Islamic nations that would have lifted the arms embargo against the Bosnian Muslims (*New York Times*, 30 June 1993: A4). In a highly personal and emotional appeal, the Bosnian Ambassador to the United Nations, Mr. Mohammed Sacirbey

asked the representative of France whether the French people "could have been convinced that Vichy France was an acceptable alternative to the majesty of a free and sovereign France". To Sir David [of Great Britain] Mr. Sacirbey evoked the memory of Winston Churchill, who declared to the US in the dark early days of World War II, "Give us the tools and we will finish the job." "If this response is worthy of the British people, then I believe that the British people would agree it is also worthy of the Bosnians," Mr. Sacirbey said.

(New York Times, 30 June 1993: A4)*

Thus, despite their category as victims, the Bosnian Muslims are Muslims, and the category of Muslim is highly pejorative in the Western consciousness, as demonstrated by Ahmed (1992) and others. The Bosnian Muslims might be compared with another category of victims that has intruded forcefully onto the postmodern collective consciousness: the AIDS patients. The Bosnian Muslims took over the role of AIDS patients, with all of the ambivalence that AIDS invokes. Specifically, both Bosnian Muslims and AIDS patients evoke images of a completely helpless victim. Yet Americans are still Puritanical at heart, and they like winners, so they feel ambivalent about AIDS victims (sex is still taboo to the American mind), and about Bosnian Muslims as well. Hence, the great outpouring of verbal sympathy, outrage, even humanitarian aid for Bosnian Muslims, but no action that would stop their slaughter once and for all. After all, Bosnian Muslims, like AIDS patients, are tainted victims according to the unconscious standards of the Western collective consciousness.

But are not both the Croats and Bosnian Muslims victims of Serbian aggression? Officially, yes, in that the United Nations, the USA State Department, and the European Community all concluded that Serbia was the primary aggressor in the current Balkan War. But unofficially, or in parallel with this official version, the West sought to discredit the images of both the Croats and Bosnian Muslims as victims. To phrase the matter differently, the postmodern consciousness seems to demand a fictional version of the victim as a perfectly good victim that wears only the metaphorical white hat when being slaughtered by the evil Nazis – who are all bad. In this Hollywood account of Nazism, projected onto the postcommunist Balkans, there is no room for reality, in which all peoples are a mixture of good and evil. One might add that Britain, France, and the USA, in their roles as the Enlightenment nations most involved in monitoring human rights abuses in the contemporary Balkans, could never live up to the scrutiny and absolutist standards they imposed on the Croats and Bosnian Muslims regarding human rights. One has only to think of the wartime atrocities and abuses committed by these allies in every war that they have fought.

One needs to be reminded of Freud's typically *fin de siècle* insight that sadism always co-exists with masochism, a view developed especially by Erich Fromm (1955, 1964). Thus, in the real world there do not exist the Hollywood versions of the fictitious aggressor as a pure sadist and the victim as a pure masochist. For example, and in line with this psychoanalytic line of reasoning, Serbia was engaging in an unconscious, masochistic need for punishment even as she engaged in brutal sadism (see Schoenfeld 1984). In 1993, Croatia began to collaborate openly with Serbia against the Bosnian Muslims, and thereby the masochistic Croatia exhibited sadistic traits of her own. Moreover, frustration breeds aggression, so the Bosnian Muslims also engaged in terrorist and inhumane acts against Croat and Serbian civilians. In sum, none of these developments should have been surprising. What is much more surprising is the unrealistic expectation by well-educated Western diplomats that the Croats and Muslims would behave as perfect victims, as ideal masochists.

In 1993 the Muslims were still maintaining their image as helpless victims, while the Croats were the "bad guys" – not as bad as the Serbs, but bad nonetheless. And the Serbian side, while regarded in official circles as the aggressor, nevertheless scored brilliant points in public relations. The West negotiated with Serbian leaders it labeled as war criminals much as it negotiated with Hitler. Western diplomats were photographed shaking hands with, smiling with, and obviously enjoying themselves with Messrs. Milošević and Karadzić in ways that were an eerie reminder of similar meetings with Hitler. Albert Wohlstetter writes, "The same satellites that again and again over the past two years have transmitted from Bosnia horrifying pictures of children with missing limbs and burned-out faces have also shown the unashamed faces of the Western mediators, ever hopeful that the next test of Milošević's sincerity will succeed" (*Wall Street Journal*, 1 July 1993: A14). The West looked to the Serbian-born American, Milan Panić, to bring peace to the Balkans, even though Mr. Panić was the Prime Minister of a country involved in war crimes, ethnic cleansing, concentration camps, and genocide. Mr. Panić was admired in the West even though he served as the leader of Serbia during a time in which the worst atrocities were being committed. This irony never penetrated the Western consciousness. On the other hand, Dr. Franjo Tudjman, who took Croatia on the path of freedom and independence – one might argue, in the footsteps of the American war for independence two hundred years ago – was referred to in the American media as the "butcher's apprentice" (to Slobodan Milocević, the "butcher of the Balkans").

When the Clinton Administration took over the reins of American power in 1993, it was clear that it spoke the language of liberalism, anti-Fascism, human rights, cosmopolitanism, pluralism, and other pro-Western, Enlightenment values. The irony is that these values were co-opted by the Serbian side – a side branded officially as the aggressor – at the same time that they worked against the victims, Croatia and the Bosnian Muslims. Thus, any instance of the suppression of human rights or the freedom of the press in Croatia was reported instantly and analyzed thoroughly in the Western media as evidence that Croatia was not a real democracy. Such instances constituted evidence that Croatia was not worthy of Western support. The question was never raised whether it was unrealistic to expect that Croatia, as a young democracy, or any other democracy for that matter, could live up to these high ideals so completely. At the other extreme, a headline in the *New York Times* read, "The US and Serbia, Suddenly on the Same Side" (20 April 1993: A6). Slobodan Milošević praised Mr. Clinton for not intervening in the Balkans, and for not allowing the US to become the world's policeman (ibid., 7 April 1993: A6). At a news conference, a reporter asked President Clinton, "Is it strange to have Milošević on your side?" and the President replied, "Yes, it's an unusual feeling, and I hope he'll stay there" (ibid., 18 April 1993: A8). Perhaps

William Safire had a point when he asked, "How gullible can be we?" (ibid., 10 May 1993: A15). This is because "Milošević must pretend. He announced to the East and West: I'm on your side: don't hold me responsible for the continuing conquest I set in train" (ibid.). Mr. Safire added that Lord David Owen, the chief negotiator for the European Community, "all but embraces this war criminal [Milošević] as a new hero" (ibid.).

The final irony I shall consider here is that the reality of anti-Semitism has been lost in the postmodern, postcommunist hunt for fictitious Nazis. Ahmed (1992) is right to remind us that both Jews and Muslims are Semitic peoples. The world's collective conscience has been sensitized to the anti-Jewish variety of anti-Semitism, but it continues to be insensitive, even racist, toward Muslims. It is as if anti-Semitism did not disappear but was merely transformed. The depth-psychological reasons for anti-Semitism analyzed by Charles Schoenfeld in his essay, "Psychoanalysis and Anti-Semitism" (1966), appear to be active despite almost a hundred years of psychoanalysis.[33] To these reasons one should add what might be called depth-sociological reasons, that both Judaism and Islam attempt to preserve tradition alongside modernization. For this reason, modernists – who abhor tradition – fall easily into the habit of anti-Semitism.

The hunt for Nazis exposed by Baudrillard holds much more meaning than he attributes to it. It is a symptom of how fiercely Westerners want to cling to narratives spun from the Enlightenment, including nostalgia for communism, and how threatened they feel by postmodern developments that challenge modernity itself.

Chapter 3

Unwelcome alternatives

Thus far in this discussion we have seen that the dominant Western response to the collapse of communism, conceived as a modernist system, has been typically modernist. The West assumed, quite incorrectly, that the communist utopia would be replaced by the modernist utopia of capitalism and perhaps by the postmodern utopia of tolerance. Instead of criticizing the evils of communism, and yanking communism out by its roots, the West embarked on a veritable orgy of Nazi-hunting, as if the 1990s were really the late 1940s, and Nazism, not communism, the real threat to world security. The postcommunist foreign policies of Britain, France, and the USA – the three primary countries in which Enlightenment narratives took root – were characterized by nostalgia for the former Soviet Union and by what might be called Yugonostalgia. Gorbachev was supported by the West until it had no choice but to back Boris Yeltsin. And for all its protests against Slobodan Milošević, the West took steps to make sure that Milošević would win against the Croats and Muslims. As a result, the West alienated the Islamic world, and caused formerly communist nations in Eastern Europe and the former Soviet Union to wonder why they ever admired the West. What is the basis for this affinity between so-called postmodernism and communism conceived as a modernist system?

Let us review and rephrase the argument thus far: postmodernism – whatever it is – is being built on the ruins of a vanquished modernity. Modern culture, in turn, was built on the utopian hope for total human emancipation from culture, history, and tradition (Gellner 1992a). One can conceive of communism as a distinctly modernist system in the sense that it also sought this same utopian dream of complete emancipation from culture (Bauman 1992). But modernist emancipation became totalitarianism in formerly communist nations. And the collapse of modernism in some communist countries gave rise, not to efforts to find an alternative to modernist assumptions, but to nostalgia. In formerly communist nations, one found nostalgia for pre-communist national identities; in capitalist nations one found nostalgia for communist nations and Marxist ideologies; and in Islamic nations, one found nostalgia for the alleged purity of a Golden Age. Hence, the West continues to mourn the demise of Yugoslavia and the Soviet Union even as the Islamic peoples in these former Empires are clamoring for their cultural identities. In particular, modernity sought to create out of Western European tradition a *tabula rasa*, an absolutely new and "better" civilization compared with traditional European communities or tradition in general (Tönnies [1887] 1963). In this sense Hitler was a modernist, for he sought to wipe the slate clean and to erect a new civilization. In this same sense Stalin was a modernist, in that he too tried to eradicate Slavic culture and to replace it with his version of a modernist utopia. Hence the secret attraction, disguised affinity, and tacit collaboration of capitalism, Nazism, and communism in this century. All of these oppressive "isms" sought to exterminate tradition and nationalism.

More importantly, for the purposes of the present discussion, the 1990s quest for a Greater Serbia is also modernist. The Serbian war against its neighbors is a total war against space, memories, tradition, community, family, and religion – against everything that represents the pre-modern.[1] Because Islam is still a very traditional culture, it is regarded by Serbia as well as many other modernists as an entity that must be destroyed. Thus, the Serbs blow up the foundations of mosques when they conquer Muslim towns. They also destroy Catholic churches. They forcibly separate the men from the women and children when they occupy villages. The Serbs rape Muslim and Croat women in the most humiliating manner possible, to scar them for life so that they will not want to return to their villages or bear children in the future. The West knows about these events because they have been documented on television. To be sure, the West protested against Serbian aggression and barbarism, much as it protested against atrocities by Hitler and Stalin, but it not only refused to stop Serbia, it made sure that Serbia would win by not allowing the nationalist Croats and Muslims to defend themselves. All the rationalizations in the world will not alter the historical fact that the modernist West gave tacit support to the modernist Serbian goal of wiping the slate clean in the Balkans.

The West's main response to this Balkan tragedy was labeled "humanitarian." Secretary of State Warren Christopher, for example, claimed that the USA had no vital interests in the Balkans, although it had humanitarian interests.[2] As if vital interests cannot be humanitarian and humanitarian interests are not in America's long-term security interests! I agree with Albert Wohlstetter that "if this gives humanitarianism a bad name, neither does it help the reputation for realism of Western negotiators who think of themselves as pragmatists" (*Wall Street Journal*, 1 July 1993: A14). This was a highly organized, abstract, and typically modernist version of humanitarianism in that the Bosnian Muslims were presumed to have a right to a naked biological existence, but not their collective past (tradition) or a viable future. This is the philosophical significance of the Washington Peace Plan of May 1993, in which a promise was made to establish fictional "safe havens" for the Bosnian Muslims.[3] These safe havens were compared with the Indian reservations upon which the USA forced Native Americans to live without a real past or future. If the postmodernists who equate modernity with oppression, even genocide, are right, then it is important to note that despite all the talk about postmodernism, modernity is alive and well in the world.

The claims that have been made thus far raise some serious new issues in the postmodern discourse as it pertains to postcommunism, including the following: far from being just the abstract antithesis to capitalism, Soviet and Yugoslav communisms may have existed as disguised Russian and Serbian imperialisms respectively. After all, if Max Weber ([1904] 1958) was right to claim that capitalism is rooted in particular cultural traditions, it should follow that communism, too, had various cultural, even nationalist roots (Meštrović, Goreta, and Letica 1993b). And if the Enlightenment project had truly and finally come to an end in the present *fin de siècle*, one would have been confronted with the unexpected choice between "good" and "bad" nationalisms and traditions. But how does one determine the standards for distinguishing good versus bad given the fact that many postmodernists would find such categories – or for that matter, any dualisms – oppressive? Yet without the dualism good/evil, for example, the postmodern world found itself helplessly condoning genocide in the Balkans. These are the issues to be addressed in this chapter. As I write, modernity is alive and well despite the shallow rhetoric of protest found in postmodern discourse, and the only true challenges to modernity are to be found in Islamic and other traditional cultures.

Suppose that we are right to claim that the communism which ruled Europe up to the 1990s was actually a disguised "bad" version of Russian and Serbian nationalisms. It would follow that the collapse of communism in the former Soviet Union and former Yugoslavia would not alter Russian and Serbian authoritarianism in appreciable ways. Instead, one would expect that the Russian and Serbian forms of imperialism that animated their respective versions of communism would merely transform themselves into new forms of imperialism. Indeed, one could argue that the quest for a Greater Serbia made itself painfully apparent in the early 1990s, in line with my predictions. But Serbia's aggression toward its neighbors was not interpreted primarily as the result of the same program for a Greater Serbia that animated Yugoslav communism and that reduced the other Yugoslav republics to the status of internal colonies. Similarly, the West failed to interpret as imperialistic or ominous Russia's March 1993 proclamation that it would prevent the other republics in the Commonwealth of Independent States (formerly the Soviet Union) from secession. Publicly, not a single Western diplomat made the connection that Serbia's role as the policeman of the Balkans was a prelude to Russia's coming role as the policeman of the former Soviet Union.[4] In fact, the West seemed to welcome Russia's offer, and painted President Boris Yeltsin as the James Monroe of Russia:

"What's wrong with a Russian Monroe Doctrine?" one high Clinton official asked rhetorically. "And what's terrible about Russians being regional peacekeepers in an area where no other country can and will prevent future Yugoslavias? And why shouldn't they have the same right to act under a general UN mandate the way we did in Iraq?"[5]

ANTI-MODERN OR AFTER MODERNITY?

Intellectuals have not yet resolved the question whether postmodernism constitutes rebellion against or an extension of the Enlightenment narratives that constitute modernity. In other words, is postmodernism anti-modern or just something that comes after modernity? An excellent illustration of the former position is Aleksander Solzhenitsyn's (1993) essay, "The Relentless Cult of Novelty and How it Wrecked the Century." An equally compelling defense of the latter position is given by Anthony Giddens in "Uprooted Signposts at Century's End" (1992). Solzhenitsyn argues that postmodernism's wholesale rebellion is but the latest "recurrence of one and the same perilous anti-cultural phenomenon, with its rejection of and contempt for all foregoing tradition" (1993: 3). He believes that the formerly communist nations as well as the Western nations are suffering the evil consequences of this rebellion.[6]

On the other hand, Giddens rejects the term postmodernism altogether, and opts instead for the concept "high modernity" to capture some problematic aspects of late twentieth-century modernism. But he believes that modernity is a Western product, can be repaired, and is inexorable: "Rather than speaking of post-modernity, let us say instead that certain key traits of modernity are becoming radicalized and globalized. . . . It is no longer purely Utopian to anticipate the possible emergence of a truly global order, a global cosmopolitanism" (Giddens 1992: 22). I have no intention of trying to resolve the issue that divides followers of Solzhenitsyn versus Giddens in these abstract terms, for such an effort succumbs to circular reasoning in which modernity's abstractionism is analyzed in abstract terms. Instead, let us recast this polemic in relation to the problem at hand, namely, postcommunism.

If one were to seek out concrete examples of what a postmodern rebellion against Enlightenment narratives might be like, one would point to nationalism, fundamentalism, and other passionate, anti-globalist, anti-cosmopolitan, phenomena in postcommunist lands. This is because passion, faith, and fanaticism are typically understood to be characteristics that one finds in traditional cultures, that lead to particularism, and that are the obverse of the modern effort to be guided strictly by rationality. This is commensurate with the general formula put forth by Ernest Gellner (1992a) that rationality opposes culture. One might be tempted to compare such an understanding of postmodernism with Jürgen Habermas's (1987) expressed desire to complete the Enlightenment project, and to regard post-modernism as threatening to this project. But here again, one has already prejudged the Enlightenment project as something benign, and rebellion against it as something dangerous. One has already assumed that there exists only one form of rationality, and that traditional cultures do not exhibit their own sorts of rationality or logic. Let us not follow Habermas in haste. For now, let us hold the thought that the nationalism, religion, and other explosions of passion in postcommunist nations constitute excellent illustrations of rebellion against the modernist system that was communism. If that is true, then Solzhenitsyn's position is inherently conservative and oppressive.

In addition, one would arrive at the tentative yet surprising hypothesis that postmodernism – understood as rebellion against the Enlightenment narratives – took place in formerly communist countries, not the chic and faddish centers of postmodern discourse, such as Paris and New York, which have certainly not succumbed to nationalism or particularism (at least not yet). This is surprising because Americans and Western Europeans have become so used to thinking of Eastern Europe and the former Soviet Union as economically backward, that one would not expect *them* to rebel at what limited modernity they enjoyed. (This attitude is as arrogant as Hegel and Marx refusing to consider the Balkans and Russia in their grand schemes concerning the end of history.) It is surprising also because the dominant Western response to the fall of communism has been to offer the postcommunist nations still more modernity, this time in the form of democracy and capitalism. More on that later.

What about the alternative understanding of postmodernity as an extension of the modernist fragmentation of meaning and other problems that Giddens subsumes under the rubric of high modernity? In this context, one thinks of the postmodern discourse that pertains to some of the following phenomena (among others): the world as text, cultural and moral relativism, kitsch, the circulation of fictions, America as the world's Disneyworld, fun-culture, the behavior of cultural traits as if they were the symptoms in a patient suffering from hysteria, and other phenomena up to and including nihilism. If the modernists are right that one should abandon all tradition and culture, then the end-point of such a quest seems to be Baudrillard's (1986) vision of the individual lost in a sea of circulating fictions, none of which is grounded in any sort of permanence at all. Life becomes a cultural desert, and America the penultimate symbol of the postmodern desert landscape (see Rojek and Turner 1993). Gellner (1992b) regards this postmodern outcome as nihilistic. Yet many authors follow Giddens (1990) to defend it as liberating and as holding the potential for heightened tolerance, pluralism, and democracy (Bauman 1991, Rosenau 1992).

In fact, the debate whether high modernity is liberating or oppressive already seems outdated in the few years since the Berlin Wall was torn down. Instead of globalism and cosmopolitanism, the world is beset by fragmentation and Balkanization. Any visitor to or consistent student of postcommunist nations will probably agree that the other benign phenomena drawn from the trajectory represented by the writings of Anthony Giddens are not very likely to be found in nations that emerged from under the yoke of communism. For example, Eurodisney was built in Paris, not Budapest. The charm of McDonald's in Moscow has already worn off, and in general, the citizens in postcommunist nations had to struggle just to make a living, which is not a condition conducive to developing the consumer mentality that capitalism needs. Far from promoting the globalism envisaged by Giddens, postcommunist nations have tended in the opposite direction, of particularism. If it is true that communist doctrines have been exposed as great lies, Eastern Europeans *do not* share the West's typically cynical reaction to this high modern discovery, such that the Western postmodernist concludes that "Absolute truths do not exist anyhow, and trying to find them is pointless. Nor is it worth the trouble to strive for some kind of higher meaning" (Solzhenitsyn 1993: 3). Instead, the citizens in many postcommunist nations have embarked on a search for absolute truths, primarily in nationalist and religious traditions, among others. The Eastern European individual is not lost in a sea of circulating fictions, but is smothered by traditions. Far from being a cultural desert, life in formerly communist nations constitutes a rich and often overwhelming experience of cultural symbols drawn from previously repressed national, religious, and other traditional sources.

This tentative conclusion is surprising because it exposes the fact that modernity's course in formerly communist nations was different from its course in capitalist and socialist nations usually referred to as the West. Proof that we are on the right track lies in the incredible naivety and total lack of embarrassment among all those American, French, and British diplomats who ostensibly, loudly, and ostentatiously tried and failed to negotiate peace in postcommunist Yugoslavia, as well as all those many Western intellectuals who predicted a quick and easy transition to capitalism in the former Soviet Union. If communism were just another modernist system, or merely a modernist system and nothing more, then these diplomats and intellectuals might have been justified in assuming that one model of modernity – the one that took root primarily in the USA, France, and Britain – fits all cultures. One might term this the McDonald's approach (from Ritzer 1992) to postcommunist foreign policy: if a universal McDonald's hamburger can be put together rationally in any city in the world, then a universal version of capitalism and democracy can be built just as rationally and easily. At the time of writing, most Western intellectuals as well as diplomats have not grasped the obvious, namely, that (1) the Western brand of modernity that is derived from the Enlightenment is not only rational, benign, and conducive to human rights, but might also be barbaric and savage in many aspects, and (2) the formerly communist brand of modernity might have had cultural roots even as communism eschewed culture every bit as much as the Enlightenment project was opposed to culture.

Much has been written already about McDonald's and Disneyworld as centers of a postmodern blend of Weberian rationality as well as fun-culture (Baudrillard 1990; Ritzer 1992; Rojek 1993). I would add a new dimension to this discussion in the light of the preceding. Using Freud's original *fin de siècle* insights, the widespread popularity of McDonald's, Disneyworld, *Sesame Street*, and other icons of Western fun-culture may be interpreted as symptoms of infantile regression. The fact that foreign policy, law, and many other Western institutions lend themselves easily to comparisons with McDonald's and Disneyworld philosophies suggests that postmodernists have refused to grow up in Freud's sense of growing up. Instead of seriously confronting the grave issues presented by the collapse of communism, as well as late capitalism, leading intellectuals such as Anthony Giddens offer a childish retreat into something like Disney's fantasy of "It's A Small World, After All." The many diplomats', philosophers', consultants', and politicians' promises of easy transitions into the West's fun-culture remind one of the schemes for world improvement concocted by school-age children. I make these analogies not to be insulting, but to make the serious point that infantile regression is a primitive defense mechanism. If this Freudian insight is still relevant, the question arises: what is the ominous threat that the Western world is defending itself against by regressing into childhood fantasies? I have been implying an answer all along: the threat of the collapse of modernity itself, which is not a cause for celebration, but for profound anxiety.

THE EAST–WEST DICHOTOMY

I agree with Ahmed (1992) that the East–West dichotomy is cultural, not geographical, so that Australia, for example, is often considered to be part of the West. Furthermore, Islamic nations are considered Eastern even though they span much of the globe from North Africa to Indonesia. But even as a cultural dichotomy, the East–West distinction is problematic.

For example, many writers have claimed that East meets West in the former Yugoslavia. Even if that were true, culturally speaking, in that the former Yugoslavia was home to Catholic as well as Orthodox and Islamic cultural traditions, it is notoriously difficult to find this cultural dividing-line. Thus, the Slovenes regard their border with Croatia as the border between the West and the Orient, respectively. Yet the Croatians regard themselves as Western and the Serbs as representative of Eastern culture. Moreover, even though the Slovenes claim in their media that the Balkans begin in Croatia, Croatians deny that they were ever a part of the Balkans, and they regard Slovenia as a satellite of Serbia! Thus, one hears the pejorative phrase, "Alpine Chetniks," among Croats when referring to their Slovene neighbors to the north.

Bosnia-Herzegovina became a microcosm of the tensions that ripped apart the former Yugoslavia in that its Croats, Serbs, and Muslims came to align themselves with these East–West stereotypes even though they tried to preserve a Western type of multicultural state. For example, the 23 May 1993 issue of the Sarajevo newspaper, *Oslobodjenje* (Liberation), ran the headline, "All Serbian Flags," to describe the flags of the USA, France, Britain, Russia, and Spain, the countries that came up with the Washington Peace Plan. The article went on to explain this generalization by claiming that these nations effectively allowed Serbia to destroy the multicultural state that Bosnia-Herzegovina used to be (and that Yugoslavia used to be as well). While the Bosnian Croats regard the Bosnian Serbs and Serbia in general as an Oriental menace – on a par with Islam – the Bosnian Muslims came to regard both the Croats and the Serbs as Western powers bent on the extermination of Islam.

Europe is not immune to this stereotyping. Most people seem to agree that Britain and France constitute Western Europe, but what about Germany or Russia?

And where does Eastern Europe begin? Poland? Ukraine? Whereas the Western Europeans typically refer to Russia as well as the former Soviet Union as the East, the Islamic world refers to the former Soviet Union and all of Europe – in fact, to the Christian world – as the West. And where does the "backdoor" of Europe begin? Some Western Europeans claim that it begins with Slovenia, Croatia, Serbia, Macedonia, even Germany. Many writers refer to Northern Italy as Western Europe and Southern Italy as something other than Western Europe. In general, one could argue that far from Western European influences spreading to formerly communist East-Central Europe and the Balkans, the reverse has occurred: a sort of Balkanization seems to have taken over so-called Western Europe. The dream of a United States of Europe has been shattered already by the hostility shown by Britain and France to Germany, evidenced especially in their differing policies toward the former Yugoslavia, as well as the ways that smaller European nations aligned themselves in relation to this anti-German tendency.

Arnold Toynbee (1962) confounds matters further when he declares that the term modernity is a kind of shorthand for the West and that both modernity and the West are best represented by the concept of America – the United States of America in particular. In *America*, Jean Baudrillard (1986) concurs, but adds that America has become a fictionalized center of the equally inauthentic, postmodern and fictional West. To be sure, Barry Smart[7] has a point when he argues just as convincingly that Europe or even Japan make better candidates for the role of symbols of modernity, capitalism, and/or "the West." In addition, we have seen that President Clinton and many others have hinted that the USA itself is succumbing to a sort of cultural Balkanization – an "Eastern" phenomenon – as evidenced by race riots and many other sorts of divisiveness. For example, Hispanic and African Americans forcefully criticize the logic of the predominantly white and Protestant culture that is imposed on them in the name of melting-pot America. Women and gays have taken on the status of fictional ethnic groups in the USA. There is open discussion of secession in Hawaii, Northern from Southern California, the two halves of Texas (Hispanic versus Caucasian), even the cities of New Orleans and New York as "states." Yet one suspects that "logic" has little to do with these assessments. In fact, there may exist several varieties of logic (Islamic logic, Balkan logic, emotional logic, Eastern logic, etc.) and not just the sort that is typically associated with the Enlightenment. The more important point is that America is still perceived by many Europeans, the Japanese, and others in the world as the primary symbol of phenomena typically subsumed under the rubric, "the West," including democracy, individualism, and modernity, among others.

Alexis de Tocqueville's ([1845] 1945) assertion that America is the beacon of democracy shining down upon the rest of the world is open to criticism, even cynicism – it is certain that many citizens in the USA no longer see their country's role in this light. Nevertheless, it is easy enough to verify empirically that when it comes to major political decisions that involve the United Nations or other international bodies, the USA is the motor that drives these organizations. Thus, the US led many other countries in the Gulf War, and declined to lead Europe to rescue Bosnia-Herzegovina from Serbian aggression. Europe still looks to America for leadership, even if it resents the USA for this very fact.

In assessing these many meanings and nuances regarding the East–West dichotomy, one is tempted to conclude that the distinction is illogical and meaningless. After all, it cannot be the case that Japan, the USA, Croatia, France, and Russia can all be considered Western in some senses of the term. By the standards of Western logic, it is logically incorrect to regard all these cultures as Western, for reasons discussed above. Equally true, however, is the fact that most of the postmodern world looks up to America and its cultural products as the prototype of phenomena deemed to be Western: Disneyworld and fun-culture in general, the golden arches of McDonald's (see Ritzer 1992), blue jeans, the rock star Madonna, the soap opera *Santa Barbara*, among others. Ahmed (1992) makes an important point when he claims that these and other phenomena are perceived as threatening by most of the Islamic world. It is equally true that the USA and most of Europe feels threatened by Islam, perceived as the Eastern phenomenon *par excellence*: "The Islamic peril is now seen by many as the greatest threat to the West, beside which the Red and Yellow perils pale into insignificance" (Ahmed 1992: 3). If one refuses to use the East–West dichotomy because of the contradictions it seems to entail, one will be blind to the empirical reality of the looming East (Islamic)–West (American and European) conflict that is slowly but surely emerging onto the postmodern, postcommunist scene.

For example, it is interesting that with the passage of time, Serbia's principal victims in the Balkans, the Croats and the Muslims, came to battle against each other. Slowly but steadily, Serbia drew the Western "allies" from World War II into being tacit accomplices to her aggression, whereas the Islamic world came to regard the Muslim plight in Bosnia-Herzegovina as the most important symbol of Muslim suffering since the Crusades. It does not matter that the Islamic world consistently "fails" to exhibit the kind of political unification that Westerners exhibit. Such an assessment makes ethnocentric use of the concept of "unification" in the Western sense. While it is true that the Islamic world has failed to stand up to the West thus far, and in that sense is not unified, it is also true, in the words of Akbar Ahmed, that

> In mosques from Karachi to Cairo, in the Muslim world, and Seattle to Cambridge, in the non-Muslim world, I have been struck by the universality and similarity of themes expressed in the *khutba*, the sermon delivered on Friday to the congregation.... The main themes emerging in sermons reflect the apocalyptic mood among ordinary Muslims.... Several clear themes are apparent: there is the eternal and universal struggle between good and evil. The world is seen as increasingly dominated by the power of the West, especially the United States, which represents moral and spiritual decadence. Sex, drugs and violence are what the West offers and Muslims must resist them with their piety and moral strength. Stereotypes and hearsay often pass as truth in the

arguments; the VCR and some of its more vulgar exhibits are taken as exemplifying the West. The museums, parks and libraries are seldom, if ever, mentioned.

(1992: 196)

I shall add that I came across a similar "script" during my own participant-observation research at the mosque in Zagreb, Croatia, in 1992 and 1993. Ahmed's work is laudable for sensitizing Westerners to the ways in which they threaten and feel threatened by Islamic culture. Yet neither his discussion nor any discussion of this sort can escape some fundamental ambiguities. For example, Ahmed asks, "What can Islamic civilization contribute to the world?" and replies, "It can provide a corrective and a check to the materialism that characterizes much of contemporary civilization, offering instead compassion, piety and a sense of humility" (1992: 117). Yet one must take into account that (1) Islamic civilization can be accused of its own versions of materialism and decadence; and that (2) Western civilization also has its own versions of compassion, piety, and a sense of humility, especially as these are reflected in ideal and idealized Christian dogma. In sum, all cultures are a mix of categories usually labeled as good and evil so that, strictly speaking, East and West are indistinguishable at the same time that the East–West polarity that Ahmed isolates is empirically verifiable, and therefore "real."

There is no easy solution to this dilemma. My own strategy for coping with the issues raised thus far is to keep the East–West dichotomy, but to use it in a limited and specific sense. I do *not* mean that Western culture is fundamentally superior to or essentially different from Eastern culture. At the same time, one can make sense of many postmodernist and postcommunist developments by pointing to a strong current of prejudice within the USA, France, and Britain and some other nations deemed Western against the Balkans, the Islamic world, and all other nations and cultures that oppose the Enlightenment traditions. The USA, France, and Britain are nations in which the Enlightenment traditions that are called human rights, fair play, and individualism, among other recognizably "Western" phenomena took root, even if (1) one can question how viable these traditions still are in these nations and (2) one should be sensitive to non-Western versions of human rights, fair play, and individualism. Thus, postmodernist and postcommunist developments involve Enlightenment traditions in some form – albeit, often fictitious, infantile, and used according to double standards – from the USA to Russia, versus Islamic traditions that feel threatened by these traditions even as they attempt to emulate them. But this characterization begs the question of what is meant by traditions and culture, a topic that will be addressed next.

IS MODERNITY A CULTURAL TRADITION OR AN ANTI-CULTURAL IMPOSSIBILITY?

Ernest Gellner (1992a: 13) is probably right that the Enlightenment was the beginning of a program for complete liberation from culture. Part of Gellner's analysis involves pitting the philosopher, René Descartes, as the precursor and representative of this program for liberation, versus the sociologist, Emile Durkheim, as the chief spokesperson for the doctrine that all human phenomena are rooted in some ways in culture. Durkheim even claimed that individualism itself is a cultural phenomenon, that individuals could not act out their freedoms unless their cultures supplied them with the basis for individualism (discussed in Meštrović 1988). Anyone who has read the bulk of Durkheim's writings will find that he is extremely critical of the oversimplified rationalism found in Cartesianism, the doctrine that social problems can be addressed and solved with mathematical precision and elegance.[8] Despite the rhetoric of protest at the Enlightenment found in postmodern discourse, Cartesianism still reigns supreme from academia to the halls of government to so-called popular "culture." It is a telling sign that Durkheim continues to be misapprehended as a disciple of Descartes and that his culturally oriented sociology had been eclipsed almost completely by sociologies derived from the Enlightenment program.

According to Gellner (1992b: 2), there exist three major alternatives for orienting one's self in relation to the power of culture: "Religious fundamentalism; relativism, exemplified for instance by the recent fashion of postmodernism; enlightenment rationalism, or rationalist fundamentalism." He regards religious fundamentalism as untenable, and postmodernism as the path to nihilism,[9] so he recommends rationalist fundamentalism as the least obnoxious choice.[10] One might object that Gellner is advocating a paradox: he counsels one to have *faith* (a notion that the Enlightenment sought to overcome with pure rationality) in the Enlightenment project despite all the good reasons that Gellner and others have cited for criticizing the Enlightenment project, especially that this enterprise has been linked with terror.[11] But Gellner's reply is coldly pragmatic: "Enlightenment Secular Fundamentalism has become the unwritten, but widely recognized code of cognitive conduct of many, though not all, scholars of scientific-industrial civilization" (ibid.: 76). He adds that

> We happen to live in a world in which one style of knowledge, though born of one culture, is being adapted by all of them [other cultures], with enormous speed and eagerness, and is disrupting many of them, and is totally transforming the milieu in which men live. This is simply a fact. I am not starry-eyed in the face of it.
>
> (ibid.: 78)

But the victory of what Gellner calls Enlightenment Secular Fundamentalism is not an accomplished fact. Gellner underestimates the power of Islamic fundamentalism as well as the world's many other traditional cultures to see through the cynicism of believing in an Enlightenment tradition that continues to mask colonialist and imperialist tendencies. The Enlightenment program constitutes more than a style of knowledge, because cognition colors moral, national, and other political issues. For example, at the June 1993 World Conference on Human Rights in Vienna,

So deep are divisions over the universality of human rights, a concept some belittle as excessively "Western," that delegates could not agree on condemning torture in their draft declaration. Prodded by China and Indonesia, 40 Asian countries approved a statement contending that standards of justice and fairness should be tempered by "regional peculiarities and various historical, cultural and religious backgrounds." The statement adds that human rights should never be used as "an instrument of political pressure" or made a condition for development aid.[12]

Defenders of Enlightenment Fundamentalism might be surprised that anyone in the world could question the cognitive meaning of the concept of human rights. Yet, from the perspective of individuals raised in countries that fall outside the domain of the Enlightenment project, the West has a long and hypocritical history of using the concept of human rights to further its own realist policies, and of not using this concept in an even-handed and impartial way. Moreover, most of the non-Western world regards economic survival as a much more important human right than, let us say, freedom of speech. David Riesman (1977) has already suggested that President Jimmy Carter used the concept of human rights in ethnocentric and inconsistent ways, and it seems that the Clinton Administration is following in his footsteps. To cite just a few examples from the first few months of the Clinton Presidency, China's most-favored trading status was renewed, despite the Tiananmen Square massacre; the US continued to punish the Haitian peoples with sanctions ostensibly to persuade them to overthrow their government; Turkey was promised hundreds of millions of dollars in military equipment if it would make greater strides in human rights; Serbian human rights abuses were ignored while Somali and Iraqi violations were punished swiftly. The fact that President Clinton's first military actions involved attacks on Somalia and Iraq in June 1993, but not on Serbia, was not lost on the Islamic world.

One cannot escape Durkheim's disturbing dictum that all cognitive as well as moral phenomena – for the two are interrelated – cannot exist save as cultural phenomena. There cannot be a universally valid understanding of human rights, logic, rationality, democracy or anything else. This is what the Descartes–Durkheim polemic is all about. The Cartesian option necessarily leads to terror, colonialism, and imperialism because it assumes that Western definitions are universally valid so that all those who oppose them are automatically wrong. Yet the Durkheimian, relativist position does not necessarily lead to nihilism, chaos, or anarchy, as so many defenders of the Enlightenment project claim. Instead, the Durkheimian project assumes that the world's cultural diversity can be overcome, eventually, through the power of sympathetic understanding of differences. This is the message that shines through Durkheim's *Division of Labor in Society* (1893) and *The Elementary Forms of the Religious Life* (1912) especially. In these and other works, Durkheim claims that democracy and individualism did not begin with the French Revolution or with any other Western event or culture. Rather, these can be found in some form in every culture, even that of the Australian

Aborigines. All cultures subscribe some degree of sanctity and respect to the individual, or else these cultures could not survive. In opposition to Marxist, Cartesian, and other modernist utopian projects, Durkheim was proposing a compassionate and just division of labor among the world's many diverse collective consciences. Durkheim's anti-modern aspirations are still far from being apprehended in any meaningful sort of way.

In any event, the Cartesian, Enlightenment version of human existence is untenable. Adherents of the Enlightenment project are unable to explain how Enlightenment-based values, beliefs, and other components of culture are transmitted across generations if the individual is to be completely free of all traditions, habits, and other cultural phenomena. True, the USA still subscribes officially to the natural rights doctrine which assumes that all *men* are born equal and free, but there is no need to review here the many well-known protests by women and minorities that this high-sounding ideal does not apply to them. Latter-day Cartesians must assume that individuals are born with their human rights intact, but this assumption flies in the face of common sense: if governments, religions, families, and other manifestations of cultural traditions did not protect the individual with laws, habits, and customs, the individual would be at the mercy of others bent on depriving him or her of human rights. This is not to deny that such cultural habits and customs can also oppress the individual, and we will tackle this problem in the next section.

For now, the only consistent, and genuinely postmodern conclusion regarding the problem of culture versus the Enlightenment project is the following: the Enlightenment project is itself a tradition traceable to a Northwest corner of Europe, whose habits and world-views were diffused throughout much of the world, and continue to be diffused. Yet this project does not enjoy some special sort of existence, as if all the rest of the world needed tradition but the Enlightenment project were self-begotten and self-contained. The Enlightenment tradition animates what is often referred to as the West, but the West is just one cultural tradition among many. The notions of individualism, human rights, freedom, and democracy are its proudest cultural achievements, but these are still only habits, customs, traditions, laws and other components of culture, not something supernatural. Both Western and non-Western cultures also contain oppressive traditions, but non-Western cultures are not devoid of individualism and democracy (a point argued forcefully by Durkheim in *Professional Ethics and Civic Morals*, [1950] 1983). We turn now to analyzing some issues raised by this tentative conclusion.

GOOD VERSUS BAD IN CULTURES

The Cartesian antipathy toward culture blossomed into the modernist disdain for nationalism. Communism tried to pretend that nationalism did not exist, or tried to eliminate national identity altogether. Despite these efforts, and following the collapse of communism, nationalism emerged as the most powerful social force in the world. Western nation-states are also hostile to nationalism, and for the same modernist reasons held by communists: nationalism bespeaks the power of cultural identity. Boutros Boutros-Ghali (1992) has written that the concept of national sovereignty needs to be softened, especially with regard to "failed" nation-states such as Cambodia and Bosnia-Herzegovina, so that the United Nations can fulfill its missions. But from the perspective of these supposedly failed nation-states, and other nations that experience difficulties with establishing a nation-state, Mr. Boutros-Ghali's suggestion smacks of imperialism. This is because the UN is perceived by most non-Western nations as less an international organization than the extension of Western powers. Indeed, it is not difficult to argue that the most powerful Western nation-states in the world today, the USA, France, and Britain, are highly nationalistic in their own right, even if they try to obscure this fact, or deny it outright (Greenfeld 1992). No one who has witnessed a parade commemorating American, French, or British civil religions – albeit the civil religions of the mostly white majority populations in these countries – can deny the explicit outpouring of nationalist sentiment. An excellent illustration is the celebration of the West's victory in the Gulf War. But these same Western nations have reproached Croatia and other formerly communist nations for celebrating their own national identities or independence, and make no distinction between a peaceable nationalism that seeks to live and let live versus the aggressive nationalism exhibited by Serbia, for example. All nationalism is deemed bad by the West. There is more than a touch of hypocrisy in this.

In any event, these anti-cultural and anti-nationalist positions that constitute modernism are untenable, for reasons discussed previously. Nationalism and national sovereignty are components of cultural identity that are comparable to Freud's concept of the id. Just as the id cannot be eliminated, national sovereignty is an irrational component of the collective make-up of groups that cannot be eliminated no matter how much disciples of the Enlightenment criticize it as obsolete, primitive, or dangerous. In this regard, I agree with Charles Schoenfeld:

> Appealing only to man's intellect – using logic and reason to "prove" that sovereignty is a pernicious notion that threatens the peace of the world – is not likely to result in the rejection of sovereignty. If the doctrine of sovereignty helps fulfill deeply-rooted emotional needs, then arguments alone – no matter how valid – cannot convince sovereignty's champions to abandon it.
>
> (1984: 127)

In addition, the West must confront the empirical reality of heightened nationalism and cultural identity throughout the postmodern, postcommunist world. Clinging to outmoded assumptions derived from the Enlightenment will only exacerbate existing fissures that tend toward cultural wars between West and the non-West in various forms. In sum, the postmodernist must distinguish between good versus bad nationalisms and good versus evil in all cultures. Otherwise, disciples of the Enlightenment project will assume that all nationalisms and cultural traditions are evil, an assumption that supports the tendencies toward terror, oppression, colonialism, and imperialism that have been the object of postmodern criticism. These anti-cultural tendencies by the West, such as the insistence that the West's definition of human rights is universally valid, lead to paranoia among non-Western nations in which it is presumed that the West uses the language of human rights and democracy to mask its still existing and more subtle imperialism.

But are not the categories "good" and "evil" themselves oppressive? They can be, but do not have to be. I follow Durkheim's lead in holding that good nationalism and other cultural phenomena are those that promote compassion within a culture and in relation to other cultures.[13] Evil is a category reserved for those cultural phenomena that promote egoism within and external to cultures, such that individuals and nations are aggressive or even violent toward their neighbors. In sum, a good form of cultural and national identity seeks to live and let live, while the bad forms seek to live at the expense of other cultural and national groups. And in line with Durkheim's adherence to the notion of the dualism of human nature, it is important to note that good will never triumph completely over evil. Individuals as well as nations and cultures will always constitute a relative mix of these good and evil traits. Durkheim was not a utopian dreamer, and neither am I.

As I have argued elsewhere,[14] by compassion I do not mean to imply pity, charity, humanitarianism, or any other organized, modernist, effort to promote one's egoism in the guise of contemptuously and ostentatiously helping others. Pity, charity, and humanitarianism can be and often are oppressive, and they are often resented by both individuals and nations at the receiving end of such condescending goodwill. But this is because these cheap imitations lack the most essential ingredient of genuine compassion, co-suffering or the complete identification of one's humanity with the rest of humanity. When one acts out of pity, charity, or humanitarianism, one is looking down upon the victim. This basic contempt is not lost on the victim, who reacts with a volatile mixture of gratitude and hostility. Consider, for example, the highly ambivalent and often very angry reactions to United Nations humanitarian efforts by the recipients of such aid in Bosnia-Herzegovina and Somalia, two highly publicized humanitarian spectacles of the 1990s. What I am calling compassion refers to something completely different, and quite rare in the world.

Synonyms for compassion might be sympathy, sympathetic understanding, empathy, caritas, group-libido, and other terms with similar assumptions in the writings of Emile Durkheim, George Herbert Mead, Max Weber, Georg Simmel, Marcel Mauss, Thorstein Veblen, Sigmund Freud and other precursors of the social sciences from the previous *fin de siècle*. These and other sociologists (such as Pitirim Sorokin) tried to promote sympathetic understanding of the other, and to warn against knee-jerk ethnocentrism. Compassion cannot be oppressive, at least when it is genuine. This is because compassion, in the sense used by Durkheim and like-minded colleagues, is the glue that holds societies and cultures together. Without compassionate identification by the individual with other individuals to some extent, it is impossible for any society to exist. Durkheim never seems to tire of writing of how religion, language, and other cultural phenomena promote this sense of mystic sympathy, identification with others, integration and solidarity (see Meštrović 1992). Without compassion, one is reduced to acting in the role of a naked ego in opposition to other naked egos, a gladiator poised to fight other gladiators in a Nietzschean quest for power. But such a condition is the famous Hobbesian war of all against all, and cannot sustain social or cultural life in the long term. As such, genuine compassion cannot be oppressive because without it the cultural conditions for societal existence are completely impossible.

I regret that the word compassion is held in low esteem by the postmodern world in which I live and work, but it is difficult to find an alternative word. Durkheim's nephew and collaborator, Marcel Mauss, experienced a similar frustration, writing,

> At the risk of seeming old-fashioned and a purveyor of commonplaces, let me appeal once again to the old Greek and Latin concepts of *caritas*, for which the modern "charity" is such a poor translation . . . the necessary "friendship," the "community" that constitute the delicate essence of the City.
>
> ([1925] 1992: 196)

Using *caritas* would not be an improvement on compassion, and charity has taken on the connotations of contempt that oppose the original meanings of *caritas*. The important point is that societies are bound together by derivatives of charity and love, by devotion, and by sentiments, not by self-interest, ambition, hate, and strife. The Enlightenment tradition simply cannot offer a formula for keeping societies integrated because it promotes narcissism, and narcissism is inherently divisive.

In fact, it is a point in favor of my argument that one has to search high and low for a suitable contemporary substitute for compassion or *caritas*. According to the *Oxford English Dictionary*, the word charity is derived from *caritas*, which originally implied Christian love as opposed to *amour*. Old English meanings of charity implied God's love for humanity; one's love of God and one's neighbor; Christ-like conduct; spontaneous goodness and kindness; large-heartedness or making allowances for the shortcomings of others; and fairness or benevolence. With the passage of time, these dimensions of charity as *caritas* were subsumed under the rubric, love, which involved non-Christian, amorous, and selfish forms of passion. The fact that these Old English meanings are rare suggests that modern societies have, indeed, lost much of the societal integration uncovered by the Durkheimians in traditional societies. Yet without affectionate regard for others, how is a society to persist?

Note that I am doing more than restating the functionalist interpretation of Durkheim put forth by Talcott Parsons (1937) and other modernists. I do not mean the same thing as the functionalists by such terms as social solidarity, integration, and social order, nor do I share the modernist assumptions that prop up functionalism. Some of the differences between the two positions include the following: the functionalists assume that all social order is justifiable and that social order is maintained through the cognitive internalization of norms. By contrast, I draw on Durkheim's insistence that social order must be fair and just, and that it is maintained through emotional bonding. The functionalists often depict social order as something that can be put into practice and maintained independently of culture. Again, I draw on Durkheim's assumption that culture is the bedrock upon which all other sorts of social order must be built. Thus, it is possible to accuse functionalism of maintaining the status quo and even of promoting oppression. But Durkheimian sociology, in its original form, does not lead to functionalism, even though functionalism tried to make use of Durkheim's prestige to justify its modernist assumptions. In sum, I am trying to reach back and beyond functionalism to recover the original assumptions in Durkheimian sociology in order to lay the basis for a sociology responsive to present needs.

Nor should the reader confound or judge my use of compassion or *caritas* *vis-à-vis* culture with the usage of these terms by the structuralist school of thought. For example, two well-known structuralists, Jean Piaget and Lawrence Kohlberg, follow Kant and other Enlightenment philosophers in positing a *universal*, rational developmental sequence in cognitive as well as moral development. Their assumption that some cognitive and moral reasoning is "higher" than other forms is inherently ethnocentric, and therefore not conducive to compassion. Nor do I mean to imply that compassion is anything like the universal principles that disciples of Piaget and Kohlberg claim to have found. This is because even Kantian "universal" principles of morality must be rooted in some particular group or cultural standard. Gandhi, Jesus Christ, Buddha, Martin Luther King, and others who are typically cited as morally superior beings by disciples of the Enlightenment turn out, in my reading, to be thinkers who invoked key traditions from particular cultures and thereby appealed to the broad spectrum of people in those cultures. The fact that most of these allegedly super-moral leaders preached some variation of compassion is not due to their having discovered a "higher" or universal principle, but to the fact that they acted on the "lowest" common denominator essential to collective life, namely, compassion.

All cultures, Western as well as non-Western, promote some variety of compassion in their cultural make-up, even though most of this activity is taken for granted. Indeed, the very notion that one's cultural group is superior to others is automatically non-compassionate and conducive to narcissism, because compassion or *caritas* presupposes that all humans are equal by the very fact of their humanity (Schopenhauer [1841] 1965c). Note that various derivatives of this compassion are routinely taught by all the world's major religions, as well as by parents. It is difficult to imagine a viable culture in which children are not taught to share, say they are sorry when they hurt someone, be considerate, work with others, etc. Indeed, the popular writer, Robert Fulghum (1990), has turned this insight into kitsch with the claim that one generally learns in kindergarten all that one needs to know for getting along in the world.

Postmodernist kitsch aside, the question of how or even whether compassion can be taught is a serious one. If parents and kindergarten teachers have been transmitting compassion for centuries, then it is not evident how they have been doing it, because intellectuals from Plato through Schopenhauer to Durkheim have argued that compassion cannot be learned like geometry, but must be absorbed through example. Yet if it is true that Western societies tend toward narcissism such that parents and teachers no longer have the time or inclination to teach compassion through example, then these same Western societies are in serious danger of extinction, because narcissism cannot sustain social life. It is entirely beyond the scope of the present discussion to treat this issue with the depth it deserves. The point of bringing it up at this juncture has to do with sketching a line of inquiry for the future. If Western Enlightenment narratives are no longer viable because they promote oppression, ethnocentrism, colonialism, imperialism and other terrible things; and if anti-Enlightenment phenomena such as nationalism and cultural identity as well as cultural relativism are going to grow stronger as these Enlightenment narratives wane; then present-day or future intellectuals will have to make a serious and sobering search for non-modernist bases for social order. That day has not arrived, because most contemporary intellectuals as well as diplomats are still pushing the modernist notions of universal human rights, peace through negotiation, United Nations peacekeeping, and other *failed* concepts and policies on the basis of outmoded Enlightenment assumptions concerning human nature and the nature of societies.

This is not meant to imply that human rights, negotiation, and the UN are bad ideas. On the contrary. Rather, and as illustrated by the outcome of the Vienna Human Rights Conference in June 1993, the West tends to push these ideas in an ethnocentric manner onto non-Western cultures who tend to resent them. If standards for human rights are to be genuine, they have to be applied consistently to all the world's peoples, and not, as they frequently are now, on the basis of what suits Western, political self-interest at a particular time in history. Genuine negotiation has to imply standards of justice and fair play, not the military imbalance found in the Balkans at the present time. And so on. For genuine sympathetic understanding to occur among the world's many diverse cultures, the West must stop patronizing non-Western cultures. This is the significance of the concept of compassion, highlighted by Emile Durkheim as part of his forgotten dream that sociology should be the science of morality.

Again, Durkheim's use of the concept of morality holds nothing in common with the oppressive yet typically contemporary usage of this idea as a cover for self-interest. For Durkheim, the moral is that which promotes harmony, cooperation, integration, and other peaceable social values derived from compassion. For example, in arguing against United States military intervention in Bosnia-Herzegovina, Dimitri K. Simes writes that "there's no oil in Bosnia" and that "we don't even have a moral interest there" (*New York Times*, 10 March 1993: A15). From Durkheim's perspective, a war for oil – which is how the Gulf War has been characterized in most of the American news media – can never be moral, and the term "moral interest" is an oxymoron. An issue is moral precisely when it draws upon self-abnegation and sacrifice, *not* self-interest. Mr. Simes writes in a typically Western format which presumes that moral issues in the Balkans, such as genocide, are of secondary importance compared with the self-interest of Western nation-states. From the perspective of Enlightenment narratives, the West acted morally in choosing not to act in the Balkans. But Durkheim was far ahead of the postmodernists in criticizing these Enlightenment narratives because they promote selfishness, and therefore international divisiveness in the long run.

Or consider the question posed in the *New York Times* by Anthony Lewis: "How far will Bill Clinton bend his knee to the murderous thugs who lead Serbian aggression in Bosnia? How far can they push him without a response that preserves American honor?" (5 March 1993: A17). Lewis's questions presuppose collective standards of right and wrong according to which certain actors can be labeled as thugs and certain actions as honorable or dishonorable. Despite the fact that postmodernists have declared these and other distinctions as oppressive categories that should be rejected, these distinctions are perfectly straightforward and necessary for social life to exist. Without the categories of crime, punishment, honor, and dishonor, among other distinctions that all societies have made, victims cannot be protected from the law of the jungle. There is simply no good reason to expect that the postmodern rebellion against all differences will lead to tolerance. Such an attitude is far more likely to promote the tolerance of extremely intolerant acts, including appeasement in the international realm. I agree with Lewis's analysis of one important chapter in the 1990s Balkan War:

> Instead of more vigorous action to stop Serbian aggression, as he promised during the campaign, Mr. Clinton made a purely humanitarian move: to airdrop food and medicine to besieged civilians in eastern Bosnia. To avoid offending the aggressors, the President said relief supplies would go to all parties – to the attacking Serbs as well as their victims. . . . To that deferential policy, the Serbian aggressors replied with these among other actions: when starving Muslims in the Cerska area came out of their villages to collect the few relief bundles that had fallen anywhere near them, Serbs shelled them. Serbian forces used the airdrops as a cover for a major offensive against the Cerska enclave. . . . A United Nations official called it a "massacre." Dr. Radovan Karadzić, self-styled President of the Serbs in Bosnia, issued an "open letter to the American people" from the United Nations in New York. In it he denounced the airdrops, saying that land relief routes were "perfectly adequate" – though his forces have continually blocked them. . . . He as good as warned the United States to stop even humanitarian help to his victims or face Serbian terrorist attacks in this country. . . . The United Nations looked pathetic in this week's tragic events. The Security Council condemned the Serbs, but they know the strong words will only be words.

> (ibid.)

Compassion does not preclude violence in the name of just causes, provided that the concept of justice is something other than disguised self-interest. Nor does it mean that violence is the only way to promote just causes. However, compassion does mean that one will empathize with the victim and try to stop the aggressor. If the distinction between victim and aggressor is not crystal clear, one is obliged to make the distinction as far as one is able. Otherwise, one is a vicarious participant in sadism. In relation to Bosnia's plight, as well as many other historical events that called for compassion, such as the Holocaust, the West comes up with a host of rationalizations to justify inaction. Yet Durkheim's point that morality must involve something other than self-interest is exemplified by the fact that the world's intellectuals and diplomats cannot point to their tolerance of Serbian aggression with any degree of pride, or even solidarity with other nation-states. Instead, most writers as well as politicians seem embarrassed by their inaction, and the West's many alliances – left over from the Cold War – are slowly beginning to unravel. Moreover, comparisons with the Holocaust would not go away even if, as we have seen in Chapter 2, genocide in the former Yugoslavia cannot be compared objectively with the Holocaust. The more important point is that the world's Jewish community is prone to experience compassion as co-suffering for victims of genocide because of the terrible suffering that it endured.

One more dimension of compassion as co-suffering needs to be mentioned. If one takes Durkheim seriously on this issue, it seems to follow that nothing promotes social solidarity more than communal suffering while, conversely, narcissistic self-interest leads to social disintegration. Thus, and quite paradoxically, President Clinton's turning away from international affairs in order to promote American self-interest caused *more*, not less divisiveness within the USA. And the sanctions that were imposed upon Serbia in order to promote internal divisiveness with the expectation that the Serbian people would overthrow Slobodan Milošević caused *less* of the desired divisiveness and more unexpected social solidarity among them.[15] As a general principle, Durkheim's claim that nothing can compare with the integrative power of suffering can hardly be surpassed. This is why initiation rites, sacrifice, and communal pain bond people together while hedonism causes social disintegration. Even though my discussion of this and related issues is intended to be cursory, it seems reasonable to suggest that far from abandoning Durkheim's insights, President Clinton and politicians in general should receive more training in classical sociological theory, especially Durkheimian theory.

THEIR NARCISSISM AND OURS

Throughout this chapter, we have been uncovering a number of alternative explanations for understanding what is occurring in postcommunist events within a postmodern context. Any explanation that is welcome to Western followers of the Enlightenment project will be unwelcome to non-Westerners. Indeed, we found that even the East–West dichotomy is unwelcome and problematic, yet unavoidable for the simple reason that it is used. The Western notion of universalism is ethnocentric, and it denies the very notion of cultural rootedness that gives universalism its particularly Western flavor. Cultural relativism has been blamed by some for leading to nihilism, yet any alternatives to relativism clearly tend toward ethnocentrism and its attendant evils, such as terror, imperialism, colonialism, and so on. Disciples of the Western, Enlightenment project are fond of accusing non-Western people and especially traditional fundamentalists of ethnocentrism, and it cannot be denied that all peoples are susceptible to ethnocentrism. Yet the West is blind to its own "fundamentalism" when it comes to the notions of universal human rights, freedom, and democracy. I pointed to compassion as a way to overcome ethnocentrism and as a new, non-Enlightenment-based strategy for eventually finding a common humanity. But I caution, again, that the reader should not misread my use of compassion as pity, charity, humanitarianism, social order, or any other equivalent drawn from a functionalist or structuralist theoretical nexus. The assumptions for my argument are drawn from the milieu of the previous *fin de siècle*, and in particular, what Emile Durkheim really wrote about social integration (as opposed to how he has been dressed up by the modernists).

In any event, a good way to place the preceding discussion in context is to close with a discussion of the obverse of compassion, namely, narcissism. In *Culture of Narcissism*, Christopher Lasch (1979) does an admirable job of juxtaposing these two opposing notions – culture and narcissism – and demonstrating that narcissism is becoming the new "cultural" standard in Western societies. David Riesman (1950) had already achieved something similar in his *Lonely Crowd* by analyzing another oxymoron, the modern, Western, "other-directed" individual who is not really directed toward others but toward his or her self. Hence, the mass society that consists of lonely, atomized, isolated, narcissists.[16] Robert N. Bellah *et al.* (1985), Allan Bloom (1987), and many other writers have analyzed postmodern narcissism and its consequences. Western narcissism is all too evident in the context of the present discussion: Western intellectuals and diplomats talk about universal human rights but refuse to act on the basis of these allegedly binding principles unless self-interest is involved.

However, very little if anything has been written about narcissism in formerly communist nations, and the consequences of that narcissism. Clearly, communist writers and diplomats had been as narcissistic and ethnocentric as their capitalist counterparts with regard to justifying their respective ideologies. In the USA as well as the formerly communist Soviet Union, Yugoslavia, and other communist nations, popular sentiment held that one system was superior to the other and that, in fact, one system would bury the other. Such sentiments were the basis for the Cold War that had supposedly ended. If Bauman (1992) is right that the supposed death of communism signals the death of modernity, one would expect that the capitalist version of modernity would also be dying. Instead, the West had declared itself the winner of the Cold War, and its collective narcissism was exacerbated. And I have been hinting all along that Bauman, and others who had declared communism to be dead, have been deceived by appearances. The culture of narcissism that had propped up communism did not expire, and led to the next logical manifestation of that narcissism, the virulent, aggressive forms of nationalism that led to Balkanization and that may lead to further ethnic conflict in the former Soviet Union. A sort of "Balkanization" may already have begun to tear apart Western culture.

The closest counterpart to a Riesman or Lasch or Bellah of postcommunist nations is Jovan Rasković. In *Luda Zemlja* (1990) [Crazy Land], this psychiatrist who became leader of the Croatian Serbs offers a serious analysis of communism as a narcissistic ideology. Rasković notes that communist ideology had convinced an entire generation that they were "the best in the world," that they were setting an "example for others," and that in a myriad of other ways, they, the communists, had reached the end of history that Francis Fukuyama would later ascribe to the capitalists. The collapse of communism involved more than the collapse of a political or economic system. It constituted the ontological collapse of hope and faith. However, narcissism is not a condition that can tolerate such an affront to grandiose feelings of self-worth. Thus, the collective narcissism that had buttressed communism transformed itself practically overnight into nationalistic narcissism. Now, Croats, Serbs, and Muslims in the former Yugoslavia still thought of themselves as "the best in the world" and as an "example for others." I would add to Rasković's analysis that along with these former Yugoslav republics, capitalist modernists across the Atlantic in the USA and over the Slovene border in Western Europe also displayed a high degree of narcissism in assuming that formerly communist nations would now adopt their ideological system. In the final analysis, the narcissism on both sides of the former Iron Curtain prevented the desired outcome of a peaceful transition to democracy and free-market institutions.

Rasković's explanation supplies the missing link for understanding why the collapse of communism did *not* lead to anything like postmodern tolerance or the end of history or even the victory of capitalism as so many Western thinkers had predicted (among them, Bauman, Fukuyama, and Brzezinski). Instead, the collapse of communism set the stage for racism and violence. Relying on Freud, Rasković explains that this is because narcissism is necessarily an aggressive ideology that needs an other to demonize, against whom one can feel superior. As illustration, I recall a Muslim woman interviewed in besieged Sarajevo who denounced the West for not rescuing Sarajevo from the Serbs, and then added that she did not care, because she thought that Bosnia was the best country in the world. One can empathize with this woman's need for a defense mechanism under intolerable conditions, yet I recall many other Croats and Serbs, as well as Muslims, saying something similar.

The introduction of narcissism into a discussion of this sort helps to resolve another modernist dilemma. We have seen that Westerners tend to attribute the cause of violence in the Balkans to some fictitious "tribalism" (in the heart of modern Europe) and nationalism at the same time that they are blind to their own nationalisms. However, it could be that narcissism, not nationalism *per se*, is the real culprit. This is because benign nationalism might be the result of the dominance of compassionate tendencies, discussed above, while aggressive nationalism is fueled by narcissism. This explanation also holds the advantage of accounting for the West's passive aggression toward the formerly communist Balkans and especially the Muslims in the Balkans. This passive aggression (whose motto might be that the Slavs can't be helped because of their tribalism) is the result of the West's own narcissism, and it serves the end of "proving" that the West is superior to the former communists and Muslims.

However, Rasković probes deeper still, citing differences among the varieties of narcissism found in former Yugoslavia and, by extension, the former Soviet Union. Rasković claims that in his experience as a psychiatrist, he arrived at the conclusion that the constituent peoples of former Yugoslavia exhibit distinct social characters. He claims that the Croats are characterized by castration anxiety, the Muslims by anal frustration, and the Serbs by Oedipal conflicts (Rasković 1990: 105). He adds that his characterization of the Orthodox Serbs applies in large measure to the Orthodox Russians.[17] Hence, according to Rasković, Russians and Serbs tend to be aggressive and authoritarian in dealing with other peoples, and betray an all or nothing attitude (ibid.: 128). Croats are driven by fears that something terrible will happen, that they will lose all that they worked for, that they will be humiliated, and finally, that they will be tricked into giving up what they own. Muslims seek to be clean, pure, and "good" *vis-à-vis* authority. Even if one wants to reject Rasković's explanation, it is intriguing that his characterization captures the major lines of development in the current Balkan War: the Muslims were the "good boys" who naively trusted the West's promises to protect them, and were betrayed completely by the West; the Croats were most concerned with guarding every square inch of Croat territory, but not particularly interested in conquering Serbian territory; and Serbian actions definitely betray an aggressive tendency to take whatever lands they could, to defy the West, and to submit to the authoritarian rule of Slobodan Milošević.

Rasković feels that the interaction between Serbian Oedipal complexes and Croat castration complexes is the worst of all possible worlds (ibid.: 130). Both have a difficult time with authority, although he claims that the Serb acts out of fear and the Croat out of hate (one could just as well reverse these attributes: see p. 133). Serbs identify with Yugoslavia while Croats feel that the existence of Yugoslavia detracts from their national identity (ibid.: 157). The Orthodox faith becomes the myth of the Serbian people so that they identify with Orthodoxy on the level of ideology much more than with the strictly religious dimension (ibid.: 166). It is interesting to note that the circumstances of Rasković's death in 1991 remain mysterious: was he killed by Milošević's supporters because he betrayed too much knowledge of the Serbian position and compromised too much with the Croats, or did he commit suicide? The press in former Yugoslavia is unable to arrive at a satisfactory reply, yet the question is interesting because Rasković may have hastened his own death as the result of his keen insights into the social character of the former Yugoslavs.

In sum, Rasković has conceptualized three forms of cultural narcissism and predicted, accurately, that violent aggression was the logical outcome of this state of affairs. There was no possibility of maintaining a federal Yugoslavia so long as the Serbs identified with Yugoslavia and the Croats and Muslims feared it. Each group's collective narcissism led to demonization of the other two groups. But there is more. If one stays on the level of a psychoanalytic analysis of culture, to which Rasković subscribes, one will assume that the world's other collective actors perceived these differences, albeit unconsciously, and acted accordingly. Rasković only hints at this when he identifies Russian with Serbian interests, a connection that became very apparent in 1992 and 1993 especially, and also when he comments that the British always talk with the strongest chief (ibid.: 187). In the Balkans in the 1990s, the strongest chief (assuming the tribal metaphor for the sake of discussion) was Serbia. There is no doubt that Great Britain not only talked with but tacitly supported the Serbian-Yugoslav position, as did France, and the United States. It could well be the case that Serbia, Russia, the USA, France, and Britain continue to display remarkable affinities because they share some significantly similar dimensions of cultural narcissism. Contrast these nations with Croatia's friends in the world: Germany, Austria, Portugal, the Vatican, and Italy versus the Islamic friends of the Muslims in Bosnia-Herzegovina.

The American form of cultural narcissism deserves special mention. In *America*, Jean Baudrillard (1986) mocks America as the world's Disneyworld, a fun-culture in which the world's have-nots and the world's problems are relegated to oblivion or at least non-consciousness. Baudrillard's characterization is entirely compatible with David Riesman's (1950) earlier description of other-directed Americans as fun-loving, self-centered, conformists; e.g, the "lonely crowd." While some authors have characterized Presidents Reagan and Bush as the penultimate postmodern Presidents because they lived in a fictitious political world of their own making, I believe that President Bill Clinton deserves this label most of all. From the beginning of his campaign to his inauguration, President Clinton associated himself with symbols of postmodern, fun-culture: McDonald's, Disneyworld, and late-night talk shows. He threw the most expensive inauguration ball in US history and constantly tried to project the "other-directed" image: the good listener, consensus builder, nice guy. He criticized President Bush on the issue of military intervention in Bosnia when his "radar" told him that this would help him get elected, but he later abandoned the Bosnians and did not keep his word on a multitude of promises. In these and other ways, he mirrored the culture of narcissism and other-directedness that so many authors have ascribed to the American people. And the connection between American narcissism and the previous discussion is that, in the end, narcissists value naked power over ideals that require self-sacrifice. It was no surprise that, in the end, the USA went along with its European allies and gave tacit support to a Serbian victory.

Chapter 4

The postmodernist as voyeur

Suppose, for the sake of argument, that Jean Baudrillard is right to claim that old-fashioned reality has been replaced by rootless, circulating fictions such that the postmodernist consumes simulations of reality. In effect, the postmodernist becomes a voyeuristic consumer of abstract fictions because the distinction between fact and fiction has been lost. If one accepts this assumption as a starting point for analysis, it is not difficult to find illustrations from postcommunist events. Thus, instead of acting decisively in the name of the principles it espouses (universal human rights, the sovereignty of nations), the West has responded with still more ineffective, even perverse, voyeurism. For example, as part of its thirteen-point "peace plan" (an unlucky number, Freud might have noted) announced in Washington DC in May 1993, the West proposed to send still more monitors to the Balkans, and to protect the monitors, but not the civilian population under fire from Serbian attacks. The monitors already in place literally monitor – but do little other than bear witness[1] – the devastation of so-called Muslim "safe havens" by the Serbian side. United Nations *monitors*, European Community *observers*, Western journalists, Helsinki Watch *watchers*, Amnesty International observers, all those television camera crews and even book writers on the Balkans (such as Robert Kaplan and his 1993b *Balkan Ghosts*), are now engaged in the business of war-watching. And this perverse, postmodern response to the human suffering in the Balkans is big business, indeed. Millions upon millions of dollars have been and continue to be spent on one of the biggest intellectual exercises in recent years, Balkan war-watching in its many forms – including the supervision, regulation, and overseeing of a host of bureaucratic exercises sponsored by the United Nations – while Balkan people continue to suffer, and the West preaches to the world about the importance of agreeing on a universal standard of human rights.

Or consider the opening lines from Alan Riding's report on the world human rights conference that was held in Vienna at the height of the current Balkan War:

> In an atmosphere strangely removed from reality, the first World Conference on Human Rights in 25 years opens here [Vienna] on Monday with a broad mandate to discuss human rights in the world – as long as it avoids naming any

government known for abuses. Under the rules adopted for the two-week conference, the fate of civilians caught in wars, in, say, Bosnia and Herzegovina, Angola and Liberia will probably never be mentioned. Nor is any discussion expected of political prisoners in, say, China or Cuba. Instead, 5,000 delegates from 111 countries will debate human rights in the abstract.

(*New York Times*, 14 June 1993: A3)

Borrowing from Baudrillard's predictable writing style, one is tempted to characterize the aim of this conference as hunting human rights and losing reality. And one should note that the focus on abstractions as opposed to concrete realities is a typically Western strategy. Concrete issues pertaining to human rights abuses tug at the heartstrings, and ever since Immanuel Kant, the West has regarded emotionalism as a sign that one is not being serious or professional.

Several other aspects of the postmodernist discourse are highlighted if one treats the fact–fiction dilemma as central. The role of the media in disseminating fictions and simulations becomes an important issue (Glassner 1991). In fact, and following Adorno (1991), the role of the entire "culture industry" and the promulgation of propaganda to sway the "masses" also becomes important. The postmodern conclusion that truths, as such, no longer exist leads straight to moral and cognitive relativism, paralysis in decision-making, and perhaps even nihilism (Gellner 1992b). And one would be led to the conclusion that postmodernism is a mere extension of modernity, because modernity had already accentuated the fragmentation of meanings, abstractionism, the role of propaganda in indus-trialized societies, and relativism. Thus far, we have merely summarized the central issues pertaining to the trajectory of the postmodernist discourse that seems to assume that postmodernism is an extension of modernity.

But Barry Glassner is right to question whether television fictions are really as rootless and aimless as postmodernists claim: "Television may have occasioned postmodern culture, but is there space for radically postmodern television? Can a TV show survive whose form of speech is decentered and pluralistic in style, in which the border between the fictional and the real is blurred, and the ordinary conventions of other television programs are undermined to such an extent the program has an unnatural feel to it?" (1991: 53). Glassner's reply is negative. This is because television in the purportedly postmodern era continues to stress a conventional format in which the anchorperson or the medium itself plays the role of the moral agent in the universe. There can be no doubt that in covering the current Balkan War, or any other war, media personalities invoke traditional distinctions between good and evil, as well as other traditional distinctions. Yet the media wizards refuse to concede that their roles are traditional, and seek to imply that the television "anchor, like the scientist, speaks from the mythic position of the non-participant observer" (ibid.: 64). Thus, television tries to convey the illusion that it presents a perspective from nobody's point of view. The result is a truly new, and probably postmodern, mix of feigned hyper-objectivity and old-fashioned moralism.

For example, consider the ways that television and the other news media presented the current Balkan War to Western audiences: all three sides (Serb, Croat, and Muslim) were presented as equally blameworthy despite the massive evidence to the effect that the Serbian side had committed most of the atrocities.[2] Far from siding openly with the Serbs, Croats, or Muslims, the media gave the appearance of taking nobody's point of view. In taking this objective stance, the media unwittingly reproduced the oppressive tone of the Enlightenment narratives under discussion here. This is because in pretending to take nobody's side, the media did not take the side of the victims, and thereby did side tacitly with the aggressor.

The current Balkan War itself was presented in the conventional format of the "infinite story" that is familiar to viewers of soap operas. Indeed, this Balkan War became a soap opera with its recurrent and stereotypical characters: Lord David Owen, the testy but determined English gentleman who seemed obsessed with trying to get all parties to negotiate; Dr. Radovan Karadzić, the psychiatrist turned suspected war criminal and leader of the Bosnian Serbs; Slobodan Milošević, nicknamed the "butcher of the Balkans," to whom Western diplomats eventually turned for help in restraining the murderous policies of Dr. Karadzić; Alija Izetbegović, the kindly but bungling Islamic leader suspected of secretly harboring fundamentalist views; Cyrus Vance, the distinguished-looking Wall Street lawyer and former Secretary of State; General Philippe Morillon, the United Nations commander in Sarajevo whose French accent was reminiscent of that other famous French television celebrity, Jacques Cousteau – among others. The world knew little about the men except for these stereotypes, and the never-ending format of the "peace process." For weeks and months on end, these characters met in various cities throughout the world to try to reach a "negotiated settlement." According to Chuck Sudetic, writing for the *New York Times*,

> In some ways, this might seem outrageous. The United States has included Mr. Milošević's name on a list of potential war-crimes suspects, and much of the outside world has expressed revulsion at Serb tactics in Croatia and Bosnia and Herzegovina. Besides, Mr. Milošević has a dismal record for seeking compromise and keeping his word. But the overriding fact remains that he is firmly in charge and the man who must be dealt with.

> (14 March 1993: E6)

Despite their feigned objectivity, television anchors and reporters who covered this Balkan War definitely came across as moral agents. They referred to the "warring parties" as representatives of primitive "tribal" and "ethnic hatreds."[3] On the other hand, Lord David Owen, Cyrus Vance, General Morillon and all of the United Nations personnel were portrayed as rational, calm, cool and collected, the very embodiment of Enlightenment traditions. Indeed, weren't the West's key players from Britain, France, and the USA, where the Enlightenment took root? These Enlightenment-oriented "good guys" would try to bring the "tribal" warring parties "to the negotiating table." Day after day, week after week, and month after month, the West's television-viewing audience was exposed to the failure of the good guys to achieve these lofty-sounding aims. Indeed, Croatian, Slovene, German, and Bosnian television portrayed the West's "good guys" as Serbian collaborators or bunglers because of these failures.[4] But the Western media did not conclude that Messrs. Owen, Vance, and Morillon were exhibiting blind faith in the Enlightenment dream of using negotiation and other rational means to end a war. On the contrary, these good guys were portrayed as heroic in their efforts to bring the three warring parties – listed consistently as Serb, Croat, and Muslim – to their senses. The important point is that far from presenting random, circulating fictions, Western media presented the war in conventional, stereotypical images of the Enlightenment nations trying to bring rationality to primitive Balkan "tribes."

To be sure, television played a vital role in this war, and not only outside Serbia. According to Sudetic,

> In a land where much of the population is bound to the soil and functionally illiterate, and where newspapers are too expensive for many people, Mr. Milošević holds full control of the only news outlet that matters: Television Serbia. Its 7:30 evening news broadcasts, which surveys show is the only source of current-affairs information for about 65 percent of the population, has functioned since 1988 to instill fear and a siege mentality.
>
> (*New York Times*, 14 March 1993: E6)

My own experiences with viewing Serbian television confirms this observation. For example, Serbian television would use the same footage of Serbian artillery shells bombarding Sarajevo that would be broadcast by CNN and other Western media. However, the Serbian commentators would explain that this was Muslim artillery shelling the Serbs in Sarajevo.[5] This tactic is nothing but old-fashioned propaganda that Adorno (1991) and others attribute to the Enlightenment tradition. There is no need to resort to the postmodern idea, found in Baudrillard's writings, that the siege of Sarajevo was a fiction simply because it was on television.

However, it is true that in the early 1990s humanity was afforded the ability to watch the very *real* murder that occurs in war – often live, and always in color – on television. "The bloody shelling of a market in Bosnia by Serbian irregulars was broadcast around the globe by CNN" (*Wall Street Journal*, 28 May 1992: A10). Bosnia-Herzegovina became "prime time horror" (ibid.). War became a media spectacle in the 1990s – and this had not always been the case. World War II, Vietnam, and other wars up to and including the Gulf War horrified audiences with their gruesome images. Yet in these pre-Balkan wars, the horror led to action, from intervention to the peace movements that finally ended the Vietnam nightmare. The current Balkan War horrified audiences, but did not move them to intervention or large protests. And this is the aspect of postmodern voyeurism that is most interesting yet most neglected in the current literature, not the fictitious problem whether television deals in fictions or reality (for it deals with both).

BLASÉ VOYEURISM

The new element that we shall introduce into this discussion is the issue of voyeurism, reconceptualized in the context of social theories from the previous *fin de siècle*. If one takes seriously Baudrillard and others who reduce social reality to circulating fictions that are played out primarily on the television screen, then it seems to follow that postmodern humans have been reduced, at least in large measure, to passively sadistic voyeurs. Without a doubt, Baudrillard delights in presenting a portrait of the postmodernist as one who consumes primarily sordid, sexual, scandalous, even violent images. Yet Baudrillard fails to follow up on the psychoanalytically informed implications of this insight. A voyeur is one who obtains sexual and aggressive gratification from visual stimulation. If one follows Freud's understanding of voyeurism as a vicarious form of sexually aggressive behavior, one is led to the conclusion that the postmodern voyeur is obtaining vicarious sado-masochistic pleasure from his or her apparently passive yet passionate consumption of images. Furthermore, if one combines this Freudian insight with Durkheim's emphasis on collective representations as expressions of the collective consciousness, one is led to the hypothesis that the postmodern obsession with the consumption of images betrays a collectively abnormal bent toward sado-masochism that is prevalent in late industrialized societies. Is this televised Balkan War a prelude to a future in which audiences will have been reduced to postmodern Romans watching bloody spectacles in the electric arena comprised of televised images?

Despite Baudrillard's reputation as a provocateur (Rojek 1993), he would never go this far. Neither Freud nor Durkheim, nor their typically *fin de siècle* arsenal of concepts – the unconscious, the id, anomie, the abnormal, symptomatology, etc. – plays a role in Baudrillard's writings. Moreover, even old-fashioned modernists have rejected most of the concepts that seemed to be standard in the social science of the previous *fin de siècle*. Neither the avant-garde postmodernists nor the traditional modernists venture into the implications of the postmodernist conceptualized as voyeur. For the purposes of the present discussion, the major implication is that media coverage of the current Balkan War did *not* lead to a compassionate desire to end the slaughter, but to a passive state of vicarious sadism *vis-à-vis* the consumption of truly horrifying images and concepts.

There can be little doubt that the concepts introduced by Freud and Durkheim lend themselves easily to the sort of analysis being proposed here. And Freud's and Durkheim's theories are commensurate with the thought of their colleague, Georg Simmel. In *The Philosophy of Money* ([1900] 1990) and other works, Simmel argued that modernity eventually leads to the blasé attitude in which one "has completely lost the feeling for value differences" (p. 256). Yet the road to this blasé indifference consists of modernist abstraction such that the world is seen as "a huge arithmetical problem" (p. 444) and modernists come to be characterized by the "measuring, weighing and calculating exactness of modern times" (ibid.). Because modernists seem to understand everything in the abstract, they "are inclined to condone everything" (ibid.: 432). The modernist becomes a "mere spectator" to the world and this stance leads to cruelty: "There is something callous about the purely rationalistic treatment of people and things" (ibid.: 434). This pure rationalism leads to an advocacy of egoism and ruthless individualism (ibid.: 438).

Simmel's sociology of modernity lends itself easily to an analysis of what is called the postmodern coverage of the current Balkan War. In this case, post-modern really implies hyper-modern, because the news media in general and television media in particular convey hyper-abstract, rational images of reality that lead to the blasé attitude. The very terminology used in watching, monitoring, and observing "reality" suggests that the object of one's inspection is interchangeable. After all, there exist air pollution monitors, blood glucose monitors, baby monitors, carbon dioxide monitors, and all sorts of monitors up to and including human rights abuse monitors in the Balkans. In the end, one reacts to the findings of human rights abuse much as one reacts to the finding that there is too much smog over Los Angeles – with indifference. This is the horrifying implication – for those who are still able to feel horror – of Simmel's *Philosophy of Money*.

Thus, the television camera does not really bring one closer to reality. It actually distances the viewer from what Simmel called the aura of the object. And the television camera does this because it is part of a larger trend in modern cultures toward abstractionism. The television camera is for Baudrillard what money is for Simmel: the symbol of a larger movement toward indifference. Yet Baudrillard and Simmel need Durkheim and Freud to give us the full story, because modernist indifference is not purely indifferent. Both Baudrillard and Simmel hint that the blasé attitude thrives on cruelty and callousness, what Freud called sadism. In these senses, again, the postmodern scene is simultaneously anti-modern and hyper-modern, emotional and highly abstract.

Even a cursory glance at the contents of what passes for postmodern, visual culture suggests that much of it is violent, sexual, and sordid. My university students tell me that they often hold parties in which they watch rented video movies, such as *Faces of Death*, that depict actual executions, suicides, automobile wrecks, and other graphic images of "real" death. In the US contemporary television programs such as *Hard Copy* try to imitate "real" news programs by adopting the format of two serious-looking anchorpersons, but in the end such programs engage in gossip and voyeurism concerning sex scandals, murder, and other such topics. Far from needing new data for this proposed analysis – as if we needed still more mathematical exactness in an age in which people talk to each other primarily in numbers – one requires a fresh approach to existing data that involves the self-conscious use of existing theoretical orientations. In sum, the data is everywhere. It merely needs to be interpreted in a new way.

In the remainder of this chapter, I shall invoke selected aspects of the media coverage of the current Balkan War as illustration of the new conceptualization proposed above. This is an important step in the overall discussion which seeks to move beyond the impasse reached by many participants in the current postmodernist discourse that concerns the conceptualization of postmodernism as an extension of versus rebellion against modernity. This overly tidy and pedantic problem is trivial when compared with the long-term implications of the sadistic content of many postmodern images, and the fact that they are consumed almost as a matter of course.

WHAT CONSTITUTES A REAL WAR?

Anyone who has faithfully and systematically followed the news media's coverage of the current Balkan War will probably be led to ask some variation of the following question: which is more remarkable, the explosion of the savage id in the Balkans that would have shocked even the cynical Sigmund Freud, or the refusal of the world's television-viewing public to put an end to the barbarism? Regarding the first question, it is important to remember that the passive viewing of someone else's suffering is considered sadistic in most traditional understandings of the meaning of sadism. Regarding the manifestations of the id, this Balkan War offered rape, sodomy, decapitation, bodily mutilation of all types, mass executions, genocide, concentration camps, bordello concentration camps, the murder of babies and children, mass starvation, snipers, the desecration of cultural monuments – to name just some of the many variations of lust and aggression that were reported in the media. Whereas Hitler's Final Solution was carried out largely in secret and the full extent of the Holocaust was not known for many years following the end of World War II, most of the atrocities in this Balkan War were documented, studied, monitored, observed, witnessed, reported, and above all, televised. Surviving victims of Serbian aggression in the 1990s would ask, "Doesn't the world know what is going on?" The question implies that had the world outside the Balkans known the reality of the horrors that were occurring, it would have put a stop to them. The answer seems to be that yes, the world did know, but it stood by passively while Serbia conquered its neighbors and committed atrocious war crimes.[6]

In part, this seems to be the gist of Baudrillard's contribution to the sociology of war: like all other social phenomena, postmodern war has been reduced to the simulation of war. For Baudrillard, war is a fiction precisely because it is televised, and thereby blends in with other fictions on television. Thus, according to Baudrillard (1991), the Gulf War was not real. Similarly, he writes that the Vietnam War was just a "television war":

Left brittle by the Vietnam War, which was as unintelligible to [Americans] as the irruption of little green men in a cartoon strip – and which, incidentally, they dealt with as though it were a cartoon, as something remote from them, *a television war*, with no understanding of the world's condemnation of their actions and only able to see their enemy, since they are the achieved utopia of goodness, as the achieved utopia of Evil, Communism – they have taken refuge in the tranquillity of the easy life, in a triumphal illusionism.

(1986: 108)

There is something cruel, in a Nietzschean sort of way, in Baudrillard's dismissal of the very real suffering and death in the Vietnam and Gulf Wars. To the best of my knowledge, he has not written on the Balkan War of the 1990s, but his position on it can be inferred from his writings on other televised wars. No doubt, Baudrillard's unusually cruel attitude toward the reality of war has led many intellectuals to criticize him severely, even dismiss him from academic discourse (Gane 1992, Kellner 1989, Rojek and Turner 1993). Another obvious flaw in Baudrillard's reasoning is that television is not the exclusive domain of postmodern fiction-making. Nevertheless, if one grants that the postmodern news media in general (not just television) creates a stereotyped version of the world in which the West lives in a utopia based on the fiction of the Enlightenment project while the rest of the world is mired in hatred, then Baudrillard has a point. Postmodern war has been reduced to a cartoon strip, or better yet, a comic book. In particular, when one has reviewed all the many rationalizations for the West's actions and inactions in relation to the Balkan War that began in 1991, one is still left with the sobering conclusion that the West allowed Serbia to win and to commit crimes against humanity that were not supposed to be tolerated ever again (see Leslie Gelb's 1992 essay "Never Again"). Moreover – but against Baudrillard's cool sadism – one is led to consider an issue that is vital to the post-communist world dominated by the news media: what is the moral responsibility of the postmodernist consumer of images?

The West (which refers, as I said, primarily to the established Enlightenment traditions in the USA, France, and Britain) has put up a good show of moral concern, but all of its actions ensured that the atrocities in the Balkans continued and that Serbia would win its racist, imperialist war. For example, UNPROFOR (United Nations Protective Forces) humanitarian aid fed victims of Serbian aggression, but did not protect them from being killed before or after being fed. The presence of UNPROFOR forces in Croatia enabled the Serbs to consolidate their territorial gains in the Krajina region, and declare these UN-protected areas of Croatia to be a part of Serbia. UNPROFOR forces in both Croatia and Bosnia helped in the Serbian campaign of ethnic cleansing by conveniently transporting Muslims and Croats so that Chetniks could move in. Nowhere was this UN collaboration in Serbian ethnic cleansing more noticeable than in the forced UN evacuation of Srebrencia, Bosnia-Herzegovina in the Spring of 1993. The arms embargo that the West had imposed on all of former Yugoslavia meant that the Croats and Muslims could not defend themselves against Serbia, which had confiscated almost all of the military arsenal of the former Yugoslav army (Biden 1993). In sum, despite its rhetoric of protest, the West had created the socio-political circumstances that favored Serbian success in its racist campaign to establish a Greater Serbia. Well-documented Serbian atrocities – especially on television – against Muslims and Croats did not move the Western heart to stop the horror. Instead, the West had become a voyeur.

The cool contemplation of someone else's suffering has traditionally been considered sadistic. To be sure, such passive sadism is not usually considered as morally culpable as directly inflicting pain and suffering on a victim. Nevertheless, most of the world's religious and legal codes condemn the passive observer of a crime – particularly a sadistic crime – in some fashion. But tradition offers no guide for the confusing dilemma of how the human agent – deemed responsible and free by narratives spun from the Enlightenment – should respond to the *images* and simulations of cruelty, crime, and sadism that are produced by the culture industry (from Adorno 1991). And this dilemma is compounded by the fact that the West's culture industry labeled itself as humanitarian even as sadistic images came pouring in from the Balkans, and thereby blended in with the sadistic imagery that has become the staple of Western television entertainment.

Yet the West is not an ordinary, but a postmodern, voyeur. Postmodernism refers to the most recent, faddish blend of cultural relativism, nihilism, lack of seriousness, and emphasis on media images that is discussed earnestly by Western intellectuals. The postmodern voyeur is adept at rationalizations. According to William Safire,

> The Balkans mess fairly shouts out to defeatists everywhere: never in American history have so many reasons been given for staying out of such a confusing conflict so far away. Only one lonely and embarrassingly idealistic reason might compel us to risk American lives in this bad case: hundreds of thousands of human beings will die unless the US shames the world into making this generation's latest Hitlerism unprofitable.
>
> (*New York Times*, 15 February 1993: A14)

According to a cynical twist to the tenets of cultural relativism, all parties involved in this current war are equally guilty: "There are no good guys among the leaders in Bosnia, only bad guys and bystanders" (*New York Times*, 20 February 1993: E1).

It certainly seems as if the current war in the Balkans is being perceived as a fiction that is being broadcast in Disneyworld. Serbian looting, rape and pillage – why, that's Disney's *Pirates of the Caribbean* (down to the beard and sword that have come to symbolize the Serbian Chetniks). But there is no "as if" for the postmodernists, no reality that lies beneath surface reality. This Balkan War is fiction, as are all unpleasant realities of life, which are relegated to the "fourth world" that "must exit" (Baudrillard 1986: 111). There is no need to feel guilty, or ashamed, or to feel at all.[7] Jean Baudrillard, in particular, has painted a happy face on sadism, but the cool contemplation of someone else's suffering remains sadism. What about all that humanitarian aid that the West sent to the Kurds, Somalians, Bosnians, and others since 1989? It was charity that never addressed the social conditions that made charity seem necessary in the first place. Moreover, charity is always tinged with contempt and an air of superiority. In the Croatian and Bosnian cases, the West absolutely and resolutely refused to shut down the Serbian war machine, which would have made all charity unnecessary. Why? Serbia's victims came up with an answer.

It is that the West is secretly, unconsciously glad that Serbia is oppressing the

Muslims, and in general taking on the role of the policeman in the unruly Balkans. France, Britain, and the USA, all formerly imperialist powers that now tout human rights and tolerance, exhibit a remarkable sympathy and affinity with Serbia, their former "ally." (This, too, is a fiction, for Serbia was a Nazi puppet state during World War II, and a Western "ally" for only about seven months from 1941 to 1946.) The West obtains vicarious gratification from watching Serbian atrocities on television. The West can no longer openly espouse racism and imperialism, but Serbia can act out its ugly fantasies. This is Thorstein Veblen's ([1899] 1967) "vicarious consumption" with a new twist: the consumption of images, not material goods, and not just any images, but sadistic images. One might label the West's behavior as vicarious barbarism.

DOING SOMETHING

Yet the world put up a good front of "doing something" in response to the horrors of the current Balkan War. Even so, the West's efforts can be described readily as the simulation of concern, the fiction of humanitarianism, and make-believe diplomacy. The news media's coverage of the West's responses could hardly conceal the fragmentation of the efforts that were made. It really seemed as if circulating fictions, not realities, were at work. For example, soon after the fighting broke out in 1991, the West imposed an arms embargo on all of former Yugoslavia. Because Serbia had confiscated most of the military armaments of the Yugoslav Federal Army, the arms embargo hurt the victims, Croatia and Bosnia-Herzegovina, while it benefited Serbia, which was labeled the aggressor by the same Western powers that had imposed the embargo on Serbia's victims. In effect, this Western action gave tacit support to Serbian aggression, resulting in the Serbian conquest of one-third of Croatia and two-thirds of Bosnia-Herzegovina by 1993.[8] "The Yugoslav military was probably the best armed in Europe, aside from the Soviet Red Army," a US State Department official said (*New York Times*, 5 July 1992: A6).

Or consider the much touted humanitarian relief effort carried out by UNPROFOR. The humanitarian aid consisted primarily of military rations left over from the Gulf War. (And many of them consisted of pork products, adding insult to injury from the perspective of the Bosnian Muslims.) From the Bosnian perspective, what good was it for the United Nations to feed the Bosnians if these same recipients of the aid would be shot, tortured, or driven from their homes later by the Serbs? Moreover, at least one-quarter of the humanitarian aid was skimmed off the top by the aggressor Serbs before it reached the primarily Muslim victims in Bosnia-Herzegovina (*New York Times*, 24 February 1993: A6).

"Humanitarianism without a heart" is how the *New York Times* referred to the humanitarian efforts in Bosnia (22 February 1993: A1). "Aggression and its consequences cannot be stopped by charity" (ibid., 12 July 1992: E3). "A local [Muslim] military statement said of the US aid [in Bosnia]: 'We feel like animals to whom food is being thrown to exterminate us with grenades' " (*Bryan/College*

Station Eagle, 4 March 1993: A1). "False humanitarianism" is what Leslie Gelb called it, adding:

> Western policy is merely to provide enough humanitarian relief for Bosnian Muslims to quiet Western public opinion. . . . In other words, the idea is not to fight for Muslim survival, which Western officials believe to be beyond practical means. It is rather to feed them until they become refugees or get shot – or until they realize, hopefully much sooner, that they must surrender. Thus Western leaders look to the Bosnian Muslims to recognize that their cause is hopeless, come to the bargaining table and accept defeat. To drive that point home, they are telling the Muslims to forget dreams of being rescued by Western cavalry. . . . In behalf of realism, Western policy punishes the principal victims. In the name of peace, it shames any sense of justice.
>
> *(New York Times*, 6 August 1992: A11).

In December 1992, President George Bush ordered a humanitarian mission to feed the starving people of Somalia even though he would not enforce then existing UN resolutions to secure humanitarian relief missions to Bosnia-Herzegovina. President Bush's critics pointed out that the US-led humanitarian mission to Somalia deflected the West's guilt that stemmed from not helping the Bosnians (*Wall Street Journal*, 7 January 1993: A15). Furthermore, President Bush was criticized for "humanitarian imperialism" in Bosnia (ibid., 1 February 1993: A12) and "selective morality" for using military force to help Somalis but not Bosnians (ibid., 11 February 1993: A16).[9] The important point is that in the early 1990s, "humanitarianism" became a postmodern cliché, euphemism, cover for other motives, and spectacle far removed from the traditional overtones of compassion that are supposed to guide genuine humanitarianism.

Another example of the world's doing nothing in the guise of doing something in the Balkans was the sending of United Nations Protective Forces. The role of the UNPROFOR troops was spelled out clearly as one of "peacekeeping" as opposed to "peacemaking." But how does one keep peace in the midst of an active and brutal war? In effect, UNPROFOR "observers" merely and literally observed the "ethnic cleansing" (a Serbian euphemism for genocide) and other atrocities that were carried out in territories under its supervision, because they lacked the power to enforce any of the resolutions of the United Nations. "UN officials seemed helpless to stop the firing of Serbian guns they had been assigned to oversee. 'We can't control the situation,' conceded Captain Patrick van Hoorebeke, one of the UN officers. 'But we do monitor it' " (*New York Times*, 15 September 1992: A3). Turkish envoy to the UN, Mustafa Aksin had this to say about UN monitoring of Serbian crimes: "I'm sure they [the UN] were observing. Perhaps they should have been doing something more than just observing" (ibid., 9 January 1993: A4). Not surprisingly, the Croats and Bosnians nicknamed UNPROFOR as SERBOFOR, because they concluded that the United Nations was delivering humanitarian aid as a pretext for allowing the Serbs to carry out their aggressive aims and to conciliate the West's guilty conscience for allowing Serbia to do so (*New York*

Times, 14 June 1992: A11). The facts are that during the UN tenure in former Yugoslavia, Serbia carried out its territorial and racist campaigns with relative ease.

Many other Western actions seemed to be fictitious in Baudrillard's sense of the term. In fact, the West's actions seemed so groundless that they gave the appearance of a tragicomedy. For example, Western powers arranged for the signing of over forty cease-fires, and each one was broken. Some were broken even as the cease-fire was being signed. For example,

> Just as UN commanders were gaining confidence that the quiet would hold, the Serbian forces launched an artillery attack tonight on Sarajevo's old town, with at least five shells hitting one mosque as Muslims gathered for evening prayers at the start of the holy month of Ramadan. Reports from the district said at least five people were killed, and about 20 wounded.

> (ibid., 24 February 1993: A6)

In March 1993, after a long and documented string of Serbian deceit regarding cease-fires, General Morillon pronounced,

> Srebrenica is safe. He also said he believed that General Ratko Mladic, the Serbian nationalist commander, was sincere in pledging on Friday not to attack the town again, and to court-martial the local Serbian commander for having ordered the attacks that killed scores of people in Srebrencia and nearby villages [in Bosnia]. . . . He added, "I think that at the present time everybody has to understand that the time of ethnic cleansing and the taking of hostages is finished. There is a big, deep desire for peace in the whole population, and their leaders, I am sure, have understood that."

> (ibid., 29 March 1993: A5)[10]

A few days later, the Serbs opened fire on Srebrenica, forbade the shipment of food, and rejected the much touted Vance-Owen peace plan (ibid., 3 April 1993: A1).

After many meticulous studies and the review of scrupulously documented evidence, the West came up with a list of suspected war criminals, most of whom were Serbs. The President of Serbia, Slobodan Milošević, and the President of the self-proclaimed Bosnian Serbian Republic, Radovan Karadzić, were included on this list. But far from issuing a warrant for their arrest – as the UN had done in Muslim Somalia for a "warlord" suspected of war crimes – Western powers included Messrs. Milošević and Karadzić in peace negotiations. In one particularly tragicomic moment, the United States Secretary of State, Lawrence Eagleburger, was denouncing Mr. Karadzić as a chronic liar and possible war criminal even as Karadzić was wandering the halls of the very building in Geneva in which Eagleburger spoke (*New York Times*, 17 December 1992: A10). In February 1993, the United States went along with the EC and the UN in granting Mr. Karadzić immunity from prosecution so that he could negotiate with Croats and Bosnians in

New York City (ibid., 23 February 1993: A1). The irony of negotiating with a suspected war criminal was rationalized by Messrs. Vance and Owen as just one of those things that negotiators must do: "It may go against the grain to let criminals go unpunished, but no major country has any intention of dismantling the Serbian Government by force and arresting its leaders" (ibid., 22 February 1993: A1). The *Wall Street Journal* quoted a Muslim as saying that inviting Mr. Karadzić to negotiate was "as if the international community had invited Saddam Hussein and the Emir of Kuwait to talk it out two years ago" (27 August 1992: A7). George Kenney called the peace talks "a charade that will fail unless military muscle is employed against Serbia" (*New York Times*, 27 August 1992: A14).[11]

When many Islamic nations criticized the West for its apparent double standard in bombing Muslim Iraq and Somalia for violating UN resolutions while it allowed Serbia to violate UN resolutions, Western diplomats responded with the excuse that the war in former Yugoslavia had to be ended through negotiation, not military means. When many efforts at negotiation failed, Cyrus Vance (representing the United Nations) and Lord David Owen (representing the European Community) worked out a "peace plan" that was criticized for rewarding Serbian aggression by granting them many of the territories they had seized by force. On 18 June, 1993, Lord David Owen dropped this peace plan and urged the Bosnian Muslims to accept Serb-Croat proposals to divide Bosnia into three ethnic zones (*Wall Street Journal*, 18 June 1993: A1).

In sum, from its beginnings in 1991, this Balkan War has been conceptualized in euphemisms, clichés, and other terms that lend credence to the charge that it came across as the simulation of war. The news media characterized it as ethnic conflict, a civil war, and an instance of tribalism. In fact, it was none of these things, because it involved clear-cut aggression by Serbia against nations recognized by the United Nations. The racist notion of tribalism is particularly ridiculous, because this war occurred in the heart of modern Europe, which cannot be described as tribal. Finally, it was not even a "war" in the traditional sense of armies equipped for military battles. Instead, the Serbian army outgunned its victims by a ratio of 10 to 1, and carried out its military strategies primarily against civilians.[12] Thus, the most correct designation for this "war" might really be slaughter. In the words of the Bosnian Minister of Foreign Affairs, "My country has turned into a slaughterhouse" (*New York Times*, 20 May 1992: A7). In an essay entitled "What Has the World Done for Bosnia? A Diary of Disgrace," the editors of the *New York Times* write,

> But even now Washington, and London, and the EC, and NATO and the UN shrink from forceful actions to counter the Serbs' aggression and *slaughter* in Bosnia. . . . After a year of *savage slaughter*, mass rapes, ethnic cleansing and undoubted genocide, the world has responded with all the right words.
>
> (20 December 1992: E2; emphasis added)

Other euphemisms flourished: the Serbian term, "ethnic cleansing" tended to be used in place of the more powerful term, genocide. "What we Muslims are undergoing is genocide," said a victim of Serbian aggression (*New York Times*, 29 September 1992: A4), but initially, the United States concluded that the killings were "too random to be genocide" (ibid., 16 August 1992: A1). Yet according to George Kenney, while it is true that the US "State Department was not able to confirm reports of Serbian genocide in such camps – it did not try very hard. Had it done so, the US and the UN would have been obliged under the Geneva Convention to intervene" (ibid., 27 August 1992: A1). In general, Akbar Ahmed (1993: 26) seems to be right when he claims that "What has to be clearly pointed out – both to Muslims and non-Muslims – is that this is not just a civil war or tribal war as is seen by the Western media but determined, brutal and savage genocide."[13]

The use of the term humanitarianism covered up the West's very inhumane tolerance of grisly horrors. The word peacekeeper camouflaged the fact that there was no peace, and that UN peacekeepers were the passive observers of war and genocide. Negotiation became a euphemism for collaboration with Serbia. "Transporting refugees" is a term that covered up the fact that the UN assisted the Serbs by removing Croats and Muslims from territories conquered by Serbs. References to the Nuremberg war crime trials were used ostensibly as threats to deter Serbian crimes in the future, even though the function of trials is primarily one of punishment and justice, not deterrence. Even the sanctions imposed on Serbia were a fiction, because Russia, Romania, Greece and other Serbian allies broke them freely and with impunity, and also because "the Serbs' weapons are so abundant, the [Central Intelligence] agency said, that they are exporting arms to raise cash" (*New York Times*, 4 April 1993: A8).

Even the concept of the Holocaust was used and misused so that Serbia associated Croatia with the Holocaust but managed to cover up completely its own collaboration with World War II Nazis (Cohen 1992). According to the *Brooklyn Jewish Weekly*, "Many Jews see parallels between the Holocaust and the suffering of the Bosnians under Serbian ethnic cleansing" (19 February 1993: 2). But up to the Spring of 1993, Elie Wiesel and other survivors of the Holocaust publicly regarded such parallels as efforts to cheapen the Holocaust. Thus, in the Fall of 1992, Mr. Wiesel took up Serbia's invitation to visit the prison camps (initially called "concentration camps") run by the Serbs so that he could be convinced that Serbia was not perpetuating the evils of the Holocaust.[14] Mr. Wiesel complained later that the Serbs had lied to him when they assured him that the camps had been closed, and concluded, "All I know is that, besides everything else, as far as Serbian authorities are concerned, I feel betrayed" (*New York Times*, 25 February 1993: A11). The "everything else" presumably refers to the news media's efforts to evaluate Serbian crimes against its victims in relation to the Holocaust.

It is important to understand clearly what lends a tragicomic aspect to these Western responses to the Balkan War that began in 1991, and makes them all seem to be fictions or mere imitations of actual cease-fires, contracts, negotiations, and reactions to crime. Durkheim's sociology tends to ground all of these phenomena in social traditions. Thus, a cease-fire or any other contract must involve society's commitment to the proposed agreement in addition to the intentions expressed by the individual actors who participate in the agreement (Durkheim [1950] 1983). But this primary social condition for a contract simply did not exist in this particular Balkan War. Despite well-documented and repeated deceit by the Serbian side regarding cease-fires and other agreements,[15] the West continued to negotiate with Serbs, even those Serbs who were prominent on lists of suspected war criminals. When the two Serbians, Borislav Herak and Sretko Damjanovic, were found guilty of war crimes by the Bosnian government primarily on the basis of their confessions,

> there was an uneasy feeling among many in the courtroom that these two were serving, in effect, as substitutes for the men they consider the real villains of "ethnic cleansing" – men like Radovan Karadzić, the Bosnian Serb leader; Ratko Mladić, the Bosnian Serb military commander, and their mentor, Slobodan Milošević, President of Serbia. All three continue to meet Western negotiators who are attempting to end the war, even as their names sit atop a list of potential war criminals the United States has handed to the United Nations for consideration by the war crimes tribunal that the Security Council has voted to convene.
>
> *(New York Times*, 4 April 1993: E2)

According to Durkheim ([1893] 1933), a crime is that which offends the collective consciousness, and must be punished in order to preserve the moral order. If a crime is tolerated to any degree, it ceases to be a crime, and the collective consciousness has been weakened. From this Durkheimian perspective, it is no excuse to claim, as Messrs. Vance and Owen explained, that they had to negotiate with suspected war criminals. Negotiation immediately lends an aura of moral respect to those who participate in it, and negates the collective indignation that is supposed to be the defining feature of society's reaction to crime. Finally, no collective consciousness of the world exists as of yet (Durkheim [1925] 1961), so that these efforts at applying the notions of contract, negotiation, and criminal law to a set of international crimes may have been doomed from the start. Ever since Nuremberg, war crime trials are far from being anything more than victors' trials.

Thus far, it seems that we would agree with Baudrillard that old-fashioned grounds and referents for truth and morality no longer apply in the postmodern world. Baudrillard would have one believe that the West in general, and America (as the primary symbol of Enlightenment-based utopia) in particular can take the attitude, "Long live the Fourth World, the world to which you can say, 'Right, utopia has arrived. If you aren't part of it, get lost!' " (1986: 112). Thus, the Croatians and Muslims in former Yugoslavia were "condemned to oblivion, thrown out to go off and die their second-class deaths" (ibid.). But I disagree with Baudrillard that the West can get away with living in its self-imposed conceptual cocoon characterized by vicarious sadism. Instead, I agree with Ahmed (1992) that the Islamic world came to regard the West as decadent and evil as a result of observing the perceived pattern in which the West would invoke moral principles primarily against Muslim nations, but not against Christian nations. Ahmed (1993) has added to his analysis the fact that the Islamic world also failed to come to the aid of the Muslims in Bosnia-Herzegovina.[16] Yet what could the Muslim world really do? It has lost its will to fight due to many years of losing every battle it had fought against the West. While attending Friday prayer services in the mosque in Zagreb, Croatia – where the worshipers were mostly pitiful refugees from Bosnia-Herzegovina – I heard the repeated message in the sermons that the plight of the Muslims in Bosnia-Herzegovina was the last straw in the West's perceived pattern of oppressing Islam in Afghanistan, Palestine, Kashmir, Iraq, Iran, Libya, and elsewhere. Thus, Islam might well become the Evil Empire for the West as a replacement for the Cold War that had just ended. But such a conclusion definitely supposes that social reality consists of more than circulating fictions. It consists of traditions of decency, standards of justice and fair play, and habits in which nations are expected to behave toward each other according to the same principles of a Golden Rule that is expected to guide individual behavior across diverse cultures.

It does not matter how the West excuses or rationalizes its failure to prevent crimes against humanity in the Balkans following the collapse of communism. Perhaps it is true that the West did not have to send its own troops to die for any Slav. But that is no excuse for the West's ensuring that the Croats and Bosnian Muslims could not defend themselves against the Serbian aggressors. The important point is that the powerless do not just go off and die their second-class deaths. Instead, victims invoke age-old standards of justice – which are not just television images. Other dictators will take heart from Milošević's victory. For example, in an ominous development, President Boris Yeltsin requested "special powers" from the United Nations "to stop ethnic conflicts in the former Soviet Union" (*New York Times*, 1 March 93: A1). Clearly, many republics in the former Soviet Union regard Russia's motives as suspiciously as Serbia's victims regarded her motives as part of Yugoslavia. Other nations that wanted to emulate the West will now suspect the West's motives. Serbia's victims will become bitter and desire revenge. And even Saddam Hussein, the alleged Hitler of the Arab world, came to be perceived as a victim. For example, as reported in the *Wall Street Journal*, " 'The West's reaction to the Kuwait invasion has reached such horrific proportions that the original act has lost all significance," argues Jerusalem-born Jabra I. Jabra, one of the world's most celebrated novelists and a Baghdad resident since 1948. "We're dazed: why is the Western world destroying us?' " (12 March 1993: A15).

RAPE AS METAPHOR AND REALITY IN THE BALKANS

In late 1992 and early 1993, the American media slowly began to cover the story of how Muslim and Croat women in former Yugoslavia became the victims of institutionalized rape by the Serbs. At nearly the same time that these stories of rape were broadcast, the American public was exposed to media coverage of what came to be known as "Nannygate." The two women whom President Clinton nominated for the post of Attorney-General withdrew their names from consideration because of negative public reaction to the fact that they had hired illegal aliens to babysit for their children. In response to Nannygate, editorial pages were filled with numerous articles on sexual discrimination, sexual harassment, gays in the military, and inequities with regard to how professional women struggle to raise children in modern America. But there was no comparable outcry in the editorial pages from feminists or the general public over the then well-documented rape and torture of Muslims and Croats by Serbs in war-torn former Yugoslavia.[17] One must wonder why nannies and sexual harassment should spark the interest of postmodern America – or at least why the media should choose to make these issues part of its "culture industry" (from Adorno 1991) – while the brutal rape of Muslim and Croat women during this Balkan War is relatively ignored. I am referring to news stories such as the following:

> Borislav Herak, a 21-year-old Serbian nationalist fighter, took the witness stand at his trial here [in Sarajevo] today and said that he killed and raped dozens of Muslims in Serbian "ethnic cleansing" offensives across Bosnia and Herzegovina last year. Mr. Herak, a former Sarajevo textile worker, is accused of 35 killings and 16 rapes. . . . The account Mr. Herak gave reporters over recent months was the first by a Serbian participant in "ethnic cleansing." In the techniques of killing he claimed to have used, including throat-cutting and machine-gunning, and in the apparently casual and random fashion in which most of his victims were selected, the young Serb's story closely matched accounts by thousands of Muslims who managed to escape Serbian offensives in the last 12 months.
>
> *(New York Times*, 14 March 1993: A6)[18]

Up to the 1990s, such acts were labeled monstrous, and their perpetrators were called mass murderers. But note how the reporter has removed the sting of these labels by deftly rationalizing Mr. Herak's acts as aspects of "ethnic cleansing." "Cleansing" is an agreeable action, and killing is what humans do to vermin – and animals do to each other – as opposed to murder, which is a uniquely human act of barbarism.

National differences account for some of the differences in how the Balkan rape story was disseminated and received. The German media led the way in Europe by reporting on the rapes as early as October 1992. Croatian and Slovene media also used this story as part of a negative campaign against Serbia. Britain and France were only slightly less tardy than the USA in picking up on it. Thus, a CNN producer told me on 7 December, 1992, in Zagreb, Croatia, that CNN would not cover this rape story because Americans would not be interested in it. She added that Americans would be interested only if American women were raped. An official at the American Embassy in Croatia told me that the US government was aware of the problem, but that one must keep in mind that women get raped in every war. An American newspaper reporter in Zagreb told me that he would cover this story only if he could find documented evidence of alleged Serbian-run "bordello camps" in Bosnia-Herzegovina. Presumably, these camps – in which women were alleged to be raped to death – would have to look like a "bordello camp" might be expected to appear in the postmodern movie consciousness.

These and similar statements betray a curious, postmodern blend of cynicism and "tolerance" that borders on indifference, not to mention an attitude that leads easily to yellow journalism. Postmodern Americans seem to be consumed with the issues of sexual harassment and fears of *saying* something offensive in the workplace, but are presumed not to be overly interested in systematic, documented sexual brutality against women and children in the distant Balkans. The campaign to promote tolerance between the sexes in the American workplace clashes dramatically with the tolerance of one of the most extreme forms of intolerance in the Balkans. By this I mean that rape was used by the Serbs in this Balkan War as an instrument of "ethnic cleansing, to degrade and humiliate the women and children so much that they would never want to return to their homes."[19] In an article entitled "Gynocide," Anna Quindlen interprets these events:

> Is a particularly sophisticated and brutal form of *genocide* going on in the former Yugoslavia, which relies on the psychosexual destruction of those who would bear the next generation of Bosnian Muslims, so hated by the warring Serbs? I will try not to numb you with the stories. The 10-year-old who was taken away every night to be raped by soldiers and then returned each morning to her mother. . . . The women raped in front of children, husbands and fathers to heighten the humiliation. . . . We women once liked to think that if we ran the world, there might be less emphasis on brute strength. But pacifism suddenly seems a pallid ideal beside these stories. And the timidity of American policy seems ill-suited to this brutality. It's time to reconsider American military intervention, despite the seeming intractability of this no-win war. . . . If husbands are never able to embrace again wives whom they know to have been violated, if women so violated recoil from sexual contact, if families reject daughters twice victimized, by violence and then by the strictures of a culture that esteems virginity – then it is possible that the rape policy will help wipe out the Bosnian Muslims. We will have witnessed the *genocide of these people without even recognizing it*, the killing of something inside these women that guarantees the future.
>
> (*New York Times*, 10 March 1993: A15; emphasis added)

This intolerance of non-Serbian women was tolerated by the West even as it engaged in its own, highly publicized intolerance of those who are intolerant in the workplace.

Even the word intolerance fails to capture the blend of sadism and sexuality that seems to characterize systematic rape in this Balkan War. However, in this regard as well, the documented sexual brutality was not just a random fiction broadcast on the television screen. Instead, it blended in with a veritable voyeuristic orgy of sado-masochistic themes found on American television in the 1990s, from MTV (Music Television) to soap operas. For example, that postmodern idol, the rock star

Madonna, captured the West's attention in the Winter of 1992 with sado-masochistic images in a best-selling book and a number of videos and films. In effect, blatant sado-masochism became entertainment for the masses. Even women's fashion in late 1992 came to emphasize the black leather look that Madonna had associated with sexual "mistresses." Of course, from the Durkheimian perspective in sociology, Madonna's seemingly private achievement in popularizing sado-masochistic fictions was made possible because collective representations in Western societies were receptive to these images. Meanwhile, real sadism – including sadism associated with sex – affected thousands of lives in Bosnia-Herzegovina – and neither the Western public nor its many diplomats made an effective effort to put a stop to it, or even to allow the Bosnian Muslims to defend themselves. How can one begin to explain these inconsistencies?

If one were to follow Baudrillard's lead, one would argue that real sexual brutality committed during the Balkan War of the 1990s blended all too easily with the fictionalized sado-masochistic fantasies that became increasingly popular in the postmodern world of the same time period. Reality was broadcast on the same television screen that featured sado-masochistic fictions such that the distinction between reality and fiction became blurred. In effect, the real rape ceased to exist. This explanation seems to assume that the postmodern public that watches television is not sufficiently astute to distinguish fact from fiction. Such an assumption is difficult to accept, given the obvious sophistication of postmodern people compared with their ancestors.

Other social forces may be at work. For example, the rape in former Yugoslavia was perpetrated primarily by Serbs against Croat and Muslim women and children. Herein lies the rub. At a feminist conference on wartime rape that was held in Zagreb in October 1992, Western feminists refused to endorse the position put forth by Croat and Muslim feminists that the rape was aimed against women of a particular ethnic group – in other words, that Serbs used rape as a weapon against Muslim and Croat women and children.[20] The Western feminists were willing to condemn the rape as a male phenomenon, but not as an ethnic phenomenon. Such ethnic considerations are every bit as politically incorrect as verbal sexual harassment in the 1990s. The West has erected mental defense mechanisms against the suggestion that rape can be and is used as a weapon of war or genocide. For example, Croatian and Muslim feminists point out that rape is not cited specifically as a war crime in any of the Geneva articles of war. If wartime rape in the Balkans is to be prosecuted in the future, it will have to be construed and extrapolated as torture, bodily pain, and the like, but not rape *per se*.

Yet the Geneva articles were written primarily in response to Nazi atrocities, and the Nazis committed crimes which were more clearly racist than sexual in nature. It is well known that Nazi racism was commensurate with a general drive toward eugenics and modernist control of reproduction that permeated the Western cultures of the early twentieth century (Bauman 1989, 1991). In contrast with Nazi war crimes, Serbia's atrocities in the 1990s war against her neighbors constitute conceptually new varieties of atrocities, namely, sexual, sado-masochistic acts of brutality intended to promote terror and to aid in the process of "ethnic cleansing." And this new sort of racism seems to be commensurate with a generalized, Western cultural interest in sado-masochistic themes.

In other words, much as Hitler's racist campaign might be considered as the cultural product of the modernist era of the early twentieth century, Serbia's racist campaign might be considered as the cultural product of the postmodern mood of the late twentieth century. Hence, Serbian atrocities were tolerated, not because the postmodern audiences could not tell fiction from reality, but because – following Freud – voyeurism is itself a passive act of sexual sadism. On 5 April, 1993, Anthony Lewis wrote in the *New York Times*:

> How far can Serbian leaders go in their contempt for the rules of international order without provoking a meaningful reaction from the United States Government? Is there a limit to the shame President Clinton will feel without acting?. . . . If Bill Clinton has the resolve – the courage, the determination -- I do not doubt that he could win the necessary support in Congress and the country for strong action. After all, the case is not hard to make: "My fellow Americans, nearly 50 years ago we and our allies defeated the menace of Hitler and the Nazis. We cannot allow *Nazi methods to be revived on the continent of Europe. It would be too terrible to let that specter loose again.*"
>
> (A11; emphasis added).

The existing media reports and other documentation of this new, institutional form of rape perpetrated by Serbs against their non-Serb victims are commensurate with my own research results: the mass rapes are a deliberate, systematic aspect of the Serbian campaign that is called "ethnic cleansing."[21] In Zbigniew Brzezinski's words, Serbian mass rapes of Croats and Muslims "had become almost a policy."[22] Roughly the same story is told by victims who could not possibly know each other: after the Serbs occupy a Croat or Muslim village, they haul off the men to no-one-knows-where. The remaining women are beaten and raped repeatedly, often in front of family members, and in the most savage manner possible. Sodomy, men urinating and ejaculating in women's mouths, broken bones, and bodies covered with black and blue bruises – these are the descriptions I heard, and that are found in other documented evidence (see Allman 1993, for example). But the more important point is that one will find nearly the same images in pornographic and other violent films produced in our *fin de siècle*.

For example, the following account by a Muslim survivor, published in the *New York Times,* bears an eerie resemblance to violent scenes that have become the staple of many contemporary films:

> There was silence. Then the crazy, dirty stinking Chetniks jumped at the women like animals; they tore off their clothes, pulled their hair, cut their breasts with their knives. They'd cut the belly of the women who wore the traditional Muslim baggy trousers. Those who screamed would be killed on the spot. In front of few hundred prisoners they raped and tortured women and girls for

days. It was unbearable to watch girls being raped in front of their fathers. In the evening, after heavy drinking, the Chetniks would come in the hall with lamps. Stepping on us, they would look for girls, not older than 12, 13. The girls cried, holding on to their mothers. As they were taken, pieces of their mothers' clothes remained in their hands. While doing that, the Chetniks would shoot at us. Later they would leave the girls' dead bodies in the hall, so we had to see them. We cried until morning. Then they would throw the bodies in the river. Every day the same picture was repeated; they would rape and kill in front of hundreds of us.

(13 December 1992: E17)

Many of the raped women became pregnant, but again, as part of a deliberate plan to make sure that they "bear Chetnik [Serbian] babies" (*New York Times*, 3 October 1992: A1). According to one Muslim victim, her tormentor told her, "When we let you go home you'll have to give birth to a Chetnik. We won't let you go while you can have an abortion" (ibid.). Borrowing from the Nazi focus on hygiene even in the midst of sadism, Serbian camp doctors performed gynecological examinations on the imprisoned Muslim and Croat women to determine whether the plan to make them pregnant was working. If not, they were usually returned to the camps and raped again. If they became pregnant, they were released from the camps only after they were so far along in their pregnancies that an abortion would have been illegal or unsafe. Herein lies the ultimate humiliation for the Croat and Muslim woman: to be forced to give birth to the child of her tormentor.

Despite Western knowledge and sophistication concerning psychiatric trauma, the West concentrated on sending food and clothing as part of its humanitarian relief effort in the Balkans. It did not try to send an army of psychiatrists, gynecologists and social workers to Croatia and Bosnia-Herzegovina. This is an egregious oversight, because these rape victims needed, and continue to need, more than food. They need to cope with massive psychological and bodily traumas that have resulted in symptoms that include depression, migraines, suicide, bleeding, and menstrual problems – among others. Carol J. Williams, reporter for the *Los Angeles Times*, depicts some of these traumas in the victims:

A dazed, 60-year-old woman spends most of her day staring at the wind-swept leaves around her refugee camp, waiting listlessly for the end of her life. Her wounds from gang rape by soldiers are more emotional than physical, but she has neither the strength nor the will to recover.

A 28-year-old in the fetid basement of Zagreb's mosque is too worried about her children to apply the one salve she says would end the suffering inflicted by multiple rapes. Her three toddlers, already traumatized from having witnessed the beating and violation of their mother, would be orphaned as well as homeless if she were to succumb to the urge to take her own life.

For girls like a 17-year-old Muslim waiting to give birth after nine months of sexual enslavement, there is neither professional help nor much prospect of healing. Each time a fetal foot or elbow swims across the womb, those impregnated by war rape relive the terror of the attacks. The young, unmarried ones have nothing to inspire hope for the future, psychologists and social workers say, because they will be ostracized in their tradition-bound societies once the war ends and some semblance of civil life returns to their homeland. . . . As a gynecologist attending to a pregnant Muslim teenager put it, "For them there are probably no alternatives but madness or prostitution."

(30 November 1992: A1)

Far from receiving any sort of help for their psychological traumas, most of the rape victims encountered an attitude that sociologists have already labeled as "blaming the victim" (Ryan 1967). Muslim victims of rape, in particular, are shunned by family and friends, although this cultural reaction is also shared by some Croats.[23] The Croatian government has sought not to publicize the plight of its rape victims, for fear they would be labeled as prostitutes, or be exploited by a West that seems to thrive on sado-masochistic sexual fantasies in its popular culture. Far from viewing these fears as paranoid or provincial, I believe that they are, regretfully, well-founded.

This is because from the beginning of this contemporary Balkan War, the West has behaved as a voyeur in relation to the well-documented atrocities, most of which have been attributed to the Serbs. Contrast the use of "rape" as a metaphor in the Gulf War with the total and complete absence of this concept in discussions of the current Balkan War. In 1991, the American media used rape as a metaphor to convey the image that Kuwait had been "raped" by Iraq. Partly in response to this powerful metaphor, the US led the Western world in rescuing Kuwait as the allegedly innocent victim of Iraqi aggression.

In the present Balkan War, Croatia and Bosnia-Herzegovina are also victims, and have also been "raped" symbolically, this time by Serbia. But instead of helping the Balkan victims, the West blamed the victims repeatedly. An American newspaper reporter explained the situation in the Balkans to me as follows: Bosnia is like a young woman who was told by the West to walk alone down a dark alley at night wearing a mini-skirt. "Go ahead," said the West, "We're right here behind you." (He was referring to Western assurances to Bosnia in the Spring of 1992 that Serbian aggression would be checked in Croatia, and would go no further.) Beginning in April of 1992, Bosnia was "raped" repeatedly by Serbia, despite the assurances. Not only would the West not stop the "rape," it negotiated (and as of this writing, continues to negotiate) with the "rapists," especially Slobodan Milošević and Radovan Karadzić. Croatia fared even worse: she was not "a clear cut case" because "she was asking for it." (Here he was referring to Croatia's well-publicized Nazi collaboration.)[24] And besides, the West had not made any promises to Croatia to protect her.

The important point is that both victims, Croatia as well as Bosnia-Herzegovina, came to be blamed for being "raped" metaphorically, and actual Croat and Bosnian women who had been raped were also blamed for being victims. Far from being a circulating fiction, the concept of rape is deeply rooted in collective representations that relate to the notions of sacredness versus pollution, masculinity versus femininity, and innocence versus guilt, among many others. The blame came in many varieties: western opinion-makers wrote repeatedly that if Croatia and Bosnia had not wanted independence from Belgrade, none of this would have happened. This is not even a subtle variation of the ugly, chauvinist response to the real rape of real women – now extended to whole nations – that "they were asking for it." Thus, acting Secretary of State Lawrence Eagleburger stated that the West "should wait until they [the warring parties] exhaust themselves and then move in" (*New York Times*, 27 August 1992: A14).[25] Along these lines, the Western opinion-makers assumed that Croatia could handle nearly a million Bosnian refugees who came pouring in over its borders – proportionately the equivalent of 45 million refugees in the USA. And above all, the West absolutely refused to allow Croatia and Bosnia-Herzegovina to arm so that they could protect themselves from Serbian aggression.

Despite all the rationalizations, denial, and other defense mechanisms that the West used to cover up its complicity in Serbian atrocities, in the end, at some unconscious level that still exists in all humanity, the West experienced a collective sense of guilt. This is because the notion of fair play or justice is constitutive of all social systems (Durkheim [1950] 1983), and it seems unjust that the West not only refused to help Bosnia-Herzegovina and Croatia, but actually made it impossible for these nations to defend themselves effectively by imposing an arms embargo on them. Tragically, instead of confronting this guilt honestly and constructively, the West continued throughout 1992 to engage collectively in classic mental defenses. Rape, real and metaphorical, was trivialized as something that just happens to unlucky women, and nations. The shipment of humanitarian aid – to repeat, this aid consisted primarily of leftover rations from the Gulf War – displaced the guilt into a direction that failed to address the need for humanitarian aid in the first place.

ADDING INSULT TO INJURY

1–8 November, 1992 was declared by the United Nations to be a Week of Tranquility for Children in war-torn Bosnia. The UN recruited Ms. Audrey Hepburn as spokesperson for the program, and her televised message on the importance of reaching every child in Bosnia-Herzegovina saturated the Croatian and Bosnian media. At first, Bosnian and Croatian politicians were speechless when they learned that humanitarian aid given to children as part of this UNICEF program was purchased in Serbia – and with coveted hard currency. Some of the clothing that was donated to the Bosnian children was even inscribed in the Cyrillic alphabet. The one word that finally broke through was – disgusting. I heard ordinary Croat citizens say, "I used to like Audrey Hepburn as an actress. I don't think I could ever watch one of her movies again."

Adding still more insult to injury, the UN announced that following the success – from their point of view – of the Week of Tranquility for Children, future humanitarian aid would be shipped from Belgrade to Sarajevo on a daily basis. Essentially, Serbia's victims would be forced to receive humanitarian aid from their enemies. Serbian television did not fail to exploit this development as a sign that the world finally recognized Serbia's goodwill. The UN spokesperson responded to Croat and Bosnian criticisms by acting incredulous. When Croat reporters pointed out that the UN broke its own economic embargo against Serbia by purchasing clothing in Serbia – when it could have been bought just as easily in any number of other nations – the spokesperson responded that the UN gave special permission for these particular purchases. Overall, the UN defended its actions on bureaucratic grounds, that humanitarian aid was delivered efficiently from point A (Belgrade) to point B (Sarajevo), and seemed completely oblivious to the moral callousness of its actions. Or at least such was the appearance, because this event, which became a huge scandal among Serbia's victims, was hardly covered in the American media.

The UN and the US State Department frequently associated Serbian ethnic cleansing with Nazi war crimes. For example, "UN investigators blame Serbs for the worst atrocities, from the creation of Nazi-like detention camps to forced deportations and systematic rape of Muslims" (*Wall Street Journal*, 23 February 1993: A1). The astute postmodernist might pose the question: if Hitler were alive today, and carried out his "Final Solution" in the postmodern 1990s instead of the old-fashioned 1940s, would the UN have shipped aid from Berlin to Jews and other victims of the Nazis who were imprisoned in concentration camps? (The analogy is apt because Sarajevo and many other Bosnian cities became, in effect, concentration camps, as a result of the Serbian siege that began in 1992.) And more importantly, would the so-called civilized world stand by and let the UN collaborate with Hitler?

The postmodernists seem to be right: the old distinctions between right and wrong, truth and illusion, even good guys and bad guys, no longer apply. Humanity has apparently reached the era of the end of distinction and difference. In this case, it did not matter to the UN who sent or received humanitarian aid, nor the reasons why, so long as the job got done. This particular Balkan War has been transformed into just another natural disaster. When Mr. Silajdzić, Bosnia-Herzegovina's minister for foreign affairs, made the statement that the West has lost all feeling for the Bosnian tragedy – what could that possibly mean to the West? In effect, Serbia was no more morally culpable than a tornado or flood or earthquake.

A similar scandal occurred in the middle of February 1993. The Bosnian government urged the citizens of Sarajevo to refuse UN humanitarian aid until such aid reached other areas of Bosnia-Herzegovina. According to John Burns, reporter to the *New York Times*,

> United Nations officials described the [Bosnian] Government's move as "ridiculous," as "blackmail," and as a decision to "fast to death". . . . But Mr. Izetbegović, and other top [Bosnian] officials held fast, saying it was time the world knew how little aid has reached Muslims living beyond the reach of the

mainly Western news reporters and camera crews who make their base in Sarajevo. . . . The [Bosnian] Government, in cutting off all relief supplies to Sarajevo, intended that the United Nations would put an end to the "farce of pretending that it could save Bosnian Muslims with its present approach".

(16 February 1993: A3)

Indeed, many government and media reports had documented the fact that up to a quarter of the humanitarian aid that passed through Serbian checkpoints was given to the Serbs as payment for safe passage. And up to 40 per cent of the areas that needed the humanitarian aid never received it. Thus, one could characterize the Bosnian "hunger strike" as an effort to counter the postmodern fiction of an effective UN with the hard reality, supported by facts, of its dismal failure. But clearly, one must penetrate further than the conclusion that might be drawn by some postmodernists that UN fictions were being countered by Bosnian fictions. It hardly takes an astute student of human nature to conclude that the West was using the fiction of delivering humanitarian aid to justify its refusal to rescue the Bosnians in a Kuwait-style military operation. And it seems equally obvious that the desperate Bosnians went on a hunger strike in order to humiliate the UN so that the world's collective consciousness would react to the starving Bosnians with compassion.

The final example of UN insensitivity to the dignity of Bosnian Muslims as humans that I will consider – out of many that could be discussed further – is the evacuation of Muslim refugees from Srebrenica on 30–31 March, 1993. Thousands of desperate refugees were jammed onto UN trucks – not buses or helicopters, but trucks used to transport food – for the journey to nearby Tuzla. Two children were crushed to death in the first trip, and seven people died in the panic of the second trip, among them four children. According to the *New York Times*,

The Bosnian Army commander in Tuzla criticized the United Nations for the way it undertook today's evacuation. "This method of transportation was not agreed to and was inhumane," said the statement signed by the local commander, Hazim Sadic. "We don't even transport livestock that way."

(30 March 1993: A7)

FREEDOM OF THE PRESS AS FICTION

The first week in November 1992 was marked by a feeding frenzy in the Western media on the theme, "Croatia is also the aggressor in Bosnia, alongside Serbia." The problem is that the Western media was feeding on itself; the *New York Times* took its cue from the *L.A. Times*, and so on down the line of leading American newspapers. This is another aspect of the allegedly rootless circulation of fictions that is supposed to characterize the postmodern scene. One editorial after another proclaimed that Mr. Tudjman – labeled the butcher's apprentice – was the Croatian counterpart of Mr. Milošević of Serbia; that there existed a campaign for Greater

Croatia; and that a free press in Croatia did not exist.[26] Moreover, Mr. Izetbegović was consistently suspected in the media of harboring Muslim fundamentalist aspirations,[27] and it seemed as if every charge made by the Serbs that the Muslims provoked them was dutifully reported.

Whatever criticisms one might have wished to level at Mr. Tudjman and the Croatian government, foreign affairs specialists had to concede that neither Bosnia nor Croatia attacked one square meter of Serbian territory. And Messrs. Tudjman and Izetbegović were rarely afforded an opportunity to defend themselves, as in this rare coverage of Mr. Tudjman's rebuttal:

> The world has been looking for an alibi not to take action against Serbia in Bosnia, and it found it by blaming Croatia as well. But objectively, this guilt does not exist. Croatia encouraged Croats in Bosnia to participate in the referendum that approved Bosnia's independence, and was the first to recognize Bosnia as an independent state. Where we have fought in Bosnia, it has been to defend those areas where Croats are a majority. How can anybody call this a crime?
>
> (*New York Times*, 18 December 1992: A1)

As for the allegedly total lack of an independent press in Croatia, I should point out that I regularly bought a copy of *Globus* – an independent, privately owned Croatian newspaper that is supposed not to exist – along with *Slobodna Dalmacija* and other newspapers that frequently criticized the Croatian government. In one such issue of *Globus*, I read an interview with Mr. Haris Silajdzić, the minister for foreign affairs in Bosnia-Herzegovina. It is odd that the Western media did not interview Mr. Silajdzić in order to verify the charges of Croatian aggression against Bosnia. Wouldn't the Bosnian minister for foreign affairs know of such aims? But Mr. Silajdzić stated clearly: "Croatia is not the aggressor in Bosnia-Herzegovina. Everyone knows that Croatia was and remains a victim of Serbian aggression. Croatia is Bosnia's only link to the rest of the world. . . . Croatia took care of our refugees. Because of Croatia, we were able to get some weapons. In all these ways, Croatia has shown, not aggression, but friendship." Mr. Silajdzić went on to say that the many newspaper stories in the Western media concerning Croat–Muslim conflicts are Serbian propaganda. He added: "The world knows that Serbia began this expansionist, genocidal war. Given that the world did not and does not want to stop Serbia, it had to find scapegoats. First, it blamed Bosnians for allegedly firing on other Bosnians. Now, it labels Croatia the aggressor. It's shameless, disgusting hypocrisy on the part of the West."

The important point is that the Western media, which assumes without question that it is impartial and covers all sides of a story, consistently maintained the interpretation that all sides (Serbs, Croats, and Muslims) were equally guilty in this Balkan War. And this fiction of equal guilt was maintained despite the facts and government reports that pointed all too clearly to the conclusion that Serbia was overwhelmingly responsible for the war and the atrocities.

Here again, my own observations serve as witness to the fact that the demands and dictates of Serb leaders such as Mr. Milošević and Mr. Karadzić that I watched on Serbian television reverberated a few days later in American, French, and British media outlets. "Croatia is the aggressor," and "sanctions need to be imposed on Croatia," Mr. Karadzić would claim. Typically, I found these claims printed a few days later in the *New York Times*. But when I heard Bosnian and Croatian politicians and opinion-makers complain on Croatian television about Western hypocrisy and United Nations collaboration with the Serbian enemy, I found that these criticisms of the West were not reported in American newspapers. How objective can the American media truly be?

For example, let me hark back to the UNICEF Week of Tranquility for Children scandal in which the UN bought goods in Serbia to distribute to Serbia's victims. Croatian and Bosnian public, editorial, and political opinion was one of outrage. Yet most Americans never even knew that the scandal had occurred. During that same week, 1–8 November, 1992, the Bosnians were portrayed in the Western media as seeking ties with Islamic freedom fighters from Iran, and Croats as the aggressor that would carve up what was left of Bosnia by the time the Serbs got through with it.

But there is more to this sacrimonious blaming of the victims, Croatia and Bosnia, on the part of the West, in this case for allegedly not guaranteeing freedom of the press. Any observer who is sensitive to cultural distinctions will focus on the cost of a "free" press. The issue of *Globus* that I bought in Croatia cost me 400 dinars in the Fall of 1992, or almost $1.00. That was not a problem for me, an American living in Croatia on a Fulbright Scholar's stipend. But for the average Croat, whose salary was $105.00 per month in October 1992 (as low as $50.00 per month) it was enormously expensive. In Croatia and Bosnia, it was common for one newspaper to be shared by scores of people. Who in America or Western Europe would pay the equivalent of about $40.00 for a newspaper? All this pious sermonizing by the West about freedom of the press conveniently ignored the tremendous economic hardship and sacrifice endured by Croats and Bosnians as a result of the ongoing war and hundreds of thousands of refugees.

Finally, it is worth noting that most American cities are served by only one local newspaper, if they are that lucky. The recession hit the newspaper industry hard, and many newspapers were closed in the 1980s and early 1990s. Yet in Zagreb, Croatia, despite all the hardship caused by the Balkan War, one could choose from over a dozen – including American, British, and other foreign papers. By contrast, how many urban Americans have access to or interest in foreign newspapers, particularly Eastern European newspapers, so that they can learn other people's points of view directly?

IMPLICATIONS

With regard to the media coverage of the current Balkan War, it seems that one should question that portion of the postmodernist discourse which claims that old-fashioned truths have been replaced by circulating fictions. At least with regard to the war in former Yugoslavia, this characterization of the role of the postmodern media serves as a convenient excuse for other motives and, ultimately, for the absolute refusal of the West to come to the aid of Bosnia and Croatia. Far from being random, rootless, circulating fictions, the stereotypes and clichés used by the American media point to a very coherent structure.

Among the consistent themes that are found in American coverage of this Balkan War, I focused on the following: the Yugoslav people live in a perpetual state of hatred that can be traced back for many centuries. The Serbs, Croats, and Muslims are equally guilty because all three sides have committed atrocities. The Croats and Muslims brought the wrath of Serbia on themselves – the classic "blame the victim" argument. A small group of leaders, such as Messrs. Karadzić and Milošević, are guilty of imposing ruin on innocent Serbia, but the average Serb is exempted from blame. The Croats are associated with Ustase atrocities from World War II, and the Muslims in Bosnia are associated with contemporary Islamic fundamentalism, but Serbian collaboration with the Nazis is not discussed at all by the leading opinion-makers and newspapers in the USA.

When discussions shift to Serbian war crimes and atrocities committed in this Balkan War, these crimes are mitigated by the fact that Serbian leaders are consistently shown negotiating with UN and other Western diplomats. Mr. Milošević, the "butcher of the Balkans," is also the peacemaker.[28] Mr. Karadzić is referred to in the American media as Dr. Karadzić – a sign of respect – and his demands for the right of self-determination among the Serbs in the Croatian and Bosnian lands that were taken by force are treated seriously.

There is no need to resort to the confusing, jargon-filled vocabulary of postmodernism in order to make sense of these and other themes. They all point, very consistently and clearly, to the conclusion that the West sides with Serbia – despite the rhetoric of protest. This is the conclusion reached by Serbia's victims, and is supported by Russia's open support for the Serbs as the "good guys" in this Balkan War. Nor is this conclusion shocking, even from the standpoint of Jean Baudrillard's version of postmodernism, because he claims that the Yuppie logic found in postmodernism is that all the weak and powerless "must exit." The Croats and Bosnian Muslims are the weak and powerless relative to Serbia, so they must disappear, pure and simple.

Chapter 5

The end of morality?

Up to now, moral problems in politics have usually been refracted through the prism of the idealism versus realism debate, represented by Daniel Patrick Moynihan versus Henry Kissinger.[1] The idealists point to America's role, in particular, in maintaining an international moral order, while the realists tend to view all matters in terms of national self-interest and power (Fukuyama 1992). This dated alternative seems to be insufficient for apprehending the moral crisis represented by the brutality of the current, postmodern, postcommunist conflict in the Balkans. And of course, the core of my argument is that the actual conflict in the Balkans represents the beginnings of a world-wide Balkanization process.

This is because the American version of moral idealism is simply blind to the return of history, not only in the Balkans but throughout the postcommunist world, as well as to the rampant narcissism and anti-culturalism within the USA and Western Europe. If America still holds any moral power as a symbol of freedom, this symbolism stems from its historical past, not its actions in the postmodern present. For example, President Clinton's bombing of Iraqi civilians in June 1993 in the name of lofty principles gave him a slight and temporary boost in the American opinion polls, but was labeled as an act of terrorism by many Americans and non-Americans alike.[2] On the other hand, the realists miscalculated the symbolic effects of the Balkan crisis on the dream of a united Europe, the New World Order, the possibility of a counterrevolution in postcommunist Russia, and the general prospect of peace in the world. Even if Henry Kissinger and his disciples were correct that the actual fighting would be contained to former Yugoslavia (see Isaacson 1992) – an assumption I believe will prove to be incorrect – they underestimated the symbolic and moral implications of the current Balkan War on Western nations. The EC and UN lost their credibility, the New World Order became the butt of cynical remarks, America lost its prestige in foreign affairs, and Russian hardliners kept referring to their little Slavic brothers in Serbia. In the words of Anthony Lewis, "The dream of a united Europe, powerful contributor to a better world, is dead. It died when the European Community refused to act against Serbian aggression – when it would not lift a finger to stop mass racial murder on its own continent" (*New York Times*, 29 March 1993: A11).

I have argued that postmodern discourse, in its present form, confounds one's efforts to comprehend the collapse of communism and its consequences as much as it illuminates them. As stated from the outset, communism fell during a time in which Western intellectuals were writing about the end of history, culture, and other phenomena, up to and including modernity itself. The result of all these alleged endings that make up much of the postmodern discourse was supposed to have been the triumph of liberal democracy, tolerance, and rationalism over ideology, nationalism, territorial imperialism, and totalitarianism. At the same time that Western intellectuals were engaged in these apocalyptic predictions, they were upholding an ethnocentric, up-beat – even fun – world-view concerning the universality of human rights and the absolute superiority of the West to the rest of the world. As such, disciples of the Enlightenment were engaged in a high-stakes gamble relative to postcommunist development. But if modernity is truly coming to an end in the postcommunist world, it follows that liberal democracy, rationalism, and other derivatives of the Enlightenment in non-communist lands should also be coming to an end. It seems to follow also that fundamentalism, nationalism, Balkanization and other alleged evils that are filling the void left by the collapse of modernity in postcommunist lands should also be taking over the so-called West, albeit in forms that will not make them instantly recognizable as such.

The fate of formerly communist Yugoslavia was caught up in the cultural lacunae caused by these endgames, and the destiny of the former Soviet Union will probably unfold along similar lines. However, Westerners refuse to acknowledge that a kind of Balkanization has already afflicted the West. To return to the June 1993 Vienna Human Rights Conference as illustration, many commentators were tempted "to reduce the global human rights debate today to a clash of good guys against bad guys, of Western democracies against Asian dictatorships, of countries defending the principle of universal human rights against third world attempts to water down the concept with economic, cultural and religious arguments" (*New York Times*, 20 June 1993: E5). Yet, ironically, many "lobbies in the West are now claiming special rights for say, women, children, indigenous peoples, migrant workers and the handicapped" (ibid.). Not only that, the cultural relativist position is inescapable to the extent that one takes seriously major findings from a hundred years of anthropological and sociological research. And the West has yet to concede that universal human rights are seen as a luxury by peoples in developing countries who see their most basic human right as economic survival.

Instead of the melting-pot version of assimilation in which immigrants lost their ethnic identities to become Americans, contemporary Americans refer to themselves as African Americans, Hispanic Americans, Native Americans, and other sorts of Americans. Gender and sexual preference have practically assumed the status of ethnic groups to the extent that gays demand "minority rights." American society still has a long way to go before it reaches the pitch of Balkanization in the former Yugoslavia, yet the existing divisiveness is already tinged with considerable hostility. For example, the celebration of the Super Bowl victory by the American football team, the Dallas Cowboys, in January 1993 resulted in some ugly rioting on the streets of Dallas, Texas. In some instances, African Americans pulled Caucasian Americans out of their cars and beat them up; as revenge for slavery, they claimed. Dallas is not Sarajevo, and it may never become Sarajevo exactly, but disturbing similarities exist already.

Neither Americans nor their Western partners in trade (Britain, France and Germany) tend to dwell on similar instances of ethnic hatred and other precursors of Balkanization within their borders. The Americans, in particular, have tried to put a brave face on postcommunist developments. American Deputy Secretary of State, Lawrence Eagleburger, made explicit his personal as well as the USA's national commitment to Enlightenment narratives at a conference on 26 August, 1992. Commenting on the meaning of the collapse of communism, Mr. Eagleburger asserted:

> Just three years ago, mankind began anew its long-interrupted march towards freedom, enlightenment and the rule of law. We had every reason then to hope that all nations liberated from communism would join not only the Western circle of democracy, but also the circle of peace created by the reconciliation of historical enemies. We envisaged, in short, an enlarged commonwealth of democracies poised to enter the 21st century having transcended the hatreds and rivalries which had so blighted the century we were about to leave. These hopes remain undiminished, but in the meantime events in the former Yugoslavia have confronted us with the specter of history not transcended, but relived; and of the vision of that land's future as a reenactment of its tragic past.

Against Mr. Eagleburger's naive optimism and faith in the modernist version of history as a straight-line march forward to democracy, one could point to several well-known intellectuals who acknowledged that entire cultural systems can find themselves in decline, and even expire (Sorokin 1957, Spengler [1926] 1961, Toynbee 1978). Moreover, Mr. Eagleburger was putting the credibility of the Enlightenment dream on the line. He seems to have implied that at first he thought that the Yugoslavs and the Soviets subscribed to the same Enlightenment narratives which he believes are still inspiring the West. Yet he overlooked the fact that Marxism and communism were Enlightenment narratives, but they crashed in the former Soviet Union and Eastern Europe. When the actions of the Yugoslavs and Soviets did not seem to meet Western expectations of how nations should behave in accordance with the so-called Western version of the Enlightenment narratives, Mr. Eagleburger and other diplomats changed their argument. Surprised by the eruption of nationalism in postcommunist lands, Western diplomats argued that supposedly universal Enlightenment narratives would apply only to Western nations, while the rest of the world chose to remain mired in history, including hatred and "tribalism." This is also the gist of Francis Fukuyama's argument in *The End of History and the Last Man* (1992). But it is as untrue that Westerners are as completely rational and free of hatred as depicted by disciples of the Enlightenment as it is that the South Slavs are capable of practically no emotions except hatred.[3]

Mr. Eagleburger's and Mr. Fukuyama's arguments amount to little more than a latter-day version of colonialist philosophy. The South Slavs have now become the Western man's burden. In reality, the turmoil in the Balkans and the former Soviet Union constitutes more than a chaotic eruption of hatreds and rivalries. Mr. Eagleburger and many other disciples of the Enlightenment were deaf to the voices crying out for freedom from the former Yugoslavia and former Soviet Union. As of 1993, almost everyone seems to have forgotten how the Slovenes, Ukrainians, Croats, Bosnians, Latvians, and others depicted the West in their information media as a symbol of pure democracy, and did not see the cultural narcissism and other shortcomings in Western culture. Yet for Western diplomats, all postcommunist nations fell short of Western ideals and therefore were deemed unworthy of Western support. In particular, all parties in the Balkan conflict were treated as if they were equally guilty of anti-democratic actions.[4] One might adopt an American colloquialism to make the point that, for the West, there were no good guys or bad guys in the postcommunist eruptions of nationalism and violence. Again, the Western notion of universal human rights was used as a weapon with which to discount the fledgling democracies in postcommunist lands. But was the West ever sincere in demanding that Croatia, the Ukraine, Bosnia, and other new democracies conform to perfect records (by Western standards) of human rights, freedom of the press, and minority relations so soon after they made their first transitions to democracy? One could retort that Western democracies did not achieve democracy overnight.

In addition, Western diplomats and intellectuals failed to see that the Yugoslav and Soviet communist systems were also internal Serbian and Russian Empires. That is, Serbia and Russia dominated the ranks of the communist parties in their respective Empires, as well as the military officer corps, educational, business, and other social institutions, not to mention the nations that constituted these Empires. The collapse of communism meant that these internal Empires were threatened with extinction as well, because the republics they had dominated throughout the Cold War suddenly demanded freedom. For example, neither the Ukraine nor Croatia wanted to submit any longer to the internal colonialism emanating from Moscow and Belgrade, respectively. Serbia responded to the defiance from Croats and Muslims with an open, military campaign to establish Greater Serbia, and Russia began to threaten its neighbors from what used to be the Soviet Union with warnings that it would not permit a repeat of Yugoslavia within the Commonwealth of Independent States.[5] Far from being characterized as one hue of undifferentiated hatred, postcommunist conflict can be perceived as a struggle between self-determination and imperialism. Interestingly, old-fashioned Serbian imperialism and massive human rights abuses, compared with the poor record on human and civil rights on the part of Serbia's victims, were treated on the same plane by the West.

It took a very long time for any portion of these insights to penetrate the thick prejudice of anti-nationalist sentiment in the West's public consciousness. For example, the editors of the *New York Times* waited until 19 June 1993 to come to a conclusion that was evident to others as early as 1991:

Seeing that no outside power means to deny it total military victory, Serbia now drops all pretense. Yes, its real goal is to destroy and dismember Bosnia, not merely to protect the interests of Bosnian Serbs. Yes, it fully intends to keep most of the territory it has forcibly seized and to turn it into an ethnically cleansed Serbian state.... Western governments aren't about to intervene militarily, but they need not endorse this trashing of the rules of international behavior.[6]

The West preached universal human rights, democracy and other Enlightenment narratives to the republics within former Yugoslavia that wanted to break away from Serbian domination as well as other postcommunist nations. At first, Slovenia, Croatia, Bosnia-Herzegovina, Georgia, Lithuania, the Ukraine and other newly formed nations that broke away from the Yugoslav and Soviet Empires believed the Enlightenment-based rhetoric, and expressed their unabashed desire to join the orbit of Western European and American social values. But it slowly dawned on these fledgling democracies that the West was not going to receive them with open arms. In fact, and despite the loud rhetoric of supporting self-determination, the actions of the Western powers tended to support, first, the preservation of communist Yugoslavia and the Soviet Union, and then the preservation of the police powers of Serbia and Russia. This is not meant to question the sincerity of Mr. Eagleburger's expressed faith in the Enlightenment project, for his personal motives can never be determined with any finality, and are irrelevant in a sociological discussion of this sort. Rather, it is to state that these same Enlightenment narratives might well cover imperialistic, colonial aspirations, which, even if they can no longer be fulfilled as openly as before (because of the climate of political correctness), continue to affect international relations in contradictory ways.

By 1993 it was already clear that Britain, France, and Russia were not prepared to end the agony in Bosnia-Herzegovina, and would not allow military action to stop Serbian aggression.[7] But Britain, France, and Russia are usually regarded as Serbia's allies against Germany (even though both France and Serbia were guilty of extensive Nazi collaboration), and all of these nations had formed Empires in the not so distant past. The traditional enemy of these once openly imperialist powers, Germany, aligned itself with and supported the new nations that were never imperialist powers: Slovenia, Croatia, Bosnia-Herzegovina, the Baltic Republics, and other republics that were trying to break the grips of Moscow and Belgrade. Germany's moves were attacked bitterly in the British, French, and even American media as efforts to revive a new sort of German imperialism. Indeed, one could argue that France and Britain blocked Slovene, Croat, and Bosnian independence in order to block German interests (Garde 1992). In the 1990s, and in the midst of efforts to establish a European Community, European newspapers were engaged in bitter diatribes concerning the fairness of the Versailles Treaty. The United States acted out its equally traditional isolationism, yet it clearly tended to side with its former allies, Britain and France, and to act against its former enemy, Germany. Meanwhile, Islam was treated by all these nations as a threat, and dealt with accordingly, from Palestine and Bosnia to Iraq and Somalia.

The overall point is this: none of these developments fits the scenarios associated with postmodernism conceived as either the continuation of the Enlightenment narratives or as something that comes after modernism, a scenario that emphasizes kitsch, fragmentation, confusion, the circulation of fictions, and so on. Instead, the alignment of the various actors (nations) is very clearly along traditional alliances, affinities, and international relations. For example, the governments of France, Britain, and Russia displayed remarkable sympathy for Serbia despite their public condemnation of Serbian aggression against her neighbors (*New York Times*, 31 January 1993: E18). Yet these traditional affinities and alliances (the USA, Britain, France, Russia, and Serbia) are *not* consciously acknowledged by politicians, diplomats, or opinion-makers, for that would be tantamount to admitting that imperialism and colonialism have not been overcome. Instead, one finds a hypocritical, modernist rhetoric of support for universal human rights, self-determination and democracy even as such support was withheld from many nations that tried to break free from imperialist powers that had wrapped themselves up in communist ideology. It is this confluence of modernist consciousness and seemingly traditional and oppressive behavior that is distinctive in the present political situation in the world, and that deserves to be appreciated as a postmodern phenomenon, not as the straightforward extension of old-fashioned imperialism.

THE CASE OF YUGOSLAVIA'S BREAKAWAY REPUBLICS

I stated at the outset that even though the present discussion is applicable to many postcommunist nations, in the interest of making the argument manageable, former Yugoslavia will be the primary focus of discussion. Moreover, we have seen that so many opinion-makers and intellectuals interpret the current Balkan War as the symbol of the end of Europe, NATO, the UN, the New World Order, and other phenomena that one feels compelled to address the break-up of Yugoslavia as something that holds deep implications for the future of the postcommunist world. Thus, it is important to note that Germany pushed the rest of the reluctant European Community to recognize Slovenia and Croatia as independent nations, a fact Secretary of State Warren Christopher used to reproach Germany (*USA Today*, 17 June 1993: 11A). The United States waited until April 1992 to recognize Croatia, Bosnia-Herzegovina, and Slovenia as independent nations even though forty-three other nations had recognized them, finally, on 16 January 1992, almost six months after they had declared their independence. And the United States acted primarily on the basis of *Realpolitik*: Bosnia-Herzegovina had been invaded by Serbia in April 1992, and the United States acted to recognize all three breakaway republics (Slovenia, Croatia, and Bosnia-Herzegovina) at this time in order to "send a message" to Serbia. But what was the message? And why should something as serious as recognizing a new nation be used as a tool for postmodern communication?

The United States continued to express publicly its intention to work with the

European Community and the United Nations to resolve the Balkan crisis through diplomacy and negotiation, even though these and other modernist entities and tactics had proved to be ineffective in dealing with Serbian aggression (*New York Times*, 17 April 1993: A1). For example, on 10 July 1992 the West rebuffed the plea by the President of Bosnia-Herzegovina, Alija Izetbegović, to rescue his country by using a Kuwait-style military intervention[8] or, at the very least, to lift the arms embargo against all the former Yugoslav republics so that the Bosnians and Croatians could defend themselves against a vastly better-armed Serbian aggressor – in other words, to allow for a fair fight. According to Leslie H. Gelb:

> The main problem with my idea of limited Western intervention to create a fair fight in Bosnia is that I can't sell it to anyone in power. Even if President Clinton bought it, he would have a very tough time getting Western Europe, Russia or the United Nations to go along. . . . Diplomacy without force is farce, but that is the present Western–UN course. It is cynical farce, for all the realists and neo-isolationists who espouse it know they are winking at Serbian genocide and merely delaying their inevitable confrontation with Serbia, at unforgivable cost in Muslim lives. [President Clinton] has no policy, and every one of his aides knows that.
>
> (*New York Times*, 28 February 1993: E15)

Similarly, Senator Robert Dole asserted that the West had no real foreign policy toward former Yugoslavia: "All we're doing is standing by while the Serbs mop up Bosnia and divide it into 11 little pieces and slaughter all the women and children. In my view, that's not a policy" (*New York Times*, 20 April 1993: A6).

Let us cast a critical eye on the Western efforts to resolve the Balkan crisis strictly through negotiation or other political means. These efforts are consistent with Jürgen Habermas's (1987) version of a Western tradition derived from the Enlightenment in which a premium is placed on rational communication as opposed to the use of force. The warring parties in the Balkans were repeatedly advised to lay down their arms and talk. It is extremely important to note that these advisors were primarily British, American, and French – in other words, *men* (not women) steeped in Enlightenment traditions – not, let us say, Nigerian, Polish, or Mexican traditions. But the negotiators forgot, or acted as if they did not know, that just truces depend on a pre-existing social order that ensures that contracts will be honored and promises will be kept (Durkheim [1893] 1933). These societal conditions were clearly lacking in the Balkan War. Moreover, the Serbs held a decisive advantage at the negotiating table due to their superior military strength. The so-called negotiations were a sham, because the parties involved were never on an equal footing. Editorials in the *New York Times* characterized the Balkan War as slaughter of the Bosnians and Croatians by the Serbs (*New York Times*, 20 December 1992: E2). Serbia's victims were compelled by the European Community to negotiate with the aggressor. In fact, Bosnia-Herzegovina was being compelled to give up its sovereignty, which is a direct affront to the Enlightenment narratives concerning the rights of nation-states.

In January 1993, the Bosnians and Serbs rebuffed the "peace agreement" offered to them by Cyrus Vance and Lord David Owen. Yet, in a seemingly counter-Enlightenment move, Messrs. Vance and Owen decided to force the Bosnians and Serbs to accept their peace proposal by having it imposed on them by the United Nations Security Council. The benign face that the Western powers had tried to paint on negotiation obviously hid the uglier aspects of Enlightenment narratives that many postmodernists had warned against. First, the peace proposal was characterized by many opinion-makers as appeasement,[9] because it rewarded Serbian seizure of territory by force: "Why would Cyrus Vance be pressing the victims to accept such an arrangement? For a year now, Western Europe and the US have appeased Mr. Milošević and his killers, refusing to draw the line" (*New York Times*, 3 January 1993: A11). Second, the peace proposal dismantled the sovereignty of Bosnia-Herzegovina – which was a duly recognized nation-state by then, and a member of the United Nations – by depriving it of a central government and army (*New York Times*, 3 February 1993: A7). In other words, the Western powers were behaving as colonial powers of old that callously bartered national sovereignty and changed national borders to suit their imperialist interests, not the interests and sovereignty of the nations that were directly involved in these changes (see also Boutros-Ghali 1992). Finally, Lord David Owen abandoned this peace plan in June 1993 in favor of carving up Bosnia into three ethnic zones and forcing her to give up her national sovereignty:

> Europe's mediator, Lord Owen, has quickly accommodated himself to this final jettisoning of the Vance–Owen peace plan. Preserving the territorial integrity of a United Nations member state, supposedly the very rationale behind the Vance–Owen approach, turns out to have been just one more disputable detail. "I'm a realist," proclaimed Lord Owen, echoed by the Governments in London and Paris that employed him to create the illusion of principled diplomacy.
>
> (*New York Times*, 19 June 1993: A14)

George Kenney accused Messrs. Vance and Owen of collaboration with the aggressor:

> United Nations "negotiations" over Bosnia are so utterly obscene they do not warrant serious comment. Only force on the ground counts. Lord Owen, abandoning the peace plan he co-authored with Cyrus Vance, admitted as much, despite his naive plea for negotiations to continue. Both diplomats bear a heavy responsibility for collaborating with Serbian aggression.[10]
>
> (Kenney 1993a: E17)

Another example of the ugly side of what appeared to be Western evenhandedness is the arms embargo that was imposed on all the former Yugoslav republics shortly after fighting first broke out in 1991. This arms embargo did not hurt Serbia, which had seized almost all the military hardware of the former Yugoslavia, but made it impossible for Bosnia and Croatia to defend themselves. Even the economic embargo that was imposed on Serbia – but was never enforced effectively – did not stop Serbia from openly importing petroleum and other goods that it needed, so that Serbia's victims felt that the West was, in effect, punishing them, not Serbia. For example, the ongoing Balkan War prevented Croatia from making use of her once lucrative tourist industry along the Adriatic Coast, so that even without official sanctions of the sort that were imposed on Serbia (but not enforced), Croatia was hurt by Western refusal to stop Serbian aggression. Moreover, Serbia had been stockpiling weapons for just this occasion for years, and in one publicized instance had purchased at least 14,000 tons of weapons despite the United Nations sanctions (*New York Times*, 6 July 1992: A4). In fact, Serbia had stockpiled so many weapons that it was able to sell them on the open market for hard currency. Serbia's victims did not stand a chance against such military superiority, and yet the Croats and Muslims were frequently blamed for defending themselves to the best of their abilities (*New York Times*, 24 April 1992: A4).

The West's behavior could be described in terms of Enlightenment narratives as being even-handed, objective, non-partisan, and scrupulously "fair" in that all parties were treated equally. But such objectivity and fairness presuppose democratic and just conditions that simply did not exist in the Balkans. As a result, Western policy toward the Balkans actually damaged the peace process and gave tacit support to Serbia, who was labeled the aggressor (*New York Times*, 10 July 1992: A1).[11] This is because the West's refusal to take sides in the Balkan crisis gave support to the better equipped Serbs, who conquered most of Bosnia while the West continued to engage in its high and mighty discussions of the value of negotiation.

WHAT WAS REALLY AT STAKE?

Despite Western efforts to preserve the unity of former Yugoslavia, in Summer 1992 Yugoslavia became a thing of the past. What was called the Yugoslav "civil war" – a euphemism for slaughter, because Serbia's victims never had a fighting chance – was actually a struggle for Slovene, Croatian, and Bosnian self-determination against Serbia's imperialist quest for a Greater Serbia, revenge, and territorial aggrandizement. In 1991, Germany – the great counter-Enlightenment alternative to the French and British traditions – stepped back into history to fill the leadership void left by American and Western European equivocation by pushing for the diplomatic recognition of these breakaway republics which no longer wanted to be a part of the Serbian Empire masquerading as communist Yugoslavia. But neither Germany nor the rest of the European Community took a decisive, military stand against Serbian aggression, even after Serbian "ethnic cleansing" – a euphemism for genocide that was invented by the Serbs and adopted by Western news media – and other atrocities were well documented. When he resigned on Christmas Eve, 1991, President Mikhail Gorbachev warned that the fate of the former USSR was to be found in the bloody unraveling of what used to be Yugoslavia. As the war dragged on from 1991 to 1993, it became increasingly clear that Yugoslavia was becoming the symbol of the destiny of many

postcommunist nations as well as of the failure of the so-called New World Order
to replace the enmity of the Cold War with a world democratic movement. "Instead
of a new world order, there is a great deal of disorder," George Melloan wrote
(*Wall Street Journal*, 1 June 1992: A13). And in an essay entitled, "Bush's New
World Order Evokes Only Cynicism," Anthony Lewis wrote:

> The greatest failure, the one that will forever stain George Bush's reputation,
> has been in the former Yugoslavia. Bold American leadership, exercised in a
> timely way, could have prevented much of the political and human disaster. Mr.
> Bush wrung his hands. He is still wringing them. . . . How is it possible to square
> the feeble, feckless Bush of these events with the gung-ho President who rallied
> the world against Saddam Hussein? Does the difference come down to oil?
>
> (*New York Times*, 28 September 1992: A14)

As late as 14 June 1992 – when Serbia had already conquered one-third of Croatia
and two-thirds of Bosnia – the United States Ambassador to Yugoslavia, Warren
Zimmerman, predicted for the *New York Times* (p.E9) that the Yugoslavs "will
come back into some form of an association." The continued clinging to the
Yugoslav idea exhibited by the United States as well as Western European powers
constitutes a serious instance of cultural lag or inertia, an unrealistic response to
the world-wide implications of the socio-political crisis in the Balkans, and the
shirking of Enlightenment-based traditions that honor the quest for democracy.

Despite the fanfare that greeted the idea of a sort of United States of Europe, the
Europeans would not help Serbia's victims. This is understandable if one considers
that, traditionally, Europeans have regarded the Balkans as a sort of Third World
on the doorstep of Europe. United States foreign policy on the Balkans was divided
between a Congress that was sympathetic toward granting diplomatic recognition
to Slovenia, Croatia, Bosnia-Herzegovina and the other breakaway republics and
that called for an active – including military – American role in stopping the
Serbian conquest of its neighbors, versus a State Department that acted to preserve
Yugoslavia or otherwise to present a neutral position. Deputy Secretary of State
Lawrence Eagleburger was accused of being soft on Serbia due to his business and
other ties with Serbia (Glynn 1992).[12] As a result of this internal conflict and
resultant paralysis, the United States quickly lost its position of leadership in the
post-Cold-War world. The overall indecisiveness led to a passionless indifference
toward human suffering in the Balkans that could be characterized as sadistic. Each
passing day brought reports of atrocities that were documented by respected
organizations such as the Helsinki Watch Committee and the American State
Department in a matter-of-fact manner. Rapes were investigated, concentration
camps were studied, and murder was confirmed, but the world was not moved.
Here again one should be reminded of Georg Simmel's ([1900] 1990) searing
critique of objective culture: its penchant for quantification at the expense of
subjective, emotional reactions.[13] In a pathetic display of pedantry, the West's
response to reports of atrocities was to study them,[14] not to put a stop to them and
then to study them. The concentration camps that were discovered by the news

media in mid-1992[15] were still operating in the Spring of 1993, but by then, they were no longer discussed by politicians or journalists.[16] And this vicarious sadism was not lost on the Islamic world, which concluded that had the roles been reversed such that Bosnian Muslims were attacking Christian Serbs, the Christian West would have acted swiftly to save its own kind.

The following question was posed repeatedly in editorials in the *New York Times*: how could the West stand on the sidelines and allow the murder in the Balkans to continue?[17] One reply is that the Cartesian tradition which was incorporated into Enlightenment narratives is unsuited for action in the face of moral dilemmas. Rationality is best suited for rationalization, including the rationalization of viciousness, and is not an adequate basis for moral decision-making (Schopenhauer [1841] 1965c). In a most Cartesian manner, Western analysts took their time to study, analyze, and gather data when confronted with reports of Serbian atrocities. And even when these atrocities had been documented in a scientific manner – as if affronts to moral consciousness constitute a role for science, and as if video documentation obtained by journalists was insufficient – the West did not act in accordance with its publicly proclaimed quest to protect human rights. Despite the refrain heard following the Holocaust – Never Again! – genocide in the former Yugoslavia continued despite massive news coverage (Brzezinski 1993b). The news media interviewed scores of Muslim and Croat women who had been raped brutally by the Serbs, yet there was never an organized outcry from the West's many feminist organizations. Similarly, the postmodern promises of tolerance and respect for cultural and moral relativism led to moral and political paralysis.

For the purposes of the present discussion, it is important to emphasize that rationalism is not the only or even the most important tradition in Enlightenment narratives. These same narratives include the Judeo-Christian traditions of compassion and justice, as well as the tradition first cited by Alexis de Tocqueville ([1845] 1945: 31), that America is the beacon of democracy in the world. The symbol of America as the New World or New Jerusalem that would achieve the promise of democracy that floundered in the Old World of Europe continues to exert its influence in the present *fin de siècle*, even if it is highly controversial (for more on the controversy, see Rojek and Turner 1993). For example, it is well known that the United States typically leads forceful actions taken by the United Nations as well as its allies, most notably Britain and France. And as we have noted already, compassion as empathy, *caritas*, or co-suffering is fundamentally different from pity, humanitarianism, and bureaucratic charity, which are tinged with an air of superiority but fail to ameliorate the conditions that cause suffering and the need for charity in the first place. Humanitarian efforts in the late twentieth century, such as the delivery of food and clothing to Bosnia-Herzegovina and Somalia in the 1990s, are bureaucratized, thinly disguised vestiges of colonialism. The Bosnians, in particular, interpreted Western humanitarian aid – which often consisted of military rations left over from the Gulf War – as an excuse for inaction relative to the agenda sought by the Bosnians, namely, military intervention against Serbia.

Today's Cartesians as well as the Baudrillard-type postmodernists are likely to reject these other Western traditions (Judeo-Christian compassion and justice) as an adequate basis for foreign policy. In the first place, these phenomena are traditions or habits, and the postmodernists, along with the modernists, abhor tradition. Second, compassion seems laughable in a world dominated by the will to power – one thinks of Gandhi's letter to Adolf Hitler asking him to please stop his aggression. Yet, compassion and the image of America as the beacon of democracy were invoked unabashedly by President Bush in 1991 in order to justify the military effort to rescue Kuwait from Iraq. Indeed, and in line with Robert N. Bellah's (1967) concept of American civil religion, President Bush frequently invoked God to justify the bombing raids on Iraq, characterizing them as "God's work." Why, then, was it suddenly embarrassing to invoke these same cultural ideals and American civil religion in the Balkans? The Bush Administration tried to explain that the atrocities in the Balkans were not of the same order as the atrocities committed by Saddam Hussein, but this line of reasoning did not convince the opinion-makers and pundits. The editors of leading American newspapers concluded, and I think correctly, that President Bush had no coherent post-Cold-War foreign policy to offer.[18]

In 1991, it was taboo to raise the question whether the United States acted in the Gulf War from the publicly touted motives of defending human rights and democracy – or for oil. A year later, editorials in the *New York Times* (21 May 1992: A14) and other leading publications claimed routinely that the United States led the West against Iraq for the sake of oil. For example, "though their leaders usually spoke loftily of reversing aggression and enforcing a new world order, Americans understood why they should get involved in Kuwait: it was to make the world safe for Saudi Arabian oil" (*New York Times*, 16 July 1992: A4). Another year later, in 1993, the opinion-makers could not defend any of the public motives or justifications for the Gulf War – nor the repeated bombing of Baghdad in the final weeks of Mr. Bush's Presidency – save for Mr. Bush's personal animosity for Mr. Hussein. Steven Graubard (1992)[19] gives another explanation: President Bush was imitating Margaret Thatcher's tidy and "successful" Falklands War – not a war for oil, but a war for image. Oil could have been protected by keeping the troops in Saudi Arabia, but President Bush, his "manhood" challenged by Margaret Thatcher, had to have his own neat and tidy, perfect (in the postmodern sense) war.

Even if any of these or other equally cynical assessments[20] of the motives for the Gulf War are correct to any degree, the true motives for the Gulf War were nevertheless shrouded, loudly and ostentatiously, in the moral and compassionate language of standing up for human rights and democracy. The average American could never concede publicly that he or she would send a son or daughter to die in a war for the sake of a barrel of petroleum. Such a notion is still highly offensive to the tenets of American civil religion. Yet the rhetoric of standing up for human rights and democracy, which dominated the Gulf War, was conspicuously absent in public political discourse concerning the Balkans. This fact eventually left many Americans feeling as if they had been deceived, and unsure when real democracy and human rights are at stake. And this cynicism made it even more difficult to involve the American people seriously in stopping Serbian or any other post-Gulf-War aggression. For example, on 22 April 1993, fully 68 per cent of the American people were *against* the bombing of Serbian military targets in order to stop the atrocities in Bosnia-Herzegovina.[21]

In sum, and notwithstanding United Nations resolutions against Serbia as well as the West's rhetoric of protest against Serbian atrocities, Serbian President Milošević achieved what the Islamic President, Saddam Hussein, was not allowed to achieve, namely, the change of international borders through the use of brute force. The rationalization that Mr. Hussein attacked a bona fide country, Kuwait, while the war in former Yugoslavia was a civil war is a lame explanation. By the legalistic standards of the West, this contemporary Balkan War was never a civil war, but a war for territory waged by Serbia against the sovereign and duly recognized nations of Bosnia-Herzegovina and Croatia.

The Islamic nations drew their own conclusions from these hypocritical efforts by the West to justify its willingness to let the slaughter in Bosnia-Herzegovina continue, week after week, one bloody month after another, year in and year out. From the Islamic point of view, the Christian West had pitted itself repeatedly against Muslims in Iran, Iraq, Afghanistan, Kashmir, Azerbaijan, Palestine, Somalia, and Bosnia. The conceptual distinction between Christian and Islamic nations became so powerful that Croatia came to be perceived as the enemy of Bosnian Muslims even though the Croats and Muslims were allies against Serbia for much of 1992. From the Islamic point of view, it seemed as if the West would not tolerate any infraction of UN resolutions on the part of Muslims, but tolerated all sorts of infractions of similar UN resolutions committed by the Christian Serbs.

For example, the United Nations and the Western powers took no military action against Serbia when, on 7 February 1993, Serbian gunners downed a United Nations relief flight bound from Zagreb, Croatia to Sarajevo, Bosnia-Herzegovina. There did not exist any doubt that Serbian gunners hit the airplane. According to Chuck Sudetic, reporter for the *New York Times*: "The United Nations said its peace-keeping troops witnessed the Serbs shooting at the German plane with a 23-millimeter antiaircraft gun set up in the village of Kosijersko Selo, which lies in a Serbian-occupied swath of Croatia under United Nations protection" (9 February 1993: A6). The United Nations issued a verbal protest, but negotiations continued in New York City, and so did the violence and ethnic cleansing in former Yugoslavia. Yet, a month prior to this event, the United States, Britain, and France bombed Iraq merely for turning on their radar while Allied flights were in the area. Christian Croats and Muslim Bosnians shared a similar fate.

What was really at stake in the Balkan War of the 1990s? The credibility of the West and the values derived from the Enlightenment, including the West's standards of morality.

SERBIAN ACTIONS AS CRIMES AGAINST HUMANITY

Despite the public efforts by the United States and the European Community to help the Yugoslavs settle their differences through negotiation, war broke out in the Summer of 1991, first between Serbia and Slovenia, and then between Serbia and Croatia. Fighting spread to Bosnia-Herzegovina in the Spring of 1992. The annexation of Vojvodina and Kosovo by Serbia occurred silently and secretly from 1991 to 1993. The Helsinki Watch Committee and other neutral sources have estimated that the war in the Balkans has resulted in at least 150,000 casualties and over three million refugees.[22] Most of the casualties are civilians, including many women and children. Croatian and Bosnian newspapers noted that the Serbian regime was more brutal and destructive than Hitler, Mussolini, Napoleon, or other dictators who had attacked the same territories in the past. These other dictators did not destroy cultural treasures such as Dubrovnik, whereas the postmodern world watched the Serbian bombing of Dubrovnik and other cities on television – and did absolutely nothing to stop it. When the war spread to Bosnia-Herzegovina, the cultural destruction was just as deliberate:

> Undercutting denials by [Serbian] government leaders that there is no official policy behind the forced expulsion of Muslim Slavs and Croats from the Serbian Republic [of Bosnia], Mr. Simo Drljaca speaks frankly of how to "cleanse" undesirables. "With the mosques, you must not just break the minarets," he said. "You've got to shake up the foundation because that means they cannot build another. Do that, and they'll want to go. They'll just leave by themselves."
>
> (*New York Times*, 22 August 1992: A3)

Serbian snipers repeatedly and deliberately targeted civilians – including children. Slobodan Milošević's regime waged a military campaign to obtain territory by terrorizing, torturing, starving, murdering, and raping civilians.[23] In effect, the Serbs had organized criminal activity into a quasi-military strategy. "It is just like killing rabbits," said a Serbian sniper of killing civilians in Sarajevo, and added, "I feel nothing" (*Wall Street Journal*, 16 September 1992: A1). "The whole idea of the [Serbian] attack is to humiliate, to punish and to subjugate the population" (*New York Times*, 9 June 1992: A6).[24]

The fighting was particularly brutal. In its report entitled *War Crimes in Bosnia-Herzegovina*, the Helsinki Watch Committee warned:

> The findings in this report, and the reports from Bosnia-Herzegovina by independent news media, provide at the very least *prima facie* evidence that genocide is taking place. The "ethnic cleansing" that is being practiced by Serbian forces is directed particularly against Muslims and Croats on the basis of their religion and ethnicity. The victims of such "ethnic cleansing" have been expelled from their homes and villages, rounded up and held in detention camps; deported; killed in indiscriminate attacks; and summarily executed. . . . Genocide is the most unspeakable crime in the lexicon. The authorization that

the Convention provides to the United Nations to prevent and suppress this crime carries with it an obligation to act.

(1992c: 1–2)

But the United Nations did not act to prevent and suppress this crime, only to deliver humanitarian aid to the victims who had escaped with their lives. A standard rationalization for not acting was that all sides were equally guilty of atrocities. For example, the Croatian and Bosnian governments were also accused of human rights abuses.[25] Yet according to the USA State Department, Croatian and Muslim atrocities paled in comparison with those of the Serbians. Even as the United States was gathering facts for its reports, the city of Sarajevo was bombed daily by the Serbs. Even when the West's accusations against Croats and Muslims became a self-fulfilling prophecy by the summer of 1993, in that Croats and Muslims did engage in large-scale ethnic cleansing against each other, one can scarcely discount the desperation and sense of betrayal that drove them to imitate the Serbs (*New York Times*, 26 February 1993: A15).

In sum, the frequent efforts to equalize the aggressor with the victim in the Balkan War will doubtless go down in history as one of the West's most pathetic hypocrisies. Western criminal law makes fine distinctions in degrees of guilt, but refused to apply these distinctions to the Balkan War. Moreover, from the Muslim point of view, it is of interest that the deliberate bombing of civilian targets in Iraq during and long after the Gulf War – an action that is, technically speaking, a war crime – never received the scrutiny with which the West assessed non-Western atrocities.

A reporter for the *New York Times*, John F. Burns, cites numerous instances of Serbian barbarism, such as the one in which Chetnik soldiers dispassionately cut the throats of all citizens whose names indicated that they were Muslim (10 July 1992: A1). In addition, the Serbian-backed armies had destroyed hundreds of cultural landmarks, and had bombed hospitals, schools, and churches that could not possibly have been construed as military targets. A visitor to the war zone found evidence of random bombardment of civilian homes. European Community observers and other neutral parties had documented deliberate shooting of civilians and, in some cases, of the observers themselves. And all this despite the deployment of United Nations peacekeeping troops. The Croatian as well as the Bosnian press claimed that the Serbian government counted on the United Nations to legitimize its territorial gains. From the perspective of Serbia's victims, it was little wonder that UNPROFOR (United Nations Protective Force) was labeled as SERBOFOR by the Croats and Muslims, and that United Nations Secretary-General, Boutros Boutros-Ghali, was jeered when he visited Sarajevo. Despite its rhetoric of protecting values that stem from the Enlightenment narratives, in practice, the United Nations gave tacit support to the Serbian aggressor. In general, United Nations presence in former Yugoslavia did not detract from Serbia's openly proclaimed policy of establishing a Greater Serbia (*Wall Street Journal*, 28 May 1992: A10). On the contrary, the UN frequently aided Serbian aggression. A case in point is the proud announcement by the UN on 22 April 1993 that they had demilitarized and disarmed Srebrenica so that it could be surrendered to the Serbs (ibid.: A1).

Ever since the conflict began in former Yugoslavia in the Summer of 1991, each successive cease-fire was followed by an exponential increase in the number of casualties. Cease-fires came and went – the media stopped counting after the fortieth one was violated – and were apparently taken seriously only by the Western diplomats who had negotiated them. Despite all the negotiations as well as the presence of United Nations troops, the Serbs had created racially "pure" areas in formerly Croatian and Muslim territories by evacuating or executing all non-Serbs along the fronts (*New York Times*, 10 May 1992: A3; 3 June 1992: A10). Given this colossal failure of the United Nations and other modernist, Western institutions to halt Serbian aggression, one must confront the question: is the West implicated in Serbian war crimes?[26]

THE CULTURAL ROOTS OF THE WEST'S IMPOTENCE

Suppose that one seeks to discount the argument put forth above that the West shared – at least vicariously, and perhaps secretly, even secretly from itself, in a Freudian sense – in Serbia's blatant imperialism. How can one explain the mighty West's impotence and incompetence in dealing with a third-rate dictator such as Slobodan Milošević? (a question also posed in the *Wall Street Journal*, 20 May 1992: A14.) In the past few decades, Western discourse in diverse fields, including politics, has been dominated by a cultural movement labeled postmodernism. Contributors to the *political* discourse on postmodernism tend to conclude that it results in moral and governmental paralysis, even nihilism (Heller and Feher 1988). Consider the views put forth by Jean Baudrillard (1981): if postmodern social life in Western countries consists of ideas, simulations, and "circulating fictions" that have no firm origin, referent, or roots, then nothing is true, and no position is morally superior to another. The postmodern stance is an extension of the extreme cultural relativist position that flows from the West's Cartesianism and neo-Kantianism, and that has been documented and criticized by many notable authors (Gellner 1992a). Yet there is more to the claim that postmodern reality consists of fictions played out on the television screen, a theme that we explored in the previous chapter. The implication seems to be that the West's seemingly high standards of human rights apply only to the comfortable few, while the rest of the population "must exit."

Yet this cruel attitude toward the powerless is not fundamentally different from colonial and imperialist attitudes toward the many peoples that were exterminated by white Europeans in the name of some glorified ideal that was eventually associated with Enlightenment narratives. Baudrillard's critics have accused him of unwittingly promoting a cruel and inhumane stance, for the dismissal of all social events as fictitious ignores the very real brutality imposed by Saddam Hussein, Slobodan Milošević, and other dictators upon their victims. But one could argue that regardless of what Baudrillard's personal motives might be, his characterization of postmodern sadism suggests why the West implicitly chose to align itself with the Serbian aggressor in the contemporary Balkan War.

In addition, if one focuses on the aspects of the postmodern argument that pertain to power relationships rather than epistemology (as in the previous chapter), it seems to contain an important kernel of truth. For example, one might speculate that had Kuwait failed to purchase the services of a competent public relations firm prior to the Gulf War, the American public could not have been manipulated into displaying its traditional compassion (cited by Tocqueville [1845] 1945) for victims of human rights abuse for the simple reason that it would not have been able to distinguish the victim from the aggressor. After all, Iraq was a former ally of the USA, and Kuwait had been blatantly hostile to the United States for many years prior to the Gulf War.

This fact exposes a neglected aspect of the sociological "construction of reality" (from Berger and Luckmann 1967) in the current Balkan War. The comparatively wealthy Serbian government had purchased the services of a competent American public relations firm, while the relatively poorer Croatian and Bosnian governments were not able to do so. The results were entirely predictable: the Serbian propaganda machine associated the Croatians with the pro-Nazi Ustase atrocities of World War II, and monopolized the American news broadcasts, which originated more from Belgrade than from Zagreb. The obvious historical fact that Serbia also collaborated with the Nazis during World War II was almost completely suppressed (Cohen 1992, Vuković 1991).[27]

Only the siege of Sarajevo changed the Serbian domination of the news media, because it was the site of the 1984 Olympics and is recognizable to a good deal of the world's population – especially the American population of avid television watchers. Nevertheless, at least initially, the American public was far more likely to sympathize with the plight of the Serbs, who claimed that their civil rights were violated or in danger of being violated, than with the Croats and Muslims, who accused the Serbs of genocide (*New York Times*, 9 June 1992: A6). Subsequent documentation of Serbian genocide against the Croats and Muslims by fact-gathering organizations such as the International Red Cross, the Helsinki Watch Committee, and the American State Department, among others, did not change this set of circumstances. Serbia had won the propaganda war, not on the basis of objective facts, but because it could purchase the ability to sway public opinion.

Philip J. Cohen (1993) has documented the fact that the Serbian side had misappropriated the history of the Holocaust in its propaganda campaign. According to Cohen, Serbia also collaborated with the Nazis during World War II, and its puppet dictator, Milan Nedić, boasted to Hitler that Serbia was the first country in Europe to achieve the final solution by exterminating 94 per cent of the Serbian Jews. Yet the connection between the Serbian Chetniks and the Holocaust remains practically unreported in coverage of the background context of the current war. Serbia, the aggressor, succeeded in presenting itself to the world as the victim.[28]

Germany is a major exception to this generalization. The Germans know the history of Nazism more directly than other Europeans. When exposed to the media reports of *contemporary* and self-proclaimed *Chetnik* forces that were backed by the Yugoslav Federal army and the Serbian government, a majority of the German public came to the conclusion that something like the Holocaust was re-emerging in Europe. Probably as an effort to overcome the collective guilt of its Nazi past, the German government decided as early as 1991 that Germany should step back into history and do something good for Europe – which was translated into supporting the Croats, Bosnians, and Slovenes against the Serbian government.

This German move was interpreted by other Western nations – especially Britain and France – as Germany's attempt to revive its old dreams of Empire-building. Even if the British and French are correct to some extent, the important point is that Serbian propaganda did not work on the Germans. For most of the rest of the world, it worked all too well. The cynical conclusion that follows from the preceding is that sympathy for one or the other party in the present conflict depends mostly on the selling of video images, not "reality." The widespread use of public relations firms to package and sell a nation's position in a war places moral causes on the same level as selling toothpaste or beer. This assessment flows from applying Adorno's argument in *The Culture Industry* (1991), and the insights of the Frankfurt School in general, to an aspect of the postmodern focus on fictions that is not accounted for by Baudrillard. Power, not epistemology, still lies at the basis of transnational relations.

THE FATE OF AMERICA'S ROLE AS LEADER OF THE DEMOCRATIC REVOLUTION

In his *America and the World Revolution*, the historian Arnold Toynbee (1962) wrote of America's historical role as a world leader in the democratic revolution ever since the firing of the shot that was heard around the world in Concord in 1774. He treats the terms American, Western, and modern as synonyms. But, writing in 1962, Toynbee claimed,

> Today America is no longer the inspirer and leader of the World Revolution, and I have an impression that she is embarrassed and annoyed when she is reminded that this was her original mission. No one else laid this mission upon America. She chose it for herself. . . . By contrast, America is today the leader of a world-wide anti-revolutionary movement in defense of vested interests. She now stands for what Rome stood for. . . . Playing Metternich is not a happy role. It is not a hero's role, and not a winner's, and the player knows it.
>
> (1962: 91)

For the purposes of the present discussion, it is important to analyze the implicitly sociological argument in Toynbee's historical analysis. Toynbee comes very close to making the Durkheimian argument that America used to be a moral symbol because she stood for derivatives of *caritas*, including justice and fair play, but that she lost this role by succumbing to blatant narcissism. According to Toynbee,

The paramount aim of the people of the US is the protection of their own vested interests, and they are not concerned for social justice except in so far as this can be made to serve a purpose that is, in truth, the opposite of what social justice stands for.

(ibid.: 217)

Toynbee supports his claim by noting that Americans ignored Hitler, but hated the communists, who could have affected their pocket-books (ibid.: 94). America became rich, hence conservative: "The American people are now feeling and acting as a champion of an affluent minority's vested interests, in dramatic contrast to America's historic role as the revolutionary leader of the depressed majority of mankind" (ibid.: 97). In general, "since 1917, American has reversed her role in the World. She has become the arch-conservative power instead of the arch-revolutionary one" (ibid.: 102). It is important to note that Toynbee's characterization of America coincides with Jean Baudrillard's portrait in *America* (1986), even if their explanations differ. For example, Baudrillard does not bother to make a value judgment concerning America's transition to heartless narcissism.

It is as true now as it was when Toynbee claimed it, that most of humanity remained poor as America and the West grew rich. All Western countries have "gone American" (1962: 144), but what is the purpose of this trend? Toynbee's answer is that the purpose is to consume and to possess, not to be moral. He asks, "Why has Western Christianity been less successful than Western science?" (ibid.: 43). This, too, is an implicitly Durkheimian question, so long as one notes that neither Durkheim nor Toynbee saw any essential differences between American, Hindu, Muslim or any other versions of morality as some sort of refraction of *caritas*. The important point seems to be that America lost her power as the symbol of morality as she slowly but steadily "succeeded" materially.

For our purposes, it is completely beside the point whether America "really" stood for justice and freedom in the past. Many historians have claimed, in contradistinction to Toynbee, that only a third of the American population wanted freedom from Great Britain in the 1760s.[29] A postmodern discussion of the sort being offered here is not going to pursue "reality," whatever that might be. The more important points, for our purposes, are that (1) America was *perceived* in her old-fashioned role as symbol of freedom by many postcommunist nations, and (2) the Balkanization of America stems from the dominance of narcissism, consumerism, and blatant egoism at the expense of *caritas*.

For example, Croats, Slovenes, and Bosnians expected the Americans to receive them with open arms when they declared their independence from Serbian domination. After all, weren't they imitating the American thirst for freedom? In trying to explain to its peoples why the United States waited for months to grant them diplomatic recognition, and made them defenseless against the hardline Serbian government by imposing an arms embargo on them, the press in Croatia, Slovenia, and Bosnia-Herzegovina arrived at the following conclusions: the United States acted in the Gulf War for the sake of petroleum, not democracy; it recognized the Ukraine because of the threat that the nuclear weapons on its territory might fall into the "wrong hands" (those of nationalists and Islamic fundamentalists); it forgave China for the Tiananmen Square massacre so that China would not veto its proposals against Iraq that were put through the United Nations Security Council; and in general, that the United States and Western Europe act on the basis of cold pragmatism that protects the status quo, not the democratic principles they espouse. Self-determination in Bosnia-Herzegovina, Croatia, and Slovenia threatened this status quo, and set a precedent for the dissolution of covert Empires throughout the world. Thus, diplomatic recognition was delayed, moral support was denied, and these fledgling democracies were abandoned to fend for themselves.

Western politicians rationalized their inaction by claiming that the Balkan crisis is complex. Actually, it was brutally simple and clear at the beginning: well-documented Serbian aggression and barbarism constituted an affront to internationally recognized standards of human rights, national sovereignty, and political behavior – the very things that the West claimed it stood for. The solution should have been equally straightforward: the international collective conscience should have acted decisively on behalf of historically rooted and traditional values regarding the sanctity of human life and national sovereignty. Instead, the international community acted (or failed to act) in order to promote vested interests. These vested interests included, but were not limited to, discouraging the break-up of nation-states; supporting the role of Serbia as policeman in the Balkans; and making international organizations such as the United Nations, the European Community, and others look effective, when, in fact, they had proven themselves to be impotent in many regards.

In other words, the West should have acted *on purely moral grounds*, because the fate of the postcommunist world was at stake. Given the course of postcommunist developments *vis-à-vis* Western rhetoric concerning democracy and universal human rights, why in the world should postcommunist nations want to emulate the West? What will our children say about us when they read about Balkan genocide in their history books? These are the questions that the West must weigh in its seemingly rational deliberations in these postmodern times.

DOES THE WORLD HAVE A COLLECTIVE CONSCIOUSNESS?

A discussion of this sort is necessarily incomplete if one fails to invoke Emile Durkheim's neglected concept of the collective consciousness. In *The Division of Labor in Society*, Durkheim claimed that "the totality of beliefs and sentiments common to average citizens of the same society forms a determinate system which has its own life; one may call it the *collective* or *common conscience*" ([1893] 1933: 79). Durkheimian scholars have not yet resolved three issues that are central to the present discussion: (1) Does Durkheim's use of the French term *conscience* imply epistemological consciousness or moral conscience or both? (2) Does the collective consciousness disappear with the development of individualism? (3) Is it true that an act ceases to be criminal if it is not punished by the collective consciousness, along the lines of Durkheim's assertions that

> An act is criminal when it offends strong and defined states of the collective consciousness. In other words, we must not say that an action shocks the common consciousness because it is criminal, but rather that it is criminal because it shocks the common consciousness. We do not reprove it because it is a crime, but it is a crime because we reprove it.
>
> (ibid.: 80–81)

I do not hope to resolve these purely academic issues within the confines of the present discussion, although I have addressed them elsewhere (see Meštrović 1988, 1991, 1993). Let us translate Durkheim's use of the French *conscience* as conscience, with the understanding that consciousness is also implied – thus, collective conscience. And let us entertain the hypothesis, without hoping to resolve it here, that it may be true that with the development of narcissism the postmodern West has, indeed, languished in social solidarity and morality, e.g., the collective conscience. This leads to the most disturbing hypothesis of all, that the West's failure to punish Serbian aggression within the heart of Europe in the postcommunist and postmodern contexts may indeed signal the end of morality. If acts are criminal only if punished, then failure to punish Serbian aggression means that this aggression and its attendant crimes are not really crimes.

Note that Durkheim's assumptions fly in the face of the West's Enlightenment-based assumptions. The West had behaved in the Balkans as if acts are criminal if they are labeled as such by the United Nations or other legal bodies whose legitimacy the West recognizes. But Durkheim claims that if the collective conscience tolerates crime, the crime ceases to exist as such. The question arises: whose collective conscience is involved? It is true that throughout *The Division of Labor* Durkheim discusses the collective conscience in particular societies, not the international "community." Yet, to the extent that the term, international community, is not yet another postmodern euphemism, it seems to follow that the same principles that Durkheim ascribes to particular societies should apply to a cosmopolitan society of the world, namely: "Crime is not simply the disruption even of serious interests; it is an offense against an authority in some ways transcendent. But, from experience, there is no moral force superior to the individual save collective force" (ibid.: 85).

Durkheim upholds the cultural relativist position that today's disciples of the Enlightenment criticize, as when he writes that "an act is socially bad because society disapproves of it" (ibid.: 82). He adds that "what characterizes crime is that it determines punishment" (p. 85). Thus, crimes will vary tremendously from one society to the next and across historical time periods, yet, paradoxically, "as numerous as the varieties are, crime is everywhere essentially the same, since it everywhere calls forth the same effect, in respect of punishment, which if it can be more or less intense, does not by that change its nature" (ibid.: 83).

The punishment to which Durkheim refers must involve cruel vengeance, to some extent:

> It is an error to believe that vengeance is but useless cruelty. . . . We avenge ourselves only upon what has done us evil, and what has done us evil is always dangerous.
>
> (ibid.: 87)

> And in truth, punishment has remained, at least in part, a work of vengeance.
>
> (ibid.: 88)

> What we avenge, what the criminal expiates, is the outrage to morality.
>
> (ibid.: 89)

Charles Schoenfeld (1966b) finds a similar emphasis on retribution in punishment within psychoanalysis, and also, albeit unconsciously, within Western law itself (see Schoenfeld 1974). To be sure, Western intellectuals will point to the Enlightenment legacy as one in which punishment of the criminal is supposedly less cruel than it was in the past. But Schoenfeld (1974) is right to point out that even the so-called humane, modern prison system is nevertheless vengeful and cruel in that it exposes convicted criminals to the stress of monotony, forced homosexuality, and a bare-minimum biological existence that in no way prepares them for subsequent assimilation into modern society. The important point is that cruelty is an integral aspect of punishment, even in the West, and despite the fact that many Westerners would never admit this.

But one would be missing Durkheim's point if one regarded any and all state-sponsored acts of vengeance as moral actions. For example, I believe that Durkheim would not have regarded President Clinton's bombing of Iraqi civilians in June 1993 as a moral act of the collective consciousness. This is because President Clinton and his Administration justified this act with reference to the Enlightenment principle of self-interest. For Durkheim, self-interest is never moral, because it is based on egoism, and egoism is a disintegrative force that works against *caritas*.[30] The moral vengeance must be applied on behalf of the collective principle of compassion or *caritas* – and contemporary humanity is far from being able to make out what such standards might be, practically speaking.

Let us apply Durkheim's insights to the present discussion of the West's reaction to crimes against humanity in the Balkans. The West imposed sanctions against Serbia, not to punish her, but ostensibly to try to convince her to stop her campaign for a Greater Serbia (and this effort failed). Secretary of State Warren Christopher has stated repeatedly that punishing Serbia is not in America's self-interest. In sum, Serbia's crimes against humanity have not been punished by the world's collective conscience, and therefore have ceased to be crimes. On the contrary, the world has accepted the methods by which Serbia acquired territory, namely through force.

If Durkheim is right that crime determines punishment, and if his analysis concerning individual societies is applied to the world community, then it seems to follow that Serbia ought to be punished through military action against Serbian military targets, even if the military analysts are right that such action would not meet the test of having tangible military or political goals relative to Western self-interest. The goal ought to be to preserve the moral integration of the world community: punishment in the name of *caritas* for all the innocents who continue to be slaughtered in the Balkans. Disciples of the Enlightenment might label this conclusion as traditional, cruel, vengeful, and contrary to the principles of the Enlightenment. (But they are much more likely to conclude that it is not in the West's interest to stop Serbian aggression.) On the other hand, Durkheim might have claimed that today's disciples of the Enlightenment have undermined the moral power of the world community by their inability and unwillingness to punish Serbian aggression. One cannot have it both ways.

If crimes – collective or individual – are not avenged, if expiation is not exacted, then the collective conscience is weakened, which gives rise to other crimes in the future. The source of moral outrage only appears to be psychological or derived from the individual. In fact, if one follows Durkheim, the true source of moral outrage is collective and is based on the compassion or *caritas* previously discussed. The social fabric is disrupted if crime is tolerated within individual societies, and likewise if collective crime is tolerated within the world community. The probable reason why the USA and Western Europe have not been able to make a convincing moral argument, or even to exhibit genuine moral outrage at Serbian aggression, is the prevalence of doctrines that stem from narcissism, utilitarianism, self-interest, the Me-generation philosophy and other end-points of the Enlightenment legacy. For Durkheim, morality must be pursued for its own sake, not as the means to some other end, and not on the basis of self-interest.

The West's collective actions in the Gulf War were presented by the media wizards and politicians as inspired by moral outrage but are believed by most analysts to have been motivated by self-interest. The Islamic world perceives itself to be the evil that the West seeks to punish. Durkheim might have predicted such an outcome, for genuine punishment must involve collective, not utilitarian, interests in order to preserve moral unity. One may be tempted to dismiss Durkheim, but his principles do suggest that the West failed to act morally in either the Gulf War or the Balkan War. And for the sake of completeness, Durkheim's critical stance toward the Enlightenment legacy ought to be acknowledged.

To drive this last point home, one has merely to contrast Durkheim's group-centered approach to morality with Lawrence Kohlberg's (1981) Enlightenment-based theory of moral development. Like so many other cognitive structuralists (such as Jean Piaget and James Fowler), Kohlberg begins with the Kantian, Enlightenment assumption that all persons are born with morality inscribed in their minds, but that some progress to "higher," post-conventional stages while others remain stuck in "lower," pre-conventional and conventional stages of morality. Note the ethnocentric bias in Kohlberg's theorizing that characterizes other ideology derived from the Enlightenment: morality is universal, yet some forms of morality are better than others. Thus, Kohlberg (1981) dismisses Durkheim's ([1925] 1961) writing on morality as aiming toward merely conventional morals, doing that which is required by the group.

But against Kohlberg's arrogant dismissal of Durkheim, note that post-conventional thinking automatically presupposes the commission of crime for the sake of "higher" principles. This linkage between universal principles (glorified by the Enlightenment) and ordinary crime is evident in the question that Kohlberg asks in his test to determine one's stage of moral development: should a man named Heinz steal a drug that he needs to save his dying wife, given that the druggist is overcharging for the drug and refuses to give it to him? It is incredible that other, non-violent options are not given to Heinz in Kohlberg's scheme of things, or that the question is not open-ended, "What should Heinz do?" One's level of moral development is scored by Kohlberg and his followers based upon how one reasons and develops a rule for answering whether or not Heinz should steal.

Discussions with my students concerning the Heinz dilemma invariably lead to the axiomatic response, yes, of course Heinz should steal the drug. Further discussion typically reveals that contemporary students feel that they should resort to violence if their desires are frustrated in general. It is the extremely rare student who reasons that perhaps Heinz should work out some sort of compromise or understanding with the druggist. By invoking these examples, I do not mean to offer a critique of Kohlberg on Kantian terms. On the contrary, I hope to make the point that violence is built into Enlightenment-based theories of morality, from Kant to Kohlberg. If Kohlberg assumes that Jesus Christ, Buddha, Martin Luther King, Socrates and other post-conventional thinkers were morally superior to the rest of humanity because they chose to break social norms for the sake of universal principles (as if such principles could exist without culture), then there is little to prevent one from regarding the common criminal as a post-conventional thinker. This is because, in the postmodern context, what one regards as a universal principle is entirely subjective anyway – based on perceived self-interest – given that no principles are presumed to be rooted in one's culture.

And, in fact, most of the post-conventional moral leaders on Kohlberg's list were treated as criminals by the societies in which they lived or the cultures with which they clashed. That is entirely understandable from Durkheim's perspective, as is the fact that they subsequently *became* moral leaders because changes in social circumstances led various collective consciences to endow them with dignity and respect.

More important, for the purposes of the present discussion, the contrast between Kohlberg's Enlightenment-based theory of morality and Durkheim's anti-Enlightenment theory of morality illuminates a hidden aspect of the West's collaboration with Serbian aggression. The mystery of the West's affinity with and sympathy for Serbia's acts in the current Balkan War can be cleared up if one compares Serbia's "moral reasoning" with that of Heinz in the Kohlberg dilemma. Serbia reasoned, very much like Heinz, that certain territories in Croatia, Bosnia, and Kosovo really belong to Serbia. "Should Serbia steal the territories?" is analogous to asking "Should Heinz steal the drug?" In both cases, self-interest is the primary issue. Had Serbia opted for negotiation or some sort of compromise with her neighbors, she would have been merely conventional. But by defying world opinion for the sake of a desire for territory that might as well be a universal principle (in the postmodern bastardization of Kant), Serbia has earned the secret admiration of countries that subscribe most openly to the Enlightenment-based principle of self-interest, including the USA, France, and Britain.

In other words, the end-point of morality based on the Enlightenment in my classroom in Texas is reflected among the West's diplomats: it may be difficult to make out universal principles (as Kant taught), but there are desires, and if someone gets in the way of my desires, I can resort to violence, provided I am prepared to suffer the consequences of that violence. Such is the postmodern version of post-conventional moral reasoning.

IMPLICATIONS

Western intellectuals, diplomats, and politicians engaged in a high-stakes gamble following the collapse of communism. They gambled the credibility, legitimacy, and power of moral principles derived from the Enlightenment. Most of these principles can be reduced to enlightened self-interest, which Durkheim held could never provide a stable basis for moral order. Messrs. Fukuyama and Eagleburger wrote and spoke nobly of how postcommunist nations would automatically follow the Enlightenment path to democracy, free markets, and universal markets. They were wrong, in general, and particularly with regard to the Balkans. Perhaps this Balkan War would have been just another little war and yet another forgotten instance of genocide and unspeakable crimes against humanity were it not for the context in which it occurred: in the heart of Europe, following the collapse of modernist communism, under the postmodern glare of television cameras, and with so much rhetoric concerning Enlightenment ideals.

Because it occurred in these particular circumstances, this Balkan War resulted in the Balkanization of the West. As of 1993, Western opinion-makers write with cynicism when they address the topics of Europe, America's role in the post-Cold-War world, NATO, the UN, moral outrage, humanitarianism, universal human rights and other topics, symbols, and phenomena that pertain to Western culture and societies. I predict that not only will the current Balkan War spill beyond the borders of the former Yugoslavia, but that the Balkanization of the West will also continue unabated. Sociology itself will continue to be Balkanized, and stray further from the noble path that Durkheim envisaged for it a hundred years ago as the moral counselor to the modern world.

Chapter 6

What went wrong with the Enlightenment project?

Jean Baudrillard observes that Alexis de Tocqueville contrasted the "good" America of freedom, democracy, and high regard for the individual with the "bad" America that institutionalized slavery and exterminated the Indians (Baudrillard 1986: 88–9).[1] Of course, Baudrillard and other postmodernists reject Tocqueville's distinction between good and bad traditions, supposedly because such a distinction involves privileged access to truth and morality (Smart 1992: 219). Nevertheless, it is interesting that despite this postmodern disdain for making moral distinctions, many contemporary writers focus on the particularly American and by extension generally Western vices of consumerism, anomie, narcissism, and superficiality as they continue to co-exist with moral ideals of democracy that most of the modern world seems to applaud (Bellah *et al.* 1985, Bloom 1987, Lasch 1991, Riesman 1980a). Baudrillard and the postmodernists have not really transcended Tocqueville.

How does the diverse system of contradictory cultural meanings that make up the modern landscape get transmitted across generations, given that both modernists and postmodernists reject the traditional notion of culture as a system of habits? I agree with Norman K. Denzin that "the major contemporary American (and British) social theorists want to either absorb postmodernism into existing 'modernist' frameworks, or ignore the [cultural] perspective entirely" (1991: 20). Denzin is probably also correct to conclude that "this anti-totalizing stance stems from the belief that terror resides in any attempt to conceptualize societies as coherent, integrated entities" (ibid.). Notwithstanding the actual motives of postmodern intellectuals, the end result is that the postmodernists are unable to explain coherence, continuity, or even the viability of their own, ostensibly pro-democratic, liberating program – not to mention the glaring contradiction we have uncovered so far in the modernist project.

The postmodern program is largely a refraction of the modernist project, namely, Jean-Jacques Rousseau's, John Stuart Mill's, and other Enlightenment glorifications of the lonely individual who wants to eradicate culture, which is, almost by definition, poised against the individual. The American doctrine of "natural rights" (which cropped up in the confirmation hearings of Supreme Court Justice nominee Clarence Thomas) owes its intellectual moorings to this anti-cultural doctrine. Thus, Rousseau (1975) took up the by now well-known position that the human animal is naturally good until the forces of government, society, school, and family warp and cripple him or her.

Similarly, John Stuart Mill ([1859] 1974) argued that liberty is paramount, and can be taken away by the state only to prevent harm to others. In general, according to Mill, "Over himself, over his own body, and mind, the individual is sovereign" (ibid.: 20). In general, "the despotism of custom is everywhere the standing hindrance to human advancement" (p. 136). Ernest Gellner (1992a) has already fleshed out the anti-cultural stand that is inherent in the rest of the Enlightenment project.

Up to now, I have argued that the Western postmodern discourse is not very different from a revival or extension of the Enlightenment project, as opposed to the more genuinely anti-Enlightenment, and therefore more genuinely postmodern movements to be found in Islamic, Balkan, and other cultural movements that oppose the West. Postmodern discussions of tolerance and universal human rights are not very distinct from the teachings of Descartes, Rousseau, Locke and other luminaries from the Enlightenment. Such rhetoric is inadequate because it has not dealt with Durkheim's devastating observation that even individualism is a cultural product or tradition in that no one is born as an individual endowed with natural rights. For proof, one has only to consider the many cultures that do not recognize the Western version of individualism. In such cultures, the individual suffers grievously compared with the rights that he or she enjoys in Western cultures.[2] On the other hand, such traditional cultures also do not suffer as much as Western cultures from the ill-effects of narcissism.

In addition, Barry Smart is probably correct that "increasing rationality cannot guarantee increases in freedom, and to that extent the 'utopian' modern project is in trouble" (1992: 219). One should also consider the completely anti-Enlightenment position voiced by the philosopher, Alfred N. Whitehead: "Unless society is permeated, through and through, with routine, civilization vanishes. So many sociological doctrines, the products of acute intellects, are wrecked by obliviousness to this fundamental sociological truth."[3] This is because without the social organization imposed by civilization and its customs, the human animal's life is reduced to the solitary, poor, nasty, brutish and short experience made famous by Hobbes. Closely related, there exist problems that stem directly from excessive individualism, namely, narcissism, selfishness, and egoism, which are detrimental to the individual as well as to the larger society (Lasch 1979). Finally, the anti-cultural disciples of the Enlightenment philosophers cannot escape the conclusion reached by Gellner (1992a) and others that their position is not universal, but is itself a cultural tradition that began in a tiny Northwest corner of Europe. Any other explanation has to assume that the values that stem from the Enlightenment are self-begotten, *a priori* entities. This position is absurd, and in any event is completely negated by the horrifying anti-individualism and oppression found in human history.

Even if partially true, all of these criticisms are overly intellectual, and do not touch directly enough on the major problem that concerns us in this book (the affinities between postmodern narcissism and postcommunist violence). For example, Christopher Lasch's (1979) criticisms of narcissism do not leave one with much more than the conclusion that narcissism is not nice. A much more forceful criticism of the Enlightenment legacy is to be found in a neglected and still untranslated book by Jovan Rasković entitled *Narcissism* (1988). Mr. Rasković, the previously mentioned psychiatrist[4] and leader of the Serbs living in Croatia, argued that narcissism is an ontological category that demonstrates its power in various forms of aggression, overt as well as covert. Narcissism cannot exist without aggression and fear. Rasković applies his psychoanalytic interpretation to this century's worst narcissists: Mussolini, Hitler, and Stalin. He argues that the narcissist is always ready for battle and that even when he or she has everything, he or she does not have enough enemies. Narcissism will lead to individual as well as collective paranoia, megalomania, racism, and obsession. Yet by virtue of being a narcissist, this pathological type will not be able to admit these faults – in a most paranoid fashion, the racist is always someone else.

It is ironic that this Serbian psychiatrist's analysis also fits the one dictator that he does not mention, the Serbian President, Slobodan Milošević. And no one can read Rasković sensitively without realizing that the paranoia, megalomania, and racism that he attributes to narcissists seem to coincide with the fact that many Serbs see themselves as the world's victims even when confronted with the crimes perpetrated under the leadership of Mr. Milošević (see especially Kaufman 1992). If Rasković is correct in his ingenious linkage of narcissism and aggression, the consequences of his insight apply not only to Serbia, but also to the consumer-based, Western cultures that did not try to stop Serbian aggression from the outset. Here again, we confront the issue of vicarious barbarism in the West, already discussed to some extent, as well as the insight that the postmodern West is drowning in violence, racism, and various forms of aggression against its own citizens. Rasković's insight is a direct challenge to the illusion that modern as well as postmodern freedom from tradition and culture leads to tolerance and democracy. On the contrary, such narcissistic freedom may lead to forms of aggression that will become increasingly worse as narcissism grows in Western cultures.

Still, neither narcissism nor barbarism are black-or-white concepts. One cannot escape Freud's ([1901] 1965) observation that some degree of narcissism is healthy or at least functional, especially in newborn infants, who need to regard themselves as centers of their universe in order to survive. And Durkheim ([1925] 1961) is probably right that healthy individualism is compatible with social obligations, such that moral and healthy forms of individualism should be contrasted with unhealthy forms of egoism and narcissism. Many contemporary social critics fail to make this distinction, and either praise or condemn all forms of individualism.

An analysis of this sort leads implicitly to the question, "Are Westerners superior morally to the Serbs and others who perpetrated atrocities in

Bosnia-Herzegovina?" Not only have Westerners committed genocide in the historical past – and usually in the name of some glorified Enlightenment ideal – but I have pointed to vicarious, silent, conspiratorial elements in the West's tacit support of Serbia. One must take seriously the Muslim perception of the narcissistic-prone West, as echoed by Mustafa Ceric, the Grand Imam of the mosque in Zagreb, Croatia:

> "We feel betrayed by Europe." Like many Muslims here as well as those visiting from Arab countries, he pointedly asked whether the world is silently conspiring or acquiescing in the "final elimination" of Muslims from this corner of Europe. They see Orthodox Christians, Serbs and Catholic Croats pressuring the Muslims, with the West mouthing platitudes, essentially standing aside.
>
> (*New York Times*, 23 August 1992: A8)

BACK TO HISTORICAL EXPLANATIONS

Group and cultural differences have intensified in the postmodern, postcommunist era, culminating in a world-wide explosion of nationalisms. The present-day postmodern version of nationalism is not the sort found at the previous turn of the century. Alvin Toffler is probably correct that a century ago, "beneath the nationalism lay the familiar imperative of industrialization: the desire toward integration" (1980: 75). There was a movement away from tribes, clans, principalities and other small units toward huge blocs and Empires that fulfilled the industrial need for integrated marketplaces. All that has changed in the current *fin de siècle*. Nowadays, large Empires, trading blocks, and other huge national chunks are disintegrating into ever smaller units, from the Balkans proper to California, which is threatening to break up into three chunks. The fruits of modernist, previously global culture co-exist in an unhappy balance with anti-global, provincial, particularistic social forces.

Even if one grants to the postmodernists that present-day humanity is living in apocalyptic times – despite or because of the resurgence of this new form of nationalism – such a state of affairs is neither new nor incompatible with the co-existence of anti-modern tendencies. For example, in *Decline of the West*, Oswald Spengler ([1926] 1961: 26) compared the phase of Western civilization that led to World War I with Rome in its last, dying stages: unspiritual, unphilosophical, brutal, commercialized, egoistic and therefore profoundly amoral. In Spengler's (ibid.: 32) words, the transition from culture – based on the soul or the heart – to civilization – the domain of the intellect – occurred in the Western world in the nineteenth century. Spengler regarded as decline this shift from culture to rational society, which is depicted by modernists as progress.[5] We have pointed to a similar paradox in the postmodern program, such that modernity co-exists with forces directly inimical to it, from nationalism to fundamentalism, in an unhappy and tense balance.

Spengler's argument is corroborated by scores of writers who noted similar paradoxes in the modernization process, even if they used slightly different terminology. Thus, Ferdinand Tönnies (1887) documented the change from *Gemeinschaft* or community based on "natural will" and the mother–child archetype to *Gesellschaft* or society based on the "rational will" and commerce. Scholars still debate whether Tönnies defended or condemned these profound changes in social organization. Schopenhauer (1818), Georg Simmel (1907), Nietzsche (1901) and other intellectuals from the previous *fin de siècle* also noted the transition from culture based on sentiments, sympathy, and feelings, or the heart, to society or civilization based on utilitarian principles, commercialism, and egoism. Thorstein Veblen (1899) even distinguished between "habits of the heart" – applied to a mythical, matriarchal culture in the remote past – and "habits of the mind" or thought used to explain modern forms of barbarism.[6] Durkheim ([1893] 1933) argued that the same division of labor that was the engine that drove modernity also produced unhappiness, anomie, and alarming increases in suicide and crime. Freud ([1930] 1961) capped these typically *fin de siècle* assessments with his infamous phrase, civilization and its discontents.

Arnold Toynbee is another voice from the past whose pessimistic historical reading of the civilizing process needs to be incorporated into the postmodern discourse. According to Toynbee, "the rise of the doctrine of human perfectibility and progress obscures human nature which expresses itself in devious ways" (1978: 282). Far from making the world a better place, the Enlightenment legacy has worsened various crises in the world. Toynbee offers the following summary: "The West has sold to the world a civilization that has turned out not to be what either the seller or the buyers believed it to be at the time of the sale" (ibid.: 284). One could argue that this assessment still applies to the West's efforts to "sell" the Enlightenment legacy to the postcommunist world.

In a passage that is directly relevant to the current Balkan crisis, Toynbee seems to echo Spengler in his treatment of imperialist tendencies in various civilizations as they come into contact with one another:

> Belgrade passed out of Ottoman hands in 1866 to become the capital of the Serbian "successor-state" of the Ottoman Empire; and it was recovered by the Serbs from the Austrians in 1918 in order to become the capital of Jugoslavia, which is a "successor-state" of the Hapsburg Power as well as of the Ottoman.
>
> (1978: 27)

Toynbee seems to have captured the contemporary character of Serbian aggression in the Balkans as a blend of Habsburg imperialism and suppression of nationalism with Ottoman cruelty. Toynbee's characterization is much more apt than the fictitious comparisons to Nazism that we analyzed in Chapter 2, and also genuinely postmodern in that he refers to the co-existence of cultural trends that genuinely oppose each other.

An integral aspect of Toynbee's overall view of historical developments in the world is that "Civilization, as we know it, is a movement and a condition, a voyage and not a harbor. No known civilization has ever reached the goal of civilization yet" (ibid.: 11). What a contrast to the arrogant claim found in the works of many postmodern writers that the West had truly reached the end of history, which is to say, the goal of civilization.

The important point is that modernity produces its own nemesis. In seeking to establish order and eliminate sentiment, modernity paradoxically produces disorder, fragmentation, and heightened passions – in a word, the anti-modern (or the genuinely postmodern). This process is captured better by unorthodox historians such as Spengler and Toynbee who followed in the wake of Arthur Schopenhauer's ([1818] 1965a, 1965b) formula that heightened rationality exacerbates the will (or passions) than by Kant's, Rousseau's, Comte's or the Cartesian formulas that rationality can eventually control or even eliminate the passions. A popular rendition of this boosterish faith in rationalism and technology is found in Alvin Toffler's *The Third Wave*:

> We must, as a first step, launch the widest public debate over the need for a new political system attuned to the needs of a Third Wave civilization. We need conferences, tv programs, contests, simulations, exercises, mock constitutional commentators to generate the broadest array of imaginative proposals for political restructuring, to unleash an outpouring of fresh ideas. We should be prepared to use the most advanced tools available to us, from satellites and computers to video-discs and interactive television.
>
> (1980: 420)

To some extent, Toffler's advice has already been put into practice. President Clinton has made skillful use of television to simulate the American "town meeting" made famous by Tocqueville – albeit, an electronic town meeting in which there is no sense of community. Thus far, instead of eliminating the supposed evils found in traditional cultures, the postmodern television camera has only exacerbated these evils. Far from replacing the need for faith as expressed in religion, modernity fosters a desperate quest for faith as expressed in fundamentalism – and fundamentalists have made skillful use of television. The intrusion of the electronic media into nearly every societal institution has not yet appreciably lessened racism, sexism, violence, or any of the other evils found in modern as well as pre-modern societies. Riane Eisler (1987: 194) is probably right to say that Alvin Toffler merely promotes the change from one dominator system (the chauvinist, industrial one) to another (technological but equally chauvinist).

Eisler adds a genuinely new dimension to this discussion in that she implies that feminine civilization has always been distinct from masculine civilization. More-over, she implies that feminine civilization fosters partnership and is "good" or at least better than the masculine, dominator type of civilization. Her overall argument is that humanity must elevate "feminine virtues" from a secondary or supportive to a primary and central position (1987: 121). Elsewhere, I have expressed my agreement with Eisler's thesis overall (see Meštrović 1992). But taking a cue from Toynbee, one wonders whether Eisler has also succumbed to utopian thinking: might not feminine culture be too much of a good thing? And the moment that one thinks of arriving at any sort of final, good society, one is poised to repeat the errors of the many totalitarian systems of the past.

This cautionary note applies also to the writings of Pitirim Sorokin, who claimed that the survival of the human race "becomes doubtful if the egotism of individuals and groups remains undiminished; if it is not transcended by a creative love as Agape and as Eros – love as a dynamic force effectively transfiguring individuals, ennobling social institutions, inspiring culture, and making the whole world a warm, friendly, and beautiful cosmos" (1950: v). There is no doubt that excessive egoism is harmful to individuals as well as to whole groups of people. Nevertheless, a society that is perceived as warm, friendly, and beautiful by some will undoubtedly be perceived as oppressive by others.

Sorokin's *Russia and the United States* (1944) deserves special attention in a discussion of this sort. It is amazing that Sorokin saw the ghosts of communism *and* capitalism in 1944. He argued that wars are usually fought between cultures that hold very different values, but that the United States and Russia are very similar and, in fact, were converging in their value systems.[7] In the conclusion, he laid down four "indispensable conditions for a lasting peace" between these two superpowers:

> First, a fundamental reintegration and transvaluation of most of the contemporary cultural values; second, effective promulgation and inculcation among all states, nations, and social groups of a set of fundamental norms and values which shall be universally binding; third, explicit limitation of the sovereignty of all states in regard to war and peace; and fourth, the establishment of a supreme international authority vested with the power of obligatory and enforced decision in all international conflicts.
>
> (1944: 235)

When it comes to prophecy, Sorokin's genius breaks down, and his views betray a naive optimism in modernism. The United Nations has tried to take on the role of a sort of super-policeman of the world,[8] and has tried to downplay the sovereignty of nations, especially the newly recognized nations in the Balkans (Boutros-Ghali 1992). But national sovereignty is one of those *irrational* human phenomena that cannot be eliminated even if it is illogical and often seems to get in the way of world peace (Schoenfeld 1984). Besides, Sorokin assumes that some supreme, modernist international authority would be fair and just in its dealings with all of the world's nations. There is no body of evidence to support such an incredibly optimistic and naive view.

Lewis Mumford is another voice from the past who thought about the prospects of civilization. Like Toynbee and Schopenhauer, he takes the pessimistic position that civilization cannot conquer human evil. In this vein, Mumford regards Herman Melville's *Moby Dick* as a parable on the mystery of evil and the accidental nature of the universe (1955: 38). In general, for Mumford, "the whole tale of the West is a tale of this effort to combat the whale – to ward off his blows, to counteract his aimless thrusts, to create a purpose that will offset the empty malice of Moby Dick" (ibid.: 39). Far from being successful, this aim to subjugate and control evil has resulted in new and stronger versions of evil, from genocide to the almost routine targeting of civilian targets during wars.

For example, Mumford agrees with Toynbee that up to World War I, wars were fought with limited means for equally limited objectives.[9] According to Mumford, "Military power, though used for irrational political purposes, was still subject to moral control. Nobody held the fallacious notion that war itself was so bad it could excuse any degree of violence or butchery" (1955: 236). But in World War I, the bombing of civilians came into vogue, and "this general moral disintegration paved the way for the use of the atomic bomb" (ibid.: 238). What is distinctive in Mumford's analysis, however, is that he blames the "civilized" victors over Nazism for this newly sanctioned and widespread barbarism: "Nihilism produced the bomb" (ibid.: 241).

Clearly, the deliberate targeting of civilians was made practically routine in the two most publicized wars since the fall of communism, the Gulf War and the Balkan War that began in 1991. While much has been written on the bombing of civilians by Serbs, very little attention has been paid to US, British, French, and other "Allied" bombing of Iraqi civilian targets, including civilian water supplies, sewage facilities, and communication networks, not to mention the use of "uranium depleted" but still radioactive artillery shells. Clearly, many of the postmodern West's military actions against Iraq constitute war crimes every bit as much as the actions of the Serbian dictator, Slobodan Milošević, against his Balkan neighbors. In other words, seemingly "primitive" barbarism is an integral aspect of two very important wars that have occurred in the postmodern, postcommunist era and that were waged by a group of nations that usually refer to themselves as the "Western allies."

In general, one should be suspicious of the overly neat and tidy depictions of postmodernity as either rebellion against or an extension of modernity. As noted from the outset, it could well be the case that the previous *fin de siècle* got it right, and that modernity co-exists with its seeming opposites, postmodernism and traditionalism. It is a safe assertion that sociology was born about a century ago in Western Europe as humanity began to feel the consequences of these dramatic shifts and paradoxes.

HABITS OF THE HEART

The phrase, "habits of the heart," and the focus on "habits" as the essential ingredient of culture in general by Alexis de Tocqueville (1845), William James (1890), Thorstein Veblen (1899), Max Weber (1904), Emile Durkheim (1893), Georg Simmel (1907) and other founding fathers of sociology was replaced, beginning in the 1920s, with a vocabulary of rational social action, rational choice theory, utilitarianism, and other abstract derivatives of positivism (Spengler [1926] 1961: 108). The original study of culture as a manifestation of social consciousness that was popular in the previous *fin de siècle* was replaced with an approach to society as a social system devoid of culture that could be studied using methods established by the natural sciences. All this is in keeping with Spengler's thesis in *Decline of the West* ([1926] 1961: 353–424) that the ascent of science signals the death of culture. It may be true that recently contemporary sociology has grudgingly conceded the importance of culture to some extent with the advent of *some aspects* of the postmodernist movement (Rosenau 1992). Even so, postmodernism thoroughly permeated philosophy, literature, the arts, and architecture before it was admitted into contemporary sociological discourse. Furthermore, some versions of postmodernism hold to Nietzschean and modern nihilistic overtones that might be considered anti-cultural, if one conceives of culture as habits and traditions derived from the collectivity (Kroker and Cook 1986: 1–19).

In sum, it seems that contemporary sociologists are suspicious of the concept of "social character" and its original precursor, Tocqueville's "habits of the heart."[10] When confronted with these concepts, many sociologists ask, in a positivistic vein: how do you operationalize social character? How do you test the hypothesis that social character "causes" behavior? Contemporary social scientists do not seem to know or bother with the fact that from Schopenhauer to Spengler, it was argued that these questions, which belong to the realm of the natural sciences, *should not* be asked of history and cultural studies, since: (1) the scientific concern with facts and natural laws is itself a manifestation of late civilization; (2) history and culture are living, organic phenomena such that one cannot move forward and backward in history, as if history were static and dead; and (3) passions and other phenomena pertaining to the Schopenhauerian will give rise to scientific conceptions, which are secondary, not primary phenomena (see Bellah *et al.* 1985: 227–307; Magee 1983; Scrinton 1988).

Even the leading critics of Western societies do not seem to realize the full extent of the subtleties of using the concepts "habits of the heart" and "social character" in discourses that involve the concept of culture. For example, Bellah *et al.* (1985), Allan Bloom (1987), and Christopher Lasch (1991) cite many problems with Western modernism, from cultural and moral relativism to cancerous individualism or narcissism. All of these authors call for a conservative return to community, the republican tradition, or some other nostalgic remnant of the "good old days." The intellectual movement that they represent is sometimes called communitarianism, and is typically depicted as the obverse of liberalism. What they fail to realize is that they are applying a modernist, liberal, positivistic solution to problems that lie at the heart of the modernist project. This is because, if one follows the anti-Enlightenment trajectory from Schopenhauer to Spengler, one cannot retrieve the past, and one cannot use social engineering to solve a cultural problem – in this case, to bring back the supposedly good old days. In sum, the habits of the heart of the past have already been replaced by contemporary habits of the mind, and even if *new* habits of the heart will emerge in some idealistic cultural phase in the future, as Sorokin (1957) and others have argued, this sensate culture cannot retrieve its youth. In fact, Spengler, Toynbee, Sorokin, and some postmodernists cite this nostalgic longing as a major symptom of the decline of the Western, modernist project.

Consider, for example, that the most dominant response to the fall of communism among capitalist nations has been euphoria at the alleged victory of capitalism over communism coupled with nostalgia for some fictitious golden age of capitalism from yesteryear. This reaction stems from motives that run deeper than relief that Khruschev did not bury the capitalist West, as he had promised. It stems from the West's tendency toward expansion, a new imperialism based on the market, and assimilation that is inherent to the modernist project (Bauman 1992: 226–8, Spengler [1926] 1961: 24–47), as well as a false remembrance of benign capitalism. For whatever faults one might have found in the works of Karl Marx, his searing criticisms of the evils, injustice, and suffering caused by capitalism were on target. Yet Michael Novak (1982), Joshua Muravchick (1991), Francis Fukuyama (1992), and others who proclaim the unequivocal moral virtues of capitalism are hardly able to disguise the underlying, ethnocentric assumption that it will be the American brand of capitalism that will save the world from history. They seem oblivious to the fact that when he introduced the concept *end of history*, Hegel ([1899] 1965: 128) argued that only Germany would achieve this supposedly desired state of affairs. The German ethnocentrism that led to so much conflict in the twentieth century is merely being replaced with American ethno-centrism at the end of the present century, along with many smaller ethnocentrisms in the rest of the world.

In addition, at least two questions left over from the previous *fin de siècle* need to be asked: can the Western, modernist project be simply and quickly transplanted into the *cultures* that had survived communism in Eastern Europe and the former Soviet Union? The automatic answer in the West seems to be a resounding "yes," despite the failure, thus far, of capitalism to take hold in Poland, Russia, and other postcommunist countries. Moreover, a genuinely cultural approach to the problem would suggest that every nation's economic system must be related to that nation's particular culture or habits and traditions. And *should* the Western modernist project be forced onto the peoples who had just endured the communist version of the modernist project?

IN WHAT WAYS IS CAPITALISM VICTORIOUS?

In the previous *fin de siècle*, intellectuals predicted that socialism would eventually eclipse capitalism. This attitude is found not only in the works of Karl Marx, but in works that range from Edward Bellamy's (1888) best-selling *Looking Backward: 2000* to H.G. Wells's (1935) depiction of a *socialist* New World Order. Socialism's compassionate overtones flow from Romanticism and the previous *fin de siècle* belief in the power of the heart over the mind, but in addition flow from the Nietzschean concept of will to power. Socialism as well as communism tried to impose "compassion" systematically, with brute force if necessary (Spengler [1926] 1961: 361). In that sense, both doctrines are modernist products of late *civilization* but not culture, for both exhibited extreme intolerance, universalism, and the nature of the imperative command as opposed to Christ's original message of tolerance and ethics as an end in itself that invites, but does not command.[11] The important point is that both capitalism and socialism may be inadequate blueprints for the good society.

For example, Michael Novak (1982: 10–14) claims that there is no democracy without free markets (capitalism), and no freedom without democracy. However, since capitalism is based on the utilitarian doctrine of self-interest, one must take issue with Novak (1982: 80) and others who claim that self-interest can be a moral doctrine (cf. James Madison in *Federalist No. 51* on human nature). Novak is correct only if one tunes out Western history. However expedient and useful capitalism and self-interest may be, they have never been considered unambiguously moral in the Western tradition that pointed to the doctrines of self-abnegation and asceticism found as the moral bedrock of Christianity. For this reason, Durkheim ([1928] 1958: 240) criticized both capitalism and socialism for trying to derive morality from the doctrine of self-interest as a futile strategy that attempts to get "the most from the least, the superior from the inferior." Veblen (1943: 299) seems to be more accurate in his claim that the secret of the West is that it promotes pecuniary self-interest enshrined by capitalism *as well as* Christian asceticism and self-abnegation. Remove one or the other tradition from Western history, and it is no longer recognizable. The history of the West teaches that the human animal is a *homo duplex*, simultaneously higher than the angels but lower than the beasts (Durkheim [1914] 1973). One can trace this doctrine in various forms throughout Western history, from Plato through Pascal to Durkheim ([1914] 1973: 159). Its consequence is that *all* economic doctrines promote selfishness, which is the basis of immorality, and must be offset by a moral structure that resides in other societal institutions, not just government. These institutions include the family, religion, neighborhood, and other secondary groups that ideally foster altruism more than egoism (Durkheim [1950] 1983). In line with Durkheim's emphasis on secondary groups, Tocqueville's ([1845] 1945: 338–46) central claim is that democratic freedom degenerates into license unless it is restrained by religion, the community, and other conservative factors. Despite these compelling arguments in favor of a healthy conservatism that should act as a brake on unbridled liberalism, the *homo duplex* concept suddenly disappears in various postmodern doctrines. With the end of history, one jettisons the traditional notion of sin. The human animal is now perfectible.

It is true that capitalism has not resulted in Gulags. The Marxist critique of capitalism has been discredited so many times that we will not add to existing criticisms here. The more important point is that all the debates for and against Marxism and for and against government regulation of markets fail to address the point that capitalism does not exist as an abstraction, but as a cultural phenomenon embedded in the rest of a particular culture. Any capitalist system or mechanism minus the habits of the heart endemic to it constitutes a "public danger" to society, according to Emile Durkheim ([1950] 1983: 12). Drawing upon the doctrine of *homo duplex*, Durkheim ([1897] 1951) accused Western, capitalist as well as socialist, nations of promoting anomie, a state of unlimited desires whose end results include rampant consumerism, high suicide and crime rates, disenchantment, and other forms of discontent that accompany progress (cf. Meštrović 1988: 54–75). According to Durkheim, anomie is offset by *moral* – but not only or even primarily governmental or legal – regulation that stems from a variety of secondary groups. But he noted that religion, the family, and the workplace are less able to fulfill this regulatory role in modern societies (Durkheim [1897] 1951: 366–92). Consider that in hoisting capitalism onto postcommunist nations, one is imposing anomic consumerism that is problematic even in the West, *minus* any regard for the traditional, cultural, moral networks that are supposed to contain it. Unlimited desires without moral checks spells a disastrous dose of anomie if one takes Durkheim seriously.

Contemporary social scientists sell their services as consultants to newly elected, democratic governments in former communist nations with the aim of teaching their citizens the principles of free-market economics practically overnight. In most cases, no compromise is sought with socialist principles or existing cultural mores. It is classical economic theory or nothing, imposed as a sort of shock therapy. The human cost has been great already, and is bound to grow: massive unemployment, disillusionment and hunger among the masses, inflation, and political instability. If the shock therapy fails, the highly paid consultants will retire to their offices at Harvard and other leading Universities in the West, and rationalize their failure by citing obstacles to the market forces they tried to unleash. But the suffering caused to millions of people might be fantastic. No one has yet asked the cultural question: what are the habits of the *heart* of the nations that used to be ruled by communism, and what system is best suited to their *cultures*?

The cynicism among Western, capitalist individuals has been well documented, from David Riesman's *Lonely Crowd* (1950) to Peter Sloterdijk's more recent *Critique of Cynical Reason* (1987). Capitalism *does* have its faults, including a tendency to promote predatory, barbaric habits of the *mind* that lead to selfishness and connectedness to others based almost solely on consumerism (at the expense of being productive), as argued by intellectuals from Veblen (1899) and Erich Fromm (1955) to Baudrillard (1988a: 22).[12] And one must reckon with Horkheimer and Adorno's *Dialectic of Enlightenment* (1972), in which these two key leaders of the Frankfurt School indict the Enlightenment for the rise of Fascism in the bourgeois West. One must confront the question: why would the West want to transform Eastern Europe and the former USSR into its image in all its manifestations? After all, the West does not present an unequivocally pretty picture.

Furthermore, Eastern Europe and the former USSR are not responding according to the modernist plan that calls for enlightenment, the rule of law, assimilation, and social order (see Bauman 1992: 221). Instead, Balkanization, nationalism, fundamentalism, religion, and worse, ethnocentrism and racism, are erupting in formerly communist nations (albeit not due to capitalism). These same phenomena are also erupting in Germany, France, Britain, the USA and the so-called Western nations. The borders of nations that had been consecrated by the Helsinki Accords are dissolving quickly into increasingly smaller republics that exhibit paranoia toward the intentions of their neighbors almost as soon as they declare their independence. Examples include the war between Croatia and Serbia, the tragic conflict in Bosnia-Herzegovina, the dispute by Macedonia with its Balkan neighbors over its identity and borders, and the many conflicts among the newly enfranchised Soviet republics.

I contend that the original conceptual vocabulary of sociology from the previous *fin de siècle* serves as a more adequate basis for analyzing and comprehending contemporary heart-over-mind – genuinely irrational – postcommunist manifestations. In the absence of a liberal tradition – and that is a key point, that liberalism is a tradition, not the negation of tradition – that harks back to the Enlightenment philosophers in the West, the vacuum in postcommunist nations has been filled by those cultural traditions that barely survived communism: nationalism, religion, and other centripetal forces that bespeak the power of "habits of the heart." In line with Tocqueville's ([1845] 1945: 49) distinction between "good" versus "bad" habits of the heart in America, a similar distinction may apply to Balkan and other postcommunist lands. The negative "habits of the heart" include authoritarianism, intolerance, anti-Semitism, bigotry, provincial- ism, envy, the search for scapegoats, and an institutionalized cult of hatred. Hardly any social scientific literature exists on the good habits of the heart.

For example, the cultural sociologist, Dinko Tomašić (1948a, 1948b, 1953) argued that most of the negative Slavic habits of the heart are confined to the mountain-dwellers in the Dinaric and Ural Alps. His theory is not very different from Tocqueville's argument that in the USA the aristocratic South should bear the brunt of the responsibility for America's vices, especially slavery. A modernist might be tempted to retort that this is pure nonsense, because these vices are universal. Nevertheless, it is interesting that in line with Tomašić's theory, the fighting among the Croats, Serbs and Muslims in the 1990s is confined to a crescent-shaped region known as *Krajina* as well as alpine regions of Bosnia-Herzegovina in which Dinaric residents have been committing atrocities against each other for many centuries.

THE FALL OF COMMUNISM

The fall of communism in Eastern Europe and the former USSR is one of the most significant events of the twentieth century. In general, Western scholarly and popular presses have been reluctant to publish anything on the subject that is not descriptive or ideological. The ideological statements usually involve diatribes against Marxism, or boosterism for Western capitalism and clichés about universal human rights. In contrast to these ideological and mostly ethnocentric interpretations, the present analysis points to an alternative view not found in current literature. Communism fell of its own accord because it represented a modernist, civilizational force in its autumnal, "late" stage that clashed completely with an underlying culture that is still in the Spring of cultural development.

This hypothesis is commensurate with the broad outlines of what we know sociologically about Eastern Europe and the former Soviet Union. Compared with the modernist West, the nations that used to be ruled by communism are still predominantly rural and are dotted by Hansel and Gretel cottages more than suburban homes. In general, they are closer to what used to be medieval culture in the West than what passes for modernity today. Fromm and Maccoby's (1970) analysis of mother-centered, Catholic Mexico resonates in many ways with the cultural values found in Catholic Croatia, Poland, and other Eastern European countries. Even the postcommunist lands that subscribe to various Orthodox faiths have little in common with Max Weber's ([1904] 1958) cultural description of the linkages between Protestantism and capitalism in the West.

But Max Weber's famous *Protestant Ethic and the Spirit of Capitalism* ([1904] 1958) has not been read primarily as a treatise on culture. Instead, and based on their modernist reading of Weber, Western sociologists have shown great interest in the supposedly causal connection between Protestantism and capitalism. Recent scholars have been pointing to Weber's ambiguity in this regard (Kasler 1988, Sica 1988). Indeed, Weber wrote ([1904] 1958: 91):

> We have no intention whatever of maintaining such a foolish and doctrinaire thesis as that the spirit of capitalism (in the provisional sense of the term explained above) could only have arisen as the result of certain effects of the Reformation, or even that capitalism as an economic system is a creation of the Reformation.

Notwithstanding the controversies that still surround Max Weber's thesis, my point is that sociologists know next to nothing of how Slavic Catholicism and Orthodoxy relate to any doctrines of worldly success, much less Western, Protestant-based capitalism. Why in the world should such cultures be conducive to communism *or* capitalism or any other modernist project exported from the predominantly Protestant West?

Consider Robert Bellah's concept of American civil religion (1967). In developing this controversial concept, Bellah borrowed from Rousseau, Tocqueville, and the Durkheimian ([1912] 1965: 343) idea that a "religion" can exist independently of bona fide churches so long as it involves representations of the sacred and the profane. This means that political ideas, institutions, and symbols become artificially charged with religious overtones. Even the very modern, liberal notions of human rights and dignity become the object of a sort of religious worship. In this way, again, modern ideas such as liberalism are conjoined with traditional concepts such as religion. Hence, Durkheim's conceptions of the "cult of the individual" and "moral individual" – modern, liberal ideas that are treated as sacrosanct even in ostensibly non-traditional societies.

This Durkheimian insight seems to have escaped Bellah, who focused instead on the rather ethnocentric idea of American civil religion as the celebration of American holidays, ideals, and images of America as the beacon of democracy blessed by God (cf. Tocqueville [1845] 1945: 32). It is true that American civil religion was revived significantly by American Presidents from Abraham Lincoln to Ronald Reagan and George Bush. Mr. Bush depicted the fall of communism as well as the Gulf War in the vocabulary of American civil religion, to the effect that America, as a nation blessed by God, was able to achieve these victories. Indeed, it is remarkable that many if not most American intellectuals whose writings influence public opinion view the collapse of communism as a victory of the American way of life that was ordained by God.

Yet Bellah's conception of American civil religion never transcends these power-hungry, imperialist dimensions of modernity. Against Bellah, but in line with Durkheim ([1912] 1965), one should assume that every people has its civil religion – including the Eastern European and formerly Soviet nations that were ruled by communism. But what do we know about their civil religions? Next to nothing with regard to formal, published sociological or otherwise cultural studies.

Bellah (1967) acknowledged that the American celebration of national identity leads easily into ethnocentrism and imperialistic adventures of many sorts. He cites the extermination of the Native Americans and the "misadventure" in Vietnam as examples. But he never resolved how the "good society" (Bellah *et al.* 1991) that is supposed to promote tolerance is possible given the imperialistic tenor of the American civil religion that he hopes to revive. In fact, Bellah (1989) simply stopped using the term, American civil religion, while he kept its conservative overtones and goals of recovering the American republicanism of bygone days.

So it is interesting that in the present *fin de siècle*, the revival of civil religions seems more noisy than ever, and in many cases has spilled over into intolerance of other people's civil religions. For example, American civil religion is intolerant of Islamic civil religion, which tends to be dismissed as Islamic fundamentalism. Serbian civil religion seeks to exterminate Islamic as well as Croatian civil religions. In sum, a key aspect of the postmodern rebellion against the grand narratives of the Enlightenment has been that traditional religion has allied itself with nationalism. The result is a highly combustible mixture of religion and politics that is anti-modern in the sense that it is based on passion and faith, yet has preserved the modernist tendencies toward imperialism.

In fact, a close analysis of the events that triggered the current Balkan War reveals that the conflict began largely over symbols. In 1991, Serbs objected passionately to Croatian symbols as depicted on flags and uniforms, as well as Muslim mosques as symbols of Turkish rule in the Balkans. Both the Croats and Bosnian Muslims lost all sense of reason when confronted with the Serb symbol of the letter "S" used four times, which, when translated, stands for the phrase, "Only Unity Saves the Serbs." Western diplomats were simply naive when, following the economic model of the human person as motivated solely by rational self-interest, they concluded that everyone in the Balkans would determine that war was not in their self-interest. Religious fervor combined with political symbols produces a new alloy that cannot be reduced to either one alone. All the world's major religions teach compassion and tolerance, but when mixed with the uniquely modernist ideas of self-determination, the result is paranoia and imperialism charged with fanaticism.

Let us pause here to take our bearings in the present discussion. I began this book with the claim that postmodernism, conceived as a cultural phenomenon peculiar to the latter half of the twentieth-century West, might exist simultaneously with modernism and traditionalism. Civil religion is one of the clearest illustrations of such a curious phenomenon. Far from leading to the desired end of tolerance, thus far at least, civil religions in postcommunist lands have led to extreme intolerance, up to and including genocide. Moreover, Western civil religions have cloaked themselves in the rhetoric of tolerance, negotiation, universal human rights, rationality, and other narratives spun from the Enlightenment to such a great extent that, paradoxically, they have come to tolerate intolerance. For example, well-documented Serbian genocide – which is an extreme form of intolerance – was tolerated by the West despite specific articles in the United Nations charter that call for the prevention and punishment of genocide (Helsinki Watch Committee 1992c: 2). This state of affairs in the post-Cold-War world is neither modern nor traditional, but a new combination of both that deserves to be called postmodern.

If one takes seriously this new formulation of a devastating tendency in contemporary international relations that is frequently dismissed as mere tribalism, then one is led to ask the following question: how and why did the *modernist*, communist *system* take root in a *traditional*, *cultural* nexus that was opposed to it? An answer seems to be that portions of the underlying, traditional cultures in formerly communist nations exhibited an affinity – a sort of "strange attraction" (from chaos theory) – with communist modernism. In other words, the imperialist, terrorist, and otherwise oppressive aspects of modernity that have been exposed by some postmodernists were commensurate with some barbaric, terrorist, and otherwise oppressive aspects of traditional culture that preceded communism. The advantage of such a cultural approach is that it focuses on underlying, chronic, and *persistent* factors that cast the surface events into their proper context. One important consequence of this formulation is that the fall of communism was only illusory. Beneath the surface of this seemingly dramatic event, the same cultural and anti-cultural forces are still festering in some postcommunist nations, and may produce a new authoritarian social system.

It is possible to argue that beneath all the apparent transitions the underlying culture in some specific portions of Eastern Europe and the former Soviet Union is unsuited to democracy, and that there exists a real danger of regression to previous undemocratic forms of government. The reasons are historical: the developments of democracy in the USA, France, Britain, Germany and other nations that made the transition from aristocracy to freedom were characterized by regressions, uneven progress, even civil wars. With regard to the USA, we have cited as illustration Tocqueville's widely acclaimed account of the American experiment in democracy. One should also note Tocqueville's ([1845] 1945: 264–80) major warning concerning American democracy's quest for equality: that it necessitates the centralization of power, thus endangering individual liberty. For example, Tocqueville wrote, "I know of no country in which there is so little independence of mind and real freedom of discussion as in America" (p. 273). Given the weight of history, why should the West suddenly follow Fukuyama's (1992) Hegelian claim that history has come to an end, and that the postcommunist lands will have an easier time in making this difficult transition to democracy?

Based on his review of the formation of political states in Eastern Europe from the Middle Ages to 1948, Tomašić concludes that "the origin of these states can be found in the personality traits of the [Slavic] predatory herdsmen and the military whose power-seeking traits have remained basically unchanged throughout the centuries" (1948a: 115). If Tomašić is correct, and the cultural approach to this problem holds merit, one has to fear the possibility that "all new Eastern European state formations which are organized along the same lines, will undoubtedly share the fate of their predecessors" (p. 116). Of course, people have the capacity to change, but not before the power of previously established habits is broken through self-conscious reflection.

Tomašić does not claim that the entire cultural infrastructure in Eastern Europe and the former Soviet Union is unsuited to democracy. Rather, he cautions that those who were drawn to communism in the Balkans and the former Soviet Union tend to have been raised in the same geographical regions that drew pre-communist authoritarian types. The communist type of imperialist has tended to be Serbian and Russian – although not exclusively, of course. I have already indicated that the Yugoslav and Soviet communism systems were actually disguised Serbian and Russian Empires, respectively.

When one considers that most of the democratically elected officials in former communist lands are themselves ex-communists, one should at least pause to wonder whether this argument might hold some merit. One might object that the communists' political–economic monopoly of power is more immediately relevant than culture. But our point is that excessive yearning for power is itself a cultural trait that differs from more peaceable cultural types. If this line of reasoning holds some merit, there is the dangerous possibility that the ex-communists in democratic clothing will soon begin to exhibit autocratic, authoritarian, and anti-democratic tendencies that are rooted in their cultural upbringing. From some existing contemporary indicators, it is possible to arrive at the tentative conclusion that this ominous process is already underway.

CONCLUSIONS

Since the alleged fall of communism in 1989, one and only one scenario for the future of postcommunist lands seems to have dominated Western media as well as intellectual treatises, namely, that market economy, democracy, and pluralism will prevail. This scenario is commensurate with Fukuyama's (1992) thesis that with the alleged fall of communism, the West had witnessed the *end of history*, by which he means the end of nationalism, totalitarianism, and imperialism. Yet Balkanization, nationalism, and territorial expansionism – humanity's historical vices – have already reappeared in postcommunist lands.

Instead of admitting that they were wrong in their naive, optimistic predictions, Fukuyama and like-minded intellectuals responded by dismissing former Yugoslavia from their rosy theories. Liberal democracy would spread everywhere except Yugoslavia. Over and over again, one found opinion-makers referring to the "tribalism" in former Yugoslavia. This is a Eurocentric, even racist characterization because of its clear implication that the Yugoslavs behave like the tribes in Africa, who are assumed not to have mastered European self-restraint. The lack of understanding and communication between the West and the newly liberated nations may itself contribute to negative scenarios. When postcommunist nations fail to live up to Western expectations, the result is not always one that is in keeping with the high image that the West has of itself as *rational*. Consider, for example, former US Ambassador to Yugoslavia David Anderson's (1992: A15) cruel dismissal of all the Yugoslavs:

> The problem, I fear, is the Yugoslavs themselves. They are a perverse group of folks, near tribal in their behavior, suspicious of each other (with usually sound reasons), friendly on the outside but very cynical within, ever ready for a war or a battle, proud of their warrior history, and completely incapable of coming to grips with the modern world. . . . So, I would say, a plague on both houses [the Croats and the Serbs].

It is remarkable that the *Wall Street Journal* published such a racist statement. No society anywhere in the world could exist if it were so totally hostile and "completely incapable" of coming to grips with modernity. After all, former Yugoslavia exists in Europe, which is assumed to be modern. And Yugoslavs love their children, have friends, and participate in other social activities that characterize humans in all societies. In general, as the proponents of the Enlightenment project came to realize that their predictions did not square with the facts, they revealed an ugly racism. Not just Yugoslavia, but other countries were dismissed. Consider the following statement by Mr. Fukuyama:

> While Yugoslavia crumbles and newly liberated Hungarians and Romanians torment each other endlessly over the status of the Hungarian minority in Transylvania . . . most *advanced* European states would seek to avoid entanglement in such controversies like a tar baby, intervening only in the face of *egregious violations of human rights or threats to their own nationals*. Yugoslavia, on whose territory the Great War began, has fallen into civil war and is disintegrating as a national entity. But the rest of Europe has achieved considerable consensus on an approach to settlement of the problem, and on the need to *insulate* Yugoslavia from larger questions of European security.
>
> (1992: 274; emphasis added)

If one took Fukuyama seriously, one would conclude that the Yugoslavs, Hungarians, Romanians and others were infected with a virus such as AIDS, and must be quarantined. The Western Europeans are assumed to be so "advanced" that entanglement in the Balkans is beneath them, unless the violations of human rights become "egregious." Yet, since 1992, when Fukuyama's words were published, the human rights abuses in Yugoslavia became horrifying, yet the "most advanced Europeans states" still refused to stop the atrocities.

The West continued to mourn the dissolution of communist Yugoslavia, despite the well-documented atrocities committed by Serbs day in and day out, and even though only Serbia and Montenegro apparently wished to preserve Yugoslavia. One frequently came across the lament to the effect that, if only Slovenia, Croatia, and Bosnia had not wanted independence, then none of these awful things would have happened.[13] That seems an apt summary of many articles written on this contemporary Balkan War. The Slovenes, Croatians, and Bosnians, in turn, felt betrayed by the West whose orbit of values they thought that they had sought to join, and began to express public suspicions about the discrepancy between the West's *actions* to preserve the status quo or further its self-interest, versus its rhetoric of supporting freedom and democracy.

Fukuyama's thesis assumes that *one*, universal history operates in the world, that it cannot be improved, and that it can be studied in a scientific manner. These assumptions are in keeping with the Enlightenment faith in progress that has prevailed in the West. But it is arrogant and foolish to conclude that our present-day system of democracy cannot be improved by our grandchildren and their descendants. For the postmodernists, on the other hand, the Enlightenment is oppressive, not liberating. Yet, neither doctrine lived up to its own promises of promoting tolerance and democracy. The modernists betrayed their truly oppressive superiority complex by simply dismissing as tribalists any peoples who did not live up to their expectations. The postmodernists were so wary of committing themselves to any narrative, standard, or cultural ideal that in the end they simply tolerated the intolerance that is called genocide. Meanwhile, the virulent nationalists exploited both the modernist tendency to act only on the basis of self-interest and the postmodern refusal to take a stand by practicing naked aggression and almost unspeakable brutality without fear of punishment from the world community.

There are other lacunae in the prevalent Western attitude toward the fall of communism and its aftermath. First, Western optimism and faith in liberal democracy, the end of history, and the free market betrays a sort of imperialism that is characteristic of late civilizations. The West likes to claim that it has outgrown imperialism, yet it seeks to promote the fruits of its Enlightenment-based tradition exclusively on its own terms – or else. Second, the majority of Western analysts seem uninterested in attaining a *cultural* understanding of the cultural "habits of the heart" of the people who were ruled by communism, and who are now assumed to be willing recipients of the fruits of modern, Western *civilization*. Finally, contemporary analysts of Western civilization in general and American civilization in particular such as Bellah, Lasch, and Riesman note problems with contemporary liberal democracy, including narcissism, excessive consumerism, paralyzing cultural relativism, cynicism, and continued problems with race relations.

The important point is that democracy and the free-market are not unequivocally benign, free-floating, ahistorical abstractions, but are rooted in culture. As with all other cultural traits, democracy and the free-market will have their benign as well as destructive characteristics. Similarly, there can be no doubt that postcommunist cultures contain their own unique blend of good versus bad habits of the heart. The conclusion that follows from the present analysis is that the good, peaceable, pro-democratic habits that lead to liberty should be nurtured, while the negative ones should be the objects of conscious reflection and collective self-examination.

Chapter 7

What would a genuine post-Marxism be like?

As stated from the outset, one of the most important world events that occurred in conjunction with the postmodern era in the late 1980s was the gradual crumbling and eventually the "final" collapse of communism in Eastern Europe and the former Soviet Union. The finality of the collapse may have been only apparent, however. The cultural habits that had sustained the communist system were not and could not be eradicated completely, thereby leaving open the possibility that a new form of authoritarianism could take the place of the former system. Moreover, even if communism, conceived as an *economic* system, did collapse, the cultural system that buttressed communism quickly betrayed its persistence by its transformation into *nationalism* and various sorts of *civil religion*. Russian, Serbian, Croat and other nationalisms that had survived communism became noisier than ever, and were tinged with sacrosanct language concerning the alleged holiness and spirituality of the Russian soil, Serbian blood, Croatian history, and so on. One is tempted to refer to these religiously charged nationalisms as "civil religions" (Bellah 1967), yet this term has been used primarily to investigate American civil religion, and may not be wholly applicable to other nations. Moreover, Robert Bellah *et al.* (1985) abandoned the use of the concept of civil religion because of the controversies surrounding it. Nevertheless, and because Bellah was inspired by Rousseau, Tocqueville and Durkheim in his original formulation of the concept, one might learn something new and directly applicable to the postcommunist, postmodern scene by going back to the previous *fin de siècle* in order to seek out the original sources of this important concept. This is what I propose to do in this chapter.

The importance of analyzing the religious dimensions of politics is twofold: first, Marxism and communism sought to eradicate religion as an unnecessary fetishism in their quest for rational utopias. Yet religion returned with a vengeance in the postcommunist, postmodern context. I am aware that many contemporary Marxists deny any connection between Marxism and communism. But I agree with Marcel Mauss that "Nevertheless, socialism, and especially Marxist socialism, has no right to repudiate its direct kinship with Communism, and its relative responsibility for the latter" (Mauss [1925] 1992: 168). Second, the current Balkan War quickly degenerated into a three-way religious war of sorts involving

Muslims, Catholic Croats, and Orthodox Serbs. To be sure, all religions preach love of neighbor, so that it is wrong to attribute the hatred in this Balkan War to religion directly. On the other hand, sociologists of religion have known for a long time that religion often correlates with prejudice (Roberts 1990). If religions teach love of neighbor, they are also often implicated in wars of ethnic hatred, from the Crusades to the Hindu–Muslim clashes in contemporary India. This is an important topic that needs to be investigated.

I shall be leading to the conclusion that something like civil religion seems to exist in all societies at all times – even modern and postmodern societies – and may be thought of as an alloy of political, economic, and religious elements that cannot be reduced to any one of them alone. Instead of taking on the conceptual baggage that comes with Bellah's use of the term, civil religion,[1] I shall hark back to Durkheim's original usage of the terms civic religion and civic morals – which are related to each other – from his *Elementary Forms of the Religious Life* ([1912] 1965) and *Professional Ethics and Civic Morals* ([1950] 1983), respectively. The distinctive, and most important aspect of the present analysis is that a focus on civic religion and morals counters the tendency in Marxist as well as so-called classical economics – not to mention modernist thought in general – to reduce all phenomena, including religion, to economic variables and factors. By contrast, from Tocqueville through Durkheim to Veblen, one finds the tendency to reduce most phenomena – including economics – to religion. Now that the postmodern revolution has called into question the Enlightenment narratives that had dismissed religion's importance in modernity, and also because events since the collapse of communism have highlighted religious factors, it seems that Durkheim's neglected formulation may be more relevant than Marxist and other modernist attitudes toward religion.

Civic religion and morals are implied in the postmodern discourse that arose in response to the apparent collapse of communism, even though these precise phrases are not used, and even though modernist narratives are still used to describe events. For example, the purported victory of capitalism over socialism is being presented by the New Right as vindication, even a *moral* triumph, given that only a century ago most intellectuals had predicted the triumph of socialism over capitalism. Recall that H.G. Wells's New World Order was going to be a socialist society of the entire world that would promote compassion and justice in opposition to the evils that were attributed to capitalism. President Bush's use of the phrase, New World Order, reversed Wells's high regard for socialism – in that it posited the victory of capitalism and democracy – but it kept the moral temper of the original formulation. The important point is that in these and similar socio-political formulations, religious imagery and terms were and continue to be used freely in quasi-religious ways: the contemporary world is still searching for a *common faith*, a workable *ethic*, *codes of conduct* for men's working relationships with women, and *principles* such as justice that hark back to religion. And these usages are attributable to mainstream leaders and intellectuals in postmodern societies, not to fringe groups of fundamentalists.

For example, a headline in the *Wall Street Journal* of 2 May 1991 read, "The Pope Affirms the New Capitalism," which is actually supposed to be the old-fashioned, free-market capitalism. Michael Novak (1991) compares Pope Leo XIII's 1891 encyclical *Rerum Novarum* with Pope John Paul II's 1991 encyclical *Centesimus Annus* to conclude that both Popes condemned socialism and praised – at least in principle, despite some misgivings – free-market capitalism. No sooner did the dust begin to settle from the fall of communism, so to speak, than the USA, Western European governments, businesses, and advocates of the free market assumed that they could begin to export their brands of capitalism and democracy to Eastern Europe and the former Soviet Union as part of a quasi-moral crusade. The new dogma became, "The market will cure all social ills." Despite the modernist rhetoric of value-free positivism regarding economic issues, the moral and religious aspects of economics are inescapable, even if most modernists refuse to admit this fact.

The utilitarian assumption that self-interest promotes the greatest social good forms the bedrock of modern economic theory. This assumption is hardly questioned in contemporary times, yet in the previous *fin de siècle*, Durkheim, Veblen, and others criticized its use by *both* socialism and capitalism, because both economic doctrines are erected on the utilitarian premise that morality will flow automatically from rational self-interest. Durkheim and Veblen, by contrast, held that the market caters to predatory, competitive, pecuniary, egoistic interests, which can never serve as an adequate basis for morality. Thus, Durkheim ([1893] 1933: 370–82) wrote extensively on the need for modern markets to ensure justice *and* mercy, not profit alone (see Cladis 1992; Schoenfeld and Meštrović 1991). Veblen ([1899] 1967: 212–45) pointed to an alternative to the emulatory, predatory, ceremonial, and wasteful aspects of capitalism and socialism that he thought would be found in a revival of "archaic," pre-barbaric traits of altruism, love of peace, and even Christian morals (see Leathers 1986). To take Durkheim, Veblen, and some of their other colleagues from the previous *fin de siècle* seriously is to regard our tumultuous *fin de siècle* as the watershed for a truly revolutionary (not in a violent sense) transformation of politico-economic systems from a barbarism shrouded in modernist rhetoric of rugged individualism to a new era of peace, justice, and non-alienating production. This is what would be involved in a genuinely postmodern and post-Marxist revolt against the narratives from the Enlightenment. But all this is essentially old business from the previous *fin de siècle*, in which the idea of a New World Order was first conceived.

The economist turned sociologist, Thorstein Veblen ([1910] 1943), wrote openly that he hoped that the Christian principle of love would overcome – though not necessarily replace – the morals of pecuniary competitive business. Durkheim's writings are crammed with similar allusions to the remnants of matriarchal religion, such as altruism, mutual sympathy, love, *caritas*, compassion, and justice, which he hoped would replace anomic economic structures based on egoism and what has come to be known as narcissism. Both Veblen and Durkheim, along with many of their contemporaries, assumed that habits are the essential building blocks of culture. They also thought that the Enlightenment habit of associating egoistic self-interest with morality was mistaken. Their proposals for social reform called for a rearranging of existing cultural habits that could be found in a given society's religious, political, and family institutions to include the derivatives of compassion.

But orthodox economic theory does not include the concept of "habits" in its vocabulary, because it assumes that all behavior is rational, an assumption that precludes the possibility of considering non-reflective behavior. Habits that pertain to compassion are never discussed, and the habitual association of self-interest with social well-being is not questioned. Moreover, contemporary orthodox economic theory is primarily positivistic in its orientation and quantitative in its methodology. As such, it is not likely to search for evidence that might call its assumptions and methods into question – the dramatic rise of incidents of murder, drug abuse, suicide, sexual molestation and various other sorts of barbarism thrive alongside modernity in cultures guided by the habit of self-interest (Meštrović 1993). In sum, the assumptions found in classical economic theory are part of the Eurocentric, Enlightenment narratives that postmodernism purports to rebel against (Murphy 1989). The more important point, for the purposes of the present book, is that Durkheim's sociology, as it relates to the spirit of the previous *fin de siècle*, offers the possibility of making the postmodern rebellion genuine. Moreover, Durkheim's thought constitutes a genuine alternative to Marxism.

From a Durkheimian perspective, the confusing discourse that followed the dramatic collapse of communism in the late 1980s is a repetition of the debates concerning the moral import of communism, socialism, and capitalism that concerned him, Veblen, H.G. Wells, Pope Leo XIII, and many others in the previous century. This time around, humanity is offered a new opportunity to transcend the limitations of unjust, barbaric, predatory forms of economic association.

ECONOMIC SYSTEMS AS CIVIC RELIGIONS

Before proceeding further, it is important realize that by the term "religion" Durkheim did *not* mean to imply church attendance, adherence to religious beliefs, strength of commitment to one's denomination or any of the other standard connotations of religion used by contemporary sociologists of religion as well as laypersons. Durkheim ([1912] 1965) meant simply that religion involves sacred versus profane representations of images and symbols. For Durkheim, phenomena as diverse as the scientific idea of causation, the high value placed on private property in capitalist nations, the high regard accorded to individuals in those same capitalist nations, the awe and respect shown to political leaders, even the air of sanctity attributed to discussions of Rationality (with a capital R) by nations with an Enlightenment tradition, all betray a religious character. Any and all discussions of awe, respect, initial force, sanctity, and similar phenomena involve the social category of the sacred and are therefore discussions of religion, broadly defined.

Modernists have not admitted that this is the central message of Durkheim's *Elementary Forms of the Religious Life*, of course. Such an admission defies too strongly the Enlightenment-based dogma that science and rationality are independent of and superior to religion. Yet, given the postmodern context of the present discussion, one should consider the strength of Durkheim's argument: if the rationalists and fanatical disciples of the Enlightenment truly seek to eliminate any and all vestiges of religion, then how will their purely secular society provide for respect, devotion, duty, patriotism, and all the other derivatives of the category of the sacred that are taken for granted in any social order? The important point is that pure, secular rationality does not inspire faith, awe, or respect of and by itself. Indeed, one of Durkheim's most devastating criticisms is that the Enlightenment legacy itself is a civic religion, even if its adherents seek to deny this.

One of Durkheim's disciples, Celestin Bouglé, elaborates on the consequences of Durkheim's extreme emphasis on religion in a comparison and contrast of Marx and Durkheim entitled "Marxism and Sociology" (in Bouglé 1918). This essay is important because it supplements Durkheim's own neglected writings on socialism, and because it compensates for the comparisons of Marx and Durkheim by contemporary writers who tend to cling to Marxism despite its acknowledged flaws (for example, see Pearce 1989). According to Bouglé (1918: 186), the postulate of all truly sociological research is the idea that genuinely social phenomena are something other than the sum of their parts. This is obviously true for Durkheim, but Bouglé believes that for Marx, too, social phenomena are not the mere enumeration of society's individual phenomena. New values are created through association. Even Marx's version of historical materialism in no way negates a collective psychic life in this sense. In this regard, Marx and Durkheim begin their analyses with somewhat similar philosophical assumptions, at least according to Bouglé.

Bouglé thinks that another important point of convergence between Marx and Durkheim is that both believe that the motives humans ascribe to their behavior are often an illusion, and that the real forces at work are mostly unconscious. This is a significant contrast to the general tendency to comprehend social life in terms of conscious, rational "human action" (from Parsons 1937).

Another point of convergence, according to Bouglé, is that both Durkheim and Marx were philosophers of social disarray and disharmony that was embedded in the very structure of society. Bouglé's typically *fin de siècle* opinion contrasts sharply with the contemporary views of Marx as a "conflict theorist" who opposed Durkheim's "functionalism." Indeed, Durkheim *did* focus on the social malaise experienced by individuals as a result of incorrect social arrangements in both capitalism and socialism (see Durkheim [1928] 1958). One could even argue that Durkheim was more sensitive to social malaise than Marx and the Marxists, because Durkheim faulted Marx for being biased in favor of the suffering of the proletariat while ignoring the suffering present in the entire society. The Durkheimians felt that anomic economic structures caused pain to the total social body, including the bourgeoisie. According to Durkheim:

The malaise from which we are suffering is not rooted in any particular class; it is general over the whole of society. It attacks employers as well as workers, although it manifests itself in different forms in both: as a disturbing, painful agitation for the capitalist, as discontent and irritation for the proletariat. Thus the problem reaches infinitely beyond the material interests of the two classes concerned. . . . [one should] address, not those feelings of anger that the less-favored class harbors against the other, but feelings of pity for society, which is suffering in all classes and in all its organs.

([1897] 1986: 143)

According to Bouglé, Durkheim and Marx also part intellectual company when it comes to the practical consequences of their doctrines. Bouglé claims that Karl Marx was "the authentic ancestor of pragmatism" (1918: 211) because his materialism lends itself to immediate action. By contrast, Durkheim was highly critical of pragmatism (see Durkheim [1955] 1983), because he regarded it as an affront to the "cult of truth," what he regarded as an almost religious quality ascribed to the complexity of reason and truth. Of course, Durkheim has been criticized by Marxist intellectuals for not preaching revolution or any other form of violent social change. But given the evil consequences that have resulted from taking Marx too seriously on immediate social action, it seems more reasonable to commend Durkheim's doctrine for its essential prudence.

Another difference cited by Bouglé (1918: 222) is that Durkheim did not believe that, by itself, the "will" of the working classes could ever bring forth social harmony. Schopenhauer ([1818] 1965a) also regarded the "will" as inherently unruly and as the source of all social strife, never its solution. Similarly, Bouglé dismisses Marxism on the grounds that it is *solely* a "philosophy of will" (1918: 225). In fact, Bouglé invokes both Schopenhauer's and Nietzsche's notions of "will" to make the point that historical materialism must, by its over-emphasis on the will of the working classes, promote egoism, not social harmony (ibid. p. 230). Again, history seems to vindicate the Durkheimians, because many inhumane programs were carried out by Marxist regimes in this century in the name of the will of the working classes.

But the most important point of divergence of Marx and Durkheim, according to Bouglé, has to do with the philosophical notion of representationalism. Here we arrive, finally, at the religious dimensions of economic and political systems with which we began this chapter. Bouglé claims that for Marx, collective representations are mere illusions, "religious hallucinations" and myths that oppress the proletariat (1918: 239). Marx and Durkheim differ most sharply on the issue of religious representations. For Marx, religion is the opium of the people, an epiphenomenon of psychological processes (ibid.: 240). In this regard, both positivists and orthodox economists share Marx's disdain for religion, although for slightly different reasons. But according to Bouglé, Durkheim regarded religious representations as the most basic social phenomena such that, "in principle, *everything is religious*" (ibid.: 241; emphasis added). Indeed, Durkheim claimed that "religion is in a word the system of symbols by means of which society becomes conscious of itself; it is the characteristic way of thinking of collective existence" ([1897] 1951: 312).[2] In keeping with Durkheim's high regard for the power of religious representations, Bouglé (1918) claims *that economic evolution is preceded by a long period of religious evolution*. Here is still another aspect of Durkheim's ([1912] 1965) belief that religion is the "womb" from which all other institutions are derived, including economic institutions (discussed in Meštrović 1991). The question to which this neglected aspect of Durkheim's sociological theory leads is the following: has religion (in the Durkheimian sense) evolved to the point at which a "religion of humanity" can sustain a just and humane economic system?

Bouglé (1918: 245–6) concludes with an interesting contrast of metaphors regarding Marx and Durkheim. For Marx, representations in general and religious representations in particular are *reflectors*, epiphenomena of other processes, primarily materialistic and economic forces. But for Durkheim, representations in general and religious representations in particular are *prisms*, cultural phenomena that illuminate almost everything else that occurs in society.[3] The relevance of this crucial distinction for the present discussion should be obvious: Marxism and communism both tried to derive the good society from an economic rearrangement which downplayed or was even hostile to religion. Communism failed, but instead of admitting defeat, Marxists as well as classical economists are bent on another program of deriving the good society from economic restructuring – this time, capitalism, in the West as well as the former communist countries. The Marxists may be wrong in their modernist assumption that religion is relatively unimportant. But the Durkheimians may turn out to be right that almost everything in societies, including political and economic phenomena, are refractions of society's pre-existing religious arrangements.

APPREHENDING DURKHEIM'S POLITICAL AND ECONOMIC THEORY IN THE POSTMODERNIST ERA

Most of the commentators on Durkheim's stance on communism, socialism, and Marxism – whether their orientation is to the political left or right – tend to grudgingly concede a few insights to Durkheim, and then proceed to criticize him on the basis of Marxist, positivistic, or other Enlightenment assumptions. The tenor and drift of these criticisms have already been explored in Chapter 1. For the purposes of this chapter, it is important to note that Durkheim offers a fresh alternative to the debate between socialism and capitalism, one that is profoundly relevant to the postmodernist discourse that has called into question Enlightenment narratives and assumptions. This is because he regards both socialism and capitalism as modernist doctrines that are doomed to fail because they try to derive the good society from egoism (what we call narcissism), and he felt that this was an impossible undertaking (Durkheim [1928] (1958)).

For example, in *The Radical Durkheim*, Frank Pearce (1989) points to the obviously liberal strand that binds Durkheim to Marx. This is a welcome alternative to the incorrect depictions of Durkheim as a status quo functionalist. But again, Pearce criticizes Durkheim's sociology for being inadequate compared with Marxism. Now that Marxism is in turmoil, and has been discredited at least to some extent by the failure of the communist experiment, it seems more reasonable to take Durkheim seriously and to apply his thought to the post-modernist debate. In general, most scholars who comment on Durkheim's socio-political thought approach him from the bias of Enlightenment narratives that are being questioned here, and so fail to appreciate the contribution that his sociology can still make to contemporary problems.

In *Capital* (1858), Marx's ostensible aim is to demystify what he considers to be vulgar economic understandings of commodities, perverted understandings that transform social relations into properties of commodities. (Both Veblen and Adorno appreciate this aspect of Marxism to question reification.) For Marx, "every commodity is a symbol, since, in so far as it is value, it is only the material envelope of the human labor spent upon it" ([1858] 1977: 90). Marx adheres to the peculiar claim that value is an "objective" expression of the human labor that was expended upon making a product (ibid.: 43). Commodities in which equal quantities of labor are "embodied" should have the same value (ibid.: 39). Labor is "crystallized" in a commodity such that the value of a commodity actually represents human labor – though vulgar economists are blind to this supposedly obvious fact, according to Marx. Contrary to one's intuitions, Marx claims that the less labor is expended in the production of an article, the less is its value (ibid.: 40). Marx tries to make his notion that commodities embody labor seem reasonable by invoking Aristotle, and many contemporary Marxists are trying desperately to resuscitate his rational theory of value (see, for example, Postone 1993). But Henry Adams, H.G. Wells, and many other intellectuals from the previous *fin de siècle* commented that they could not follow Marx in his strange efforts to quantify value and make it seem entirely rational. Against Marx, I agree with Marcel Mauss, who wrote:

> I do not think there can, for a long time, be a purely rational society. . . . Why should one expect the domain of the economy, the domain of needs and tastes, to be one of pure reason? Why should one expect that a world with such crazy values, where a clown's buffoonery is worth as much as the patents of the finest inventions, why should one expect that world suddenly to abandon its scale of values? . . . Why should that world suddenly be governed by the fairy tale of the masses' intelligence or the intelligence imposed on them by the magic and force of a Communist elite?
>
> ([1925] 1992: 190)

Neither Marx's followers nor his critics are certain what he meant by his claim that value embodies the average amount of labor that was expended in creating a commodity. What is important from the perspective of the present discussion is that in this regard, Marx is betraying an extreme tendency to spin his economic theory off the grand narratives of the Enlightenment. His supposedly demystified, hyper-quantitative, hyper-rational rhetoric appealed to positivists and economists who would not otherwise agree with the specifically socialist aspects of Marx's overall thought.

Missing from Marx's excessively rationalistic understanding of value is the notion of non-rational desire. Humans value fancy cars, beauty, expensive homes, prestige, and luxury regardless of the labor or utility that these represent. For Schopenhauer, as for Durkheim, the will that animates desire is blind, a pure hunger that knows no bounds. This is the insight that apparently inspired Veblen's cynical and sarcastic *Theory of the Leisure Class* ([1899] 1967). Yet Marx attacks classical economists for treating money, diamonds, and pearls as if they were inherently valuable, as if these commodities were *religious* fetishes. Marx traces the basis of this bourgeois "stupidity," as he calls it, to the "religious reflex" that causes humans to worship Nature ([1858] 1977: 79). His overall aim is to strip away these fetishes and illusions, to make human relations with other humans and with Nature intelligible and reasonable (Fromm 1962). Schopenhauer, Durkheim, and many other *fin de siècle* thinkers regarded such aims as impossible from the outset. According to the *fin de siècle* spirit, one can never really rid humans of their sense of mystery, metaphysics, prestige, and reverence for Nature, all that goes into the non-rational aspects of social life, and that is crystallized most clearly in the social institution of religion.

Durkheim took up Marx's concept of value directly, and criticized it:

> This is how we escaped the fallacies of the classical economists *and* the socialists. . . . As we have said, it is not the amount of labor put into a thing which makes its value; it is the way in which the value of this thing is assessed by the society, and this valuation depends, not so much on the amount of energy expended, as on the *useful results* it produces, such at least as they are felt to be by the collectivity, for there is a *subjective factor which cannot be ruled out. An idea of genius, flowering without effort and created with joy, has greater value and merit than years of manual labor.*
>
> ([1950] 1983: 216; emphasis added).

Veblen (1899) and Adorno (1991) are two among many thinkers who pursued this Durkheimian line of thinking (even if they were not inspired directly by him). However, Riesman (1953) has exposed an interesting ambiguity regarding Veblen's social thought in this regard: Veblen is Marxist in his assumption that a strictly efficient and objective system of value can be established even as he exposes the subjective factors that are involved in value. Veblen ([1899] 1967: 97) calls "waste" that which "does not serve human life or human well-being on the whole" even though he admits that a certain amount of wasteful, "idle curiosity" is indispensable for innovation. A similar ambiguity exists in Durkheim's attitude toward anomie as a wasteful state that is essential to "the spirit of progress." Durkheim never specified how much anomie is healthy and how much is pathogenic.

Nevertheless, the problem is not insoluble. The important point is that Durkheim's sociology presents intellectuals with a problem to be solved that is relevant to the postmodernist age: given that human desire cannot be made rational and "efficient," how shall society establish the *just* limit of what individuals ought to desire for their own psychological and sociological well-being? How much prestige, conspicuous consumption, and conspicuous waste is appropriate to an individual and society? This seems to be a more realistic problem than the free-market assumption that spontaneous order will emerge in the market on the one hand, and the Marxist assumption that desire can be made rational on the other.

In sum, Marxist economics betrays its modernist assumptions in its hostility toward religion and in its aim to explain value in completely rationalist terms. Durkheimian economics, by contrast, betrays its anti-modernist assumptions in its hostility toward Marxism and in its aim to accept a certain amount of irrationality in economic as well as other aspects of social life, but contain these irrational tendencies within "just" limits. But justice itself is a moral concept derived from religious thought, which is why Durkheim ([1893] 1933) referred to his version of sociology as the science of moral facts.

WHAT SHALL BE DONE WITH THE DIVISION OF LABOR?

Karl Marx captured the imaginations of generations of intellectuals with his dream of a classless society. He singled out the division of labor as the culprit of oppression, and presented a utopian vision in which virtually anyone would be able to do what he or she wanted while living in perfect harmony with others. In a famous passage, Marx writes:

> For as soon as labor is distributed, each man has a particular, exclusive sphere of activity, which is forced upon him and from which he cannot escape. He is a hunter, a fisherman, a shepherd, or a critical critic, and must remain so if he does not want to lose his means of livelihood; while in communist society, where nobody has one exclusive sphere of activity but each can become accomplished in any branch he wishes, society regulates the general production and thus makes it possible for me to do one thing today and another tomorrow, to hunt in the morning, fish in the afternoon, rear cattle in the evening, criticize after dinner, just as I have a mind, without ever becoming hunter, fisherman, shepherd or critic.

(1983:177)

Ironically, only the leisure class holds the luxury of being able to do one thing today and another tomorrow. Minimizing the division of labor and over-regulating production not only stifled communist economies. Social solidarity was weakened and the seeds of Balkanization were sown because Marxism unwittingly promoted what Durkheim ([1893] 1933) called "mechanical solidarity," which is brittle compared with the "organic solidarity" based upon the division of labor. Knowing what we know now, how naive Bellamy (1888) seems, and all the many others who took Marx seriously in this regard. And it is high time to take Durkheim seriously on the question of whether an advanced division of labor really does promote a high degree of social solidarity *as well as* individualism.

Contrary to many false depictions of him as a conservative thinker, Durkheim ([1893] 1933) argued that the division of labor, in its normal, non-anomic state, would actually liberate the individual, and in any case was a process that could not be stopped or reversed. Note the key point that for Durkheim ([1893] 1933: 171), it is individualism, not socialism, that is modern and inevitable: "Individualism, free thought, dates neither from our time, nor from 1789, nor from the Reformation, nor from scholasticism, nor from the decline of Graeco-Latin polytheism or oriental theocracies. It is a phenomenon which begins in no certain part, but which develops without cessation all through history." Moreover, Durkheim never associates the development of individualism with the rise of the so-called West. Rather, he argues that individualism is promoted anytime and anywhere that the division of labor develops.

Additionally, individualism itself comes in two varieties, what Durkheim called higher or moral individualism versus egoism, or what we call narcissism (Meštrović 1988). And both forms of individualism are actually rooted in cultural habits, representations, and other social phenomena. In other words, Durkheim rejects the Enlightenment dogma that individualism is derived from the individual. Social development involves *homo duplex* or the dualism of human nature, a dialectic of forces, such that "there are in each of us . . . two consciences: one which is common to our group in its entirety . . . the other, on the contrary, represents that in us which is personal and distinct, that which makes us an individual" ([1893] 1933: 129). Thus, "there are, here, two contrary forces, one centripetal, the other centrifugal" (ibid.: 130).

Given his reliance on *homo duplex* as the ground for social development, Durkheim could not follow Marx in proposing unequivocal progress into liberation of the individual from culture – a centripetal principle. For Durkheim, there will always exist a push and pull relative to individualism versus the awesome power of the collectivity. So Durkheim sought a social standard of justice to temper inequality and other imperfections in social life that he felt would never be eliminated completely. He felt that "the moral conscience of nations is in this respect correct; it prefers a little justice to all the industrial perfection in the world" (ibid.: 51). Even if the ideal of equality were approached, "one sort of heredity will always exist, that of natural talent", because "intelligence, taste, scientific, artistic, literary or industrial ability, courage and manual dexterity are gifts received by each of us at birth, as the heir to wealth receives his capital or as the nobleman formerly received his title and function" ([1897] 1951: 251). Thus, "a moral discipline will be required to make those less favored by nature accept the lesser advantages which they owe to the chance of birth" (ibid.). Compulsory equality in the name of individual freedom was out of the question for Durkheim.

While Durkheim never specified exactly how this moral discipline can be imposed in a just manner, the more important point is that his incomplete thinking on this matter deserves to be taken seriously now that Marxist utopianism has been called into question by the fall of communism. Given his concept of *homo duplex*, Durkheim assumed that individuals cannot control their desires of their own accord, that "they cannot assign themselves this law of justice" ([1893] 1933: 249). He elaborates:

> So they must receive it [justice] from an authority which they respect, to which they yield spontaneously. Either directly and as a whole, or through the agency of one of its organs, society alone can play this moderating role; for it is the only moral power superior to the individual, the authority which he accepts. It alone has the power necessary to stipulate law and to set the point beyond which the passions must not go. . . . As a matter of fact, at every moment of history there is a dim perception, in the moral consciousness of societies, of the respective value of different social services, the relative reward due to each, and the consequent degree of comfort appropriate on the average to workers in each occupation. . . . [Thus] the man of wealth is reproved if he lives the life of a poor man, but also if he seeks the refinements of luxury overmuch. Economists may protest in vain; public feeling will always be scandalized *if an individual spends too much wealth for wholly superfluous use, and it even seems that this severity relaxes only in times of moral disturbance.* A genuine regimen exists, therefore, although not always legally formulated, which fixes with relative precision the maximum degree of ease of living to which each social class may legitimately aspire. However, there is nothing immutable about such a scale. It changes with the increase or decrease of collective revenue and the changes occurring in the *moral ideas* of society. Thus what appears luxury to one period no longer does so to another; and the well-being which for long periods was granted to a class only by exception and supererogation, finally appears strictly necessary and equitable.
>
> (ibid.: 249–50; emphasis added)

Note again the emphasis on religious conceptualization even in discussions of economic and political life. The Marxists as well as many postmodernists have sought to eliminate all such religious and moral concerns as oppressive mystification. But they overlook the fact that even in communist societies the masses did perceive the injustice of their leaders living in luxury while they could barely make ends meet. A moral conscience survived communism, much as Durkheim described, and the fall of communism was not due just to economic mismanagement and failure – as if only modernist, utilitarian principles counted. Ordinary people in communist countries were angry at the perceived moral injustice brought on by the communist system.

Durkheim noticed that even in decadent societies – capitalist, socialist, or dominated by some other economic system – the moral conscience of humanity is offended by conspicuous waste and infinite, anomic consumption at the expense of others. Durkheim's critics have accused him of promoting Fascism because of his high esteem of society (see Ranulf 1939). But this is a patently false charge when one considers that, unlike the Fascists, Durkheim was trying to promote the individual (see Giddens 1977). And as Turner and Kassler (1992) point out, post-Durkheimian sociologists have apologized for or condoned Fascism despite their anti-Fascist rhetoric. Other critics have charged that Durkheim is defending the status quo, but again, the careful reader will note that he is critical of societies and epochs that promote immorality, decadence, and injustice, and that he consistently upholds the moral ideals of justice and humanity. Despite all the criticisms levelled at him, an unbiased reader will probably agree with Durkheim's argument above, in the context of his overall theory: the poor in postmodernist USA would be considered wealthy by the standards of a developing country, and the postmodernist middle class has access to more comforts than the leisure classes of yesteryear. He is completely sensitive to the fact that societies change, but he is always mindful of liberal, individualist ideals. In the present *fin de siècle*, homelessness is frequently discussed as a consequence of the Reagan and Thatcher eras, along with the massive shifting of wealth from the poor and middle classes to the wealthy. It seems to be the case that part of the postmodernist cultural program is to bring forth a greater class consciousness of the class divisions, conflicts, and inequalities that are present more than a century following Marx's writings. (Although the opposite current also exists: the belief that class divisions are less important than "lifestyles," which presumably cut across classes.) But is the Marxist solution of a classless society or the liberal emphasis on equality the only alternative to capitalist exploitation? Durkheim's sociology offers a neglected alternative that is as sensitive as the Marxist focus on class differences, yet avoids the unwelcome solutions offered by the Marxists, liberals, as well as neo-conservative capitalists.

The role of the division of labor in modernity lies at the heart of discussions of this sort. Durkheim (1893) began his career with the thesis that the division of labor is a natural process that pertains equally to the biological and social worlds. It is a force that regulates at the same time that it liberates the individual, and it cannot be put into motion, stopped, nor controlled by humans. In Schopenhauerian terms, it has a "will" of its own that works through humans, and its origin is the will to life, the struggle for existence. But unlike Spencer, and more in line with Kropotkin and Veblen, Durkheim could see that cooperation as well as competition are forces that result in the division of labor: "The division of labor is, then, a result of the struggle for existence, but it is a mellowed *denouement*. Thanks to it, opponents are not obliged to fight to a finish, but can exist one beside the other" (Durkheim [1893] 1933: 270).

Durkheim was sensitive to the inequalities and injustices of his day that seemed to accompany the progress of the division of labor, but he steadfastly refused to admit that these were due to natural and normal development. Instead, he referred to these problems as effects of the anomic, abnormal, or "forced" division of labor, and thought that these abnormalities could be repaired or at least controlled within tolerable limits by humans. All this is well known to anyone who has studied Durkheim's *Division of Labor* (1893). Equally evident are the unfounded charges by most of Durkheim's commentators that he was a conservative defender of the status quo because he refused to adopt the Marxist attitude toward the division of labor.

But humanity has now witnessed the results of almost a century's worth of tampering with the division of labor by many Marxist regimes. Of course, intellectual Marxists deny that these regimes "really" understood Marx's intentions. Let us return to Marx's famous passage on the supposedly evil effects of the division of labor, quoted above. The educated postmodernist reader knows that all of the activities depicted by Marx are actually much more complex, time-consuming, and bureaucratic in modern societies than Marx could have imagined. One cannot simply be a critic, artist, or anything else at will. These things require education or a license or permits or some other contact with an advanced division of labor. Even the seemingly simple chore of purchasing and finding a parking spot is an onerous chore in most postmodern universities. In this regard, I agree with Pearce (1989) that Marx's theories cannot possibly apply to any societies that have moved beyond peasant or otherwise traditional culture. Durkheim's theory of the division of labor needs to be reappreciated as a viable alternative to Marxist concerns.

THE SPIRIT OF CASTE DESPITE MODERNITY

One of the most ironic aspects of the communist system is that it reproduced the class inequalities characteristic of capitalist systems even as it tried to eradicate all class distinctions. Bouglé's (1908) neglected *Essays on the Caste System* is an excellent illustration of the Durkheimian explanation for this and other ironies, because it is a quest for a synthesis of opposing forces, and for treating an essentially Marxist problem in a non-Marxist way. The focal point of Bouglé's discussion is the notion of the "spirit of caste" (le régime des castes). Bouglé's reliance on the metaphor "spirit" reminds one of Max Weber's controversial use of the idea of the "spirit of capitalism." Might not the use of "spirit" be another echo of the German *Geist*? And one should make the connection to Veblen's insistence that modern economic practices are derived from barbaric "habits of the mind" that are essentially exploitative. Although he focuses on the caste system in India, and does not refer to Veblen directly, Bouglé argues that the spirit of caste persists, albeit in a diluted form, in modern Western societies.[4] The essential argument is that the spirit of caste is centripetal: it works against the normal develop ment of the division of labor in modern organic solidarity, and against the eventual, natural developments of justice and moral individualism. The spirit of caste pertains to all social forces that repel this natural development of justice, that lead the individual to retreat into his or her particular group rather than society as a whole, that prevent alliances and contracts, and that atomize and divide (Bouglé [1908] 1971: 9). With so much concern expressed by postmodern opinion-makers and politicians over "tribalism," Balkanization, and divisiveness in the present *fin de siècle*, it is obvious that Bouglé's interpretation of Durkheim is still fresh and relevant.

In the context of Schopenhauer's ([1818] 1965a) anti-Enlightenment philosophy, Bouglé seems to be claiming that the spirit of caste works against the social will to life as it works itself out in the division of labor. Durkheim ([1893] 1933: 130) dealt with aspects of this problem under the rubric of centripetal forces that oppose the centrifugal forces of the division of labor, which has come to be known as the opposition between particularism versus universalism. Here is another aspect of Durkheim's own sensitivity to the dialectics involved in Enlightenment narratives, including the narrative of unilateral progress that emerged later in Adorno's (1991) writings. Durkheim did not favor the development of one force to the detriment of the other, but sought their reconciliation and the production of new social forms.

According to Bouglé, all specialization holds the dangerous potential of preserving the spirit of caste. In more contemporary language, Bouglé seems to be arguing that the specialization required in an advanced division of labor can degenerate into a narcissistic loyalty to one's particular profession, firm, class, or other reproduction of ancient tribes. Durkheim seems to have implied this in the sections of his *Division of Labor* devoted to the abnormal forms of the division of labor ([1893] 1933: 353–73) as well as to the sections of *Suicide* devoted to anomie within capitalist societies ([1897] 1951: 241–58). Like Durkheim, Bouglé seems to believe that this abnormal form of association is not inherent to the division of labor. Rather, it is a phase which the West outgrew "in antiquity" but which recurs periodically during periods of anomie and other abnormal developments in the West (Bouglé [1908] 1971: 14). However, "India has prolonged, indefinitely, a phase that other civilizations have only passed through" (ibid.: 61).

Given the Durkheimian assumption that religious representations are the most important kind of representational life, it is not surprising that much of Bouglé's discussion centers on religion, especially Indian religions. In Bouglé's view, the caste phenomenon is essentially religious, and this dimension of social inequality pertains to Islam, Christianity, and Hinduism, as well as to the civil societies derived from them. (Compare Veblen's [1899] 1967 mocking treatment of devotional observances by the predatory leisure class.) These religious, collective representations express a collective reality as well as the subjective experience of individuals, although all this occurs for the most part unconsciously. In Bouglé's words, "The tree bears leaves while knowing nothing of the roots" ([1908] 1971: 125).

Bouglé believes that both Hinduism and Buddhism are examples of a kind of "political neurasthenia" because of their emphasis upon flight from the world (ibid.: 74). "In a word," Bouglé adds, "Buddhism retains and reinforces that in Hindu thought which turns away from life" (ibid.: 75). In these religious systems, present injustices are accepted because the rigid hierarchy is accepted as the expression of a secret justice (ibid.: 76). For example, one's low social status is a just punishment for evils committed in a previous life. It is difficult to avoid making a connection here with Erich Fromm's (1955) discussion of passive acceptance of injustice in traditional as well as capitalist societies. Indeed, the defenders of capitalism are equally guilty of using the secret justice of Adam Smith's invisible hand to rationalize the real injustices and hardships often caused by unregulated markets.

The spirit of caste is not only unjust, it is inimical to any true social solidarity. (Durkheim [1893] 1933 also held that primitive forms of social solidarity are brittle and subject to easy dispersion.) There can be no genuine patriotism in societies characterized by the spirit of caste because "respect for the caste system is the patriotism of the Hindus. They enact a paradox in that they can only unite in the cult which divides them" (Bouglé 1918: 142). Bouglé's assessment is in keeping with Durkheim's claim that modern forms of association should, in their ideal states, transcend ethnocentric particularism and be oriented toward universalism and cosmopolitanism. At the same time, centripetal forces will be transformed into a high, collective regard for the family and the "cult of the individual."

In his conclusion, Bouglé refers to Durkheim's *Division of Labor* to make the point that "the role of the division of labor is precisely to substitute an organic solidarity which liberates the individual from the mechanical solidarity which oppresses him" ([1908] 1971: 167). It is interesting that, according to the Durkheimians, primitive forms of association, such as refractions of the caste system, persist despite and within modern forms of association. This is another *fin de siècle* assumption that differentiates Durkheim's legacy from the Marxists as well as from the utilitarians and modernists, who optimistically assume that one can achieve a complete break with the past. It seems that Durkheim's assumptions are more realistic and certainly more relevant to the contemporary discourse in postmodernism.

This is because, for Durkheim, it is possible for a society to be simultaneously very modern *vis-à-vis* the latest technology and the dominance of an advanced division of labor and extremely traditional *vis-à-vis* all sorts of fundamentalist movements, religious fanaticism, and a caste-like devotion to one's immediate group, among other postmodern paradoxes and ironies. From a Durkheimian perspective, the persistence of the primitive and originally religious "spirit of caste" is the cause of present-day inequalities, injustices, and anomie in modern societies. Ultimately, the spirit of caste contributes to the Balkanization process that we have been tracing outside the Balkans as well as within the former Yugoslavia. But this centripetal force is also the source of religion, family life, nostalgia, patriotism, tradition, and other aspects of the collective conscience that must be *transformed*, not eliminated by social progress. Bouglé's interpretation of Durkheim seems to extend Schopenhauer's (1818) depiction of the simultaneously destructive and constructive aspects of the will to life. And as suggested repeatedly, it is entirely consistent with Veblen's (1899) analysis of modernity as a fundamentally ambiguous phenomenon, part barbaric and part civilized. As such, it offers a complex alternative to the simplistic Marxist formula for and solution to class conflict.

THE DURKHEIMIAN ALTERNATIVE TO MARXISM

Durkheim's pacifism, his groping for a brand new solution to the barbarism that exists within the heart of the modernist project, has been missed by his commentators on both sides of the political spectrum. Durkheim did not advocate revolution, and he wanted to modify, soften, and temper the advanced division of labor that is the backbone of all market economies. The Marxists accuse him of supporting the status quo, and "conflict theorists" teach solemnly that, contrary to Durkheim's peaceful intentions, conflict is an inevitable aspect of social life. The functionalists and rational choice theorists cannot accept Durkheim's call for regulation of the market even if they subscribe to the need for "the rule of law" and "social order." The law and order they have in mind is not attuned to Durkheim's notions of social justice or altruism. Rather, they call on the state to insure their rights to self-interest, and dismiss Durkheim's charge that self-interest is anomic. And it is still true in our *fin de siècle* that most legislators are wealthy, so their self-interest naturally tends toward promoting wealth for the leisure class, not the weak and powerless members of society.

As early as 1886, Durkheim had predicted the demise of socialism *and* communism:

> Production will be abundant only if the individual is stimulated to produce. The soil may be fertile, the people intelligent, and science in progress. But for the indispensable lever of individual action, which puts these things in motion, there will be not a single atom of value created, and all these riches of nature and intelligence will be as if they never were. Socialism makes society into an army of functionaries paid at more or less fixed rates. Consequently, each worker, no longer being directly interested in his work, performs only mechanically. Precision might be asked of him, but not zeal. Absorbed in society, he will consider himself too insignificant to dare to undertake anything. What good is it to exhaust oneself in efforts which will be lost, anonymous and invisible, in this enormous mass of the state? Besides, the state is too massive a machine for such delicate operations.
>
> (Durkheim [1886] 1990: 28)

Durkheim prophesied accurately the crisis of motivation and legitimation that occurred in Eastern Europe and the former Soviet Union, and that is slowly creeping into "capitalist" countries as well, as they embrace some elements of socialism in the guise of the welfare state. But he was equally critical of the *laissez-faire*, unregulated, free-market capitalism that was popularized by Ronald Reagan, Margaret Thatcher, and George Bush in the 1980s, and promulgated by the New Right. The word deregulation captures the ethos of the 1980s and 1990s in politics and economics, as well as in popular culture. The rich irony here is that contemporary conservatives and liberals agree that productivity and the overall social good occur when the government's interference with individual freedom is minimized. This assumption places faith in the bankrupt notion of Adam Smith's "invisible hand", which may have "worked" in Adam Smith's time due to the many cultural constraints placed on individual greed, but proved to be disastrous when applied to the Me-generation of the 1980s and 1990s. The result has not been an increase in overall prosperity, but deep recessions related to unprecedented economic and political scandals, as well as narcissism and increased divisiveness in the social fabric as a whole. These are exactly the things that Durkheim predicted about a century ago.

In contrast to the boosterish but flawed views that make up modernist narratives, Durkheim ([1950] 1983) conceived of the state as a potentially benign, moral entity that could and should act to guarantee human rights and general morality:

> The fundamental duty of the State is laid down in this very fact; it is to persevere in calling the individual to a moral way of life. . . . If the cult of the human person is to be the only one destined to survive, as it seems, it must be observed by the State as by the individual equally. This cult, moreover, has all that is required to take the place of the religious cults of former times. It serves quite as well as they to bring about that communion of minds and wills which is a first condition of any social life.
>
> ([1950] 1983: 69)

Several aspects of Durkheim's formulation require explication. First, Durkheim's reference to morality escapes the cultural and moral relativist's objections, "Whose morality shall be imposed?" By morality, Durkheim referred to that minimal amount of human sympathy and what might be termed communalism without which society could not exist. This is because a society based exclusively on egoism would annihilate itself. Second, Durkheim's reference to the *cult* of the human person is obviously religious in the broadest sense of the term, and is part of his career-long focus on "moral individualism." Moral individualism is a set of cultural beliefs, values and other "collective representations" that ascribe worth, dignity, and respect to the human person living in modern (but not just Western) societies. Third, this respect for human rights – which is taken for granted in modern societies, but is not explained except for the untenable reference to "natural rights" – is religious in nature, and is an extension of earlier religious habits, including the habit of synthetically attaching sanctity to various phenomena. In this case, the social category of "sacredness," which is the staple of religions as defined by Durkheim, attaches itself synthetically to human persons. But there is nothing inherently sacred about humans: society must sanctify them in this religious manner for them to be treated with respect by their fellows. In sum, Durkheim regards individualism itself (but not egoism) as a civic religion in modern times.

Durkheim's view of the state's role in promoting this new civic religion is an alternative to Herbert Spencer's atomistic individualism as well as to Hegel's state absolutism, the two doctrines that have animated capitalism versus communism and socialism, respectively. If the state does not intervene or regulate business activity in some fashion, the end result will not be long-term prosperity – almost all economists admit the necessity of periods of inflation and recession alternating with short-term prosperity in capitalist systems – but overall anomie. Durkheim's view that the modern state must regulate the individual is consistent with Arthur Schopenhauer's ([1818] 1965a: 133) earlier claim that "without such checks and in view of the infinite number of egoistic individuals, the *bellum omnium contra omnes* [war of all against all] would be the order of the day, to the undoing of all." The tremendous political and business scandals of the 1980s and 1990s cause one to at least give pause to Durkheim's view.

On the other hand, according to Durkheim,

> If the State is not everything, we must not conclude that it is nothing. It should not do everything, but it must not leave everything undone. It has some specific economic functions and obligations. If it can, by itself, neither produce nor distribute riches, at least it can and ought to regulate circulation. Its duty is to oversee the health of society. Now, among all living beings, the equilibrium of forces, the just proportion among its parts, is the condition of health.
>
> ([1886] 1990: 28)

It is important to note that by using the word "regulation," Durkheim did *not* imply the kind of vast, bureaucratic, welfare state that often impedes individual initiative and that neoconservatives loathe. Instead, he thought of the spontaneous, emotional "regulation" that occurs in families and small groups, and that is not perceived as oppressive. Furthermore, he thought of the state as a small, centralized brain-center whose function is to "think" more than to act, whose task is "to ensure the most complete individuation that the state of society will allow of. Far from its tyrannizing over the individual, it is the State that redeems the individual from society" ([1950] 1983: 69). The essential difference from free-market assumptions is Durkheim's insistence that "It is not this or that individual the State seeks to develop, it is the individual *in genere*, who is not to be confused with any single one of us" (ibid.).

It may be helpful to connect Durkheim's version of soft socialism, in which the state is the brain and the people are the heart, to a similar vision found in H.G. Wells's socialism. In *The Fate of Man*, Wells (1939: 216) could see already that both communism and Western socialism were heading in what he thought was the wrong direction:

> Both Roosevelt and Stalin were attempting to produce a huge, modern, scientifically organized, socialist state, the one out of a warning crisis and the other out of a chaos, and the lack of a brain organization to give that state consciousness and coherence was a difference not in nature, but degree.

The reference to the state as a brain, a kind of consciousness but not the center of activity is one more bit of unfinished business from the previous *fin de siècle* that we shall pursue in this Durkheimian analysis.

In the remaining pages of this chapter, I shall sketch Durkheim's theory of the state as it pertains to economic interests in order to point the way to a viable alternative to both socialism and orthodox capitalism. But given the space constraints of this book, it is nothing more than a sketch. The postmodern rebellion at narratives spun from the Enlightenment – and the doctrine of self-interest is one such narrative – demands that one take Durkheim seriously, at long last, in relation to an alternative to old and dying systems of thought.

In his *Professional Ethics and Civic Morals*, Durkheim ([1950] 1983: 96) links his discussion of political anomie with a discussion of economic anomie. The causes of both types of anomie are rooted in socialist and classical capitalist conceptions of the state and market because both of these seek to unfetter the human will. But in line with Schopenhauer's insistence that the human will is by nature infinite and insatiable, Durkheim writes that "to the extent that the individual is left to his own devices and freed from all social constraint, he is unfettered too by all moral constraint" (p. 7). And,

> It is not possible for a social function to exist without moral discipline. Otherwise, nothing remains but individual appetites, and since they are by nature boundless and insatiable, if there is nothing to control them they will not be able to control themselves.
>
> (p. 11)

He elaborates on the passage above:

> The unleashing of economic interests has been accompanied by a debasing of public morality. We find that the manufacturer is aware of no influence set above him to check his egoism. He is subject to no moral discipline.
>
> (p. 12)

Note that in keeping with his holistic approach to society, Durkheim links economic habits with habits in other areas of social life. He concludes that "There is no form of social activity which can do without the appropriate moral discipline" (ibid.). The shadow of Schopenhauer's thought is evident in Durkheim's argument: society (and not just the state, but all of society) is the system of collective representations that must restrain the human will, which is by nature insatiable. If society fails in this moral task to restrain these desires and aims, and fails to turn at least some of them into an altruistic direction, "it is inevitable that these aims will become antisocial" (ibid.: 15). Centrifugal forces must be offset by centripetal forces, and vice versa.

Durkheim writes that all the professions except business have their code of ethics. This fact, in itself, contributes to anomie. In addition, all the major social functions have been made secondary to economic functions (an insight shared by Veblen 1899). Even the government, which ought to regulate economic life, has instead "become its tool and servant" ([1950] 1983: 283). The only rule in modern economics is that of self-interest, which is insufficient for morality:

Even from the strictly utilitarian standpoint, what is the purpose of heaping up riches if they do not serve to abate the desires of the greatest number, but, on the contrary, only rouse their impatience for gain?

(ibid.: 161)

The consequences of cultural narcissism affect the *entire* social body, not just one particular class, resulting in crisis, suffering, anarchy, evil, disorganization, disaggregation, trouble, disarray, and anomaly (ibid.: 16–30). In short, anomie as it is exhibited in the economic institutions is an amoral condition that amounts to a "public danger" (ibid.: 18).

In general, along with the classical economists, the socialists and the Saint-Simonians are all accused of unwittingly promoting anomie, by advocating the reversal of *homo duplex*: the lower, egoistical pole of the dualism of human nature is established as the basis for market economics and for democratic institutions. Perhaps this assumption could and did work up to a point in the early stages of industrialization, but Durkheim is probably right that the postmodern individual will can never serve as the basis for morality. Scores of writers, from David Riesman to Christopher Lasch, have documented the eruption of narcissism, egoism, and flagrant decadence in postmodern societies.

For Durkheim, the state is an organ of social thought, a set of collective representations, that exists in a relationship of cybernetic "feedback" with the people, the nation it rules. The people and the nation are conceived as a bundle of chaotic desires, as "will." The formula for *homo duplex* is reproduced here, with the state representing the "higher" aims and the nation representing the "lower." The state's responsibility is to act as *conscience* and "to work out certain representations which hold good for the collectivity" ([1950] 1983: 50). Durkheim's vocabulary in describing the state includes the following words: deliberation, reflection, conscious, clarity, organized, and ego. "The people," on the other hand, are depicted in terms of what is obscure, unconsidered, automatic, blind, prejudiced, diffuse, sub-conscious, unconscious, and indefinite. One can scarcely avoid summing up Durkheim's characterization of the benign state and the people in Freud's terms of "ego" and "id," respectively – and to some extent, even consciousness versus the unconscious. But this Freudian terminology is also a refraction of Schopenhauer's opposition between idea and will, mind and heart, which we have established was the vocabulary characteristic of the *fin de siècle* in which Durkheim, Veblen, and Freud wrote. Durkheim reflects Schopenhauer's philosophy even to the extent of claiming that the state is the weak force and the nation the strong force in this dualistic scheme of things (ibid.: 95) – exactly the opposite of how these entities are described by postmodernists. Political anomie occurs when the people's unrestrained, unreflective will rules the state.

It follows that Durkheim does not regard the role of the state as administrative, as one of action. This is a key point that speaks to the heart of neoconservative reactions against the meddling of the state in private affairs. On the contrary, its role should be one of "consciousness and reflection" (ibid.: 50). Moreover, Durkheim disagrees with the popular view of democracy as society governing itself: "It is often said that under a democratic system the will and thought of those governing are identical and merge with the will and thought of those governed" (ibid.: 91).

Durkheim attributes this erroneous view to Rousseau (p. 99), and proceeds to criticize it: if everyone is to govern, then in fact no one governs, because the will of the masses in the political arena is as insatiable and unstable as it is in the economic arena. Because the human will is egoistic, it leads to divisiveness: "It is collective sentiments, diffused, vague and obscure as they may be, that sway the people" (p. 83). Democracies ruled by the will of the people are "pseudo-democracies" characterized by chaos, stormy changes in politics, instability, even "evil" (pp. 95–100 *passim*). The will is inherently unstable. Durkheim writes:

> How does the fact of having willed a certain law make it worthy of my own particular respect? What my will has done, my will can undo. Mutable as it is in its nature, it cannot serve as a foundation for anything stable.
>
> (p. 107)

Examples to support Durkheim's contentions may be found on both sides of the Atlantic. After the fall of communism, Eastern European nations held "democratic" elections that often swept into power populist, nationalist, and sometimes right-wing candidates in landslide victories that took away many civil liberties. In many cases, the former Bolshevik systems were replaced by almost equally oppressive forms of government. Indeed, many if not most of the "democratically" elected officials in formerly communist nations were ex-communists, whose habits of governing could not have changed from authoritarianism to democracy overnight. Similarly, on this side of the Atlantic, Americans often voted against their long-term best interest with regard to funding schools, prisons, roads, nuclear reactors for power, and made other, similar decisions based on short-term, economic self-interest that they will no doubt come to regret. In the present *fin de siècle*, Americans balk at paying even slightly higher taxes that would contribute to the common good. Historically, democratic sentiments had kept in place a host of racist, sexist, or otherwise inhumane policies that were candid expressions of the will of the people at the time, and that later generations had to abolish. Durkheim is not against democracy; but he does not believe that the core of democracy lies in the ballot box. Rather than follow in the wake of the will of the masses, the state must superimpose reflective thought on their desires. For Durkheim, democracy is not unreflective rule by the people, but effective "*communication*" between the state and the people:

> The more that deliberation and reflection and a critical spirit play a considerable part in the course of public affairs, the more democratic the nation. It is the less democratic when lack of consciousness, uncharted customs, the obscure sentiments and prejudices that evade investigation, predominate.
>
> ([1950] 1983: 89)

It is no surprise, therefore, that Durkheim puts little faith in mandate theory or universal suffrage: the voting behavior of the masses is subject to the instability of the will, or the conservative factor based on previous habits of the mind (from Veblen), or the manipulation of the culture industry (from Adorno). In any case, only a small fraction of the American population votes, so that its democracy is not, strictly speaking, an affirmation of the will of the people. Nor does Durkheim see any fundamental difference between various forms of government – monarchies or elective. The essential principle is for the state to rule by reflection, consciousness, the collective representation, discussion, and elaboration of the will of the people, *not* by action, sentiment, aspirations, or other derivatives of the will. Using the heart–mind dualism, one could characterize Durkheim's position as insisting that the state is the mind, not the heart of a people. Most so-called democratic nations follow the opposite principle: the state acts; its sphere of activity grows seemingly without check into an unruly bureaucracy; and the people respond to, elaborate upon, or otherwise follow in the wake of the state's actions. Freud's maxim that the ego should rule where the id dominates applies to Durkheim's thought. Durkheim concludes that the primary task for the future is "to work out something that can relieve us by degrees of a role for which the individual is not cast" (ibid.: 109). He never made clear what this "something" could be. But given that he was writing during the previous turn of the century, it seems unreasonable to expect more from him. It is far more surprising that his cogent criticisms of the cultural lag he was witnessing even in his time have been neglected.

Note that Durkheim was against making the individual's egoistic will the centerpiece of modern economic or political institutions. In these ways, his sociology is decidedly anti-Enlightenment, anti-modernist, and of course, anti-Marxist. His position is directly inimical to the received but old-fashioned wisdom that the atomized individual should be the ultimate basis for Western democratic and market institutions – and that this "wisdom," responsible for so much Western narcissism and decadence, should now be exported to formerly communist nations! It is little wonder that Durkheim's sociology has generally received a hostile reaction. All innovation is met with hostility or neglect, especially if the innovative doctrine criticizes egoism. Nevertheless, it is important to keep in mind that Durkheim's version of collectivism is commensurate with individualism, and that he was a champion of liberal, democratic values. But he sought the basis for this new liberalism outside the individual for the straightforward and convincing reason that no one is born with human rights unless their culture in general and state in particular are prepared to guarantee those rights.

It is certain that such a benign image of the state is radically new relative to its depictions by the political left and right. From a Durkheimian perspective, the Marxists erred in making the state the supreme organ for action, and mutilated completely its proper role of communication and consciousness. But the functionalists err in the opposite direction of making the state an appendix to the actions of the economic institutions, and thereby made the communication one-sided. Durkheim wants the state to dip into the lower layers of society, receive their input, and then elaborate that input through rational treatment by virtue of its expertise. Two-way, cybernetic communication is the essence of Durkheim's new proposal for democracy. And is not communication one of the buzzwords in the postmodernist discourse? Additionally, according to Daniel Bell and many other forecasters, communication and information, not industry, will become the hallmarks of future Western societies. In the face of this tide toward communication, it seems that the clinging to old-fashioned, predatory, egoistic versions of economics and politics that promote narcissism constitutes an aberration, an instance of widespread cultural lag that will be realized sooner or later.

In Durkheim's ([1893] 1933: 13) sweeping view of history, the moral conscience of nations will increasingly prefer justice to all the industrial perfection of the past. The true function of the division of labor is to create a "sentiment of solidarity" based on justice, *not* a social order that serves the interests of the powerful and the few (ibid.: 19). For Durkheim, the division of labor is more than an economic phenomenon: it is a moral phenomenon that upholds the value of genuine individualism, and protects the individual from predation (ibid.: 50). Like Veblen, Durkheim was hoping that pre-barbaric altruism – which is the true basis for solidarity, not egoistic individualism – would be refined in modern societies (ibid.: 174). Egoistic self-interest is an aberration, a particularistic mode of relating that is incompatible with a modern society's universal, transnational tendencies and need for communication (ibid.: 275). "The task of the most advanced societies is, then, a work of justice. . . . Just as ancient peoples needed, above all, a common faith to live by, so we need justice" (ibid.: 382).

Durkheim concludes his classic *Division of Labor* with the claims that the social ethics of the future demand that we be kind and just to our fellow humans, fulfill our tasks to the best of our abilities, and receive the "just price" for our efforts (ibid.: 404). It seems to be a reasonable and decent conclusion that balances justice with mercy, that is not ethnocentric in that the division of labor is not peculiarly Western, and above all, that is commensurate with the demands for justice expressed by most developing countries today. It is an ethic worthy of attention on both sides of the Atlantic, by the anomic societies that are currently preoccupied with postmodernist discourse as well as Eastern Europe and the former USSR as they attempt to emerge from tyranny. In sum, Durkheimianism is the most genuinely post-Marxist sociological doctrine available today.

Chapter 8

Conclusions

Based on the preceding discussion, we are in a position to make some concrete predictions and explanations that challenge the smug but probably false, optimistic faith that the Enlightenment narratives of the so-called West will help to achieve the utopian goals that were promised by Marxists and communists. These modernist, utopian goals include, but are not limited to, the victory of tolerance over racism and sexism, globalization, and the triumph of rationality over culture. Against these expectations, shared by modernists as well as some postmodernists, I predict that the process of Balkanization in the former Yugoslavia has not yet run its course and will probably cause still more fragmentation and violence; that Balkanization will spread to the former Soviet Union and that Russia will take on the role of Serbia relative to the other, formerly Soviet republics; and finally, that a form of Balkanization will tear apart and affect both East and West. The conflict between Islam and the West predicted by Ahmed (1992) will probably come to pass, but it will not replace the Cold War in the sense of a unified Islamic world against a unified Western world. Rather, the existing divisions within both Islamic and Christian nations and the civil religions derived from these faiths will probably worsen. Western Balkanization threatens not only the existence of the UN, NATO, the EC and a number of other globalizing organizations. It also threatens race relations, the relations between the sexes, and the very fabric of liberal institutions built on the remnants of the Enlightenment tradition. So Balkanization is a genuinely postmodern phenomenon, if one understands postmodernism to be a rebellion against the grand narratives of the Enlightenment.

I shall not review here all the evidence that has already been presented to arrive at this assessment. All evidence requires interpretation, in any event, and I relied on a theoretical framework based on the work of thinkers from the previous *fin de siècle* – an era that had already rebelled at the grand narratives of the Enlightenment – such as Emile Durkheim, Sigmund Freud, Georg Simmel, Thorstein Veblen, George Herbert Mead, and Max Weber, among others. I have argued that the anti-modernist, pessimistic yet pro-cultural viewpoints of these neglected thinkers has to be revived in order to perceive the process of disintegration that is already occurring, but that is masked by unconvincing, boosterish use of Enlightenment-based theories that assume linear progress, the victory of rationality over culture, and the ability to adopt a neutral point of view that is nobody's point of view, among other elements of modernism. If the reader rejects my reliance on anti-modernist sociological thinkers from the previous *fin de siècle*, then my pessimistic scenarios are called into question. But at the same time, no progress will have been made beyond the impasse found in the current literature on postmodernism, namely, whether postmodernism constitutes rebellion against or an extension of modernist narratives. This debate simply cannot be settled if one remains trapped within the assumptions of modernism that are called into question by postmodernism. One must step outside these assumptions. Let us continue to assume, for the sake of argument, and for the sake of introducing a radically new element into the postmodern discourse, that thinkers from the previous *fin de siècle* at least deserve a fair hearing. In that case, certain current events take on a significance that would otherwise not be apparent.

For example, consider the interpretation of Serbia's victory in the current Balkan War offered by Sheikh Mustafa Ceric, the top Islamic official in Sarajevo:

> "If Christians were being massacred in any Islamic country like the Muslims are being killed here," Sheik Ceric said, "the world community would have quickly found the means to condemn the Muslims as fundamentalists, and fighters of a holy war, and things would be taken care of overnight. A Muslim's life is now worth the least on the world market." "Bosnia's Muslims are the new Jews of Europe," the Muslim cleric said, "But we have no America to lean on. We have no one to lean on." ... "This is the first genocide to be committed under the protection of the United Nations," he said. "This is the first world-class crime to be carried out like a football game before the eyes of the entire world on television. And it has not helped at all. The Serbs are doing the dirty work of dealing with Bosnia's Muslims for all of Europe," he said.
>
> *(New York Times*, 25 June 1993: A3)

If one is to achieve a sympathetic understanding (from Max Weber) of this Muslim cleric's interpretation, then one has to assume that sympathetic understanding is more valuable than the purely cynical understandings offered by the modernists. If one is to make sense of the notion that the world community can act or fail to act in concert relative to a crime, one needs Emile Durkheim's notion of the collective consciousness. Otherwise, the term "world community" is just a cliché for the actions of nations that dominate the United Nations. The idea of the United Nations as an entity that can control human aggression needs to be tested against Sigmund Freud's ([1932] 1963) pessimistic prediction that such organizations will always fail to control the id. The observation that this particular instance of genocide was carried out on television can be explained by Georg Simmel's writings on how abstractionism desensitizes rather than moves or liberates the individual. If one is to take Sheikh Ceric seriously, one must learn how to take the role of the other – but that is a concept coined by George Herbert Mead. And to make sense of the suggestion that the West can be barbaric despite its achievements in the realm of civilization, one needs Thorstein Veblen's sociology, which held that modernity is actually only a latter-day barbarism.

Without the anti-modernist perspectives offered by Weber, Durkheim, Freud, Simmel, Veblen, Mead, and the entire *fin de siècle* legacy of sociology, what sense can one make of this Muslim interpretation of the tragedy of Bosnia? One is left with the boosterish, pro-Enlightenment explanations offered by the West's diplomats that are dutifully reported in all the major newspapers: the United Nations was engaged in a humanitarian mission in Bosnia; the "world community" is not responsible for the "tribalism" set loose in the Balkans; television as well as the entire "monitoring" mission of the United Nations allowed the world to "witness" crimes that will be punished at some future date – and besides, the Muslims are not pure victims in this "three-way feud with no clear aggressors and victims" (*New York Times*, 25 June 1993: A3). Eventually, the West's standards of human rights and other Enlightenment narratives will rule the entire world, and wars such as this one in the Balkans will have disappeared. The trouble with this Enlightenment-based explanation is that it fails to convince the victims, in this case the Muslims, and is blind to the savagery and violence within Western nations. An us–them mentality is set up, and exacerbated, in this case between Islam and the West, at the same time that both Islam and the West are falling victim to their own respective versions of Balkanization.

For example, I believe that the bombing of the World Trade Center in February 1993 as well as the foiled plot to bomb targets in New York City in June 1993 are a prelude to future terrorism. Such actions, by Muslim, Christian, or any other extremists, are contemptible, of course. But the West is absolutely blind to the fact that many of its actions are perceived as terrorism by Islamic victims. Thus, the siege of Sarajevo is interpreted by Muslims as Christian terrorism of Muslims supported by the West. The death of over 200 Muslims in Somalia in June 1993, caused by malfunctioning American missiles, constitutes an act of terrorism against a civilian population. Much the same can be said for President Clinton's lawless bombing of civilians in Baghdad in June 1993. Yet these Western acts of violence are almost never presented as terrorist acts in the Western media. The media wizards assume that Islam terrorizes, while the West occasionally makes mistakes. The Western reaction to Muslim terrorism is represented by the following statement by Steven Emerson, printed in the *Wall Street Journal*:

> Radical Islamic fundamentalism cannot be reconciled with the West. The hatred of the West by militant Islamic fundamentalists is not tied to any particular act or event. Rather, fundamentalists equate the mere existence of the West – its economic, political and cultural systems – as an intrinsic attack on Islam. The sooner Americans realize that no compromise or reconciliation is possible, the sooner radical fundamentalists will realize that the West cannot be manipulated.
>
> (25 June 1993: A10)

It is certainly not true that Islamic hatred of the West is not tied to any particular event – the West's collaboration with Serbian genocide against Bosnian Muslims is one such event. A statement that rules out any and all compromise or reconciliation only fuels cultural narcissism on both sides. Thus, Americans feel superior to Muslim terrorists and Muslim terrorists feel superior, in their quest for spiritual purity, to decadent Americans. This is a formula for the widespread hate and violence that consumed the Balkans in the early 1990s, not the establishment of Enlightenment-based utopia.

But the notion of cultural narcissism, derived from Freud and Durkheim, helps to explain why neither Islam nor the West is likely to achieve cultural solidarity in the near future. Narcissism promotes paranoia, hatred, and divisiveness, phenomena that cannot serve as the basis for long-lasting social solidarity even within the in-group. In fact, narcissism is conducive to the Balkanization process in that the narcissist feels that his or her religion, group, city, or other object of identification is superior to all others. Such an attitude – the narcissism of small differences – magnifies small differences even within a cultural group, thereby precluding social solidarity. The inability of Serbs and Croats to get along is reflected in the lack of solidarity between Germans and Britons, Somalis and Pakistanis, and other groups far removed from the Balkans geographically, but not metaphorically.

The delegates to the World Conference on Human Rights held in Vienna in June 1993 rejected the peace plan endorsed by the European Community and Islamic countries that would partition Bosnia-Herzegovina into ethnic divisions, and called for a lifting of the arms embargo against Bosnian Muslim forces. "The resolution was adopted by a vote of 88 to 1 with 54 nations abstaining including the United States and most European countries. Russia cast the only vote against the resolution" (*New York Times*, 25 June 1993: A3). If it is true, as many claim, that the previous conference on human rights, held twenty-five years ago, set the agenda up to the fall of communism, it may be true that the conference will set the agenda for the next twenty-five years. In that case, one can expect that the world's developing countries will oppose bitterly the West's emphasis on universal human rights – from the Enlightenment-based point of view – and keep pushing for their version of human rights, which includes the right to economic development and justice. One can also expect that with so many voices in the world clamoring for human rights and justice, very few will even be noticed in the din.

This is because the most recent Conference on Human Rights was a veritable postmodern spectacle, an ominous foreshadowing of the Balkanization that awaits the world. While former President Jimmy Carter, Secretary of State Warren Christopher, UN Secretary-General Boutros Boutros-Ghali and other delegates from powerful nations insisted on the universality of human rights as they understood them (freedom of speech, assembly, religion, and the press), delegates from other groups staged demonstrations to illustrate their plight. There were Native Americans, Kurds, Haitians, Bosnians, Croats, Palestinians, and seemingly countless others who felt that the Western standard of universal human rights had passed them by. There were so many groups expressing their plight that in the end, their cry of pain was drowned out by the common cry of pain. No one group emerged as especially worthy of notice.

REPEATING HISTORY'S MISTAKES

All along, I have been implying that capitalism is making nearly the same sociological mistakes as communism: both systems promote narcissism, which in turn degenerates easily into aggression among individuals and Balkanization among social groups. I have also been implying that far from witnessing the end of history hailed by so many postmodern intellectuals, contemporary humanity is witnessing the mindless repetition of history – and is scarcely aware of this fact. I shall attempt to drive home the second point first *vis-à-vis* Marcel Mauss's incredible 1925 assessment of Bolshevism, and lead the discussion back gradually to the first point. Most of what Mauss had to say about the communist revolution that began in 1917 also applies to the postcommunist revolution that began in 1989.

To begin with, Mauss argued that Bolshevism conquered the Russian Revolution because the terror and violence characteristic of Bolshevism did "not correspond to its soul, to the movement of the mentality of the Russian people" ([1925] 1992: 175). But so many years after the Bolshevik Revolution, the world still knows next to nothing – formally, sociologically – concerning the mentality or social character of the Russian or other peoples that emerged from the ruins of communism. Instead, Western-style capitalism and the American version of universal human rights are being applied synthetically to these postcommunist cultures by consultants and diplomats – with little success thus far.

Then as now, the West claimed that it was being neutral with regard to the momentous changes occurring in Russia and Eastern Europe. For example, Mauss notes that the Western allies (France, Britain, and the USA) "denied and still deny that they replaced the alliance with Russia with a state of war," and adds, "This is a fiction and a lie" (ibid.: 179). To counter this alleged falsehood, Mauss observes that "the French and the English blockaded the Black Sea ports, and the French bombarded Odessa," among many other illustrations (ibid.: 180). But in the 1990s, the French and the British (along with the USA) are blockading ports on the Adriatic Sea; have maintained a weapons embargo on the former Yugoslavia; contributed directly to the apartheid-like frenzy of ethnic cleansing by their insistence on carving up Bosnia-Herzegovina into ethnic enclaves; and have otherwise "committed hostile acts less violent than those of a war" (ibid.) but they did commit hostile acts now as then. I am not claiming that the parallels between the 1920s and the 1990s are anything near exact, but that is not essential to my argument. The more important point here is that the nations in which the Enlightenment traditions took hold (France, Britain, and the USA) got involved twice in this century in revolutions having to do with communism, and in both cases they feigned neutrality all the while they affected the outcome of these revolutions.

The results of Western intervention in the Bolshevik Revolution, according to Mauss, included starvation, desperation, and a terribly cruel civil war. Mauss observed that "The Russians of both sides made civil war mostly on the innocent" (ibid.: 181). Clearly, similarly cruel wars in the former Yugoslavia and Soviet Union are being waged mostly on the innocent in the 1990s. Things became so desperate in the 1920s that the Bolsheviks came to be perceived as the representatives of order and national unity. Similarly, the former communists in the Balkans and the Southern fringes of the former Soviet Union are increasingly being seen as the only ones who can restore order. When Mauss writes of the states of "real collective madness" or "siege psychosis" among the Russian people in the 1920s, he might as well be writing about the collective madness in the Balkans in the 1990s:

> States of societies in decomposition possessing only the soul of a crowd; entire populations, baffled and maddened, discover spies and traitors everywhere; they oscillate from irrational hope to limitless depression, massacring and allowing themselves to be slaughtered in succession, and demonstrating heroism, one day, cowardice the next. Even the herd instinct declines. When famine, epidemic, fear, massacres and raids are added to this, then friendships and families themselves disappear.
>
> (ibid.: 183)

Interestingly, Mauss blames the West, not the Russian people, in large measure for this tragic state of affairs: "The Allies' material blockade, the *de facto* moral, juridical and commercial blockade that followed this *de jure* blockade, has maintained this mental state in the whole Russian collectivity" (ibid.: 183). I have already cited numerous newspaper reports which suggest that the people of former Yugoslavia in the 1990s exhibit similar collective states of paranoia, bitterness toward the West, disillusionment, and despair as a result of the West's material, moral, and spiritual blockades. Mauss suggests that in the 1920s, the Bolsheviks and the Communist Party made skillful use of this collective madness because the masses believed that the capitalist nations were out to exterminate them, and therefore turned readily to the communists as saviors. In the 1990s, victims and aggressors alike in the former Yugoslavia, including Muslims, Croats, and Serbs, turned against each other and against the West. Mauss laments the resultant crisis in the 1920s that laid the groundwork for communism,

> the madness of a great people [Russia], besieged, cut off from its essential relations with the world, feeling neither within nor without the sympathy that carries societies through their crises and makes them emerge from them with glory like the England of the Protestants, the America of the Colonists and the France of the Constituents and Conventionals.
>
> (ibid.: 183).

One may just as easily lament the collective madness of the people of the Balkans, which is slowly but surely igniting a sort of madness in the Islamic world. The most common form of this collective madness seems to be widespread paranoia, the terrible fear that whole nations and groups are bent on exterminating whole other nations and groups. Of course, in some cases the paranoia turns out to be factually correct, which fuels even more paranoia and violence.

Mauss concludes that the communists took over Russia because of war and misery, not the power of their economic and social arguments. Moreover, the Bolshevik reign of terror ultimately sowed the seeds of its own destruction. If one follows Mauss's argument, communism did not fall because it could not compete with capitalism on the world market – as so many Cold Warriors claim – but because it destroyed the very basis of society. This is because, then as now,

> Terror does not bind, terror does not encourage; it makes people keep their heads down, withdraw into themselves, shun the terrorists and each other, panic and not work: "Fear and terror are weak links of friendship," as Tacitus has it, a formula that should be repeated *vis-à-vis* the first Socialist government in history. Strictly speaking they do keep states and tyrannies going; but they create neither human charity nor love, or, if you prefer, ultimately, devotion.
>
> (ibid.: 195)

We have returned to the theme of *caritas* or compassion. For Mauss as for the other Durkheimians, society consists of habits, customs, and other collective products that are forged through human sympathy, not mere legislation, and certainly not on the basis of egoism and hatred. Mauss mocked the communists: "Naive sociologists, the Communists believed that the order of sovereignty, the law, can create, like the Word of God, from nothing, *ex nihilo*" (ibid.: 198). But in the 1990s, it is the capitalists who are acting like the naive sociologists. We have seen throughout this discussion that following the collapse of communism in the late 1980s, Western consultants, diplomats, and politicians apparently believed that capitalism and Western-style democracy could be transplanted to post-communist nations practically overnight. In this sense, contemporary capitalists are every bit as naive and destructive as the communists of old.

It should go without saying that capitalists have not instigated the Gulags or other evils that are attributable solely to the communists. Still, Mauss has a point when he exposes the West's still largely denied role in the evil consequences of communism. And it is uncanny how his description of the collective madness of the Bolshevik period applies to the collective madness that is occurring in the wake of what was called the Velvet Revolution. In both revolutions, the West failed to understand the habits, customs, and culture of the people who suffered prior to, during, and following communism. And the same West that took all the credit for winning the Cold War erected a metaphorical Iron Curtain of its own against the Russians and Eastern Europeans who sought a share of Western paradise:

> Fear of foreigners, it seems, is replacing fear of nuclear war as the distraction of the decade for Western Europe's rich nations. . . . Russia and the West have swapped parts. An Iron Curtain has dropped before the majority of those wanting to enter Europe.
>
> (*Wall Street Journal*, 8 July 1993: A1)

TERROR IN THE WEST

The West's bungling during the Bolshevik Revolution also had a disintegrative effect on the West. Two world wars in the twentieth century were waged largely among Western nations. The central message of Oswald Spengler's *Decline of the West* (1926) is that the cult of rationality born during the Enlightenment has run its course and that Western culture is about to expire. Pitirim Sorokin (1957) later made much the same argument. Wars fought by the West against itself were used by both Spengler and Sorokin as evidence for their claims. But the concept of war might prove to be inadequate for capturing the gist of what they were trying to predict. It is evident that since their deaths wars have been moving steadily away from the somewhat organized affairs that they used to be, complete with rules for fighting in a supposedly civilized manner. Wars in the postmodern era almost routinely target civilians, are quite disorganized, and are fought on the basis of the rule of who is strongest in a given situation. For example, one of the most arresting visual symbols of the current Balkan War, the slamming of Serbian projectiles into civilian apartment buildings in Sarajevo, is practically indistinguishable from the slamming of American missiles into civilian targets in Baghdad.

More than that, war has become a metaphor and metaphorical wars have become almost real. As illustration of the first point, consider that the savage slaughter in the Balkans occurred despite the presence of so-called UN "peacekeepers." The reality of this Balkan War was diminished by many euphemisms of this sort (peace talks, cease-fires, sanctions, etc.). As for the second point, consider that Westerners in general but Americans in particular wage metaphorical wars on just about everything: AIDS, potholes, cancer, drugs, pollution, crime – you name it. Violence has permeated the very core of American society (Baudrillard 1986). While it would be a mistake to compare this violence with the postcommunist wars, at least in a strict sense, it is also foolish to ignore the poignant similarities. For example, the war between the sexes in the USA claims very real victims and causes tremendous damage: lawsuits cripple an individual's income-making capacity for life; children are traumatized by the loss of one or both parents; rape and violence in American homes committed by family members leave lifelong scars, every bit as devastating as those left by the rapes and violence in Bosnia. Hate crimes in the West are not appreciably different from hate crimes in the Balkans. Perhaps America is not Balkanizing along geographical lines or national divisions, but it seems to be Balkanizing along ethnic, gender, age, and other divisions. Something similar is true for Western Europe.

I have argued that the West's helpless fascination with the violence in the Balkans betrays its secret fear that despite several centuries of boosterish support for the Enlightenment project, the West too is about to succumb to a form of Balkanization. Instead of the cosmopolitan, global, rational society of the world envisaged by thinkers from Descartes all the way to today's Anthony Giddens, the world seems to be moving in the opposite direction: it is breaking up into smaller and ever smaller units that betray hostility toward each other. Furthermore, I have argued that the principle driving this Balkanization – real Balkanization in postcommunist nations, and metaphorical in the West – is cultural narcissism. The Russians and Eastern Europeans were driven to narcissism by almost a century's worth of famine, misery, and communist indoctrination, while the Western peoples arrived at narcissism via the Cartesian doctrine of individualism severed completely from culture. By a strange twist of fate, both peoples have arrived at a state in which egoism is no longer able to sustain a coherent, integrated social life. And both groups of modernists, the postcommunists as well as the capitalists, have aimed most of their hostility at Islam, arguably the most anti-modern and traditional cultural force in the world today.

To the extent that Western intellectuals grasp the paradox that the West is increasingly becoming as oppressive as the East is alleged to be, they continue to cling to the very Enlightenment traditions that have led to this dismal state of affairs. For example, consider Jonathan Rauch's *Kindly Inquisitors: The New Attacks on Free Thought* (1993). Rauch argues that the contemporary thought police that monitors political correctness in America is a form of the Inquisition. He likens the Ayatollah Khomeini's death sentence against Salman Rushdie to the new "fundamentalism" in American Universities. A couple of times in the book, Rauch admits that the new Inquisitors are "left-wingers," but most of the time he holds up liberals as the defenders of American freedom, particularly the freedom of speech. But who is really responsible for the new Inquisition? Rauch seems to imply that "true" liberals are not the Inquisitors, and that today's Inquisitors must be some sort of fundamentalists hiding in liberals' clothing. But that is not a convincing argument. American Universities are the bastions of liberal thought, and the Universities are leading this Inquisition. In sum, Rauch cannot admit to himself that the Inquisition is coming from the liberals, not the conservatives.

Rauch tries to create a context for his argument by criticizing Plato and holding up Descartes as the champion of the form of liberalism that he espouses. He suggests that Plato gives us a blueprint for Fascism in *The Republic*. But Descartes is a hero because he taught that the individual should not honor any traditional authority save his or her own opinion. Descartes as precursor to Thomas Jefferson and liberal thought? But we have seen from Ernest Gellner (1992a) that there is more to Descartes than the stereotype that he stood for rationality, skepticism, inquiry, and similar good things. He was also resolutely anti-culture, anti-tradition, and anti-society. He held up the egoistic, narcissistic, self-serving individual as the carrier of rational inquiry. Rauch fails to see that today's liberal Inquisitor is the logical end-point of this Cartesian beginning.

Today's liberal Inquisitors are less like Senator Joseph McCarthy or other fanatical right-wingers, and much more like the Marxists and communists with regard to aims, means, and style. Communism may be dead (but it may also rise up again, Phoenix-like, from the ashes), yet University liberals employ remarkably communist-like tactics in searching out bad thoughts, turning children against their parents, and denigrating any tradition that goes against their version of utopian rationalism. Unwilling to admit that their tactics promote hostility, suspicion, and divisiveness, they repeat the communist strategy of attempting to enforce a *compulsory tolerance*, and an equally compulsory humanism. I agree with Marcel Mauss ([1925] 1992) that genuine *caritas* cannot be compelled.

Rauch and other liberals never consider the role of *caritas* in the liberal tradition. On the contrary, Rauch insists that "harsh and hurtful words are an inevitable part of the search for knowledge," and he seeks to discredit the "humanitarian objection to free speech: hurtful talk, like physical violence, causes pain and thereby violates the human rights of its targets" (*New York Times*, 26 June 1993: A19). I agree with Rauch that the seemingly humanitarian (always a suspicious adjective for me) concern with hateful words should not be used as an excuse for restricting free speech. But I disagree with him and others who argue that the freedom to express hate is a healthy sign of liberalism. On the contrary, the widespread hate and hostility found in Western societies is a symptom of cancerous narcissism and the almost complete decay of social instincts and benevolence. I do not advocate the restriction of free speech, but I do not believe that this is the best of all possible worlds, nor do I believe that Descartes is the good guy compared with Plato.

Consider the television show, *Beavis and Butt-Head,* shown on the Music Television network. I invoke it because MTV is frequently used in the postmodern discourse to illustrate the circulation of visual images that is supposed to characterize postmodern culture. But this neutral assessment of MTV misses the point I have been trying to make throughout this book: narcissism leads directly to hostility and the breakdown of society. My University students spoke approvingly of this program, so I watched it regularly over a long period of time. Beavis and Butt-Head are presented as two characters who watch MTV videos and comment on them, a sort of voyeurism in the second degree. As the television viewer watches the same video that Beavis and Butt-Head are watching, one hears their simple-minded assessment. They determine that all videos are either "cool" or that they "suck." The cool videos are those that show graphic violence or suggest sex and other sordid themes. The suck videos are those that show gentle, slow, or otherwise non-violent and non-sexual images. The formula is simple, and popular: violence and hatred are cool.

Beavis and Butt-Head do not live with a family, nor do they have friends. They seem to live in front of the television set, and they are hostile to each other. "I'll beat your butt, Beavis," Butt-Head says often. They agree that old people, children, parents, pets, and neighbors all suck. It is provocative to ponder to what extent these two characters represent the beginnings of a general movement in Western societies toward narcissistic voyeurism. I have argued in Chapter 3 that narcissism and postmodern voyeurism are the two biggest obstacles to a compassionate response to the slaughter of innocents in the Balkans and elsewhere.

In any event, the important point is that narcissism may be the end-point of the Cartesian legacy. Narcissism cannot sustain social life, and it may promote Balkanization. If this hypothesis turns out to be credible to any degree, then the task for future generations is to try to find a way to preserve the virtues of individualism at the same time that *caritas* is maintained. I have argued that this was Durkheim's still misunderstood central message, the real meaning of his "cult of humanity," and his seemingly paradoxical concept of collective individualism. I shall repeat what I have stated many times before, in this book and elsewhere: this quest for *caritas* should not be reduced to old-fashioned notions of tradition and community, and it should not be made compulsory. Genuine *caritas* must be absolutely free and spontaneous. How such a liberal yet benevolent society is to be achieved is completely beyond the scope of our aims in this book. If I have convinced the reader that this is a problem worth taking seriously, then I have achieved my aims.

SCENARIOS FOR THE FUTURE

I do not anticipate any large-scale development of *caritas* in the near future. On the contrary, the present analysis leads to a very pessimistic forecast. I shall end with a somewhat detailed set of predictions for the outcome of the current Balkan War, its effects on Russia, and its meaning for the Balkanization of the West. And I hope that I am wrong on every count.

By the middle of 1993, four distinct goals emerged in the Serbian campaign in the Balkans: (1) territorial aggrandizement, (2) economic imperialism in search of natural resources, including the lucrative tourist industry on the Adriatic Coast, (3) cultural imperialism in the form of taking over or destroying cultural centers and landmarks, including Dubrovnik, Vukovar, Cavtat and later Sarajevo and Jajce, among other cities in Bosnia-Herzegovina, (4) crimes of passion and other criminal acts, including war crimes. This last aspect of the Serbian campaign includes the desire to avenge the loss of the Battle of Kosovo to the Muslims in 1389 and the Croatian Ustase crimes from World War II. The widespread looting, rape, blackmail, and "ethnic cleansing," among other criminal activities, might be subsumed under the rubric "seductions of war" (an elaboration on Katz 1988) in order to capture their irrational, lawless, even anti-civilizational characteristics.

By the middle of 1993, Serbia had achieved the following military and political objectives: it had occupied up to 25 per cent of Croatia and 70 per cent of Bosnia-Herzegovina. It had blocked Croatia's economic and political potential by burdening her with 750,000 refugees and preventing her from reaping a profit from the tourist industry along the Adriatic Coast. It should be noted that the West responded by passing restrictive refugee laws according to the "first-safe-country-principle." Because Croatia became the first safe-country for most refugees from Bosnia, it got stuck with the refugees that Western Europeans did not want:

> It means anyone seeking refuge must ask for it in the nearest safe place, even part of his own country. Those who don't, said the EC, should be bumped to the last safe country they crossed before entering the [European] community. . . .
> Thus Austria has stopped admitting Bosnians headed for Germany who arrive

via safe Slovenia after crossing safe Croatia. With 750,000 refugees bottled up there, Croatia has been forced to shut its border with Bosnia.

(Wall Street Journal, 8 July 1993: A4)

The Krajina region of Croatia had been nearly completely "ethnically cleansed," and a Serbian army, even government, had been formed in the Krajina – and this, despite United Nations forces stationed there as part of the Vance peace plan. The ethnically cleansed Krajina held elections in which the remaining Serbs voted for independence and to join a Greater Serbia. The United Nations formally declined to honor the results of this election, on the principle that it meant that borders had been changed through military force, but the election gave an air of fictional democracy to the inevitable expansion of Serbia. Similarly, most of Bosnia-Herzegovina, except for the mostly Croat-populated Herzegovina, had been "cleansed," occupied, and transformed into a satellite of Serbia.

Perhaps more importantly, Serbia had also scored victories in the propaganda war, the image-making war, and diplomacy with the West. To be sure, by the middle of 1993, Western nations in general and the United States in particular had concluded finally that Serbia was most responsible for the current war in former Yugoslavia. Nevertheless, despite sanctions, calls for war crime trials, and other political instruments of persuasion that the world community applied to Serbia, the West persisted in trying to attain a diplomatic, not a military settlement to this Balkan War. In effect, Serbian leaders such as Slobodan Milošević and Radovan Karadžić, who were suspected of condoning or committing war crimes, were engaged in diplomacy with the very powers that imposed sanctions on them. Western diplomats such as Cyrus Vance and Lord David Owen explained that they felt obliged to negotiate with Serbian leaders who are suspected of war crimes in order to achieve the West's humanitarian goals in former Yugoslavia. Yet Serbian propaganda interpreted this diplomatic activity as a moral victory, and used it to its advantage. From a strictly sociological perspective, negotiating with any suspected criminal – much less a suspected war criminal – negates the collective sense of indignation and outrage that is supposed to characterize a healthy society's reaction to crime. The result is cynicism in the so-called moral countries concerning law and order in general.

President Clinton's six-point peace plan, announced on 10 February 1993, continued the West's hitherto unsuccessful policy of trying to achieve a negotiated peace in the Balkans. The same holds true for the Washington Peace Plan announced in May 1993 by the USA, Britain, France, Russia, and Spain (all of them World War II allies, except for Spain). Moreover, by continuing to support a largely cere-monial United Nations presence in the Balkans, the West had played into the hands of Serbian strategists, and unwittingly promoted the humiliation of the United Nations. The presence of United Nations "peacekeepers" protected Serbia from direct Western military intervention – because of the West's fear for the safety of United Nations troops should fighting escalate dramatically – and enabled the Serbian side to continue its relentless campaign of ethnic cleansing in UN "protected" areas.

In the rest of 1993, and beyond, Serbia will continue to accentuate its "peacemaking" image by using UNPROFOR as the guardian of its occupied territories, and by playing on the Western fears of Islamic fundamentalism and of becoming involved in a Balkan Vietnam. Both objectives had already been realized to some extent with regard to Croatia and Bosnia-Herzegovina. Barring direct, Western military intervention under the authority of the United Nations, the history of Serbia's actions in this war leads to the expectation that she will provoke the Muslim minorities in Kosovo and Macedonia *only after Bosnia-Herzegovina is under more extensive United Nations protection than is presently the case,* as part of a negotiated peace settlement or some other arrangement. Once the UN peacekeepers are in place, they become bargaining chips for Serbian aims, and the victims of Serbia's aggression become hostages to the United Nations presence. In Kosovo and Macedonia, Serbia will claim that Serbs living in these areas are oppressed; justify its occupation of these territories based on these ethnic conflicts; and finally, call for UN intervention once she has achieved her aims. A similar scenario has already been played out in Croatia and Bosnia-Herzegovina.

Of course, this scenario is complicated by several other factors: Croatia will not renew indefinitely UNPROFOR's mandate in Serbian-held territories in Croatia, and will try to liberate these lands further by military force. The Croats complain that the terms of the Vance peace plan have not been met, especially that the Serbs were not disarmed, that refugees were not allowed to return to their homes, and that a Serbian state was allowed to be formed on Croatian territory. An important Serbian aim seems to be to gain control of the Adriatic Coast. This can be achieved fairly easily by capturing Zadar, and thereby severing Dalmatia from the rest of Croatia. In sum, fighting is likely to escalate not only in Kosovo and Macedonia, but also between Croatia and Serbia – a possibility that has received scant attention since the implementation of the Vance peace plan in early 1992.

The Muslims in Bosnia will have become the new Palestinians, a people without a nation or territory. This may have many consequences, from further ethnic conflict between Croats and Muslims in Croatia as well as in Bosnia-Herzegovina, to possible political unification among *some* Islamic nations, and to terrorism, the weapon of the powerless. Finally, the plight of the Muslim and Croat refugees, as well as the widespread human rights abuses, may provoke military action by many nations or groups of nations, from Albania, Turkey, and Greece, to Russia.

The United States does not have any vital interests in the Balkans, in a utilitarian sense, although it does have several negative interests: it wants to avoid another round of Islamic fundamentalism that might lead to terrorism and problems with obtaining petroleum from Islamic nations that may choose to show solidarity with Muslim "brothers and sisters" in Bosnia-Herzegovina. It also wants to avoid the internationalization of the current war to include Turkey, Greece, Bulgaria, Albania, and possibly Russia.

The European Community fears the impact of waves of refugees since Croatia closed its borders in 1992. It has a vital stake in the stability of the Balkans as a commercial and communication link to Greece, Turkey, and Asia. Britain and

France face competition with Germany, Austria, and Italy regarding their spheres of influence on the Adriatic, and with Germany regarding their spheres of influence in the EC. And much like the US, the EC fears Islamic expansionism and fundamentalism.

The interests of the Islamic nations can be characterized quite simply as the desire to "save" the Muslims in Bosnia-Herzegovina. After suffering perceived setbacks in Kashmir, Afghanistan, Palestine, Iraq, and elsewhere, many fundamentalist portions of the Islamic community have concluded that Bosnia is Islam's last stand against a Western civilization that it regards as decadent, evil, and above all, dangerous to its survival.

Western nations have excluded direct military intervention as a viable option for stopping Serbian aggression. As of President Clinton's announcement in February 1993,[1] it seems as if the West would intervene militarily only to ensure that humanitarian aid reached the victims of this war, and more vaguely, possibly to enforce a negotiated peace plan. In any event, a serious military reaction becomes a possibility only if all other options – including diplomacy – have been exhausted. Thus, United Nations and Western strategy for solving the Balkan crises includes the following: economic sanctions might be increased against Serbia and Montenegro, but the weapons embargo against Croatia and Bosnia-Herzegovina will not be lifted because of expressed fears that arming the Croats and Muslims might lead to increased tensions between them, an escalation in the overall fighting, and an exacerbation of Serbian aggression. In fact, many varieties of financial aid to Croatia and Bosnia-Herzegovina have been and will continue to be denied out of fear that these countries would use such money to obtain weapons illegally. In addition, humanitarian aid to the victims of the Balkan War was cut dramatically by the middle of 1993:

> The Europeans are clearly writing off the country [former Yugoslavia], said an official, who requested anonymity. The pledges are down from last year. It's not only donor fatigue, it's battle fatigue.
>
> (*New York Times*, 1 July 1993: A1)

An unforeseen consequence of this policy is that the economic hardship in Croatia and Bosnia-Herzegovina hindered the democratization process and helped push these nations further into the politically radical positions that the West had hoped publicly to avoid.

In tandem with these Western policies, the leaders of the nations that Serbia has victimized, Franjo Tudjman of Croatia and Alija Izetbegović of Bosnia-Herzegovina, were stigmatized less than, yet along with, Slobodan Milošević of Serbia. The United Nations, in particular, insisted that all three parties were guilty in this war, at times equally guilty. According to the *New York Times*, if Mr. Milošević was the "butcher of the Balkans," then Mr. Tudjman was the "butcher's apprentice" (2 November 1992: A14). Mr. Izetbegović was suspected in the Western media of harboring Islamic fundamentalist aims. Even if Western politicians, diplomats, and media demonized Mr. Milošević, it was essential that

Serbia's victims be blamed as well. Otherwise, if Croatia and Bosnia were perceived purely as victims, Western public opinion might have pressed for direct military intervention to try to end the suffering of the innocents once and for all.

Barring Western military intervention, future Serbian actions can be predicted from an analysis of its past actions. It is a very simple, albeit brilliant strategy, because it has made the United Nations and the world community seem impotent thus far. In the first phase, Serbia "secretly" occupies its future victim's territory all the while it carries on a diversionary tactic. Thus, while the world focused its attention on Serbia's half-hearted attempt in 1991 to bring Slovenia back into the Yugoslav fold, Croatia was being occupied by Serbian troops. While the world focused its attention on Vukovar and the war in Croatia in the Fall of 1992, the Yugoslav Federal Army (JNA) "withdrew" into Bosnia-Herzegovina. With the wisdom of hindsight, it seems incredible that from Mr. Izetbegović to Lord Carrington, hardly anyone noticed that Bosnia had been silently and secretly occupied by Serbian-backed forces. Similarly, while the world focused its attention on the siege of Sarajevo, in the last few months of 1992, Serbian troops had already moved into and occupied Kosovo.

In the second phase, Serbia publicly engages in "disarmament," while it arms irregular troops in the next theater of fighting. Thus, the blaring disarmament in Slovenia led to secret armament in Croatia, and the equally ostentatious disarmament in Croatia led to the arming of irregular troops in Bosnia-Herzegovina. Serbs in Kosovo and Krajina continued to be armed in the early months of 1993 even as Serbia promised to disarm Bosnia-Herzegovina. There can hardly be a better indicator of future Serbian aggression than its loud proclamations that it is working with the United Nations to disarm its troops.

Finally, in the third phase, the Serbian side engages in wholesale terrorism and criminal activity as part of its military strategy to "cleanse" whole areas of non-Serbs. Rape is an integral aspect of this strategy of "ethnic cleansing," because the aim is to so humiliate non-Serb women that they will never want to return to the scenes of their degradation. Another aspect of this final phase is to drive hundreds of thousands of refugees from their homes in order to burden Serbia's enemies with the monumental task of taking care of them, and of precluding the possibility of a war to liberate the seized territories. And especially because these territories eventually fall under United Nations protection, it is next to impossible to liberate them without endangering UN troops.

There exist at least three key elements in this Serbian strategy: (1) form irregular Serbian armies such that Mr. Milošević can deny links with or control over Serbian terrorism, (2) use Western indecisiveness, and focus on the once fictitious but now real threat of Muslim fundamentalism in Europe, (3) use United Nations troops as the guardians of Serbian-held territories and as preservers of the status quo. For example, President Bush was constrained from using American air power to enforce the "no-fly zone" over Bosnia-Herzegovina in 1992 out of fear for the safety of UNPROFOR soldiers delivering humanitarian aid, especially British and French troops in Bosnia.

Barring direct and massive Western military intervention to punish Serbia's aggression against her neighbors, and based on the foregoing analysis, I predict one of the following three worst-case scenarios:

I Preservation of the status quo. UNPROFOR will continue its mission of passively monitoring events, including "ethnic cleansing" and other violations of human rights, and delivering humanitarian aid. The Krajina region of Croatia will remain under Serbian occupation although Croatia will fight a costly war to try to recover it, and lose. In the end, Krajina will remain Serbia's staging area for a future war to claim the entire Adriatic Coast. Croatia will experience an economic catastrophe because of the refugee problem and insufficient Western financial aid (to prevent Croatia from arming itself). Croatia will be unable to offer any further assistance to Bosnia-Herzegovina, and ethnic tensions between Muslim refugees and Croats in Croatia will increase. As a result, repressive and totalitarian ideologies will become even more dominant in Croatia and Bosnia than they are now. Over a million refugees will become a threat to social order. The European Community will close its borders almost completely to all refugees and most foreigners, but will experience even more drastic waves of hate crimes than those that are presently found in Germany, France, and Britain. Despite the many proposed peace plans, Bosnia-Herzegovina will be carved up into Bosnia for Serbia and Herzegovina for Croatia. Serbia will hold onto the territories it had obtained through aggression, and will eventually be accepted back into the international community. In sum, preservation of the status quo translates into victory for Serbia. A green light will have been given to scores of would-be dictators in the former USSR, and the promise of a democratic New World Order will seem hollow. Disenchantment with the West, coupled with economic catastrophe, may set the stage for the dramatic return of communism throughout postcommunist central Europe, and throughout the former USSR. Islamic fundamentalism will be inflamed throughout the world due to the perceived inconsistency of permitting Serbian aggression against the Muslims in Bosnia while the West would not allow Saddam Hussein to violate any United Nations resolutions.

II Eruption of a Balkan–Mediterranean War. Serbia will open up a third front on Kosovo and Macedonia after a sizeable increase of UN "peacekeepers" in Bosnia-Herzegovina. A million ethnic Albanian refugees will have been added to the already large wave of refugees. Turkey, Greece, and Bulgaria will enter the conflict almost immediately. NATO will also become involved, but its mission will not be clear because Greece will ally itself with Serbia, and both nations will fight against Turkey. All post-World-War-II alliances will become problematic. In particular, tensions between Germany and Britain and France, which are already strained because of this war, will reach a boiling point. The dream of a united European Community might be shattered due to this major failure in European foreign and domestic policy. The credibility of the United Nations will have been damaged beyond repair.

III World War III. Remote as this possibility may seem at the present time, it may become increasingly likely if Russia acts on its threats and throws its military might behind Serbia. Russia will almost certainly begin to oppress Latvia, the other Baltic Republics, and secessionist republics along its southern border. China may well take on the role of diplomatic advisor, or even military supplier. Ex-communists in Russia and communists in China may come to view their alliance with Serbia as an opportunity for a counter- revolution with regard to the deceptively easy fall of communism. (After all, history teaches that most revolutions lead to counterrevolutions.) In addition, the increasingly disillusioned Islamic nations may enter such a war against both the free nations of the West and the postcommunist and some still communist nations.

IMPLICATIONS

The current crisis in former Yugoslavia is a microcosm not only of the fate of much of the postcommunist world, but of Europe and the rest of the world as well. Everywhere, it seems, postmodern forces in the sense of post-Enlightenment narratives are clashing with genuinely postmodern or anti-modern forces such as tradition, nationalism, fundamentalism, racism, and what the West calls human rights abuses. The Disneyworld dream of a united Europe is slowly but steadily unraveling as Britain, France, Germany and other EC states bicker on issues ranging from a common currency, open borders, and especially – Bosnia-Herzegovina. Balkanization is affecting the West, not just the Balkans: the large trading blocs desired by the West are becoming smaller; metaphorical wars are waged by the West against Japan and other nations in the economic sphere and against drugs, violence, and other fictions within their own borders; meanwhile, a real war in the Balkans has become a mere metaphor, its reality drowned in the euphemisms of monitors, observers, peacekeepers, peace plans, cease-fires, etc.

The countries in which the Enlightenment traditions took root will no doubt continue to rationalize their not so subtle support of Serbia and vicarious participation in Serbian atrocities. France will continue to consistently block stronger UN and EC actions against Serbia, and will thereby exacerbate its already strained relations with Germany. Weary Britain will continue its old policy of supporting a strong central government in Belgrade as the equivalent of some "pax Romana" – even though Imperial Rome was brutal, after all. And the USA will fail to overcome its Vietnam Syndrome. President Clinton's strategy of focusing on domestic issues while engaging in military actions only if they are "easy" will backfire, because cynicism and narcissism will further divide American society. Jean Baudrillard (1986) will have been proven correct: America will emerge as the center of the postmodern world in which the have-nots must exit.

Notes

1 FROM THE POSTMODERN CULTURE OF FUN TO THE GRIM REALITIES OF POSTCOMMUNISM

1 Meštrović, Goreta, and Letica (1993a, 1993b) pursue this theme. See also Dinko Tomašić (1946, 1948a, 1951, 1953).

2 Thus, Rosenau distinguishes between affirmative, skeptical, moderate, and extreme postmodernisms (1992: 3–16). Perhaps she is right, to some extent, that postmodernists "offer indeterminacy rather than determinism, diversity rather than unity, difference rather than synthesis, complexity rather than simplification.... Confidence in emotion replaces efforts at impartial observation. Relativism is preferred to objectivity, fragmentation to totalization" (p. 8).

3 See, for example, the fine discussions of this issue by Akbar Ahmed (1992), Zygmunt Bauman (1987, 1989, 1991, 1992); Daniel Bell (1976, 1977, 1988, 1990); Anthony Giddens (1982, 1987, 1990, 1991, 1992); Jürgen Habermas (1970, 1981, 1987); Agnes Heller (1990); Scott Lash (1990); Pauline Rosenau (1992); and Barry Smart (1992), among others.

4 Martin E. Marty (1992) is probably right to question whether fundamentalism is really reactionary or a remnant of some "outmoded stages of human development that are destined to wane as people become enlightened, reasonable, and scientific" (p. 56). Instead, he argues that fundamentalists are "everywhere, even in America, and they know the modern world first hand." They fight back "in the name of God or the sacred against modernity, relativism, and pluralism." I agree with him that "this calls into question most post-Enlightenment projections about the survival of religion and the question of which kinds might prosper in modern and postmodern times."

5 There can be little doubt that the "end of history" thesis guided the Bush Administration's foreign policy. Yet in 1993, Brent Scowcroft, President Bush's National Security Advisor, modified the utopianism implied in the "end of history" thesis to imply the "harnessing" of history. Thus, Mr. Scowcroft argued that only the United States could harness history, and explained away the war in former Yugoslavia:

> For the first time since the Hitler era, no would-be global dictator is working to overthrow the established order. Despite the many civil wars in the world, the US has an opportunity to mold an international system more compatible with the values we have held for two centuries.... The seemingly intractable conflict in Bosnia illustrates the complexity of the problem. The Bush Administration concluded that the situation on the ground created by the warring parties could not be significantly modified without enormous amounts of force. Even in such a case, achieving success, in any reasonable definition of that term, as in Kuwait and Somalia, appeared illusory, if not impossible.
>
> (*New York Times*, 2 July 1993: A13)

Mr. Scowcroft fails to address the following issues, among others: Hitler was a European, not a global dictator. What "established order" is being implied? Why should the rest of the world be molded in America's image? And against the characterization of the war in Bosnia as intractable, consider Albert Wohlstetter's very practical proposals for ending that war (*Wall Street Journal*, 1 July 1993: A14).

6   See, for example, John F. Burns, "New, Virulent Strains of Hatred in the Balkans and Beyond," *New York Times*, 3 May 1992: E3. He adds that "China, too, is a powder keg of ethnic discontent." The *New York Times* of 20 May 1992: A1 poses the questions, "Could the carnage in Yugoslavia have been prevented? Can it be stopped? Will it happen elsewhere?"

7   *New York Times*, 18 April 1993: A1.

8   Similarly, William H. McNeil writes: "Ultimately, this sort of word game seems silly rather than illuminating. I conclude that Back to Hegel, glitteringly refracted through the mind of Mr. Fukuyama, is reactionary in the true sense of the word" (1992).

9   Pedro Ramet (1985) addresses the case of Yugoslavia's Muslims directly, and depicts this debate as one that pits "tribalists" against pluralists. Tribalists emphasize the historical roots of ethnic consciousness and the breakdown of ethnic boundaries resulting from modernization, while pluralists expect heightened group consciousness rather than homogenization to accompany modernization in multiethnic societies. He believes that, regarding the case of former Yugoslavia, the pluralists are correct.

10 According to an editorial in the *New York Times*, "The world so far declines to defend democratic Bosnia's territorial integrity the way it did feudal Kuwait's. . . . What's still conspicuously missing is a Security Council resolution that would brand Serbian aggression a threat to international security, demand full restoration of Bosnia's sovereignty and borders, and authorize military force, if necessary, to insure compliance" (7 August 1992: A15).

11 The reasoning offered by the Clinton Administration, as set forth in the *New York Times* (28 June 1993: A1) is as follows: Iraq allegedly threatened the life of former President Bush, and as such declared war on the United States. Bombing Baghdad was therefore a defense of US sovereignty, although the US also wanted to send a "message" to Iran and Sudan as well, that terrorism does not pay.

12 According to Chuck Sudetic, writing for the *New York Times*: "A Bosnian Government official, insisting on anonymity, denounced the United Nations in alluding to the safe-haven plan and said: 'It's a farce. The United Nations will not even stand by its own resolutions. The arms embargo against Bosnia is the only resolution being enforced. The United Nations has thrown up its hands as far as we are concerned' " (31 May 1993: A4).

13 The Ambassador is referring to two events that occurred in the Spring of 1993, the terrorist bombing of the World Trade Center in New York City and the mass suicide of the self-proclaimed Messiah, David Karesh, and his followers, in Waco, Texas. It is true that Karesh and his followers were never referred to as Christians by the American media, but as fanatics and fundamentalists.

14 See also Fatima Mernissi, *Islam and Democracy* (New York: Addison-Wesley, 1992); John L. Esposito, *The Islamic Threat: Myth or Reality?* (New York: Oxford University Press, 1992); and Sandra Mackey, *Passion and Politics: The Turbulent World of the Arabs* (New York: Dutton, 1992) among many other recent works on this topic.

15 "Moscow has made it clear that its sympathies lie with the Serbs" (*New York Times*, 31 January 1993: A8). "Russia is unwilling to tolerate any military moves against Serbia" (*New York Times*, 5 February 1993: A6).

16 From a CNN broadcast on 2 April 1993.

17 For one example among many, see the article entitled "Texas Professor Who Wrote

Erotic Novel is Accused of Harassment" *Chronicle of Higher Education*, 17 February 1993: A14.

18 According to Simmel (1905: 100): "The philosophy of Schopenhauer owes its wide dissemination . . . to the decline of Christianity. . . . The philosophy of Schopenhauer is the clearest formulation of this state of affairs. To him, the Will appears to be the basis of human life as of the world in general, and indeed in the absolute sense, so that all things are simply phenomena produced by a dark, restless, impelling force, outside of which there is nothing. For that very reason is this force condemned to eternal discontent, since at every point to which it attains, it meets nothing but itself, and at every point in its development it must enter upon the same striving, upon the same state of forth-impulsion. . . . After Schopenhauer was made known in the sixties to the general public . . . it became evident, *in the profound and extended effect produced by these teachings, that for countless persons the last word had been spoken, and the formulation of their deepest needs accomplished*" (emphasis added).

19 See also *New York Times*, 14 June 1992: A11.

20 See also Nixon (1991, 1992b).

21 Similarly, Leslie H. Gelb writes: "Even as they [Western diplomats] feed the dying, they secretly seem to hope that the Muslims will give up quickly so the whole mess would go away. Then the Western leaders tried to sell the phoniest of arguments. They maintained there were only two choices: massive ground employments and thus a Vietnam-like quagmire, or what they were already doing, i.e., feeding victims" (*New York Times*, 27 August 1992: A15).

22 But perhaps this is not so surprising. See Daniel Yergin, *The Prize: The Epic Quest for Oil, Money and Power* (New York: Simon & Schuster, 1991); Ben H. Bagdikian, *The Media Monopoly* (Boston: Beacon, 1988) and James Perloff, *The Shadows of Power* (Appleton, WI: Western Islands Publishing Council, 1990). These and other authors argue that the United States Council on Foreign Affairs is soft on communism, in favor of globalism, sympathetic to Marxism, and scornful of national sovereignty. In this cynical assessment, capitalists as well as Marxists are in favor of monopolizing world markets. Hence, Wall Street and Marxism become bedfellows. Perloff, in particular, cites the fact that the Council on Foreign Relations ignored the bloodbaths in communist Cambodia and Afghanistan relative to other world problems, and that it favors the United Nations as the prelude to a world government of the future. He claims that this council is an elitist front for the international banking community, globalist, and pro-communist in its orientation (1988: 193).

23 Rodney King is the victim of a video-taped police beating that occurred in Los Angeles in 1992. The not-guilty verdict in the trial of the officers who beat him is widely believed to have sparked the riots.

24 Even though Schoenfeld does not regard himself as a sociologist, almost all of his writings touch on sociological as well as political topics. See Schoenfeld (1962, 1966a, 1968, 1974, 1984, 1988, 1991).

25 Important exceptions to the relative neglect of Tocqueville can be found, of course. See David Riesman ([1950] 1977), Robert N. Bellah *et al.* (1985), and Richard Reeves (1990).

2 STILL HUNTING NAZIS, AND LOSING REALITY

1 For example, according to Alan Riding, "Chancellor Helmut Kohl of Germany surprised and irritated his European Community partners by pressing strongly for an end to the arms embargo on Bosnian Muslims at a regional summit meeting that ended here [Copenhagen] today" (*New York Times*, 23 June 1993: A6). Apparently, French President François Mitterrand was most irritated. Kohl's only supporter was President

Bill Clinton of the USA, but according to his aides, "Clinton didn't exactly mean it" (ibid.):

> The level of indifference in the Administration's diplomacy was perhaps best articulated by a senior White House official who said Mr. Clinton never expected anything to come of his letter [to Mr. Kohl]: "We didn't expect the Europeans to take any action, but if Kohl could get them to do something, that would be O.K.," the official said.
>
> (ibid.)

See also Alan Riding's "Its Competitors Distracted, France Gets to Be a Power," *New York Times*, 27 June 1993: E3.

2 See Thorstein Veblen ([1915] 1964; 1917, 1943).

3 In almost direct response to the scene with Mr. Wiesel, President Clinton asserted the following: "The Serbs' actions over the past year violate the principle that internationally recognized borders must not be violated or altered by aggression from without. Their actions threaten to widen the conflict and foster instability in other parts of Europe in ways that could be exceedingly damaging. And their savage and cynical ethnic cleansing offends the world's conscience and our standards of behavior" (*New York Times*, 7 May 1993: A6). However, the moral outrage dissipated quickly, as Mr. Clinton decided to consult with, but not lead the Europeans in putting a stop to Serbian aggression. This dramatic shift is expressed in Senator Joseph Biden's statement to Secretary of State Warren Christopher, regarding Mr. Christopher's trip to Europe: "What you've encountered, it seems to me, was a discouraging mosaic of indifference, timidity, self-delusion and hypocrisy. I can't even begin to express my anger for a European policy that's now asking us to participate in what amounts to a codification of a Serbian victory" (*New York Times*, 12 May 1993: A4).

4 See the *New York Times*, 28 April 1993: A1: "Although some key senators have drawn parallels to the Holocaust in demanding that the US and its allies take immediate action in Bosnia, Vietnam is the dominant image evoked on Capitol Hill."

5 Of course, postcommunist reality was lost in other ways. Consider William Safire's essay entitled "Too Many Russians," *New York Times*, 14 June 1993: A14. Mr. Safire explains that because Latvia had been colonized by Russia during the Soviet era, Latvia had denied citizenship to its Russian colonizers when Latvia gained independence. While not justifying Latvia's move, Mr. Safire at least understands it, writing that Latvia's "citizenship policy seeks to compensate past unfairness with present unfairness." The entire tone of the essay is sympathetic to the Baltic quest for nationhood. By contrast, no Western opinion-maker had written of a similar situation in the former Yugoslavia, such that Serbia had colonized Croatia. Despite this fact, the Serbian minority in Croatia had been granted citizenship and explicit minority rights in the constitution.

6 In fact, prior to the postmodernists, Lewis Mumford made a poignant observation concerning museums: "The museum is a manifestation of our curiosity, our acquisitiveness, our essentially predatory culture. . . . The opulence, the waste of resources and energies, the perversion of human effort represented in this imperial architecture are but the outcome of our general scheme of working and living" (1955: 145).

7 President Bush was reported to have made this statement on NBC News on 9 July 1992.

8 *New York Times*, 24 April 1993: A5.

9 ibid., 15 April 1993: A7.

10 ibid., 18 April 1993: E19.

11 Leslie H. Gelb, "Clinton as Carter?" ibid., 25 April 1993: E17.

12 ibid., 7 June 1993: A15.

13 Suroosh Irfani, "Bosnia: Sounding Board of Soul," *News International*, 13 May 1993:
5. Mr. Irfani continues:

> Amidst the ruins, what outsiders find so striking is the dignity of Bosnian Muslims.
> A point noted by Akbar Ahmed, one of the world's leading Muslim scholars, in an
> article he wrote after visiting Bosnia. It is a dignity born of victory over chaos, of
> having endured the Dark Night of the soul, where all that Bosnian Muslims were left
> was the idea of Islam as an anchor of sanity. In their struggle for coherence and
> meaning, as Bosnians were to tell Akbar Ahmed, "had it not been for Islam, we
> would have gone mad." At its core, then, the struggle of Bosnian Muslims for
> sovereignty, pluralism and democracy became intertwined with cultural resistance.
> But only after their nominal cultural identity as Muslims became the target of
> Serbian violence.
>
> (ibid.)

14 From an opinion piece by James Chace, "Exit, NATO," *New York Times*, 14 June 1993:
A15.
15 A letter to the editor on the same page makes the following claim: "If the United Nations
continues its ineffective policy in Bosnia, it could itself to become the main casualty of
the fighting. Failure to bring a cessation of aggression and an end to the worst bloodshed
in Europe since World War II will lead to a major global loss of faith in the world
organization" (*New York Times*, 15 June 1993: A12).
16 *New York Times Review of Books*, 28 March 93: p. 3.
17 Title of an ABC news program broadcast on 18 March 1993.
18 Secretary of State Warren Christopher's characterization of the current Balkan War,
broadcast on ABC News on 28 March 1993.
19 *New York Times*, 28 February 1993: E1.
20 ibid., 31 January 1993: E17.
21 In fact, Russian support for Serbia emerges even in the small details of its involvement
in the Balkans. According to a story in the *New York Times* (12 June 1993: A3): "Russia
has 800 peacekeepers in eastern Croatia who have appeared at times to cooperate with
the Croatian Serbs, in violation of the peacekeeping mandate. In one instance in
January, the Serbs seized heavy weapons in all four UN patrol zones in Croatia. There
were suggestions at the time that the Russian troops could have done more to prevent
the raids."
22 See Anthony Lewis, "Washing Our Hands," *New York Times*, 26 March: A13, wherein
he writes, "And the President of the United States? He does nothing except order food
dropped to the victims so they can stay alive a little longer until the aggressors overrun
them. He does not even say anything about the intensifying Serbian onslaught."
Elsewhere, Mr. Lewis adds, "Britain and France have been true to the tradition of
Munich" (ibid., 26 February 1993: A15). See also, Leslie H. Gelb, "Europeans Passing
the Ball to Clinton, Hoping He Won't Act," ibid., 31 January 1993: E17; and Serge
Schmemann, "From Russia to Serbia, a Current of Sympathy," ibid.,: E18.
23 *New York Times*, 25 April 1993: E1.
24 Thus, Paul Johnson writes in the *New York Times Book Review* that "the present
involvement of the United States in Bosnia is a direct consequence of the Serbs' fear
that they could become victims of an Islamic Jihad" (9 May 1993: 7).
25 When Chetniks were mentioned in the Western media, they were described incorrectly
as anti-German and anti-Fascist forces from World War II. For example, consider the
following passage by Pulitzer Prize winning writer, John Burns: "Chetniks are Serbian
militiamen, often with unkempt beards, who have taken the name of royalist guerrillas
who fought the Germans and their Fascist collaborators in Yugoslavia during World
War II. In the current conflict, it is the chetniks, as much as any group, who have been

responsible for the bloodiest incidents" (*New York Times*, 29 December 1992: A3). In fact, Chetniks were pro-German and pro-Fascist. See Balfour and Mackay (1980), Banac (1985), Magas (1993), Poulton (1991), Ramet (1992), and Singleton (1985), among many other sources.

26 For example, on 22 April 1993 she wrote: "Holocaust survivors and historians today condemned an invitation to the Croatian President, Franjo Tudjman, who has said that fewer than a million Jews died in the Holocaust. [Croatia] became a nominally independent state allied with Nazi Germany after it dismembered Yugoslavia in 1941" (p. A1). She alleges that Mr. Tudjman has a "long history" of other "anti-Semitic" statements, and she quotes Rabbi Hier as saying, "If I had to rank the Ustashis, I might put them on the same ranking as Hitler's SS, if not above them for the atrocities committed against Jews and non-Jews" (ibid.). On 23 April 1993, and again on the front page of the *New York Times*, Ms. Schemo wrote: "Most of the visiting leaders were applauded, though guests jeered the Croatian President, Franjo Tudjman. In a book that started his political career, Mr. Tudjman wrote that estimates of 6 million Jewish dead were exaggerated, and said the 'main characteristics' of Jews were 'selfishness, craftiness, unreliability, miserliness, underhandedness and secrecy'." She also wrote that the "omission of a representative for them angered many Serbs, who had been major victims of genocide by the Ustashi puppet regime allied with Nazi Germany" (ibid.). It is worth repeating that during World War II, Serbia also had a Nazi puppet regime headed by Milan Nedić (Balfour and Mackay 1980).

27 I saw and heard Mr. Goldstein make this remark on Croatian television on 16 May, 1993.

28 Special mention must be made of the American Psychiatric Association's condemnation of Dr. Karadzić in his role as a psychiatrist:

> The American Psychiatric Association deplores and condemns Dr. Karadzić for his brutal and inhumane actions as the Bosnian Serb leader. Those actions deserve condemnation by all civilized persons, but psychiatrists issue that condemnation with particular offense, urgency and horror because, by education and training, Dr. Karadzić claims membership in our profession. In fact, his actions as a political leader constitute a profound betrayal of the deeply humane values of medicine and psychiatry. In condemning him, we affirm those values and join all persons of good will in defending the right to life and to freedom from oppression of all human beings anywhere in the world regardless of race, religion, national origin and ethnicity.
>
> (*Psychiatric News* 7 May 1993: 1)

29 He adds that the "Serbian Empire" must "be extended to Bosnia and Herzegovina," and that "special attention must be paid to the problem of diverting the peoples of the Roman Catholic faith from the Austrian influence, and evoking a sympathy for Serbia" (in Beljo 1992: 15).

30 Actually, this book is primarily the work of Mrs. Ljubica Stefan, who used the pseudonym Edo Bojović out of fear for her own safety as she was conducting research in Belgrade. I met Mrs. Stefan in Zagreb in May 1993, and she indicated that she wanted her true identity to be known at this time. It should be noted that Mrs. Stefan, a Croat who saved Jewish lives during World War II in Belgrade, is recognized by Yad Vashem as Righteous Among Nations.

31 The poem is found on pages 183–7 of the original book, *Nova Srpska Satira* (Belgrade), and was translated by Margaret Casman-Vuko.

32 Not surprisingly, even the Bosnian Muslims cooperated with the Nazis during World War II, according to Enver Redic (1987). To repeat, there is nothing unusual in this fact given Nazism's one-time almost complete victory over Europe.

33 The reasons cited by Schoenfeld (1966a) center on the emotional problems brought on

by Oedipal conflicts *vis-à-vis* Judaism as a patriarchal religion. I agree that
anti-Semitism ought to be seen, at least in part, as a psychiatric problem.

3   UNWELCOME ALTERNATIVES

1   I acknowledge that in making this interpretation, I was influenced by an article written
in *Slobodna Dalmacija*, 2 May 1993: 24, entitled "Postmodernism and War."
2   *New York Times*, 4 June 1993: A4.
3   One is obliged to question the sincerity of the USA in backing this plan. For example,
according to an article in the *New York Times* entitled "Bosnia Havens Little Help, US
Intelligence Experts Say," one found the report that "American intelligence officials
have told the White House that the plan would do little in the long run beyond creating
six impoverished refugee compounds with limited law and order and no economic
future, a senior Clinton Administration intelligence analyst said today" (10 June 1993:
A1). In the *Wall Street Journal*, Joshua Muravchik accused the Clinton Administration
of making a "calculated retreat from global responsibilities," as evidenced by the US
foreign policy toward Bosnia-Herzegovina (10 June 1993: A14).
4   See also Michael R. Gordon's article in the *New York Times* entitled "Russia, Worried
by South, Asks Arms Pact Change," 10 June 1993: A1. Russia sought exemption from
previous agreements with the US so that it could place more troops on its southern
borders to guard against an "Islamic" threat.
5   Leslie H. Gelb, "Yeltsin as Monroe," *New York Times*, 7 March 1993: E17.
6   Solzhenitsyn writes:

> For a post-modernist, the world does not possess values that have reality. He even
> has an expression for this: 'the world as text,' as something secondary, as the text of
> an author's work, wherein the primary object of interest is the author himself in his
> relationship to the work, his own introspection. . . . But let us shift our attention to
> the more complex flow of this process. Even though the 20th century has seen the
> more bitter and disheartening lot fall to the peoples under Communist domination,
> our whole world is living through a century of spiritual illness, which could not but
> give rise to a similar ubiquitous illness in art. Although for other reasons, a similar
> 'post-modernist' sense of confusion about the world has also arisen in the West.
>
> (1993: 17)

7   Barry Smart makes this argument in an essay in Rojek and Turner (1993).
8   I discuss this in the closing chapter of *The Barbarian Temperament* (Meštrović 1993).
9   According to Gellner (1992b: 70): "Postmodernism is a movement which, in addition
to contingent flaws – obscurity, pretentiousness, faddiness, showmanship, cultural name-
dropping – commits major errors in the method it recommends. . . . Postmodernism as
such doesn't matter too much. It is a fad which owes its appeal to its seeming novelty and
genuine obscurity, and it will pass soon enough, as such fashions do. But it is a specimen
of relativism, and relativism does matter. Relativism isn't objectionable because it
entails moral nihilism (which it does); moral nihilism may be hard to escape in any case.
It is objectionable because it leads to *cognitive* nihilism, which is simply false."
10   "Enlightenment Rationalist Fundamentalism, of which I am a humble adherent,
repudiates any substantive revelations," writes Ernest Gellner (1992b: 80).
11   For example, commenting on communism as a derivative of the Enlightenment project,
Gellner writes: "In the twentieth century, this more sociological, sophisticated attempt
to implement the Enlightenment ideal came to be tried out. It too ended in Terror and
dictatorship, and, subsequently, in dismal economic failure and squalor into the bargain.
That experiment reached its final end in 1989, two hundred years after the French
Revolution" (1992b: 87).

12 This passage was authored by the anonymous editors of *The New York Times*, 13 June 1993: E18.
13 The interested reader will find a full discussion in Meštrović, Goreta, and Letica (1993a).
14 See Meštrović (1991, 1992, 1993) and Meštrović, Goreta, and Letica (1993a).
15 This was brought out forcefully by William Schmidt in an article entitled "In Serbia, Sanctions Fuel Rage," *New York Times*, 15 June 1993: A7. According to Mr. Schmidt, ordinary Serbs hold the West, rather than their own leaders, accountable for the hardships caused by economic sanctions against Serbia. Milorad Vlaisavljevic is quoted as saying, "The West is not punishing the politicians, it is punishing ordinary people, and strengthening the hand of those who are the most authoritarian" (ibid.).
16 This position is compatible with many similar arguments by critical theorists, such as Theodor Adorno (1991) and Erich Fromm (1955, 1962, 1963, 1964). One should keep in mind that Erich Fromm was arguably one of David Riesman's most important mentors. Nevertheless, some readers may not be convinced that Riesman's *Lonely Crowd* can be read as a treatise against narcissism. For the sake of context, I would refer those readers to some of Riesman's other writings (see Riesman 1953, 1954, 1964, 1976, 1980a, 1980b, 1981, 1990).
17 As contemporary illustrations, consider some observations made by Celestine Bohlen in her article entitled, "Cradle of Russian Revolution a Hotbed of Disgust" (*New York Times*, 22 June 1993: A3). She quotes a Russian nationalist as making the following statements:

> Ours is a protest against the liquidation of a single, united state. The Soviet Union was viewed by Russians as their territory, a place where they felt at home. We want the restoration of a single state, call it Soviet or Russian.
>
> (ibid.)

Rasković makes similar observations about the Serbian desire for a single Serb or Yugoslavian (treated as roughly equivalent) state. Another Russian is quoted by Bohlen as saying,

> Serbs and Russians have the same mentality, and we are close by religion. I am not strong on history, but I know those are Serbian lands, and that they have been theirs for centuries. If the Muslims want to create a mythical Islamic state, let them go to Turkey. Besides, President Alija Izetbegović is no Muslim. He is a Jew.
>
> (ibid.)

Bohlen adds that "Anti-Semitism runs deep through the Russian nationalist movement," but again, Philip Cohen (1993) has uncovered a strong streak of anti-Semitism in the Serbian nationalist movement.

4 THE POSTMODERNIST AS VOYEUR

1 See Karen S. Schneider, "Bearing Witness," *People Weekly*, 5 April 1993: 30–5.
2 Consider the following excerpts from a news story entitled "Immoral Neutrality in the Balkans" by Georgie Anne Geyer that was run on Universal Press Syndicate on 11 June 1993:

> Two phrases about the war here keep popping up in the words of supposedly decent Europeans and Americans. In Brussels last week I heard over and over in one way or another in conversations about Bosnia: "Let the Serbs win quickly – then it will all be over with." Here the phrase is different but related: "The Croats and Muslims are just as bad as the Serbs – they're all the same." Both phrases make the speakers

feel better, confirming to them that no one needs to feel guilty or cowardly for not doing anything effective here ... George Orwell is alive and well in the Western world today.

In virtually every official conversation with the international and humanitarian groups here, I heard the Croatian and Bosnian Muslim victims being blamed as much as the Serb aggressors. "We now have the complete degradation of Bosnia-Herzegovina," one leading UN official told me here, typically. "Now, everyone is touched by the atrocities and becomes corrupted by them; the atrocities have become balanced." That is what some people here call, sometimes cynically, "UN neutral," and being for the use of "muscle, not force."

But it is more than that, for the international groups are not neutral. From the very beginning, their "neutral" actions have served the rampaging Serbs. When Senator Carl Levin (Democrat – Michigan) was here the first week of June, for example, and he asked his UN briefers whether the Serbs were not guilty of most atrocities, there was simply a long silence. Yet, anyone with two honest eyes can see that the Serbs have taken over 70 percent of Bosnia and now threaten the Balkans; and that at the very least 95 percent of the killings are attributable to them.

When the United Nations and humanitarian groups were put here from the Summer of 1991 onward, without the ability or mandate even to defend themselves from the Serbs, they soon became what they basically are today: hostages of the Serbs. And when you mix guilt over these policies with certain degrees of cowardice and helplessness, you get out of original idealism a bureaucratic mind-set that blames the victim.

This is the terrible legacy that outside intervention in Bosnia and Croatia is going to bequeath the world for the next crisis: Decent and idealistic people, put in an impossible situation with self-imposed restraints, give power to thugs and killers. And finally, in embarrassment and horror, they develop a rationale for it: "Everyone is guilty, so no one is guilty."

The terrible fact is that the Western and world intervention here (through the UN) does not mean non-intervention. We are involved, deeply – and inadvertently but decisively – on the Serbs' side. Every act of the international community, from prohibiting the Bosnian Muslims from defending themselves to constantly buying the Serbs time through our endless and ever-fruitless "negotiations" with them, puts us squarely on the side of the aggressors.

With that reality, created by a theater-of-the-absurd mission that renounces force against those who live by it, comes finally a real disdain and dislike for the victims. Why are they so dirty, so miserable – so repugnant? Why are they in the way of peace in our time?

Voltaire put it best two centuries ago, when he wrote, "Such is the wretched weakness of men that they admire those who have done evil brilliantly."

3 See, for example, the *New York Times*, 28 February 1993: E1 and 26 July 1992: E3.
4 "The feeling among Sarajevans is that the [UN] peacekeepers have been callous at best toward the sufferings of the city and at worst partial to the Serbian forces attacking it" (*New York Times*, 9 August 1992: A10). The Bosnian government accused the United Nations of collaborating with the Serbian aggressor when the deputy Prime Minister of Bosnia-Herzegovina was assassinated in Sarajevo by Serbs while under UN protection [and] UN troops did not fire back (*New York Times*, 9 January 1993: A1; see also *Wall Street Journal*, 11 January 1993: A1). When the Secretary of the United Nations, Mr. Boutros Ghali, visited Sarajevo, he was jeered, and called a Fascist and Hitler (*New York Times*, 1 January 1993: A4).
5 "If Western TV shows footage of a Serbian massacre of Croats or Muslims, Belgrade TV uses the same clip – saying the bodies are Serbs murdered by 'fascist' Croats.

Refugees who trudge across the screen are invariably identified as Serbs. Shells raining down on Sarajevo are, in the Serbs' version, fired by the Muslims, or 'jihad warriors.' Some Serbs are so convinced that they question whether there is a siege of Sarajevo at all" (*Wall Street Journal*, 18 September 1992: A1).

6 Of course, Muslims and Croats also committed war crimes, but I have already presented sufficient documentation to show that Serbia committed the overwhelming share of the war crimes.

7 See "The Limit of Shame," by Anthony Lewis (*New York Times*, 5 April 1993: A11).

8 Chuck Sudetic writes: "A Bosnian official, who insisted on anonymity, said, 'Ask yourself for whom Lord Owen has been working since the beginning. All these people, the United Nations, and especially Great Britain and France, have all worked for the Serbs' benefit. All their statements condemning the Serbs have been a farce. Now, when the Serbs have conquered practically everything they want, they act like kittens, like peacemakers' " (*New York Times*, 18 June 1993: A6).

9 Senator Robert Dole made similar criticisms of President Clinton's military action against a Somali "warlord" in mid-June, 1993.

10 It would truly take up too much space to document the many other instances of optimism on the part of Western officials even though they knew that Serbia had broken scores of previous promises and cease-fires. Thus, to cite one example out of scores, Mr. Cyrus Vance saw "reason for hope" that a recently negotiated cease-fire would hold even as Serbs had lobbed grenades into a funeral procession (*New York Times*, 1 September 1992: A3).

11 Commenting on the effects of another peace talk, the editors of the *New York Times* wrote: "Despite agreements reached at the London conference, Bosnian cities remain under siege, the movement of humanitarian relief convoys is still hazardous, and innocent civilians continue to be slaughtered. At London, the parties agreed to a ban on all military flights over Bosnia. Yet the bombing of defenseless population centers has actually increased. This flagrant disregard for human life and for a clear agreement requires a response from the international community" (3 October 1992: A1).

12 Creveld argues that in the twentieth century, wars in general have been transformed from Clausewitzian rules and strategies to low-intensity, brutal, protracted wars against civilians. The transformed war "will be a war of listening devices and car-bombs, of men killing each other at close quarters, and of women using their purses to carry explosives and the drugs to pay for them. It will be protracted, bloody, and horrible" (1991: 212). Perhaps the Serbian tactics in the current Balkan War are the clearest example, thus far, of Creveld's argument.

13 Ahmed elaborates: "The Serbs project themselves as a 'Christian' force wiping out the Muslims in a crusade, taking revenge for the past. The method of the Serbian forces betrays their intention. The first thing in a village that is destroyed is the mosque and all marks of it are systematically obliterated and then trees planted on the site so that there will be no memory of the mosque" (1993: 26).

14 I should add that I watched the news coverage of Mr. Wiesel's visit to Serbia on Serbian television. I can report that Mr. Wiesel's visit was portrayed by the Belgrade regime as support for the Serbian cause. It is interesting, too, that Mr. Wiesel visited Sarajevo and Belgrade, but would not visit Zagreb.

15 According to Anthony Lewis, "While Serbian leaders talk of negotiating peace, they wage undiminished war on civilians" (*New York Times*, 26 February 1993: A15). The UN Commissioner for Refugees in former Yugoslavia, Mr. Jose Meniluce, "said the commitments given by Serbian leaders to halt this 'ethnic cleansing' and to aid relief convoys had proved largely worthless" (ibid., 15 February 1993: A4). "The would-be peacekeepers describe the Serbs' behavior harshly. 'They lie to us all the time,' one said" (ibid., 10 May 1992: A3). "Mr. Milošević, who was re-elected last month on a

strongly nationalist platform, has earned a reputation among domestic and foreign officials of not keeping his word during the last 18 months of fighting in the former Yugoslav republics" (ibid., 8 January 1993: A5). "Serbia's murderous shelling of Bosnian civilians in Sarajevo and Gorazde has intensified despite last Friday's cease-fire accord. The Serbs had pledged to place their artillery, mortars and other heavy weapons under UN supervision. Instead they have continued blasting away at Bosnia, forcing temporary suspension of food and medical relief to Sarajevo" (ibid., 23 July 1992: A10). See also 14 July 1992: A1 and the *Wall Street Journal*, 17 August 1992: A1, 18 August 1992: A1, 19 August 1992: A1.

16 Ahmed writes: "It was the governments and the elite and the rich and the powerful of the Muslim lands who were responding with heartless apathy. Where were the Muslim armies? Where was the Muslim oil money, where was the Muslim power that could put effective pressure on the Serbs? It appeared not to exist" (1993: 25).

17 Of course, this characterization is a matter of judgment. Jeri Laber (1993) claims that compared with rapes committed in previous wars, the mass rape in this Balkan War has received unprecedented media coverage. And she credits feminist groups for this coverage. But my point is that compared with other women's issues, the mass rape in this Balkan War has received minimal attention. Even Laber's article was not published until March 1993, when the mass rapes that began in early 1992 had already achieved their aim of assisting with the Serbian campaign of "ethnic cleansing." Moreover, Laber keeps to the standard line of blaming all three "ethnic groups" (Serbs, Croats, Muslims) for rape, even though she acknowledges that the Serbs committed the preponderance of the atrocities. She explains this apparent contradiction with the vacuous claim that the Serbs had more of the means to commit atrocities than the other groups. The clear implication is that the Croats and Muslims would have engaged in mass rapes if they had the military means. But this is a hypothesis, and nothing more, that completely overlooks the facts that Croats and Muslims have not engaged in systematic mass rapes even in areas where they had the means precisely because, unlike the Serbs, they had no aims at territorial aggrandizement. Again, the important point is that the mass rapes in this war were a terrorist technique to achieve "ethnic cleansing" in the service of establishing a "Greater Serbia." It is pure prejudice to equate all three sides in this regard, because, at least up to the time of this writing, the Croats as well as the Bosnian Muslims did not attack one inch of Serbian territory.

18 The *New York Times* of 31 March 1993: A6 reported that Mr. Herak was found guilty "of committing genocide against Muslims, for the killings he acknowledged having committed, and of killing Muslim civilians and Muslims who were captured soldiers." He confessed to these crimes, and when the death sentence was pronounced, he said "Yes, I deserve it [the penalty]." The trial was conducted in Sarajevo by the duly sovereign Bosnian government. Yet,

> The trial and its outcome were condemned by Lieut. Gen. Philippe Morillon of France, the United Nations military commander here [Sarajevo], who is trying to consolidate a three-day-old cease-fire that continued today to bring peace across most of Bosnia. General Morillon said he had told Bosnian and Serbian nationalist leaders that it was 'not time for them to take justice into their own hands.' A better solution, he told them, would have been for the Bosnian Government to await the time when a war crimes tribunal that the United Nations plans to establish for the former Yugoslavia could place Mr. Herak and Mr. Damjanović on trial.
>
> (ibid.)

General Morillon's statements are highly offensive to Muslims regarding the crimes committed against them. First, the trial in Sarajevo was certainly not a lynch mob or some other effort to "take justice into their own hands." In fact, Bosnia-Herzegovina is a duly recognized nation that had a right to conduct this trial, a right that would have been unquestioned in France or any other Western nation. Second, the General is implicitly equating the criminal acts of revenge committed by Serbs against Muslims with the Muslim trial of a self-confessed mass-murderer. Third, at the time the trial was conducted, the Bosnians had no good reasons to believe the promises of the United Nations that it would conduct war crime trials. For almost a year, the UN had made such promises, but failed repeatedly to put into practice the mechanisms for such trials. Meanwhile, the guilty parties were escaping back to Serbia, and evidence, as well as witnesses, was being systematically eliminated.

19 A headline in the *New York Times* read, "European Inquiry Says Serbs' Forces Have Raped 20,000" (9 January 1993: A1). The rape was conducted "in particularly sadistic ways so as to inflict maximum humiliation on the victims," many of whom died after being raped. The Commission concluded that "rape cannot be seen as incidental to the main purposes of the aggression but as serving a strategic purpose in itself," namely, "the purpose of ethnic cleansing" (ibid.). In addition, Paul Lewis writes that "the UN war crimes commission has found evidence that rape has been used by the Serbs as a weapon of terror in the war in Bosnia" (*New York Times*, 20 October 1993: A1).

20 This interpretation was conveyed to me by a Croatian feminist, Gordana Letica, on 9 October, 1993, in Zagreb, Croatia. Ms. Letica attended many such all-female meetings concerning mass rapes.

21 In the words of Slavenka Drakulić, printed in the *New York Times*, 13 December 1992: E17: "What is happening in Bosnia and Herzegovina to Muslim and Croatian women seems unprecedented in the history of war crimes. Women are raped by Serbian soldiers in an organized and systematic way, as a planned crime to destroy a whole Muslim population, to destroy a society's cultural, traditional and religious integrity. . . . Mass rape is a method of genocide that should become a war crime and outlawed in all international conventions."

22 Broadcast on CNN on 22 December 1992.

23 According to Carol J. Williams, writing in the *Los Angeles Times*: "The victims of war rape are largely being ignored in Croatia, where predominantly male, Roman Catholic, conservative health officials are too discomfited by the subject to provide care or compassion. . . . Most of the rape victims have been cast out of their homes and left to fend for themselves, and sometimes their small children as well, in battle zones without food, warm clothing or shelter. Many are too shattered by the degradation or too overwhelmed by the struggle to stay alive to confide to overburdened relief workers what they have endured. For those who do talk . . . there is little reward aside from the emotional catharsis of voicing a painful truth. Their experiences are horrifying and legion. . . . Women's groups and anti-war organizations complain bitterly that nothing is done for the innumerable victims of sexual violence that has [sic] been a consequence of this war. . . .There are virtually no services for rape victims in either Bosnia or Croatia. Aid agencies, charities and religious organizations are too overwhelmed by the task of feeding and housing more than 2 million displaced by the war to devote resources to those whose injuries are not life-threatening" (30 November 1992: A1).

24 This episode in Croatia's history is undeniable. However, one must also take into account Serbia's collaboration with the Nazis, as well as what some analysts consider Serbian misappropriation of the Holocaust (see Cohen 1992).

25 In another brutal remark, Mr. Eagleburger asserted: "I have said this 38,000 times and I have to say this to the people of this country [the USA] as well: This tragedy is not something that can be settled from outside and it's about damn well time that everybody understood that. Until the Bosnians, Croats, and Serbs decide to stop killing each other, there is nothing the outside world can do about it" (*New York Times*, 1 October 1992: A3).

26 See, for example, the editorial in the *New York Times*, 8 July 1992: A12.
27 See, for example, the *New York Times*, 10 February 1993: A3; 20 February 1993: E1; and 23 July 1992: A4, among many others.
28 For example, John Burns writes in the *New York Times* that "Former Secretary of State Cyrus R. Vance, the chief United Nations mediator in the Balkans, intervened in the dispute today, calling the Serbian President, Slobodan Milošević, in Belgrade and obtaining a promise from him that he would use his influence with the Bosnian Serbs to get the aid through, United Nations officials said" (16 February 1993: A3).

5 THE END OF MORALITY?

1 For two contemporary accounts of the realism–idealism distinction in American foreign policy, see Fukuyama (1992) and Isaacson (1992).
2 See Alexander Cockburn, "State-Sponsored Terrorism, American-Style," *Wall Street Journal*, 1 July 1993: A15. Also consider that the *New York Times* published three letters to the editor concerning this action, all of them critical (5 July 1993: A18). The first one was entitled, "Again, Iraqi Babies Bear Washington's Fury." The author writes, in part:

> The people of Iraq are so hungry, sick and frightened that they cannot think about higher ideals, such as freedom and democracy. Even the middle and upper middle classes, which could think about the virtues of democracy, are too poor to aspire to such distant dreams. The West has to start looking at us as people, as a nation, and not as a regime. The United States Administration ought to stop considering Iraqi lives as tools to boost its popularity whenever the President slips in the polls. This thing has been going on too long, making the cries of the malnourished babies of Iraq too loud to be ignored by civilized nations. Please help us.

The second letter was entitled, "Might Makes Right." In it the author concludes that "the only real principle at work is that the United States is entitled to do anything it pleases to preserve its power". The author of the final letter, "Now Bomb Bosnia," writes:

> If President Clinton is the least bit serious about slowing the slaughter in Bosnia and Herzegovina, he will do to Serbian river crossings what he did to the Iraqi intelligence building. . . . I find it the height of hypocrisy that the Administration will go to such lengths to retaliate for an unsuccessful attempt on one man's life [President Bush's], while it does nothing to enforce constantly violated United Nations embargoes on Serbian military shipments to Bosnia, allowing thousands to die and continued untold suffering. . . . As the most powerful member of the United Nations and the country to which the free world looks for leadership, the United States should apply that same logic to protecting the sovereignty of Bosnia, a fellow member in the community of nations, and to defending the human rights of its people.

3 For a contrary view, see the letter to the editor in the *New York Times*, 16 April 1993: A11, which cites the Bosnian author, Ivo Andrić, who apparently did refer to an all-consuming hatred among the Balkan people. Similarly, in "A Reader's Guide to the Balkans," Robert D. Kaplan also cites Mr. Andrić as well as Rebecca West in order to portray the Balkans as a cauldron of hatred (*New York Times Review of Books*, 18 April 1993: 1). Even if there are authors who wish to make the case for the Balkan people as hateful, my point is that this position is a caricature for the simple reason that no society can exist solely on the basis of hatred. And the Balkan people do live in Balkan societies, complete with loving families.
4 Indeed, this position was often taken by an editorial writer for the *New York Times*,

Mr. A.M. Rosenthal. For example, in his opinion piece entitled "Muslims Broke the Truce," Mr. Rosenthal blamed the Muslims, who are the dominant victims in the current war, for the fact that the Serbs shelled them (16 April 1993: A15). Mr. Rosenthal went further: "Western European officials, particularly German, encouraged the break-up of Yugoslavia, beginning with Croatia, then Slovenia and finally Bosnia. Then when Serbs predictably decided to fight the secessions by grabbing as much as they could, Western Europeans looked pained" (ibid.).

5   As illustration, consider the Russian President, Boris Yeltsin's, oil embargo on Latvia as retaliation for Latvia's refusal to grant automatic Latvian citizenship to its Russian occupiers (*New York Times*, 27 June 1993: A4).

6   "Mr. Clinton: Don't Bury Bosnia," *New York Times*, 19 June 1993: A14.

7   This attitude persisted even during the extreme and well-publicized siege of Srebrenica. See the *New York Times*, 17 April 1993: A6 and 22 April 1993: A7.

8   The editors of the *New York Times* wrote on 7 August 1992: A1: "But the world so far declines to defend democratic Bosnia's territorial integrity the way it did feudal Kuwait's. . . . What is still conspicuously missing is a Security Council resolution that would brand Serbian aggression a threat to international security, demand full restoration of Bosnia's sovereignty and borders and authorize military force, if necessary, to insure compliance. . . . Success for Serbia's ethnic cleansing strategy would encourage like-minded demagogues to pursue ethnic wars from the Baltics to the Caucacus."

9   According to Anthony Lewis, "Britain and France have been true to the tradition of Munich" (*New York Times*, 26 February 1993: A15). Elaine Sciolino wrote: "Images of horror can sometimes move nations to action, but these events occurred in Bosnia and Herzegovina – terrain thus far deemed too treacherous for Western military intervention. . . . For Alija Izetbegović, negotiating with the Serbs as they systematically murder, rape, starve, and freeze his people is reminiscent of Munich in 1938, where Neville Chamberlain offered up to Hitler the territorial integrity of Czechoslovakia in the misguided hope of satisfying his territorial lust. 'There are too many Chamberlains in the European countries trying to save peace on unprincipled compromises' Mr. Izetbegovic said" (*New York Times*, 10 January 1993: E4). On another occasion, the editors of the *New York Times* wrote: "In a shameful abdication of responsibility, the US and its European allies continue to pursue a policy of nonintervention in the face of unbridled brutality" (28 September 1992: A4). On 21 May 1992, the editors wrote: "The Serbian strongman Slobodan Milošević steps up his brutal bombardment of Bosnia's capital, Sarajevo, and his 'ethnic cleansing' of Serb-occupied territory. Hundreds die, ancient towns are turned to rubble. And what is the response of the US, the EC and the UN? Sighs, shrugs, and evasions" (p. A11). On 6 January 1993, the editors wrote: "Mr. Vance and Lord Owen continue a policy of negotiation that amounts to appeasement" (p. A12). Commenting on the Vance–Owen peace plan, George Kenney wrote in the *Wall Street Journal*, "In this arrangement, Bosnia would be but a short step from having the war criminal Radovan Karadzić as president!" (18 February 1993: A18).

10   Anthony Lewis is less critical of Cyrus Vance than of Lord David Owen in an article entitled "The Price of Weakness," *New York Times*, 20 June 1993: A15. Mr. Lewis adds:

> In the week since the safe haven plan was agreed in Washington, it has turned out to be a bitter joke. The Serbs, undeterred, have devastated one of the supposed havens, Gorazde, killing many refugees. They have resumed shelling Sarajevo. The United Nations has had difficulty finding any troops for the supposed protective role. The safe haven plan is in fact nothing more than a Western cave-in to the aggressors. The havens will be, at best, overcrowded refugee camps with no viable economic life. Serbian forces, not disarmed, will still surround them. . . . Partition would

complete Serbian humiliation of the West, and especially of the United States. . . . The ugliest elements in Serbian political life, modern-day Fascists, will have been proved right in calling America a paper tiger.

11 According to the editors of the *Wall Street Journal*, "The Serbians have done a good job of making their very name synonymous in history now with something quite awful" (1 July 1993: A14).

12 See also the references to Lawrence Eagleburger's business dealings as a member of Kissinger Associates as depicted in Isaacson (1992: 732–51). Of particular significance is the fact that Mr. Eagleburger represented, among others, the makers of the Yugo automobile, whose headquarters were to be found in Belgrade, Serbia. Furthermore, David Binder wrote in the *New York Times* (27 May 1992: A4): "State Department specialists on the Balkans accused Lawrence Eagleburger, the Deputy Secretary of State, and the national security adviser, Brent Scowcroft, both of whom served in Belgrade, of holding on too long to the idea of a federal Yugoslavia even after it was clearly doomed by nationalist rivalry. Mr. Zimmerman is also criticized on this count. 'Scowcroft and Eagleburger were obstacles,' said a middle-ranking State Department official. 'Mr. Eagleburger catered to Serbia because of business connections he maintained while in private life as president of Kissinger Associates'. . . . He served on the board of directors of the now defunct American subsidiary of the Yugo automobile company, which was based in Serbia."

13 For example, Simmel asserted that in modernity, the social world comes to be perceived "as a huge arithmetical problem" ([1900] 1990: 444). The West's response to human rights abuses seems to be part and parcel of this "measuring, weighing, and calculating exactness of modern times" (ibid.).

14 For example, "State Department spokesman Joe Snyder accused Serbs of running detention centers in which inmates starve to death" (*Wall Street Journal*, 4 September 1992: A1). According to the *New York Times*, "Prisoners in Serbian-run detention camps in Bosnia face malnutrition, starvation, sexual abuse, beating, and execution, the Bush Administration said today. . . . The overwhelming response to this practice [death camps] lies with the Serbs, who are using detention centers as part of their ethnic cleansing campaign" (4 September 1992: A4). In order to downplay the emotional impact of the initial reports, on 16 August 1992, the state Department claimed that the killings were "too random to be genocide" (ibid.: A1). By 1993, it was concluded by most opinion-makers that the killings did qualify as genocide. See also *New York Times*, 5 August 1992: A6; 4 August 1992: A1; 6 August 1992: A4; 20 July 1992: A1; 14 June 1992: A4; 12 July 1992: E3; 3 August 1992: A4; 7 August 1992: A15, and the *Wall Street Journal*, 29 September 1992: A1.

15 It is ironic that whereas in April 1993 the Clinton Administration was comparing the fate of the Bosnian Muslims with the Holocaust, in August 1992 Deputy Secretary of State Lawrence Eagleburger was pointedly avoiding such comparisons. Mr. Eagleburger said: "On the basis of what we have so far, I think it's best to say there is evidence of unpleasant conditions [in the concentration camps]. A terrible thing to have happen, but I am not sure I would at this stage go to the point of saying 'death camp' if what we mean by that is an Auschwitz or a Belsen" (*New York Times*, 23 August 1992: A8). Yet even at this time, the US Senate Foreign Relations Committee "concluded that there was evidence of organized killing" (ibid.).

16 According to Mr. George Kenney, during a presentation on 13 April 1993 at the University of North Carolina at Chapel Hill, which I attended.

17 For one example among many, see the *New York Times*, 14 June 1992: A11.

18 See, for example, the *New York Times*, 3 October 1992: A1; 7 January 1993: A12; 2 February 1993: A11 and the *Wall Street Journal*, 8 January 1993: A12; 1 February 1993: A12.

19 See also the *Wall Street Journal*, 12 February 1993: A10 and the *New York Times*, 11 February 1993: A1 and 28 February 1993: A12. Of course, all of these cynical assessments might be incorrect. A relatively neglected aspect of the discussion concerning the West's motives in waging war on Saddam Hussein is his nuclear threat. It is a telling sign that following the West's victory over Iraq, the UN expended the most energy and money in inspecting and destroying Iraq's nuclear facilities. The world may never know the West's actual motives, but no matter what they were, the motive that was presented was one of defending democracy and national sovereignty.

20 For example, Kroker and Kroker (1991: xiv) refer to the Gulf War as "a sacrificial violence for the violent regeneration of American politics, and for reaffirming faith in the equivalence of freedom and technology – the civil religion of America." The Gulf War was "George Bush's term for the coming to be of Hegel's universal and homogeneous state under the hegemonic sign of the technological dynamo" (ibid.). This use of cynical ideology, cynical power, and cynical sacrifice are the "main contours of the nihilistic politics of the twenty-first century" (ibid.: xv).

21 ABC Evening News, 22 April 1993.

22 See Helsinki Watch Committee 1990, 1991a, 1991b, 1992a, 1992b, 1992c. See also Judas (1992).

23 See, for example, "A War on Civilians" by Michael T. Kaufman in the *New York Times*, 18 July 1992: A1.

24 For example, see John F. Burns, "Power and Water Lost in Sarajevo as Attacks Mount," *New York Times*, 14 July 1992: A1. And many of these attacks continued despite cease-fires: "Serbia's murderous shelling of Bosnian civilians in Sarajevo and Gorazde has intensified despite last Friday's cease-fire accord" (ibid., 23 July 1992: A10).

25 See, for example, the testimony of Jeri Laber, Executive Director, Helsinki Watch, before the Commission on Security and Cooperation in Europe on 5 February 1992, among other sources.

26 According to the editors of the *Wall Street Journal*, "left to its own devices, the UN will always be a big, expensive, rudderless boat, and without the US compass, it is headed for humiliation without end" (8 January 1993: A12). A good example of UN incompetence is the case of ten elderly people who died from exposure to the cold in a nursing home situated a half a mile from the UN headquarters in Sarajevo. The UN blamed a "mix-up in communication" for their failure to reach the elderly with blankets (*New York Times*, 8 January 1993: A5).

27 For example, the *New York Times* ran a front-page article criticizing President Franjo Tudjman's invitation to the opening of the Holocaust Museum (22 April 1993: A1). Croatia's Nazi collaboration from World War II was cited, and Mr. Tudjman was labeled an anti-Semite. Yet Mr. Tudjman was invited along with five other heads of government from East and Central Europe, all of whom had Nazi collaboration in their national pasts. Why should the European guilt for Nazism be laid almost entirely at the feet of Mr. Tudjman and Croatia?

28 "Bosnian Serb leader [Radovan Karadzić] says his people fight out of fear and in self-defense. Mr. Karadzić prefers not to speak of ethnic cleansing" (*New York Times*, 5 March 1993: A1). In an interesting article entitled, "Paranoid and Vengeful, Serbs Claim Their War is to Right Old Wrongs," Roger Thurow and Tony Horwitz quote the Serbian position as follows: "'We have always been attacked. By Turks, Bulgarians, Hungarians, Italians, Austrians, Germans,' says the [Serb] militiaman, who is clad in jungle fatigues and black boots. 'How is it that Serbs, who fought alongside America, France and the UK in World War I and II, can now be portrayed as Fascists?' In stark contrast to their menacing image on the evening news, Serbs today are a defensive, self-pitying and paranoid people. Whether they are dug in on the front lines, or waiting in the gasoline lines that snake through Belgrade, Serbs' abiding conviction is that, like

Jews, they have been persecuted through centuries of European turmoil and now are under threat again. This belief had endowed the war with both a deadly momentum and a tragic irony. Convinced they must fight to avoid being victimized again by perennial enemies, Serbs have themselves become aggressors, prompting retaliation that confirms their sense of persecution. And while rationalizing their ends with references to earlier genocide, Serbian nationalists themselves evoke eerie echoes of the Nazi era: with detention camps, ethnically cleansed towns and Hitler-like talks of a Greater Serbia and the branding of war critics as 'low-quality' Serbs" (*Wall Street Journal*, 18 September 1992: A1).

29 See, for example, the cynical assessment offered by Garrison Keillor, "In Praise of Sunshine Patriots," published on Independence Day in the *New York Times* (4 July 1993: E11).

30 For a cogent criticism of Durkheim on precisely this point, see Robert Hall's (1988) analysis.

6 WHAT WENT WRONG WITH THE ENLIGHTENMENT PROJECT?

1 One of Baudrillard's most vigorous critics is Douglas Kellner (1989). Some of Kellner's criticisms are worth noting: "Contrary to Baudrillard, I believe that there are good reasons to maintain that we still live in a society in which the mode of production dominates much of our cultural and social life" (1989: 51). Kellner depicts Baudrillard as Nietzsche's Zarathustra (p. 91) for whom history has stopped (p. 117). He also accused Baudrillard of capitulating to reification (p. 167). America becomes the simulation of Tocqueville.

2 Durkheim's teacher, Fustel de Coulanges, expresses this view poignantly in *The Ancient City* (1889): "The victory of Christianity marks the end of ancient society" (1889: 519) because prior to Christianity, every god protected exclusively a single family or a single city, and existed only for that limited entity. The state was a religious community. Patriotism was piety. "Individual liberty was unknown [and] man was enslaved to the state through his soul, his body, and his property; the notions of law and duty, of justice and of affection, were bounded within the limits of the city; men saw no possibility of founding larger societies" (ibid.: 520).

3 A quote taken from Jay Katz, Joseph Goldstein, and Alan M. Dershowitz (eds.) *Pscyhoanalysis, Psychiatry and Law* (New York: Free Press, 1967), p. 21.

4 It is worth noting here, if only in passing, that the other major Serbian leader in the current Balkan War, Dr. Radovan Karadzić, is also a psychiatrist.

5 In a cynical twist, Kroker and Kroker (1991: x) refer to postmodernism as "Spengler again: but this time the *ecstasy* of the decline of the West," the world in ruins, the *fin de millennium*. Similarly, in *The Postmodern Scene*, Kroker and Cook (1986: 8) make the following, rather disturbing claim: "It is our general thesis that the postmodern scene in fact, begins in the fourth century with the Augustinian subversion of embodied power, and that everything since the Augustinian refusal has been nothing but a fantastic and grisly implosion of experience as Western culture itself has run under the signs of passive and suicidal nihilism."

6 For a balanced analysis of Veblen, see Riesman (1953). Consider also Riesman's (1964: 391) summary of Veblen's contribution, that "modern society was, in its essential tone, only a latter-day barbarism." For an elaboration of these views in a postmodern context, see Meštrović (1993).

7 Without any reference to Sorokin, Kroker and Kroker (1991: x) echo him when they write that American capitalism and Soviet communism should be reconceptualized as "strange attractors" that "begin to slide into another, actually mutating into their opposites as they undergo a fatal reversal of meaning." They explain that communism

was "aping the economic form of primitive capitalism, and capitalism is taking on the political form of the command economy of late communism" (ibid.).

8 *New York Times*, 21 June 1993: A1.

9 Barry Smart (1992: 164) seems to agree, citing World War I as the first postmodern general war in which technological development outstripped moral and ethical development.

10 In Tocqueville's words: "I have previously remarked that the manners of the people may be considered as one of the great general causes to which the maintenance of a democratic republic in the United States is attributable . . . *the habits of the heart* . . . I comprise under this term, therefore, the whole moral and intellectual condition of a people" ([1845] 1945: 310).

11 See Cartwright (1984, 1987, 1988a, 1988b); Eisler (1987); Fromm (1963); Schoenfeld and Meštrović (1991); Spengler ([1926] 1961: 350).

12 See also Etzioni (1988, 1991a, 1991b, 1991c).

13 See, for example, Xavier Gautier (1992).

7 WHAT WOULD A GENUINE POST-MARXISM BE LIKE?

1 I discuss Bellah at great length in Meštrović (1992) and Meštrović, Goreta, and Letica (1993a, 1993b), so I will not spend much time on his concept of civil religion here.

2 See also Durkheim ([1912] 1965: 257).

3 Durkheim makes this argument explicit in *Sociology and Philosophy* ([1924] 1974).

4 However, Durkheim's follower, Maurice Halbwachs (1912, 1925, 1958), invokes Veblen directly.

8 CONCLUSIONS

1 This retreat from earlier, hawkish statements is also evident in the G–7 joint statement issued in Japan on 8 July 1993. Military intervention to preserve the sovereignty of Bosnia-Herzegovina was not mentioned.

References

Adorno, T.W. (1991) *The Culture Industry*. London: Routledge.

Ahmed, A. (1992) *Postmodernism and Islam: Predicament and Promise*. London: Routledge.

—— (1993) "Bosnia: New Metaphor in the 'New World Order'." *Impact International* 12 March: 24–7.

Allman, T.D. (1993) "Serbia's Blood War." *Vanity Fair*, March: 97–118.

Alpert, H. (1937) "France's First University Course in Sociology." *American Sociological Review*, 2: 311–17.

—— (1938) *Emile Durkheim and His Sociology*. New York: Columbia University Press.

Anderson, D. (1992) "A Diplomat Explains Yugoslavia." *Wall Street Journal*, 21 February: A12.

Arendt, H. (1966) *The Origins of Totalitarianism*. New York: Meridian.

Ash, T.G. (1990) "Eastern Europe: The Year of Truth." *The New York Review of Books*, 37 (2): 17–22.

Balfour, N. and Mackay, S. (1980) *Paul of Yugoslavia*. London: Hamish Hamilton.

Banac, I. (1985) *The National Question in Yugoslavia*. Ithaca, NY: Cornell University Press.

—— (1992a) *Eastern Europe in Transition*. Ithaca, NY: Cornell University Press.

—— (1992b) "The Exit From Communism." *Daedalus*, 121 (2): 141–74.

—— (1992c) "How to Stop Serbia." *National Review*, 18 September: 18.

—— (1992d) "Historiography of the Countries of Eastern Europe: Yugoslavia." *The American Historical Review*, 97 (October): 1084–104.

Banac, I. and Buskovitch, P. (1983) *The Nobility in Russia and Eastern Europe*. Columbus, OH: Slavica Press.

Baudrillard, J. (1981) *Critique of the Political Economy of the Sign*, translated by C. Levin. St. Louis, MO: Telos Press.

—— (1986) *America*. London: Verso.

—— (1988a) *Selected Writings*. Stanford, CA.: Stanford University Press.

—— (1988b) "Hunting Nazis and Losing Reality." *New Statesman*, 19 February: 16–17.

—— (1990) *Seduction*. New York: St. Martin's Press.

—— (1991) "The Reality Gulf." *The Guardian*, 11 January: 25.

Bauman, Z. (1987) *Legislators and Interpreters: On Modernity, Post-Modernity and Intellectuals*. Ithaca, NY: Cornell University Press.

—— (1989) *Modernity and the Holocaust*. Ithaca, NY: Cornell University Press.

—— (1991) *Modernity and Ambivalence*. Ithaca, NY: Cornell University Press.

—— (1992) *Intimations of Postmodernity*. London: Routledge.

Beljo, A. (1992) *Greater Serbia: From Ideology to Aggression*. Zagreb: Zagreb Publishers.

Bell, D. (1976) *The Cultural Contradictions of Capitalism*. New York: Basic Books.

—— (1977) *The Coming of Post-Industrial Society: A Venture in Social Forecasting*. New York: Basic Books.

—— (1988) *The End of Ideology*. Cambridge, MA: Harvard University Press.

—— (1990) "Resolving the Contradictions of Modernity and Modernism." *Society*, 27 (3): 43–50.

Bellah, R.N. (1967) "Civil Religion in America." *Daedalus*, 96: 1–21.

—— (1970) *Beyond Belief*. New York: Harper & Row.

—— (1972) *Emile Durkheim on Morality and Society*. Chicago: University of Chicago Press.

—— (1981) "Democratic Culture or Authoritarian Capitalism?" *Society*, 18 (6): 41–50.

—— (1989) "Reply to Mathisen." *Sociological Analysis*, 50 (2): 149.

Bellah, R.N., Madsen, R., Sullivan, W.M., Swidler, A. and Tipton, S.M. (1985) *Habits of the Heart*. Berkeley: University of California Press.

—— (1991) *The Good Society*. New York: Alfred A. Knopf.

Bellamy, E. (1888) *Looking Backward: 2000*. New York: Longmans.

Berger, P. and Luckman, T. (1967) *The Social Construction of Reality*. New York: Doubleday.

Biden, J.R. (1993) *To Stand Against Aggression: Milošević, the Bosnian Republic and the Conscience of the West*. A Report to the United States Senate.

Bloom, A. (1987) *The Closing of the American Mind*. New York: Simon & Schuster.

Bouglé, C. ([1908] 1971) *Essays on the Caste System*. Cambridge: Cambridge University Press.

—— (1918) *Chez les prophètes socialistes*. Paris: Alcan.

—— (1926) *The Evolution of Values*, translated by Helen Sellars. New York: Henry Holt.

—— (1938) *The French Conception of "Culture Générale" and Its Influence Upon Instruction*. New York: Columbia University Press.

Boutros-Ghali, B. (1992) "Empowering the United Nations." *Foreign Affairs*, 71 (Winter): 89–102.

Brooks, D. (1993) "A Kinder, Gentler Colonialism." *Wall Street Journal*, 15 January: A10.

Brown, C.J. (1992) "The Case of Kosovo: Keeping it Safe for Serbia." *Freedom Review*, 23 (1): 23–5.

Brzezinski, Z. (1989) *The Grand Failure: The Birth and Death of Communism in the Twentieth Century*. New York: Scribner's.

—— (1992) "The Cold War and Its Aftermath." *Foreign Affairs*, 71: 31–49.

—— (1993a) *Out of Control: Global Turmoil on the Eve of the Twenty-First Century*. New York: Scribner's.

—— (1993b) "Never Again – Except for Bosnia." *New York Times*, 22 April: A21.

Burns, J.F. (1992) "The Dying City of Sarajevo." *New York Times Magazine*, 26 July: 12–17.

Cartwright, D. (1984) "Kant, Schopenhauer and Nietzsche on the Morality of Pity." *Journal of the History of Ideas*, 45 (1): 83–98.

—— (1987) "Kant's View of the Moral Significance of Kindhearted Emotions and the Moral Insignificance of Kant's View." *Journal of Value Inquiry*, 21: 291–304.

—— (1988a) "Schopenhauer's Compassion and Nietzsche's Pity." *Schopenhauer Jahrbuch*, 69: 557–67

—— (1988b) "Schopenhauer's Axiological Analysis of Character." *Revue International de Philosophie*, 42: 18–36.

—— (1991) "Reversing Silenus' Wisdom." *Nietzsche Studien*, 20: 301–13.

Cladis, M. (1992) *A Communitarian Defense of Liberalism: Emile Durkheim and Contemporary Social Theory*. Stanford, CA: Stanford University Press.

Clark, J., Modgil, C. and Modgil, S. (1990) *Anthony Giddens: Consensus and Controversy*. London: Falmer Press.

Cohen, P.J. (1992) "History Misappropriated." *Midstream*, 38 (8): 18–21.

—— (1993) "Desecrating the Holocaust: Serbia's Exploitation of the Holocaust as Propaganda." Paper presented to the American Sociological Association.

Cooper, B. (1984) *The End of History: An Essay on Modern Hegelianism*. Toronto: University of Toronto Press.

Covic, B. (1993) *The Roots of Serbian Aggression*. Zagreb: Graphic Council of Croatia.

Coulanges, F. (1889) *The Ancient City*. Boston: Lee & Shepard.

Craycraft, K.R. (1991) "The Pope Embraces Market Economics." *The World and I*, 6 (11): 480–95.

Creveld, M. (1991) *The Transformation of War*. New York: Free Press.

Denzin, N. (1988) "*Blue Velvet*: Postmodern Contradictions." *Theory, Culture and Society*, 5 (2–3): 461–74.

—— (1991) *Images of Postmodern Society*. London: Sage.

Doherty, C.J. (1992) "Senate Passes Foreign Aid Bill Backing United States Arms for Bosnia." *Congressional Quarterly Weekly Report*, 3 October: 3066–7.

Durkheim, E. ([1886] 1990) Review of Fouillée's *La Propriété sociale et la démocratie (1884)*, translated by R. Jones. *Durkheim Studies* 2: 27–32.

—— ([1893] 1933) *The Division of Labor in Society*, translated by George Simpson. New York: Free Press.

—— ([1895] 1982) "The Rules of Sociological Method." Pp. 31–163 in *Durkheim: The Rules of Sociological Method and Selected Texts on Sociology and Its Method*, edited by S. Lukes. New York: Free Press.

—— ([1897] 1951) *Suicide: A Study in Sociology*, translated by John A. Spaulding and George Simpson. New York: Free Press.

—— ([1897] 1986) "Socialism and Marxism." Pp. 121–45 in *Durkheim on Politics and the State*, edited by A. Giddens. Cambridge: Polity Press.

—— ([1898] 1973) "Individualism and the Intellectuals." Pp. 43–57 in *Emile Durkheim on Morality and Society*, edited by R. Bellah. Chicago: University of Chicago Press.

—— ([1912] 1965) *The Elementary Forms of the Religious Life*, translated by J. Swain. New York: Free Press.

—— ([1914] 1973) "The Dualism of Human Nature and Its Social Conditions." Pp. 149–66 in *Emile Durkheim on Morality and Society*, edited by R. Bellah. Chicago: University of Chicago Press.

—— (1915) *Germany Above All*. Paris: Armand Collin.

—— ([1924] 1974) *Sociology and Philosophy*, translated by D.F. Pocock. New York: Free Press.

—— ([1925] 1961) *Moral Education*, translated by Everett K. Wilson and Herman Schnurer. Glencoe, IL: Free Press.

—— ([1928] 1958) *Socialism and Saint-Simon*, translated by Charlotte Sattler. Yellow Springs, OH: Antioch Press.

—— ([1938] 1977) *The Evolution of Educational Thought*, translated by Peter Collins. London: Routledge & Kegan Paul.

—— ([1950] 1983) *Professional Ethics and Civic Morals*, translated by Cornelia Brookfield. Westport, CT: Greenwood Press.

—— ([1955] 1983) *Pragmatism and Sociology*, translated by J.C. Whitehouse. Cambridge: Cambridge University Press.

—— (1986) *Durkheim on Politics and the State*, edited by A. Giddens. Cambridge: Polity Press.

Eisler, R. (1987) *The Chalice and the Blade: Our History, Our Future*. New York: Harper & Row.

Elias, N. (1982) *The Civilizing Process*. Oxford: Basil Blackwell.

Ellenberger, H. (1970) *The Discovery of the Unconscious*. New York: Basic Books.

Etzioni, A. (1988) *The Moral Dimension: Toward a New Economics*. New York: Free Press.

—— (1991a) "Eastern Europe: The Wealth of Lessons." *Challenge*, July/August: 4–10.

—— (1991b) "American Competitiveness: The Moral Dimension." *The World and I*, 6 (10) 465–73.

—— (1991c) "A New Community of Thinkers, Both Liberal and Conservative." *Wall Street Journal*, 16 August: A20.

Featherstone, M. (1988) "In Pursuit of the Postmodern: An Introduction." *Theory, Culture and Society*, 5 (2–3): 195–216

—— (1990) *Global Culture: Nationalism, Globalization and Modernity*. London: Sage.

Feher, F. (1988) "Crisis and Crisis-Solving in the Soviet System Under Gorbachev's New Course." *Thesis Eleven*, 21: 5–19.

Finkielkraut, A. (1992) *Comment peut-on être Croate?* Paris: Gallimard.

Freud, S. ([1901] 1965) *The Psychopathology of Everyday Life*. New York: Norton.

—— ([1915] 1958) "Thoughts for the Times on War and Death." Pp. 206–35 in *Sigmund Freud on Creativity and the Unconscious*. New York: Harper & Row.

—— ([1927] 1955) *The Future of an Illusion*. New York: Norton.

—— ([1930] 1961) *Civilization and Its Discontents*. New York: Norton.

—— ([1932] 1963) "Why War?" Pp. 134–47 in *Sigmund Freud on Character and Culture*, edited by P. Rieff. New York: Collier.

Fromm, E. (1947) *Man For Himself*. New York: Rinehart.

—— (1950) *Psychoanalysis and Religion*. New Haven, CT: Yale University Press.

—— (1955) *The Sane Society*. Greenwich, CT: Fawcett.

—— (1962) *Beyond the Chains of Illusion*. New York: Simon & Schuster.

—— (1963) *The Dogma of Christ and Other Essays on Religion, Psychology and Culture*. New York: Holt, Rinehart & Winston.

—— (1964) *The Heart of Man: Its Genius for Good and Evil*. New York: Harper.

Fromm, E. and Maccoby, M. (1970) *Social Character in a Mexican Village: A Sociopsychoanalytic Study*. Englewood Cliffs, NJ: Prentice-Hall.

Fukuyama, F. (1992) *The End of History and the Last Man*. New York: Free Press.

Fulghum, R. (1990) *All I Really Needed to Know I Learned in Kindergarten*. New York: Villard Books.

Gaffney, J. (1989) *The French Left and the Fifth Republic*. New York: St. Martin's Press.

Gane, M. (1991) *Baudrillard: Critical and Fatal Theory*. London: Routledge.

—— (1992) *The Radical Sociology of Durkheim and Mauss*. London: Routledge.

Garde, P. (1992) *Vie et mort de la Yougoslavie*. Paris: Fayard.

Gati, C. (1992) "From Sarajevo to Sarajevo." *Foreign Affairs*, 71 (Fall): 64–78.

Gautier, X. (1992) *L'Europe à l'épreuve des Balkanes*. Paris: Jacques Bouton.

Gelb, L.H. (1992) "Never Again." *New York Times*, 13 December: E17.

—— (1993a) "Surprise, Surprise, Surprise." *New York Times*, 3 January: E11.

—— (1993b) "Euro-Bosnia Games." *New York Times*, 31 January: E17.

—— (1993c) "Balkan Strategy: Part II." *New York Times*, 28 February: E15.

Gellner, E. (1992a) *Reason and Culture*. Oxford: Basil Blackwell.

—— (1992b) *Postmodernism, Reason and Religion*. London: Routledge.

Giddens, A. (1977) *Studies in Social and Political Theory*. New York: Basic Books.

—— (1982) *A Contemporary Critique of Historical Materialism*. Berkeley: University of California Press.

—— (1987) *Social Theory and Modern Sociology*. Stanford, CA: Stanford University Press.

—— (1990) *The Consequences of Modernity*. Stanford, CA: Stanford University Press.

—— (1991) *Modernity and Self-Identity*. Stanford, CA: Stanford University Press.

—— (1992) "Uprooted Signposts at Century's End." *The Higher*, 17 January: 21.

Glassner, B. (1991) "The Medium Must Not Deconstruct: A Postmodern Ethnography of *USA Today* Television Show." *Media, Culture and Society*, 13: 53–70.

Glenny, M. (1990) *The Rebirth of History: Eastern Europe in the Age of Democracy*. London: Penguin.

—— (1992) "The Massacre of Yugoslavia." *New York Review of Books*, 39 (3): 30–4.

Glynn, P. (1992) "Lawrence of Serbia." *The New Republic*, 16 February: 16.

Graubard, S. R. (1991) *Eastern Europe, Central Europe, Europe*. Boulder, CO: Westview.

—— (1992) *Mr. Bush's War: Adventures in the Politics of Illusion*. New York: Hill & Wang.

Greenfeld, L. (1992) *Nationalism: Five Roads to Modernity*. Cambridge, MA: Harvard University Press.

Habermas, J. (1970) *Legitimation Crisis*. Boston: Beacon.

—— (1981) "Modernity versus Postmodernity." *New German Critique*, 22: 3–14.

—— (1987) *The Philosophical Discourse of Modernity*. Cambridge, MA: MIT Press.

Halbwachs, M. ([1912] 1974) *La Classe ouvrière et les niveaux*. London: Gordon & Breach.

—— (1925) "Les Origines puritaines du capitalisme." *Revue d'histoire et de philosophie religieuses* 5: 132–57.

—— (1950) *The Collective Memory*. New York: Harper & Row.

—— (1958) *The Psychology of Social Class*, translated by Georges Friedman. Glencoe, IL: Free Press.

Hall, J. A. (1987) *Liberalism: Politics, Ideology and the Market*. Chapel Hill: University of North Carolina Press.

Hall, R.T. (1988) *Emile Durkheim: Ethics and the Sociology of Morals*. New York: Greenwood Press.

Hegel, G.W.F. ([1899] 1965) *The Philosophy of History*. New York: Dover.

Heller, A. (1990) *Can Modernity Survive?*, Berkeley: University of California Press.

Heller, A. and Feher, F. (1988) *The Postmodern Political Condition*. New York: Columbia University Press.

—— (1991) *Grandeur and Twilight of Radical Universalism*. New Brunswick, NJ: Transaction Books.

Helsinki Watch Committee (1982) *Yugoslavia: Freedom to Conform*. New York: US Helsinki Watch Committee.

—— (1990) *Yugoslavia: Crisis in Kosovo*. New York: US Helsinki Watch Committee.

—— (1991a) *Human Rights Abuses in the Croatian Conflict*. New York: US Helsinki Watch Committee.

—— (1991b) *March 1991 Demonstrations in Belgrade*. New York: US Helsinki Watch Committee.

—— (1992a) Open Letter to President Slobodan Milošević of Serbia. Volume 4, Issue 3, 21 January. New York: US Helsinki Watch Committee.

—— (1992b) Open Letter to President Franjo Tudjman of Croatia. Volume 4, Issue 4, 13 February. New York: US Helsinki Watch Committee.

—— (1992c) *War Crimes in Bosnia-Herzegovina*. New York: US Helsinki Watch Committee.

Hillman, J. and Ventura, M. (1993) *We've Had a Hundred Years of Psychotherapy and the World's Getting Worse*. San Francisco: Harper Collins

Hollander, P. (1988) *The Survival of Adversary Culture: Social Criticism and Political Escapism in American Society*. New Brunswick, NJ: Transaction Books.

—— (1992) *Decline and Discontent: Communism and the West Today*. New Brunswick, NJ: Transaction Books.

Holsti, K.J. (1991) *Peace and War: Armed Conflicts and International Order 1648–1989*. Cambridge: Cambridge University Press.

Horkheimer, M. and Adorno, T. (1972) *Dialectic of Enlightenment*. New York: Continuum.

Hymowitz, K.S. (1993) "Multiculturalism is Anti-Culture." *New York Times*, 25 March: A15.

Isaacson, W. (1992) *Kissinger: A Biography*. New York: Simon & Schuster.

James, W. (1890) *The Principles of Psychology*. New York: Longmans.

Judas, M. (1992) *Mass Killing and Genocide in Croatia, 1991–1992*. Zagreb.
Kantrowitz, B. (1992) "Sociology's Lonely Crowd." *Newsweek*, 3 February: 55.
Kaplan, R.D. (1991a) "History's Cauldron." *Atlantic Monthly*, June: 93–104.
—— (1991b) "Croatianism." *New Republic*, 25 November: 16.
—— (1993) *Balkan Ghosts: A Journey Through History*. New York: St. Martin's Press.
Kasler, D. (1988) *Max Weber: An Introduction to His Life and Work*. Chicago: University of Chicago Press.
Katz, J. (1988) *Seductions of Crime: Moral and Sensual Attraction in Doing Evil*. New York: Basic Books.
Katz, J., Goldstein, J. and Dershowitz, A. (1967) *Psychoanalysis, Psychiatry and Law*. New York: Free Press.
Kaufman, M.T. (1992) "Serbs See Themselves as the World's Victims." *New York Times*, 7 June: A6.
Kellner D. (1988) "Postmodernism as Social Theory." *Theory, Culture and Society*, 5 (2): 239–70.
—— (1989) *Jean Baudrillard: From Marxism to Postmodernism and Beyond*. Stanford, CA: Stanford University Press.
Kennedy, P. (1992) *Preparing for the Twenty-first Century*. New York: Random House.
Kenney, G. (1992) "See No Evil, Make No Policy." *Washington Monthly*, 24 (November): 33–5.
—— (1993a) "From Bosnian Crisis to All-Out War." *New York Times*, 20 June: E17.
—— (1993b) "The Other Clinton Test: Intervention in Bosnia." *Wall Street Journal*, 18 February: A18.
Kimball, R. (1992) "Review of *The Disuniting of America*, by A. Schlesinger, Jr." *Wall Street Journal*, 21 February: A10.
Knežević, A. (1992) *An Analysis of Serbian Propaganda*. Zagreb: Domovina.
Kohlberg, L. (1981) *Essays in Moral Development*. San Francisco: Harper & Row.
Kroker, A. (1992) *The Possessed Individual*. New York: St. Martin's Press.
Kroker, A. and Cook, D. (1986) *The Postmodern Scene: Excremental Culture and Hyper-Aesthetics*. New York: St. Martin's Press.
Kroker, A. and Kroker, M. (1991) *Ideology and Power in the Age of Lenin in Ruins*. New York: St. Martin's Press.
Laber, J. (1993) "Bosnia – Questions of Rape." *New York Review of Books*, 25 March: 3–6.
Lane, C. (1992) "When is it Genocide?" *Newsweek*, 17 August: 27.
Lasch, C. (1979) *The Culture of Narcissism*. New York: Norton.
—— (1991) *The True and Only Heaven: Progress and Its Critics*. New York: Norton.
Lash, S. (1990) *The Sociology of Postmodernism*. London: Routledge.
Leathers, C.G. (1986) "Bellamy and Veblen's Christian Morals." *Journal of Economic Issues*, 20: 107–19.
Ledeen, M. (1993) "Does the Future Look Just Like Switzerland?" *Wall Street Journal*, 3 March 1993: A11.
Letica, S. (1989a) *The Fourth Yugoslavia*. Zagreb: Dnevnik.
—— (1989b) *The Intellectual and Crisis*. Zagreb: August Cesarec.
Lewis, A. (1992) "Bush's New World Order Evokes Only Cynicism." *New York Times*, 28 September: A14.
—— (1993a) "Beware of Munich." *New York Times*, 8 January: A11.
—— (1993b) "Lessons of Yugoslavia." *New York Times*, 26 February: A15.
—— (1993c) "Yesterday's Man." *New York Times*, 3 August: A15.
Lipset, S.M. (1989) *Contnental Divide*. Washington, DC: National Planning Association.
Lukacs, G. (1980) *The Destruction of Reason*, translated by Peter Palmer. Atlantic Highlands, NJ: Humanities Press.

Lukacs, J. (1992) *The End of the Twentieth Century and the End of the Modern Age*. New York: Ticknor & Fields.

Lyotard, J. (1984) *The Postmodern Condition*. Minneapolis: University of Minnesota Press.

McNeil, W.H. (1992) "History Over, World Goes On." *New York Times Review of Books*, 26 January: 14.

Madison, James ([1789] 1988) The Federalist Papers, Number 51. Waco, Texas: Friends of Freedom Publishers.

Magas, B. (1993) *The Destruction of Yugoslavia*. London: Verso.

Magee, B. (1983) *The Philosophy of Schopenhauer*. New York: Oxford University Press.

Marty, M.E. (1992) "Explaining the Rise of Fundamentalism." *Chronicle of Higher Education*, 28 October: A56.

Marx, K. ([1858] 1977) *Capital*, Vol. 1. New York: International Library.

—— (1983) *The Portable Marx*. London: Penguin.

Mathisen, J.A. (1989) "Twenty Years After Bellah: Whatever Happened to American Civil Religion?" *Sociological Analysis*, 50 (2): 29–46.

Mauss, M. ([1925] 1992) "A Sociological Assessment of Bolshevism." Pp. 165–211 in *The Radical Sociology of Durkheim and Mauss*, edited by M. Gane. London: Routledge.

Merton, R.K. (1957) *Social Theory and Social Structure*. New York: Free Press.

Meštrović, S.G. (1982) "In the Shadow of Plato: Durkheim and Freud on Suicide and Society." Unpublished doctoral dissertation, Syracuse University, New York.

—— (1988) *Emile Durkheim and the Reformation of Sociology*. Totowa, NJ: Rowman & Littlefield.

—— (1991) *The Coming Fin de Siècle: An Application of Durkheim's Sociology to Modernity and Postmodernism*. London: Routledge.

—— (1992) *Durkheim and Postmodern Culture*. Hawthorne, NY: Aldine de Gruyter.

—— (1993) *The Barbarian Temperament*. London and New York: Routledge.

Meštrović, S.G., Goreta, M. and Letica, S. (1993a) *The Road From Paradise: Prospects for Democracy in Eastern Europe*. Lexington, KY: University Press of Kentucky.

—— (1993b) *Habits of the Balkan Heart*. College Station, TX: Texas A&M University Press.

Mihajlov, M. (1992) "Why Bosnia is Not a Quagmire." *The New Leader*, 5 August: 10–24.

Mill, J.S. ([1859] 1974) *On Liberty*. London: Penguin.

Moynihan, D.P. (1992) *Pandaemonium: Ethnicity in International Politics*. New York: Oxford University Press.

Mumford, L. (1955) *The Human Prospect*. Boston: Beacon.

Muravchick, J. (1991) *Exporting Democracy: Fulfilling America's Destiny*. Washington, DC: American Enterprise Institute Press.

Murphy, J.W. (1989) *Postmodern Social Analysis and Criticism*. New York: Greenwood.

Nietzsche, F. ([1901] 1968) *The Will to Power*. New York: Random House.

Nixon, R. (1991) "How the West Can Bring Peace to Yugoslavia." *Wall Street Journal*, 17 December: A12.

—— (1992a) *Seize the Moment: America's Challenge in a One-Superpower World*. New York: Simon & Schuster.

—— (1992b) "The Challenge We Face in Russia." *Wall Street Journal*, 11 March: A15.

Novak, M. (1982) *The Spirit of Democratic Capitalism*. New York: Simon & Schuster.

—— (1991) "Transforming the Democratic/Capitalist Revolution." Paper presented at the Karl Brunner Symposium, Interlaken, Switzerland.

Paepke, C.O. (1992) *The Evolution of Progress*. New York: Random House.

Parsons, T. (1937) *The Structure of Social Action*. Glencoe, IL: Free Press.

Pearce, F. (1989) *The Radical Durkheim*. London: Unwin Hyman.

Petrović, B. (1987) *New Serbian Satire*. Belgrade.

Pilon, J.G. (1992) "Post-Communist Nationalism: The Case of Romania." *The World and I*, 7 (2): 110–15.

Post, T. (1992a) "Help From the Holy Warriors." *Newsweek*, 5 October: 52–3.
—— (1992b) "How the West Lost Bosnia." *Newsweek*, 2 November: 62.
Postone, M. (1993) *Time, Labor and Social Domination: A Reinterpretation of Marx's Critical Theory*. Cambridge: Cambridge University Press.
Poulton, H. (1991) *The Balkans: Minorities and States in Conflict*. London: Minority Rights Publications.
Ramet, P. (1985) "Primordial Ethnicity or Modern Nationalism: The Case of Yugoslavia's Muslims." *Nationalities – Papers*, 13 (2): 165–87.
—— (1987) *Cross and Commissar: The Politics of Religion in Eastern Europe and the USSR*. Bloomington: Indiana University Press.
Ramet, S.P. (1992) *Nationalism and Federalism in Yugoslavia, 1962–1991*. Bloomington: Indiana University Press.
Ranulf, S. (1939) "Scholarly Forerunners of Fascism." *Ethics*, 50: 16–34.
Rasković, J. (1988) *Narcissism*. Belgrade: Niksic.
—— (1990) *Crazy Land*. Belgrade: Aquarius.
Rauch, J. (1993) *Kindly Inquisitors: The New Attacks on Free Thought*. Chicago: University of Chicago Press.
Redic, E. (1987) *Muslim Autonomy and the 13th SS Division*. Zagreb: Institute for the Worker's Movement.
Reeves, R. (1990) *American Journey: Travelling with Tocqueville in Search of Democracy in America*. New York: Simon & Schuster.
Riding, A. (1993) "The Painful Past Still Eludes France." *New York Times*, 13 June 1993: E4.
Riesman, D. ([1950] 1977) *The Lonely Crowd*. New Haven, CT: Yale University Press.
—— (1953) *Thorstein Veblen: A Critical Interpretation*. New York: Charles Scribner's Sons.
—— (1954) *Individualism Reconsidered*. Glencoe, IL: Free Press.
—— (1964) *Abundance For What?*, Garden City, NY: Doubleday.
—— (1976) "Liberation and Stalemate." *Massachusetts Review*, 17 (4): 767–76.
—— (1977) "Prospects for Human Rights." *Society*, 15 (1): 28–33.
—— (1980a) "Egocentrism." *Character*, 1 (5): 3–9.
—— (1980b) *On Higher Education: The Academic Enterprise in an Era of Rising Student Consumerism*. San Francisco: Jossey-Bass.
—— (1981) "The Dream of Abundance Reconsidered." *Public Opinion Quarterly*, 45 (3): 285–302.
—— (1990) "The Innocence of the *Lonely Crowd*." *Society*, 27 (2): 76–9.
Riesman, D. and Riesman, E.T. (1967) *Conversations in Japan: Modernization, Politics and Culture*. Chicago: University of Chicago Press.
Ritzer, G. (1992) *The McDonaldization of Society*. Newbury Park, CA: Sage.
Roberts, K.A. (1990) *Religion in Sociological Perspective*. Belmont: Wandsworth.
Rodrigue, G. (1993) "Politics of Rape." *Dallas Morning News*, 5 May: A1.
Roiphe, K. (1993) "Rape Hype Betrays Feminism." *New York Times Magazine*, 13 June: 26–8.
Rojek, C. (1985) *Capitalism and Leisure Theory*. London: Tavistock.
—— (1993) "Disney Culture." *Leisure Studies*, 12: 121–35.
Rojek, C. and Turner, B. (1993) *Forget Baudrillard?* London: Routledge.
Rosenau, P.M. (1992) *Post-Modernism and the Social Sciences: Insights, Inroads and Intrusions*. Princeton, NJ: Princeton University Press.
Rousseau, J.J. (1968) *The Social Contract*. London: Penguin.
—— (1975) *The Essential Rousseau*. New York: Meridian.
Ryan, A. (1992) "Review of *The End of History and the Last Man*." *New York Review of Books*, 39 (6): 7–12.

Ryan, P. (1967) *Blaming the Victim.* New York: Bantam.

Schneider, B. (1993) "Bearing Witness." *People Weekly,* 5 April: 30–5.

Schoenfeld, C.G. (1962) "God the Father-and-Mother: Study and Extension of Freud's Conception of God as an Exalted Father." *The American Imago,* 19 (3): 213–34.

—— (1966a) "Psychoanalysis and Anti-Semitism." *Psychoanalytic Review,* Spring: 24–37.

—— (1966b) "In Defense of Retribution in the Law." *Psychoanalytic Quarterly,* 35 (1): 108–21.

—— (1966c) "Erich Fromm's Attacks Upon the Oedipus Complex – A Brief Critique." *Journal of Nervous and Mental Disease,* 141 (5): 580–5.

—— (1968) "Psychoanalytic Guideposts for the Good Society." *The Psychoanalytic Review,* Spring: 91–114.

—— (1974) "International Law, Nationalism and the Sense of Self: A Psychoanalytic Inquiry." *Journal of Psychiatry and Law,* Fall: 303–17.

—— (1984) *Psychoanalysis Applied to the Law.* Port Washington, NY: Associated Faculty Press.

—— (1988) "Blacks and Violent Crime: A Psychoanalytically Oriented Analysis." *Journal of Psychiatry and Law,* 24 (Summer): 269–301.

—— (1991) "Holmes v. Bork: The Role of Unconscious Thoughts and Emotions in Law and the Politics of Law." *Political Psychology,* 12 (2): 363–75.

Schoenfeld, E. and Meštrović, S.G. (1989) "Durkheim's Concept of Justice and its Relationship to Social Solidarity." *Sociological Analysis,* 50 (2): 111–27.

—— (1991) "With Justice and Mercy: Instrumental-Masculine and Expressive-Feminine Elements in Religion." *Journal for the Scientific Study of Religion,* 30 (4): 363–80.

Schopenhauer, A. ([1818] 1965a) *The World as Will and Representation,* translated by E. Payne. Vol. 1. New York: Dover Press.

—— ([1818] 1965b) *The World as Will and Representation,* translated by E. Payne. Vol. 2. New York: Dover Press.

—— ([1841] 1965c) *On the Basis of Morality.* Indianapolis: Bobbs-Merrill.

Sciolino, E. (1993) "In Bosnia, Peace at Any Price is Getting More Expensive." *New York Times,* 10 January: E4.

Scrinton, R. (1988) "Spengler's *Decline of the West.*" *World and I,* 3 (9): 548–67.

Sica, A. (1988) *Weber, Irrationality and Social Order.* Berkeley: University of California Press.

Simmel, G. ([1900] 1990) *The Philosophy of Money.* London: Routledge.

—— (1905) "Tendencies in German Life and Thought Since 1870." *International Monthly,* 5: 93–111, 161–84.

—— ([1907] 1986) *Schopenhauer and Nietzsche.* Amherst: University of Massachusetts Press.

Singleton, F. (1985) *A Short History of the Yugoslav Peoples.* Cambridge: Cambridge University Press.

Sloterdijk, P. (1987) *Critique of Cynical Reason,* translated by Michael Eldred. Minneapolis: University of Minnesota Press.

Smart, B. (1992) *Modern Conditions: Postmodern Controversies.* London: Routledge.

Solzhenitsyn, A. (1991) *Rebuilding Russia.* New York: Farrar, Straus & Giroux.

—— (1993) "The Relentless Cult of Novelty and How it Wrecked the Century." *New York Times Review of Books,* 7 February: 3–7.

Sorokin, P. (1944) *Russia and the United States.* New York: E.P. Dutton.

—— (1947) *The Ways and Power of Love.* New York: American Book Company.

—— (1948) *The Reconstruction of Humanity.* Boston: Beacon.

—— (1950) *Altruistic Love.* Boston: Beacon.

—— (1957) *Social and Cultural Dynamics.* New York: American Book Company.

—— (1963) *A Long Journey: The Autobiography of Pitirim A. Sorokin.* New Haven, CT: College and University Press.

Spengler, O. ([1926] 1961) *The Decline of the West*. New York: Alfred A. Knopf.

Staub, E. (1992) *The Roots of Evil: The Origins of Genocide and Other Group Violence.* Cambridge: Cambridge University Press.

Stephens, B. (1993) "Hypocrisy on Rights." *New York Times*, 24 June: A13.

Tocqueville, A. de ([1845] 1945) *Democracy in America*, Vol. 1. New York: Random House.

Toffler, A. (1980) *The Third Wave*. New York: William Morrow.

Tomašić, D. (1941) "Sociology in Yugoslavia." *American Journal of Sociology*, 47: 53–69.

—— (1946) "The Structure of Balkan Society." *American Journal of Sociology*, 52: 132–40.

—— (1948a) *Personality and Culture in Eastern European Politics*. New York: George Stewart.

—— (1948b) "Ideologies and the Structure of Eastern European Society." *American Journal of Sociology*, 53 (March): 367–75.

—— (1951) "Interrelations between Bolshevik Ideology and the Structure of Soviet Society." *American Sociological Review*, 16: 137–48.

—— (1953) *The Impact of Russian Culture on Soviet Communism*. Glencoe, IL: Free Press.

Tönnies, F. ([1887] 1963) *Community and Society*. New York: Harper & Row.

Toynbee, A. (1962) *America and the World Revolution*. New York: Oxford.

—— (1978) *Arnold Toynbee: A Selection From His Works*, edited by C. Tomlin. Oxford: Oxford University Press.

Tudjman, F. (1981) *Nationalism in Contemporary Europe*. New York: Columbia University Press.

—— (1990) *Wilderness of Historical Reality: A Treatise on the History and Philosophy of Evil Brutality*. Zagreb: Matica Hrvatska.

Turner, S. and Kassler, D. (1992) *Sociology Responds to Fascism*. London: Routledge.

Veblen, T. ([1899] 1967) *The Theory of the Leisure Class*. New York: Penguin.

—— ([1910] 1943) "Christian Morals and the Competitive Sysem." Pp. 200–28 in *Essays in Our Changing Order*, edited by L. Ardzrooni. New York: Viking.

—— ([1915] 1964) *Imperial Germany and the Industrial Revolution*. New York: Sentry Press.

—— (1917) *An Inquiry Into the Nature of Peace and the Terms of Its Perpetuation*. New York: Macmillan.

—— (1943) *Essays in Our Changing Order*. New York: Viking.

Vuković, T. (1991) *The Mosaic of Betrayal*. Zagreb: St. Cyril and Methodius Press.

Vuković, T. and Bojović, E. (1992) *Overview of Serbian Anti-Semitism*. Zagreb: Alatir.

Weber, M. ([1904] 1958) *The Protestant Ethic and the Spirit of Capitalism*. New York: Scribner's.

Wells, H.G. (1906) *The Future in America*. New York: Harper & Brothers.

—— (1928) *The Way the World is Going*. London: Benn.

—— (1935) *The New America: The New World*. London: Cresset.

—— (1939) *The Fate of Man*. New York: Longmans.

Williams, C.J. (1992) "Balkan War Rape Victims: Traumatized and Ignored." *Los Angeles Times*, 30 November: A1.

Zarycky, G. (1993) "East-Central Europe: Post-Communist Blues." *Freedom Review*, 24 (1): 48–52.

Name index

Adams, Henry 159
Adorno, Theodor 79, 82, 87, 143, 160, 166, 174
Ahmed, Akbar 1, 5, 8, 52, 54, 58–61, 92–3

Baudrillard, Jean 2, 14, 18, 28–30, 82, 143, 192
Bauman, Zygmunt 18–19
Bell, Daniel 175
Bellah, Robert N. 8, 75, 140, 145–6, 150–3
Bellamy, Edward 141, 162
Bougle, Celestin 156–8, 165–7
Boom, Allan 140
Boutros-Ghali, Boutros 68, 114, 121, 138, 179
Brzezinski, Zbigniew 2, 17, 19, 32
Burns, John F. 101, 121
Bush, George x, 34, 116, 146, 153, 168, 190

Carter, Jimmy 36, 66–7, 179
Christopher, Warren 4, 28–9, 55, 112, 128, 179
Clinton, Bill ix, x, 6, 32–8, 43, 66, 73, 128, 137, 178, 187–9, 192
Cohen, Philip 44, 123
Comte, Auguste 12–13, 137
Cosic, Dobrica 45

Descartes, René x, 64–5, 133, 183–5
Dole, Robert 73, 113
Durkheim, Emile xi, 8–13, 16–17, 22, 25, 65, 97, 124–34, 142–5, 152–79, 186

Eagleburger, Lawrence 90, 101, 109–11, 116, 131
Eisler, Riane 137–8Freud, Sigmund 10–11, 18, 23–6, 52, 60, 69, 98, 134–6, 172–9

Fromm, Erich 52, 143, 166
Fukuyama, Francis 2, 4, 13–14, 20, 32, 110, 131, 141, 147–9
Fulghum, Robert 71

Garasanin, Ilija 44
Gelb, Leslie 35, 37–8, 86, 89, 112
Gellner, Ernest x, 3, 5, 13–14, 17, 64–6, 133, 184
Giddens, Anthony 2, 58, 164, 35, 115
Glassner, Barry 79
Glenny, Misha 40

Habermas, Jürgen 113
Hegel, G.F.W. 13, 15, 141, 147
Hepburn, Audrey 101
Hitler, Adolph 40, 43, 53, 55, 85, 118, 134
Hobbes, Thomas 70, 133
Horkheimer, Max 143
Hussein, Saddam 20, 36, 91, 118, 191

Izetbegović, Alija 81, 101, 104, 113, 189–90

James, William 139

Kant, Immanuel 10, 71, 137
Kaplan, Robert 40, 79
Karadzić, Radovan 43, 53, 73, 90–3, 100, 105–6, 187
Kenney, George 91, 114
Kissinger, Henry 107
Kohlberg, Lawrence 70–2, 129–32
Khruschev, Nikita 141
King, Rodney 3, 22
Knežević, Anto 40

Lasch, Christopher 75, 133–4, 140, 150, 172

Subject index